Faith, Hope, and Love

One Day at a Time

Clay Sterrett

All Scripture quoted is in italics. Unless otherwise identified, Scripture quotations are taken from The Holy Bible: New International Version®. NIV®. Copyright ©1973, 1978, 1984 by International Bible Society. Used by permission of Zondervan Publishing House. Other Scripture quotations are from the following sources: New American Standard Bible (NAS), copyright ©1973 by Creation House., Carol Stream, Illinois. The New English Bible (NEB), copyright ©1970 by Oxford Press and Cambridge University Press. The New Testament in Modern English, translated by J. B. Phillips, copyright ©1972 by MacMillan Company, New York, N.Y. The Amplified Bible (AMP), copyright ©1965 by Zondervan Publishing House, Grand Rapids, Michigan. The Living Bible (LB), copyright 1971 by Tyndale House Publishers, Wheaton, IL. The New King James Version (NKJV), copyright ©1979 by Thomas Nelson, Inc., Nashville, TN. The Revised English Bible, (REB) copyright ©1989 Oxford University Press & Cambridge University Press. Holy Bible: New Revised Standard Version (NRSV), copyright ©1989 Oxford University Press. Contemporary English Version (CEV), copyright © 1991 by American Bible Society. The Jerusalem Bible (JB), copyright ©1966 and The New Jerusalem Bible (NJB), copyright ©1985 both by Darton, Longman and Todd Ltd. and Doubleday. Holy Bible, New Living Translation (NLT), copyright ©1996 Tyndale House, Wheaton, IL. The Message, copyright ©1993 by Eugene H. Peterson, by permission of NavPress Publishing. The Holy Bible: English Standard Version (ESV), copyright © 2001 by Crossway Bibles, Wheaton, IL. The King James Version (KJ)

Extra copies and a catalog of other materials may be obtained from:
CFC Literature
P.O. Box 245
Staunton, VA 24402-0245 or check out: *cfcliterature.com* or Amazon.
ISBN 0-9760454-6-X
Printed by R. R. Donnelley & Sons, Harrisonburg, VA
Cover design by: Zoe Tennesen

"For over twenty years, the Uganda Church has been blessed by the unique approach and direct biblical teachings from brother Clay Sterrett. His teachings have greatly transformed the Uganda Church, especially in areas of balancing the gifts of God and the fruit of the Spirit. One of his best books is *Faith, Hope, and Love*. I would therefore encourage whoever desires to live a balanced Christian lifestyle to read this book."

Alex Mitala, a national leader in Uganda and for ten years the Chairman of the National Fellowship of Born Again Pentecostal Churches in Uganda, representing over 25,000 church congregations.

"Pastor Clay Sterrett has taught in many pastors' conferences in North India. His teachings are simple but profound. He has deep insight into the scripture and a very simple way of presentation. His teaching appeals to both pastors of urban and rural churches. He is very much in demand for teaching to pastors in North India.

"I have translated some of his books into Hindi and am currently translating his recent book of meditations on *Faith, Hope and Love*. I am impressed by his scholarly, spiritual, practical and expository ability on the subjects. His writings are lucid, readable and meaningful.

"It is my hope that the thinking of the readers on these subjects will be challenged and expanded."

Dr. Gabriel Massey, a spiritual father in northern India, and first Bishop of the Federation of Evangelical Churches of India.

Dedication

Over the past twenty years
a number of dear friends
have served the Lord and me
by editing my writing.
If any of my books,
including this one,
are a blessing to any readers,
I can only take a little credit for it.
My finished works include
others' insights, suggestions,
and editorial corrections.
Therefore, my sincere thanks go out
to the following servants,
several of which helped in this project:

JAMES GARRETT
JOHN MORRISON
MARY ELLEN BARRETT
DAVID HARE
and
TERESA STERRETT
(I am hesitant to put anything in print
without my wife first reading it!)

Introduction

And now abide faith, hope, love, these three; but the greatest of these is love. (1 Corinthians 13:13 NKJV)

Faith, hope, and love are three abiding realities in which we are called to excel in the Christian life. The Phillips' translation says, *In this life we have three lasting qualities – faith, hope and love.* Many virtues come and go, but these three *abide*.

We see how important these qualities are in Paul's introduction to his letter to the Thessalonians. In the first few verses, Paul wrote that he and his fellow apostles thanked God and prayed for those saints. The apostles especially remembered their...

Work produced by faith,
Labor prompted by love, and
Endurance inspired by hope in our Lord Jesus Christ.

Without these abiding realities, we would see little effective *work*, *labor*, or *endurance* in the kingdom of God.

In our day, these three words have been cheapened in their meaning. Faith is often reduced to a spiritual force that supposedly obtains whatever we want. Hope is sometimes reduced to a vague "cross-my-fingers" sort of wishing that our circumstances turn out well. Love is frequently reduced to a sentimental, romantic feeling that comes and goes like the wind. I pray that through the devotional studies that follow, these three biblical virtues will be more both clarified and appreciated.

This devotional is 312 pages in length. If you read one a day, six days a week, the book can be read in a year. If you read two pages daily, it can be read in half a year. I frequently use quotes from others but make no apology for it. I have been influenced by a multitude of godly writers – past and present – who have articulated truth much better than I have. We can all be thankful for these timeless quotations that contribute to our edification. Take time especially to meditate on any Scriptures that minister life to you. (All Scriptures are written in *italics*.)

It is my desire that these devotional studies will be used to strengthen our faith, expand our hope, and encourage our love for God and for all people. To him be the glory.

DEVOTIONS ON FAITH

1. Indispensable Faith
2. Saving Faith
3. Childlike Faith (Part 1)
4. Childlike Faith (Part 2)
5. Genuine Faith
6. Growing Faith
7. Living Faith (Part 1)
8. Living Faith (Part 2)
9. Struggling Faith
10. Perturbing Faith
11. Trusting Faith
12. Object of our Faith (Part 1)
13. Object of our Faith (Part 2)
14. God-given Faith
15. Faith and Forgiveness
16. Faith and Justification
17. Faith and Righteousness (Part 1)
18. Faith and Righteousness (Part 2)
19. Faith and Access
20. Faith and Prayer
21. Faith and Expectation
22. Faith and the Present
23. Faith and Assurance
24. Faith and Confidence
25. Faith and Simplicity
26. Faith and Reality
27. Faith and Acceptance
28. Faith and Creation (Part 1)
29. Faith and Creation (Part 2)
30. Faith and Impossibilities
31. Faith and Obedience (Part 1)
32. Faith and Obedience (Part 2)
33. Faith and Sight (Part 1)
34. Faith and Sight (Part 2)
35. Faith and Proof
36. Faith and the Future
37. Faith and Promise

38. Faith and Bargaining
39. Faith and Silence
40. Faith and Receiving
41. Faith and Facts
42. Faith and Experience
43. Faith and Feeling
44. Faith and Foundation
45. Faith and the Bridge
46. Faith and Truth
47. Faith and Substance
48. Faith and Roots
49. Faith and Surrender
50. Faith and Satisfaction
51. Faith and the Cross
52. Faith and Finished Work
53. Faith and Repentance
54. Faith and Works
55. Faith and Action
56. Faith and Commitment
57. Faith and Testing
58. Faith and Obstacles
59. Faith and Dry Times
60. Faith and Crisis
61. Faith and Suffering
62. Faith and Adversity
63. Faith and Tragedy
64. Faith and Patience
65. Faith and Endurance
66. Faith and Warfare (Part 1)
67. Faith and Warfare (Part 2)
68. Faith and Confession (Part 1)
69. Faith and Confession (Part 2)
70. Faith and Confession (Part 3)
71. Faith and Confession (Part 4)
72. Faith and Confession (Part 5)
73. Faith and Praise
74. Faith and God's Leading

75. Faith and the Holy Spirit (Part 1)
76. Faith and the Holy Spirit (Part 2)
77. Faith and Power
78. Faith and Guidance
79. Faith and Provision
80. Faith and Prosperity
81. Faith and Giving
82. Faith and Family
83. Faith and Childbearing
84. Faith and Eating
85. Faith and Sleeping
86. Faith and Signs
87. Faith and Healing (Part 1)
88. Faith and Healing (Part 2)
89. Faith and Healing (Part 3)
90. Faith and Healing (Part 4)
91. Faith and Miracles
92. Supernatural Gifts of Faith
93. How Faith Develops: Knowing the Author of Faith
94. How Faith Develops: Meditating on God's Attributes
95. How Faith Develops: Hearing the Word of Christ
96. How Faith Develops: Using What We Have (Part 1)
97. How Faith Develops: Using What We Have (Part 2)
98. How Faith Develops: Taking Risks for God
99. How Faith Develops: Standing on His Promises (Part 1)
100. How Faith Develops: Standing on His Promises (Part 2)
101. Enemies of Faith: Unbelief
102. Enemies of Faith: Self-sufficiency
103. Enemies of Faith: Seeking Honor
104. Enemies of Faith: Doubt
105. Enemies of Faith: Stubbornness
106. Enemies of Faith: Rationalism
107. Enemies of Faith: Cowardice
108. Enemies of Faith: Fear (Part 1)
109. Enemies of Faith: Fear (Part 2)
110. Enemies of Faith: Presumption
111. Levels of Faith
112. Journey of Faith
113. School of Faith

114. Keeping the Faith: Not Departing
115. Keeping the Faith: Not Depressed
116. Keeping the Faith: Not Despairing
117. Keeping the Faith: Not Destroyed
118. Keeping the Faith: Not Disappointed
119. Keeping the Faith: Not Disillusioned
120. Keeping the Faith: Not Deterred
121. Keeping the Faith: Not Distracted
122. Lord, Strengthen Our Faith
123. Faith and Encouragement
124. Faith and Fellowship
125. Faith and Dwelling
126. Faith and Reputation
127. Faith and Love (Part 1)
128. Faith and Love (Part 2)
129. Faith and Relinquishing
130. Faith and Leaving
131. Faith and Leadership
132. Faith and Humility
133. Faith and Forever
134. Faithful in Him
135. Faithful in Our Walk
136. Faithful not Fickle
137. Faithful in Small Matters
138. Faithful unto Death
139. Faithful at the End

DEVOTIONS ON HOPE

140. Understanding Hope
141. Without Hope
142. The Treachery of Hope
143. Vain Hope
144. Dashed Hope
145. Realized Hope
146. History and Hope
147. Christ Our Only Hope
148. Rediscovering Hope
149. Radiant with Hope

150. The Anchor of Hope
151. The Security of Hope
152. The Refuge of Hope
153. The Helmet of Hope
154. Temporary Hope
155. Deferred Hope
156. Delayed Hope
157. Sorrow and Hope
158. Mismatched Mates and Hope
159. Wayward Children and Hope
160. Financial Needs and Hope
161. Economic Collapse and Hope
162. Disabilities and Hope (Part 1)
163. Disabilities and Hope (Part 2)
164. Destructive Choices and Hope
165. Death and Hope
166. Heaven and Hope
167. Hope Reserved for Us
168. Hope Keeps Us Moving Forward.
169. Hope Keeps Us Optimistic
170. Hope Keeps Us Living
171. Hope Keeps a Spring in our Step
172. Hope Keeps Us Excited About the Future
173. Hope Keeps Us Renewed
174. Hope Keeps Us Praising
175. Hope Motivates Holy Living
176. Hope Comes From Christ's Resurrection (Part 1)
177. Hope Comes From Christ's Resurrection (Part 2)
178. Hope Comes From Christ's Resurrection (Part 3)
179. Hope Comes From Christ in Us
180. Hope Comes from Knowing Who is in Control
181. Hope Comes From God's Faithfulness
182. Hope Comes From the Scriptures (Part 1)
183. Hope Comes From the Scriptures (Part 2)
184. Hope Comes From Christ's Second Coming (Part 1)
185. Hope Comes From Christ's Second Coming (Part 2)

DEVOTIONS ON LOVE

186. Love – The Greatest Thing
187. Love – The Hub of Christianity
188. Love – The Nature of the Trinity
189. Love – The Expression of God's Nature
190. Love – The Reason for Salvation
191. Love – The Keynote of the Bible
192. Love – The Mark of the Christian
193. Love – The Law of the Spirit (Part 1)
194. Love – The Law of the Spirit (Part 2)
195. Love – The Building Blocks of the Church
196. Love – The Perfect Bond of Unity (Part 1)
197. Love – The Perfect Bond of Unity (Part 2)
198. Love – The Product of the Spirit
199. Love – The Motivation for Our Service (Part 1)
200. Love – The Motivation for Our Service (Part 2)
201. Love – The Goal of Our Instruction
202. Love – The Corollary to Wrath
203. Pursuing Love
204. Undeserved Love
205. Sacrificial Love (Part 1)
206. Sacrificial Love (Part 2)
207. Sacrificial Love (Part 3)
208. Giving Love (Part 1)
209. Giving Love (Part 2)
210. Future Love
211. Demonstrative Love
212. Compassionate Love
213. Inviting Love
214. Delightful Love
215. Individual Love (Part 1)
216. Individual Love (Part 2)
217. Amazing Love
218. Immeasurable Love
219. Knowing Love
220. Wedded Love
221. Verbal Love
222. Extravagant Love

223. Merciful Love
224. Reaffirming Love
225. Sovereign Love
226. Inseparable Love
227. Quiet Love
228. Chastening Love
229. Higher Love
230. Extensive Love
231. Love for God (Part 1)
232. Love for God (Part 2)
233. Love for Others (Part 1)
234. Love for Others (Part 2)
235. Love for Ourselves (Part 1)
236. Love for Ourselves (Part 2)
237. Love for our Brothers (Part 1)
238. Love for our Brothers (Part 2)
239. Love for Friends
240. Love for Sinners
241. Love for All Men
242. Love for Wives
243. Love for Husbands
244. Love for Mates
245. Love for the Prodigal
246. Love for the Unpleasant
247. Love for the Ungrateful
248. Love for the Unlovely
249. Love for the "No-good"
250. Love for the Unresponsive
251. Love for All Races
252. Love for Our Enemies (Part 1)
253. Love for Our Enemies (Part 2)
254. Love for Our Enemies (Part 3)
255. Love for Our Enemies (Part 4)
256. Painful Love
257. Unconditional Love
258. Impartial Love
259. Adoptive Love
260. Restrictive Love
261. Forsaken Love

262. Worldly Love
263. Misplaced Love (Part 1)
264. Misplaced Love (Part 2)
265. Counterfeit Love: Random Force
266. Counterfeit Love: Sentimentalism
267. Counterfeit Love: Limited Love
268. Counterfeit Love: Materialism
269. Counterfeit Love: Common Cause
270. Counterfeit Love: Infatuation
271. Counterfeit Love: Co-dependency
272. Counterfeit Love: Lust
273. Counterfeit Love: Homosexuality
274. Counterfeit Love: Sex (only)
275. Premature Love
276. Acting Love
277. Doing love
278. Practical Love
279. Voluntary Love
280. Truthful Love
281. Obedient Love (Part 1)
282. Obedient Love (Part 2)
283. Emotional Love
284. Progressive Love
285. Desirous Love
286. Prayerful Love (Part 1)
287. Prayerful Love (Part 2)
288. Putting on Love
289. The Love Chapter (Part 1)
290. The Love Chapter (Part 2)
291. The Love Chapter (Part 3)
292. Love Is Patient (Part 1)
293. Love Is Patient (Part 2)
294. Love Is Kind
295. Love Does Not Envy (Part 1)
296. Love Does Not Envy (Part 2)
297. Love Does Not Boast, It Is Not Proud
298. Love Is Not Rude
299. Love Is Not Self-Seeking (Part 1)
300. Love Is Not Self-Seeking (Part 2)

301. Love Does Demand Its Own Way
302. Love Is Not Easily Angered
303. Love Keeps No Record of Wrongs (Part 1)
304. Love Keeps No Record of Wrongs (Part 2)
305. Love Does Not Delight in Evil But Rejoices With the Truth
306. Love Always Protects
307. Love Always Trusts
308. Love Is Ready to Believe the Best
309. Love Always Hopes, Always Perseveres
310. Love Never Fails
311. Love Through Me
312. Love: Summary

Part One

Daily Encouragement
For Building

Faith

*Without faith
it is impossible
to please God.
(Hebrews 11:6)*

Indispensable Faith

*By faith Enoch was taken from this life...he was
commended as one who pleased God. And without
faith it is impossible to please God.... (Hebrews 11:6)*

Faith is one element we cannot do without in the Christian life.
Any man or woman who wants to please God and be useful in
his kingdom must live by faith.   We are saved by faith; we are
sanctified by faith; we receive answers to prayer by faith; we
overcome adversity by faith; and we are kept to the end by faith.
People today have differing ideas about faith. Some see faith as a
"force" to move the hand of God. Some see faith as a "leap in
the dark," being uncertain of what lies ahead. Others confuse
faith with mere "wishful thinking" or with a vague sense of
hopefulness.

Faith is a much larger word than most of us imagine, and
often in Scripture it is linked with other vital words. We will
examine several of these biblical partnerships with faith in the
following pages.

Faith is a foundational truth of Christianity. It is essential for
every facet of the believer's walk with God. Faith is our link to
a timeless and limitless God. Martin Luther once called faith the
"wedding ring" of the soul, by which we pledge ourselves to
Christ.[1] When we suffer severe setbacks and disappointments,
faith is what keeps us connected to a loving and sovereign God.
Faith is the prime ingredient–the bottom line in the Christian life.

Enoch, a mysterious character about whom the Bible has
little to say, was noted for his faith.[2] Along with Elijah, Enoch
was one of only two men taken up to heaven while still alive.
Few words are recorded about Enoch, but it is said he *walked
with God,*[3] and he *pleased God.*[4] Apparently, something about
his walk of faith was so pleasing to God that one day He simply
said, "Come on home!" If we, too, are to please God, we must
walk by faith, not by sight.[5] Walking with God implies that one
keeps in step with him, not running ahead or lagging behind. It
suggests we move in the same direction he is moving. Lord, help
us to walk in faith!

Day Two
Saving Faith

*For it is by grace you have been saved, through faith –
and this not from yourselves; it is the gift of God – not
by works, so that no one can boast. (Ephesians 2:8-9)*

Faith is the vehicle which brings us into contact with the grace of
God. But, we have nothing to boast about. The Greek scholar,
A. T. Robertson, pointed out that, in the verse above, the word
this refers to neither *faith* nor *grace*, but "to the act of being
saved conditioned on faith on our part. Paul shows that salvation
does not have its source in men (Greek = *not out of you*), but
from God."[6] So, we can rightly say, *it is by faith and through
Jesus that we have entered this state of grace.*[7]

Faith is the very opposite of self-dependence. When we
come to God in faith, we are saying, "Lord, I cannot make it on
my own; my own good works are woefully inadequate in
pleasing you; I cannot depend on my own natural abilities to
earn salvation." The apostle Paul would have had much to boast
about in the way of natural abilities and attainment, yet his desire
was to *gain Christ, and be found in him, not having a
righteousness of my own that comes from the law, but that which
is through faith in Christ – the righteousness that comes from
God and is by faith.*[8] This truth is also echoed in Abraham's
story: *Abraham's faith was credited to him as righteousness...the
promise comes by faith, so that it may be by grace...*[9]

Martin Luther had already been diligently serving as a
Catholic priest for a dozen years when one day he began to
meditate on a verse from the book of Romans, *For in the gospel
a righteousness from God is revealed, a righteousness that is by
faith from first to last, just as it is written, "The righteous will
live by faith."*[10] He later recalled the life-changing impact, "That
expression, *the righteousness of God,* was like a thunderbolt in
my heart."[11] We know the rest of the story – this man became
the sparkplug of the Protestant Reformation through his renewed
emphasis on justification by faith. Thank God we can know
God's salvation – simply by faith!

Childlike Faith (Part 1)

And he said: "I tell you the truth, unless you change and become like little children, you will never enter the kingdom of heaven." (Matthew 18:3)

Jesus said that if we are to experience kingdom life, we will need to become like little children. This does not mean that we remain childish in our understanding,[12] but it means that we maintain a childlike faith as we relate to our heavenly Father in faith.

What are the characteristics of a normal, little child, and how does he live? In a sense, we could say he lives by faith; he trusts others whom he knows deeply love him.

- A child knows his parents will care for him.
- A child does not worry about what he will eat.
- A child does not worry about where he will sleep.
- A child thinks little about what he will wear.
- A child trusts his teachers to guide him in knowledge and truth.
- A child immediately comes to his parents when there is a terrible storm or fearful situation.
- A child finds comfort in the arms of a parent when he is sick and feeling bad.
- A child does not have to plan his way in life.
- A child does not become troubled because of all the bad news occurring in the world. His life is secure.
- A child does not worry about his future finances.
- A child tends to live in the present now.
- A child tends to laugh a lot and enjoy the pleasures of simple things.

In summary, little children – unless they are being raised in quite a dysfunctional or abusive family – simply do not worry or live in stress. They trust. In our case – with a heavenly Father who is entirely good, loving, and righteous in all his ways – how much more should we maintain a simple faith in his care for us? God is good!

Childlike Faith (Part 2)

"I praise you, Father...you have hidden these things from the wise and learned, and revealed them to little children..." (Luke 10:21)

The life of Samuel Morris is a story of remarkable, child-like faith.[13] As a teenage boy in Liberia, he was captured by a rival tribe and held for ransom. When the high demands could not be paid, he was beaten badly, and it was decided he would be killed. One night, though, he saw a flash of brilliant light, and an audible voice commanded him to run. Amazingly, he suddenly had strength to run from his captors. The same light guided him for days through the jungle, full of danger. Samuel was led to a settlement near Monrovia, the capital. It was one of the few places that he would be safe and meet Christian missionaries.

Samuel surrendered to Christ and learned much from a missionary, Miss Knolls. He developed a simple prayer life of "talking to my Father." As he developed a hunger for more, Miss Knolls talked about her mentor, Stephen Merritt, who lived in New York City. Samuel, one day announced that "his Father had told him to go to America to meet Merritt," and he soon departed for the coastline. In child-like faith, he asked for a job on a ship bound for America and on the journey of 7,000 miles, his simple manner of praying brought conviction to many, including the drunken captain and many violent crew members. When he arrived at New York City, Samuel made a profound impression on Stephen Merritt and others he met. Samuel had come to learn and Merritt eventually made a way for Samuel to attend Taylor University in Indiana. While at Taylor, he was used mightily by God to draw people to the Lord. Late in the winter of 1892, however, Samuel came down with Pneumonia, and soon died. Samuel's life was an inspiration to many people to follow in his footsteps of faith. In one year alone, seven students dedicated themselves to serve the Lord in Africa.

Samuel's tombstone bears this inscription: "Samuel Morris...1873-1893...Famous Christian Mystic...Apostle of Simple Faith..." May we, too, have such child-like faith.

Day Five
Genuine Faith

I often think of that genuine faith of yours...
(2 Timothy 1:5 Phillips)

What words would friends likely use to describe our faith? When the apostle Paul thought of his spiritual son, Timothy, he thought of a faith that was *genuine.* The Greek word here means "without hypocrisy, sincere, without pretense or outward show." This means a faith which is not playing a part or putting on an outward layer of spirituality. People who are nonbelievers usually can spot a phony Christian, and they will be quick to reprove a man who is not genuine in the faith he professes.

Genuine faith can have great influence, more than we realize. It will even significantly affect future generations of a family. Paul, in commending the genuine faith of Timothy, mentioned two previous generations: *I have been reminded of your sincere faith, which first lived in your grandmother Lois and your mother Eunice...*[14] Notice, there is no believing father mentioned. So, women, if your husband has no interest in spiritual things, persevere and be an example of genuine faith. You never know when you will influence another "Timothy."

We are living in a day when many use the name of Christ and the word of God for selfish and material advantage. Any believer who handles the word of God must be genuine, motivated only for the glory of God and the spiritual benefit of others. *Unlike so many, we do not peddle the word of God for profit. On the contrary, in Christ we speak before God with sincerity, like men sent from God.*[15] The Greek word for *peddle* here pictures a huckster or retailer who often would put the best apples or berries on top of his basket.[16] Paul is saying that our apples should be as good on the bottom as on the top. The genuine believer is not afraid to face men with the gospel message for it is sound to the core. He is not afraid that something will be found out about his character to make him ashamed. Under the surface he has no "bad apples!" May God help us walk in such genuine faith.

Day Six
Growing Faith

We ought always to thank God for you, brothers, and rightly so, because your faith is growing more and more... (2 Thes.1:3)

Faith is like a muscle – if it is not being used, it will atrophy. Or as someone has said, "use it or lose it." In our daily lives, God will give us many opportunities to trust him and to live by faith. We may not like *all kinds of trials* that come our way, but our heavenly Father uses them to purify and develop our faith.[17]

A genuine faith is a growing faith. Faith cannot be a static thing – we are either growing in faith or we are sliding back: *My righteous one will live by faith. And if he shrinks back I will not be pleased with him.*[18] We only have two options: either move forward with God or shrink back. We can become sidetracked in fruitless discussions about, "Are we once-saved-always-saved?" Such questions miss the New Testament emphasis: we are not chosen from before the foundation of the world just to have a "salvation experience;" we were chosen to *live* by faith as a child of God. We do indeed need a starting place – a man must be born again to see the kingdom of God – but four times in Scripture it is stated, *The just shall live by faith.*[19] It is not God's will for us merely to *"get saved"* by faith, nor simply to *exist* by faith, nor only to *get* things by faith. His intention is for his righteous ones to *live* by faith. *Living* for God implies an active and growing faith affecting every facet of life.

Most of us resist growing up – both in a physical and a spiritual sense. It is easier to stay like a child and live a basically carefree and irresponsible life. It is much simpler to let Mom and Dad do the work and pay the bills. As Christians, however, *we are no longer to be children...but...we are to grow up in all aspects into Him, who is the head, even Christ.*[20] We are instructed to *grow in the grace and knowledge of our Lord and Savior Jesus Christ.*[21]

Let us not shrink back but move forward in faith.

Living Faith (Part 1)
...the righteous man shall live by faith. (Romans 1:17)

We tend to think that faith is more for religious activities – like prayer, claiming promises of God, and going on mission trips. But, faith is also active in our everyday living, even when we don't realize it. We go about daily routines – without having thorough knowledge about the instruments we use or without absolute confidence of safety – and yet it doesn't stop us from functioning. Mark Buchanan has written about our living daily by faith. "We live by faith....In one sense this is obvious. We have no other option. Just getting up in the morning requires an enormous act of faith. The food you blithely eat – even after you've seen all those science documentaries about how each bite writhes and crawls with a zillion hairy, spiny, scaly, leggy little creatures – you eat by faith. The car you drive – despite all the thousand sundry things that can go awry: brackets sheering, gas tanks exploding, lug nuts threading loose, coronary attack victims or reckless drunks careening toward you – you drive by faith. Many of us have built our houses atop the slippery joints of massive earth plates. We live astride the crack of doom. But happily, merrily, we shop and jog and go to meetings and frolic at playgrounds and lay our heads down at night beneath thin plaster ceilings – all with no perceptible speeding up of our pulses. We live by faith all day and all night long."[22]

Therefore, if we don't have great hang-ups about such everyday living – which we do with a certain level of faith – then why do we have such great hang-ups when it comes to spiritual matters? Buchanan added, "Faith is not an emergency provision for the times we're unable to compile enough hard, cold facts or weave a tight enough web of logic to explain things... It is more than a flutter in the belly or a warm glow in the heart... It is a deep certainty that sparks life into all we are and all we do."[23]

Let us be willing to exercise faith in God throughout the day – in *all* that we do – instead of just waiting for times of great crisis or need. Indeed, faith in the *everyday* matters will prepare for the greater times of need.

Living Faith (Part 2)

I will show you my faith by what I do. You believe there is one God. Good! Even the demons believe that – and shudder! (James 2:18-19)

There is a difference between mere belief and faith. Even demons believe, but they do not have faith in God. These comparisons by G. A. Bowers illustrate this distinction:

Belief is my saying to a teenager, "Yes, you can drive."
Faith is my riding along.

Belief is my saying, "You are a good mechanic."
Faith is asking you to overhaul my car.

Belief is my saying, "You are a good pianist."
Faith is asking you to play at my wedding.

Belief is my saying, "You are quite a marksman."
Faith is letting you shoot an apple off my head.

(Source unknown)

Faith is believing God's facts – that what God has said is true – but it is also the process by which we translate God's facts into personal experience. It is a belief so strong that it invokes a response from us. One unmarried young couple said they believed the biblical teaching against sexual immorality, yet they chose to regularly engage in sex. They had an empty belief in God; if it were real faith, it would invoke obedience to his word.

We say we believe in the resurrection. If so, why are we not sold-out to Jesus? We say we believe in the power of the Holy Spirit. If so, then why do we plan every detail of our lives as if he does not exist? We say we believe in the love of God. If so, then why are we so quick to criticize others and slow to forgive their offenses against us? May God help our faith to be a living faith, rather than mere belief.

Struggling Faith

When the spirit saw Jesus, it immediately threw the boy into a convulsion. He fell to the ground and rolled around, foaming at the mouth. Jesus asked the boy's father, "How long has he been like this?"

"From childhood," he answered.

"It has often thrown him into fire or water to kill him. But if you can do anything, take pity on us and help us."

"'If you can'?" said Jesus. "Everything is possible for him who believes."

Immediately the boy's father exclaimed, "I do believe; help me overcome my unbelief!" (Mark 9:20-24)

Jesus had little sympathy for unbelief. He even seems to be disgusted by it. Earlier, when the boy's father talked to him about his demon-possessed son and his disciples' inability to help him, Jesus relied, *"O unbelieving generation...how long shall I stay with you? How long shall I put up with you? Bring the boy to me."*[24] We don't get the impression here that Jesus was grinning as he uttered this rebuke.

This father was looking to Jesus for help, but his faith was struggling, *"I do believe; help me overcome my unbelief!"* Why is such struggling faith an affront to our Lord?

- Jesus was God Almighty in human flesh. Was he not able to deliver such a case? Was his power limited?
- Jesus never failed a person who was desperately seeking his help. Why think he would not help now?
- Jesus demonstrated multiple times that he was full of mercy and compassion. Why would he withhold now?

The wonderful thing about our Lord is that he is very patient with us. In this case, he rebuked the evil spirit and the boy was completely set free! Jesus never commends struggling faith (a measure of unbelief), yet in his great mercy he meets us there and brings us the help we need. Struggling faith is better than no faith! But, let us always remember Jesus' words to this father, *"Everything is possible for him who believes."*

Day Ten
Perturbing Faith

Therefore, if anyone is in Christ, he is a new creation; old things have passed away; behold, all things have become new. (2 Corinthians 5:17 NKJV)

There is something about our faith in Christ that ought to be a perturbing – or disturbing – thing. When we come to Christ, he may trouble us, or at times shake us up.

- Many of our old values will be challenged.
- Our selfish way of acting will be severely altered.
- Some relationships may need to be severed.
- Even the small details of our lives will not go untouched; even what we do for "recreation."

Our Lord does not delight in making our lives miserable; but he will disturb any area that is not rightly related to him, and his goal is to transform us into his image. *All things* will become new. This will be quite a lengthy and detailed process, and not always so pleasant. Learning to "die to ourselves" and live for God is not easy. Tozer wrote this about "perturbing faith:"

"The faith of Paul and Luther was a revolutionizing thing. It upset the whole life of the individual and made him into another person altogether. It laid hold on the life and brought it under obedience to Christ. It took up its cross and followed along after Jesus with no intention of going back...

"This generation of Christians must hear again the doctrine of the perturbing quality of faith. People must be told that the Christian religion is not something they can trifle with. The faith of Christ will command or it will have nothing to do with a man. It will not yield to experimentation. Its power cannot reach any man who is secretly keeping an escape route open in case things get too tough for him. The only man who can be sure he has true Bible faith is the one who has put himself in a position where he cannot go back. His faith has resulted in an everlasting and irrevocable committal, and however strongly he may be tempted he always replies, 'Lord, to whom shall we go? You have the words of eternal life' (John 6:68)."[25]

Trusting Faith

The message they heard did not benefit them because it was not mixed with faith [with the leaning of the entire personality on God in absolute trust and confidence in His power, wisdom, and goodness]. (Heb. 4:2 The Amplified Bible)

"Faith is then a lively and steadfast trust in the favor of God." (William Tyndale)[26]

Many people have mistaken concepts about faith and feel that trusting in Christ requires a large amount of faith. They feel faith is clenching our fists, gritting our teeth, and emphatically declaring, "I *do* believe! I *do* believe!" Faith, however, is not a matter of working up something in ourselves, but rather *trusting* or *resting* in the finished work of Christ.

When Dr. John G. Paton was a missionary in the New Hebrides Islands, he spent much time translating the Gospel of John into the local language. However, his translation work was slowed by the fact that he could not find adequate words to express *faith* and *believe*. One day, while he was in his study, one of the natives came in, hot and tired from a long walk in the hills. He sat down on one of the cane chairs, put his feet on another chair, and used a word which meant, "I am resting my whole weight right here on these two chairs." That was the word which Dr. Paton sought after, and he used that word to translate *believe* or *have faith*. Thus, the people of the Islands came to know that to believe in Christ unto salvation meant to rest the whole weight of one's mind and soul upon Christ. With this translation, John 3:16 would read,

For God so loved the world that he gave his only begotten Son, that whosoever rests his whole weight upon him should not perish, but have everlasting life.[27]

Object of our Faith (Part 1)

Let us shout aloud to the Rock of our salvation. (Psalm 95:1)

Faith is only as valid as its object. Ice comes in two basic formations: thick ice and thin ice. Thick ice is quite substantial to walk on, but thin ice you want to stay clear of. Lynn Anderson shared how his wife, Carolyn, was very suspicious of walking or driving on thick ice. "After witnessing an airplane landing on the ice, and a heavy truck meeting the plane, she felt better about it! This is the basic truth about faith, too. The most important issue is not the amount of faith we can muster, but the trustworthiness of the object of our faith."[28]

We could have strong faith in thin ice and still drown. We could have a weak faith in thick ice and yet walk securely. What counts is the reliability of the *object* in which we place our trust, not how much faith we have. If we only look to ourselves, and leave God out, we are indeed "walking on thin ice."

Jesus Christ is the object of our focus. He is as *solid* as it gets; in Scripture he is called, the *Rock of our salvation.* A. W. Tozer pointed out that we must constantly focus away from ourselves onto Christ. "Faith is the least self-regarding of the virtues. It is by its very nature scarcely conscious of its own existence. Like the eye which sees everything in front of it and never sees itself, faith is occupied with the *Object* upon which it rests and pays no attention to itself at all. While we are looking at God we do not see ourselves – blessed riddance. The man who has struggled to purify himself and has had nothing but repeated failures will experience real relief when he stops tinkering with his soul and looks away to the perfect One."[29]

So, we must not concentrate on our own faith (or lack of it); let's look instead to the *object* of our faith and we will find as we build our lives on him, that we will be standing quite securely.

Object of our Faith (Part 2)

... upon this rock I will build My church... (Matthew 16:18)

How would you answer the question, "Are you saved by faith?" Josh McDowell once challenged some contemporary thinking about this question. "The crowd was silent. You could have heard a pin drop. I (Josh) had walked down into the audience and asked one of the deacons of the church sitting near the front this question: 'How are you saved – how have you gained a relationship with Christ?'

"He answered without hesitation, 'By faith – I am saved by faith.' I looked at the entire congregation and then to him and said, 'No, you're not. No one is ever saved by faith!' That is when the crowd went deathly silent and a chill swept over the auditorium. I went on to explain my statement before the crowd branded me with a capital 'H' for heretic.

"The truth is none of us is saved by faith. If we could be saved by faith, then Jesus didn't have to die for us. We could have saved ourselves simply by an exercise of faith. Here's the question: Does faith and faith alone have any power? An entire generation is growing up today believing so. Many think that their choice to believe something has, in fact, the power to make that belief into their own truth. They seem to think if you believe something hard enough and sincerely enough, it will be the truth that will work for you.

"But when it comes to truth about your salvation, there is only one power that can change your separated and lost status before God. Your faith has no power to save. Rather, it is the *object* of your faith that has the power to save, namely Jesus Christ – because Jesus, Son of the Almighty God, is the one who died for you and rose again to purchase your salvation. 'It is by grace you have been saved, through faith – and this is not from yourselves, it is the gift of God' (Ephesians 2:8 NIV)."[30]

Let us remember, then, that faith is the instrument that connects us to God, but we are only saved by the grace of Christ. The *object* of our faith must be more important than faith itself.

God-Given Faith

God has dealt to each one a measure of faith...
(Romans 12:3 NKJV)

Faith is a gift from God; we have nothing to boast about: *What do you have that you did not receive?*[31] Judson Cornwall explained, "Faith is produced by God, not by man. Faith is a divine energy, not a religious one. It has its origin in the Godhead, not in the body of Christ. We're not capable of producing this dynamic of faith, only of receiving it. In the same manner that home owners don't produce electricity, but only consume it, we do not produce faith; we only utilize it."[32]

Realizing our faith comes from God should help keep us more humble and thankful for what we receive. If we believe God, we can be thankful he has given us the grace and the mental ability to exercise this faith. Realizing our faith is God-given should also help us in many of our struggles. Trying hard to have faith in God is quite different from expressing God-implanted faith. In his classic work, *The Real Faith,* Charles Price commented, "One of our chief difficulties is our failure to see that faith can be received *only* as it is imparted to the heart, by God Himself. Either you have faith, or you do not. You cannot manufacture it...you cannot work it up. You can believe a promise, and at the same time not have the faith to appropriate it. We have formed the habit of trying to appropriate by *belief*; forgetting that belief is a *mental* quality, and that when we try to believe ourselves into an experience, we are getting into a metaphysical realm....Genuine, scriptural faith is not *our ability* to 'count it done,' but is the deep consciousness divinely imparted to the heart of man that *it is done.* It is the faith that only God can give."[33]

So, we do not have to strive and work our faith up to a certain point. Ultimately, the faith of God is God's business; we need only to exercise it when it is freely given.

Faith and Forgiveness

If we confess our sins, he is faithful and just and will forgive us our sins and purify us from all unrighteousness. (1 John 1:9)

One of the greatest gifts God has bestowed among mankind is the forgiveness of sins. When we repent and receive the forgiveness of sins, it is a comprehensive work – including:

- Pardon of a criminal. The Judge of all men has declared us "not guilty." None of our sins will be held against us.
- All our sins – even the worst – are completely covered by the blood of Christ. God now sees us as "white as snow."[34]
- God now looks upon us as the very righteousness of Christ.[35] This is an astounding truth – we are as righteous as Jesus (because his righteousness is credited to us)!
- Our sins are not only forgiven, but forgotten. Think of a blackboard in which you list every wicked deed and every sin of omission. Then you not only erase the board but thoroughly wash it as well. Now, it is as if those things never existed! *Oh, what joy for those whose disobedience is forgiven, whose sins are put out of sight. Yes, what joy for those whose sin is no longer counted against them by the Lord.*[36]

Martin Luther once said, "To believe in the forgiveness of sins through Christ is the highest article of our faith; and it is true that whoever believes this article actually has forgiveness of sins. Therefore Satan tries so hard to rob us of this faith."[37] So, although forgiveness is a sure promise for those who come to Christ, at times we will not especially *feel* forgiven. This is where faith comes in. We must *confess* and *believe* what the Scriptures say is true for followers of Christ. We may still feel low and dirty in spirit; yet we must declare who we are in Christ, "Thank you Lord, for your grace and mercy. Thanks for the forgiveness of sins, although I sure don't deserve it. You have made me acceptable in your sight and I now have a clean slate!"

Faith and Justification

Therefore, since we have been justified through faith, we have peace with God through our Lord Jesus Christ...(Romans 5:1)

Justification basically means "to declare one righteous; to acquit." It is closely connected with righteousness and forgiveness. The importance of "justification by faith" is no small matter; many reformers paid a great price – even shed their blood – for this very doctrine. John Calvin said, "Justification is the main hinge on which religion is supported."[38]

The idea of justification carries a legal sense. Christ is the judge of all men, and his judgment carries the highest authority. When he decides a case, his authority is never to be questioned and there are no appeals. When we sinners stand before this judge, our proper response must be, "I have no basis of hope except the blood of Jesus shed on the cross for me." Whenever such a response of faith is made, the judge – with a smile on his face – declares us "not-guilty!" It does not matter how flawed our past is or what horrible sins we have committed; the blood of Jesus covers them all! We are saved from all future judgment or punishment we rightly deserve. Scripture says, *Since we have now been justified by his blood, how much more shall we be saved from God's wrath through him!*[39] This is why some define *justified* as "just–as–if–I'd never sinned." We are no longer the natural enemies of God, but are now his beloved friends.[40] Incredible! Therefore, we accept no accusation any longer! *Who would dare to accuse us, whom God has chosen? The judge himself has declared us free from sin. Who is in a position to condemn? Only Christ, and Christ died for us, Christ rose for us, Christ reigns in power for us, Christ prays for us!*[41]

Who else in the world has ever claimed to freely justify sinners? What other religion has ever offered such a wonderful gift? This all might seem too-good-to-be-true, but by faith we can freely accept what Christ has given. *Thanks be to God for his indescribable gift!*[42]

Faith and Righteousness (Part 1)

*God made him who had no sin to be sin for us, so that
in him we might become the righteousness of God.
(2 Corinthians 5:21)*

This is possibly the most astounding verse in the entire Bible,
instructing us that through Christ's work, we actually *become the
righteousness of God*. The great theologian, Charles Hodge,
wrote, "There is probably no passage in the Scriptures in which
the doctrine of justification is more concisely or clearly stated."[43]
Can we fathom the fact that as God the Father looks upon us
who believe, he sees us as the very righteousness of his Son!
Yes, it is true, and by faith we must agree it is so! ...*I no longer
count on my own righteousness through obeying the law; rather,
I become righteous through faith in Christ. For God's way of
making us right with himself depends on faith.*[44] Some have
called Christ's death on the cross, "The Great Exchange." He
took all our sin and unrighteousness, and exchanged them for his
forgiveness and righteousness.

Robert Morgan commented on the two sides to justification.
"On the one hand, our guilt is laid on Christ who bore it on the
cross in our stead. On the other hand, His righteousness is
imputed to us. The result is that when God sees Jesus on the
cross, He sees our sin, but when He looks at the justified
believer, He sees the righteousness of Christ. Think of it this
way. What if you had debts totaling 20 million dollars, a
nightmare of indebtedness that you could never overcome?
Suppose a multibillionaire said, 'I'll cover your debts; I'll wipe
out all the red ink on your ledger.' That in itself would be
tremendous. But what if he also said, 'Furthermore, I'll deposit
20 million dollars into your account, and more as needed'?
That's a picture of justification. When we receive Christ as our
Lord and Savior, the debt of sin is wiped off our books, and the
righteousness of Christ is deposited to our account. We instantly
go from being spiritually bankrupt to becoming eternally rich in
Christ."[45]

Faith and Righteousness (Part 2)

In righteousness you will be established. (Isaiah 54:14)

God himself is often described by the word "righteous." God is a God of total integrity, justice, and uprightness. *Good and upright is the Lord.*[46] There is nothing wrong, crooked or deceitful about him. The Lord *is righteous in all his ways...*[47] Scripture says, *Righteousness and justice are the foundation of his throne.*[48] Life in his kingdom is characterized by righteousness – being rightly related to the Lord. *The kingdom of God is not a matter of eating and drinking, but of righteousness, peace and joy in the Holy Spirit.*[49] Notice the order: first righteousness, then peace and joy. Multitudes in the world would love to have peace and joy, but these are the by-products of righteousness. The world is looking for peace and joy, but apart from righteousness, there is no peace; apart from righteousness, there is no true joy.

Another good definition of righteousness is simply "rightness: being made right with God – the way we are supposed to be." In the world people strive for self-improvement – both physically and spiritually, yet there is often lacking a sense of satisfaction and acceptance. Only through faith in Christ can we be made "right" in the sight of God. Only then do we become completely pleasing, favorable, and acceptable to him. Righteousness primarily concerns our standing *before God.* It means being in a state that is required by God, that answers all his demands, and that will stand his test of judgment.

If we are righteous, we are not improved, not decorated, not patched up, but made right! Consider a vinyl seat which has a bad tear in it. I used to work some in furniture repair, and I have never seen a vinyl repair kit which really does a satisfactory job. No matter what attempt is made, only a patch job is done, and the seat will never look new again. Righteousness is not God doing a patch job with us or trying to improve us; *if anyone is in Christ, he is a new creation; the old has gone, the new has come!*[50] Let us therefore have faith in Christ – the righteous One!

Day Nineteen
Faith and Access

Therefore, since we have been justified through faith,
we have peace with God through our Lord Jesus
Christ, through whom <u>we have gained access</u> by faith
into this grace in which we now stand...(Romans 5:1-2)

This word *access* is a most wonderful discovery for the believer in Jesus Christ. The Greek word cannot be fully translated by one English word. Notice the variety of translations:[51]

- *Through faith . . . we have been <u>allowed to enter</u> the sphere of God's grace . . .(NEB)*
- *Because of our faith, Christ has brought us into <u>this place of highest privilege</u> where we now stand...(NLT)*
- *We have obtained our <u>introduction</u> by faith... (NAS)*

By faith in Jesus, we gain *access* or an *introduction* to God's grace. The Greek word he used here is *prosagoge*. William Barclay said it is a word with two great pictures in it:

(1) "It is the regular word for introducing or ushering someone into the presence of royalty; and it is the regular word for the approach of the worshipper to God. It is as if Paul was saying, 'Jesus ushers us into the very presence of God. He opens the door for us to the presence of the King of kings; and when that door is opened what we find is *grace*; not condemnation, not judgment, not vengeance, but the sheer, undeserved, incredible kindness of God.'

(2) "But *prosagoge* has another picture in it. In the late Greek it is the word for the place where ships come in, a *harbor* or a *haven*. If we take it that way, it means that so long as we tried to depend on our own efforts we were tempest-tossed, like mariners striving with a sea which threatened to overwhelm them completely, but now we have heard the word of Christ, we have reached at last the haven of God's grace, and we know the calm of depending, not on what we can do for ourselves, but on what God has done for us."[52]

Because of Jesus, we have *access* – entry to the presence of the *King of kings* and entry to the haven of God's grace.

Faith and Prayer

Casting all your care upon Him, for He cares for you.
(1 Peter 5:7 NKJV)

God never intended his children to carry the weight of all their concerns and anxieties. By faith we are to bring our cares to the Lord. We can be so thankful that he cares for us.

In the Greek, the word for *cast* can also mean "to make a deposit." One expanded translation says, "...*having deposited once for all the whole of your worries upon him.* "[53] Think about how we make deposits at a bank. When I take the money to the bank deposit box, I put my deposit slip with cash and checks into the slot, and then I drive away. I don't have to stand guard over the deposit box. I don't have to go back and check with the bank every hour to make sure the money is safe. I just make the deposit and feel secure. I simply do not worry about money; I feel it is in good hands.

In the same way, when we bring cares to the Lord, we are to make a deposit. The Bible is clear – we are not to be anxious about *anything*.[54] If we continue to worry, these matters become like a heavy weight. I like the J. B. Phillips' translation of this verse. *You can throw the whole weight of your anxieties upon him, for you are his personal concern.* Charles Spurgeon also wrote, "How, then, are we to cast our care upon God? Two things need to be done. It is a heavy load that is to be cast upon God, and it requires the hand of prayer and the hand of faith to make the transfer. Prayer tells God what the care is, and asks God to help, while faith believes that God can and will do it. Prayer spreads the letter of trouble and grief before the Lord, and opens [each ailment's full] budget, and then faith cries, 'I believe that God cares, and cares for me; I believe that He will bring me out of my distress, and make it promote HIS own glory.'"[55]

Let us bring our heavy loads to the Lord. Anytime we make a deposit of our worries and leave it with him, it will require faith on our part. We should not hesitate to do this, because his love for us is incredible, and *we are his personal concern.*

Faith and Expectation

"Have faith in God," Jesus answered. "I tell you the truth, if anyone says to this mountain, 'Go throw yourself into the sea,' and does not doubt in his heart but believes that what he says will happen, it will be done for him. Therefore I tell you, whatever you ask in prayer, believe that you have received it, and it will be yours." (Mark 11:22-24)

Expectation is important in the life of faith. If we have carefully and humbly sought the will of God, we can pray boldly, expecting him to answer. It is true our prayers may be hindered because of wrong motives or selfish ambition or blind presumption. Yet, we must not allow the infirmities of the flesh to stop us nor wait for perfect circumstances before moving forward in faith.

Consider two biblical examples of expectant faith. When the nation of Israel was about to be conquered and taken captive by the Babylonians, Jeremiah bought a parcel of land. Normally, it would not make sense to buy land if you would soon have to relinquish it to your enemy! But, because God had spoken, Jeremiah fully expected that God would one day bring the captivity to an end. Jeremiah thereby acted in faith.[56]

Paul, having no natural evidence that his release from prison was imminent, wrote to his friend, Philemon, *"Prepare a guest room for me, because I hope to be restored to you in answer to your prayers."*[57] Paul, full of faith, expected to be released.

Expectation is important in receiving from God. Once I was in a special meeting where a pastor had announced there would be prayer for the sick after he preached. He proceeded to teach about faith and God's healing power. Then in the last half of the message, he outlined all the reasons some people are not healed. Needless to say, no one was healed in that meeting. Any faith which had been built up in the first half was quickly deflated in the second half! If we do not expect to see anything extraordinary in our Christian experience, then it is likely we will settle for the ordinary. Let's expect God to act in our behalf!

Faith and the Present

Now faith is.... (Hebrews 11:1)

Faith in God cannot be a vague sense of "Well, maybe if I'm lucky enough, God might sometime in the future see fit to answer my request." We must believe that *God is a present help in time of trouble.*[58] *He who comes to God must believe that He is, and that He is a rewarder to those who seek Him.*[59] God, in his sovereignty, may very well choose not to give us what we request. He is not a celestial Santa Claus, whose primary function is to distribute from his bag of treats. He is, however, a loving, heavenly Father, who is probably a lot more willing to give than we are to receive.

> *If you, then, though you are evil, know how to give good gifts to your children, how much more will your Father in heaven give good gifts to those who ask him.*[60]

> *The prayer of the upright is his delight.*[61]

> *You do not have because you do not ask God.*[62]

The Christian faith is centered in a God of the "here and now;" *Jesus Christ is the same yesterday and today and forever.*[63] Some believers tend to live in the pages of church history past and can talk only about what God did in the "good old days." Other believers live only in the pages of Bible prophecy and emphasize Christ in the future coming to rescue them from all the trouble on earth. In the Old Testament, God revealed himself to Moses and when he was asked about his name, God responded, *"I am who I am."*[64] This means, among other things, that God is actively present; that he is not limited to the past nor confined to the future: HE IS HERE NOW. As we come to him in faith, let us believe that *he is and that he is a rewarder of those who seek Him.*[65]

Faith and Assurance

Now faith is the assurance of things hoped for...(Heb.11:1NAS)

One way we know we have genuine faith is that we have an inner, confident assurance after praying. I can remember the crisis that ensued when my second son, Dave, was born seven weeks prematurely. He soon developed serious breathing difficulties. The local hospital rushed him to the infant intensive care unit at the University of Virginia Hospital. The doctor's only comment was, "It is serious. It could go either way." With my wife in our local hospital, I called several fellow believers, and we were soon on our knees in my living room. God's Spirit was present and after a time of earnestly praying, God brought the assurance to my heart. I knew – deep inside – that God had heard and all would be well with my son. The assurance was so strong, I felt I did not even need to pray any further and that I was just to give thanks. That very night my son's vital signs began to improve for the first time, and he steadily got better.

Martin Luther once defined faith as "a living, daring confidence in God's grace, so sure and certain that a man would stake his life on it a thousand times."[66] David Thomas, a leader of Overseas Missions Fellowship in Korea, was a well known London merchant. One day as he left church, his son arrived breathlessly, "Father, the store is on fire!" Mr. Thomas asked, "Are the firemen at work?" When assured they were, Mr. Thomas prayed, "Lord, it is not my store. It is thine. Put thy hand upon that fire and do it now for Jesus' sake." He then quietly said, "Now let us go to supper." Several accompanying friends protested, "What about the fire?" Thomas replied, "Didn't we commit it to the Lord? If we were to go to the store, what more could we do? He will take care of it." Halfway through their meal, the son entered the room and announced that the firemen, though feeling all would be lost, were miraculously able to stop the flames. The startled firemen could not understand the mysterious manner in which the flames were arrested, and declared it "looks like an act of God."[67] May we, too, walk in the assurance that comes with faith.

Faith and Confidence

*So keep up your courage, men, for I have faith in God
that it will happen just as he told me. (Acts 27:25)*

The following story is told by the captain of a ship on which
George Müller of Bristol was traveling in the latter part of the
nineteenth century. Müller was a renowned man of faith in his
day, who saw God provide for thousands of orphans in his care –
all in answer to prayer without advertising.

"We had George Müller of Bristol on board," said the
captain. "I had been on the bridge for twenty-four hours and
never left it, and George Müller came to me and said, 'Captain, I
have come to tell you I must be in Quebec on Saturday
afternoon.' 'It is impossible,' I said. 'Then very well, if your ship
cannot take me, God will find some other way. I have never
broken an engagement in fifty-seven years; let us go down into
the chart room and pray.'

"I looked at that man of God and thought to myself, 'What
lunatic asylum can that man have come from, for I have never
heard of such a thing as this?' 'Mr. Müller,' I said, 'do you know
how dense this fog is?'

"'No,' he replied, 'my eye is not on the density of the fog,
but on the living God who controls every circumstance of my
life.' He knelt down and he prayed one of the most simple
prayers. When he had finished I was going to pray, but he put
his hand on my shoulder and told me not to pray. 'As you do not
believe He will answer, and as I believe He has, there is no need
whatever for you to pray about it.'

"I looked at him, and George Müller said, 'Captain, I have
known my Lord for fifty-seven years and there has never been a
single day when I have failed to get an audience with the King.
Get up, Captain, and open the door and you will find the fog has
gone.'

"I got up and the fog indeed was gone, and on that Saturday
afternoon George Müller kept his promised engagement."[68]

Lord, infuse us with such confidence of faith!

Faith and Simplicity

*Has not God chosen those who are poor in the eyes
of the world to be rich in faith... (James 2:5)*

Philip Yancey related this personal story. "God often does his work through 'holy fools,' dreamers who strike out in ridiculous faith, whereas I approach my own decisions with calculation and restraint. In fact, a curious law of reversal seems to apply in matters of faith. The modern world honors intelligence, good looks, confidence, and sophistication. God, apparently, does not. To accomplish his work God often relies; on simple, uneducated people who don't know any better than to trust him...The least gifted person can become a master in prayer, because prayer requires only an intense desire to spend time with God.

"My church in Chicago, a delightful mixture of races and economic groups, once scheduled an all-night vigil of prayer during a major crisis. Several people voiced concern. Was it safe, given our inner-city neighborhood? Should we hire guards or escorts for the parking lot? At length we discussed the practicality of the event before finally putting the night of prayer on the calendar. The poorest members of the congregation, a group of senior citizens from a housing project, responded the most enthusiastically to the prayer vigil.... 'How long do you want to stay – an hour or two?' we asked, thinking of the logistics of van shuttles. 'Oh, we'll stay all night,' they replied.

"One African-American woman in her nineties, who walked with a cane and could barely see, explained to a staff member why she wanted to spend the night sitting on the hard pews of a church in an unsafe neighborhood. 'You see, they's lots of things we can't do in this church. We ain't so educated, and we ain't got as much energy as some of you younger folks. But we can pray. We got time, and we got faith. Some of us don't sleep much anyway. We can pray all night if needs be.'

"And so they did. Meanwhile, a bunch of yuppies in a downtown church learned an important lesson: Faith appears where least expected and falters where it should be thriving."[69]

Faith and Reality

...lean not on your own understanding...(Prov. 3:5)

Reality is sometimes beyond what we see with our visible eyes or what we understand with our natural minds. Faith often connects us with what is real, as Corrie ten Boom explained. "I was once a passenger aboard a ship that was being guided by radar. The fog was so dense we couldn't see even the water about us. But the radar screen showed a streak of light, indicating the presence of another ship far ahead. So, also, is faith the radar that sees reality through the clouds.

"The reality of the victory of Christ can be seen only by faith, which is our radar. Our faith perceives what is actual and real; our senses perceive only that which is limited to three dimensions and comprehended by our intellect. Faith sees more."[70]

There will be times in our lives in which everything is "cloudy" and not so clear. We might be confused, not knowing the next step to take. Our faith in such perplexing times might be somewhat shaky. All the outward circumstances might easily cause us to question (or even abandon) God, and yet this is the time that our faith needs to take deeper root. Oswald Chambers said, "Faith in God is a terrific venture in the dark; I have to believe that God is good in spite of all the contradictions in my experience...We will hang in there, as Job did, and say, 'Though things look black, I will trust in God.'"[71]

In the news recently, a massive vehicle pile-up took place on a Florida interstate that was completely darkened by a wildfire. Apparently, some vehicles continued to speed through the dark, not knowing what was ahead. God does not intend his children to walk blindly through dark times without knowing what is up ahead. *Even in darkness, light dawns for the upright...*[72] Our faith is like a radar, which lets us know what is ahead – for us, we know that at the end, we will find God himself and the fulfillment of his great and precious promises.

Faith and Acceptance

*I have chosen the way of truth; I have set my heart on
your laws.... I will answer the one who taunts me, for
I trust in your word. (Psalm 119:30, 42)*

Just before he launched into extensive gospel ministry, Billy
Graham, at thirty years of age, faced a huge faith crisis. Could
he really trust the Bible? Was it divinely inspired, or just the
words of men? Was it a book he could base his entire life upon?
In his autobiography, Graham recounted his struggle of faith. "I
had to have an answer. If I could not trust the Bible, I could not
go on....I would have to leave pulpit evangelism....I got up and
took a walk....Dropping to my knees there in the woods, I
opened the Bible at random on a tree stump in front of me
....The exact wording of my prayer is beyond recall, but it must
have echoed my thoughts: 'O God! There are many things in this
book I do not understand. There are many problems with it for
which I have no solution. There are many seeming contradictions. There are some areas in it that do not seem to correlate
with modern science. I can't answer some of the philosophical
and psychological questions others are raising.'

"I was trying to be on the level with God, but something
remained unspoken. At last the Holy Spirit freed me to say it.
'Father, I am going to accept this as Thy Word – by faith! I'm
going to allow faith to go beyond my intellectual questions and
doubts, and I will believe this to be Your inspired Word.'

"When I got up from my knees that night, my eyes stung
with tears. I sensed the presence and power of God as I had not
sensed it in months. Not all my questions were answered, but a
major bridge had been crossed. In my heart and mind, I knew a
spiritual battle in my soul had been fought and won."[73]

We can be thankful for so many apologetic works in our day
that give us greater confidence in the Bible. However, there will
always be unanswered questions and room for doubt.
Ultimately, we must take the same stand as Graham; we must
accept the Bible as the very word of God – by faith.

Faith and Creation (Part 1)

By faith we understand that the universe was formed at God's command, so that which is seen was not made out of what was visible. (Hebrews 11:3)

In this verse it says we understand creation *by faith;* it does not say we understand *by science.* Science is a worthwhile field of study, but we should not rely upon it to verify the creation. The word of God is clear – God did it – and it was not through an evolutionary process. If we cannot believe that Almighty God, by his spoken word, created the world with all its diversified forms of life, then we will have difficulties in experiencing biblical faith. A. W. Tozer stated,

"True faith rests upon the character of God and asks no further proof than the moral perfections of the One who cannot lie. It is enough that God said it, and if the statement should contradict every one of the five senses and all the conclusions of logic as well, still the believer continues to believe. 'Let God be true, but every man a liar,' is the language of true faith. Heaven approves such faith because it rises above mere proofs and rests in the bosom of God....In recent years among certain evangelicals there has arisen a movement designed to prove the truths of Scriptures by appeal to science. Evidence is sought in the natural world to support supernatural revelation. Snow-flakes, blood, stones, strange marine creatures, birds, and many other natural objects are brought forward as proof that the Bible is true. This is touted as being a great support to faith, the idea being that if a Bible doctrine can be *proved* to be true, faith will spring up and flourish as a consequence. What these brethren do not see is that the very fact that they feel a necessity to seek proof for the truths of the Scriptures proves something else altogether, namely, their own basic unbelief. When God speaks, unbelief asks, 'How shall I know that this is true?' I AM THAT I AM is the only grounds for faith. To dig among the rocks or search under the sea for evidence to support the Scriptures is to insult the One who wrote them."[74]

Faith and Creation (Part 2)

For it is by faith that we understand that the world was created by one word from God, so that no apparent cause can account for the things we can see. (Heb. 11:3 Jerusalem Bible)

If everything was created simply *at God's command,* then why is it difficult to believe that he actually created the first man, Adam out of the dust of the ground, and Eve from a rib in his side? Is this too difficult for an Almighty God? According to the verse above, God did not need pre-existing materials or natural causes to help in His process of creation: *no apparent cause can account for the things we can see.*

While Christians may have some difficulty in reconciling Scripture with the findings of science, there are even greater difficulties for those who want to insist that God created everything through billions of years in a slow, evolutionary process ("theistic evolution"). Consider two big questions:

First, did Jesus believe in a literal creation account? The Bible says Jesus was involved in the Creation. *Through him all things were made; without him nothing was made that has been made.*[75] *For by him all things were created: things in heaven and on earth, visible and invisible...*[76] So, if Jesus was there "in the beginning," then He personally knows exactly how it all happened. Scripture indicates that Jesus *did* believe in the actual persons of Adam and Eve and the account as simply told in Genesis. *"Haven't you read,"* [Jesus] replied, *"that at the beginning the Creator 'made them male and female'..."*[77]

Secondly, was the apostle Paul deceived about the creation? He wrote, *... sin entered the world through one man, and death through sin, and in this way death came to all men, because all sinned ... For as in Adam all die, so in Christ all will be made alive.*[78] Paul believed in a literal Adam and if Adam was not the "first man," then Paul's whole theological discussion would be pointless. Paul also believed that the first death came through Adam, not millions of years before. We cannot compromise this truth; let us choose to believe the words of Jesus and Paul.[79]

Faith and Impossibilities

Is anything too hard for the Lord? (Gen. 18:14)
What is impossible with men is possible with God. (Lk. 18:27)

William MacDonald encourages our faith with these words:
"Faith does not operate in the realm of the possible. There is no
glory for God in that which is humanly possible. Faith begins
where man's power ends. Müller said, 'The province of faith
begins where probabilities cease and where sight and sense fail.'
Faith says, 'If *impossible* is the only objection, it can be done!'

"C. H. Mackintosh says, 'Faith brings God into the scene,
and therefore it knows absolutely nothing of difficulties – yea, it
laughs at impossibilities. In the judgment of faith, God is the
grand answer to every question – the grand solution of every
difficulty. It refers all to Him; and hence it matters not in the
least to faith whether it be six hundred thousand (dollars) or six
hundred million; it knows that God is all-sufficient. It finds all
its resources in Him. Unbelief says, "How can such and such
things be?" It is full of "hows"; but faith has one great answer to
ten thousand "hows," and that answer is – God.'

"Humanly speaking, it was impossible for Abraham and
Sarah to have a child. But God had promised, and to Abraham
there was only one impossibility – that God could lie.

And being not weak in faith, he considered not his own body
now dead, when he was about an hundred years neither yet
the deadness of Sara's womb: he staggered not at the
promise of God through unbelief, but was strong in faith,
giving glory to God; and being fully persuaded that, what he
had promised, he was able also to perform. (Rom. 4:19-21)

"Faith, mighty faith, the promise sees;
And looks to God alone;
Laughs at impossibilities;
And cries, 'It shall be done!'"[80]

Faith and Obedience (Part 1)

By faith, Abraham, when called out to go to a place he would later receive as his inheritance, obeyed and went, even though he did not know where he was going. (Heb. 11:8)

Our natural tendency is *not* to obey the Lord; we usually seek for some clearer direction or we attempt to work out our own plans. Abraham's orders were not complete. He was just to *go* and the Lord would guide him step by step. *He did not know where he was going.* The life of faith can be frustrating because we humans like to have everything mapped out. We like five-year-plans; we don't like uncertainty. The theme for the Christian, however, is going-without-knowing.

We can delay obedience by requesting more information: "If I just knew more, then I would do God's will." God's way, however, is the opposite: *If any man is willing to do His will, he shall know of the teaching, whether it is of God, or whether I speak from Myself.*[81] It is only as we obey God that further understanding comes. In obedience to God, Abraham made a costly decision to leave his hometown of Ur. He settled in Haran, where his father died. Then, God spoke again.[82] Probably a major reason God leads us this way is so we will continually have to seek his face and hear from him. God seldom gives us the complete picture. He leads us step by step: *the steps of a man are ordered by the Lord...*[83]

Faith is linked with obedience. We criticize Peter for trying to walk on water and sinking. Yet, Peter was the only disciple willing to get out of the boat! When the master said, *"Come,"* the Scripture records, *Then Peter got down out of the boat and walked on the water to Jesus...*[84] Like Peter and Abraham, let us not stay in the comfort of our *boats* or the secure home place of *Ur*; when the Lord calls, let us step forth in obedience. Let us declare, *"We will do everything the Lord has said; we will obey."*[85]

Faith and Obedience (Part 2)

*"Why do you call me, 'Lord, Lord,' and do not do
what I say?" (Luke 6:46)*

Faith is often linked with our obedience to God. It has been said
that partial obedience is still disobedience. So, when God has
spoken to us, we must not seek to *completely* understand before
we *completely* obey. Belief and obedience come first; then the
understanding may follow (or it may not.) St. Augustine wrote
in the fourth century, "Seek not to understand that you may
believe, but believe that you may understand."[86]

Because God places such a high value on obedience, we
must continually seek his plans, and not just do what seems good
to us. Christopher Shaw has clarified this idea. "According to
Jesus' teaching, faith is tied to God's plans, not ours. Faith is not
a blank check God gives His disciples so they may ask for
anything they want. It is not an unconditional commitment to
endorse whatever we propose to do. Instead, it is the conviction
that God will give His full backing to that which He alone has
initiated.

"We only need a quick look at faith's great heroes to see that
whenever the Lord's hand moved powerfully on their behalf,
they had done no more than obey His instructions. Abraham
offered Isaac as a sacrifice because he believed God's word to
him about an heir. Moses lifted his staff over the waters of the
Red Sea because he believed the Lord would deliver the
Israelites as He had promised. He also struck the rock to obtain
water because God had told him to do so. Joshua saw the
destruction of Jericho because he accepted God's instructions
regarding that city....

"It is impossible to exercise faith in something we have not
heard directly from the Lord. Faith is only applicable when God
has clearly spoken and invited us to follow through by believing
Him. When we obey, it is clear proof of our faith."[87]

Let us therefore pray, "Lord, show me your plans, and by
the power of the Holy Spirit, I will obey!"

Faith and Sight (Part 1)

For we walk by faith [we regulate our lives and conduct ourselves by our conviction or belief respecting man's relationship to God and divine things, with trust and holy fervor; thus we walk] not by sight or appearance. (2 Cor.5:7 The Amplified Bible)

We might naturally want more tangible evidence before we walk in faith. In one sense, however, we all exercise faith many times every day. Charles Ryrie explains, "You walk into a restaurant and order a meal. It is prepared out of sight and served by people you hardly know. Without hesitation, you eat it and enjoy it. And without thinking, you have exercised faith.

"You take a prescription from your doctor – written in handwriting you can't read, containing words you can't pronounce – to a pharmacist you don't know who puts pills or tablets into a container, with words to the effect of 'Take one every four hours.' You obediently do what you are told, and then days later, hopefully, your illness is gone. Again, you have exercised faith.

"When you mail a letter, you are putting your faith in the postal service. When you fly in a plane, you are putting your faith in the airline and the professional skills of the flight and maintenance crews. On and on it goes."[88]

So, we could say that every day of our lives brings dozens of opportunities to put faith to work, even though we don't physically see the evidence or fully understand. If this is true in common matters, it should also be true in spiritual matters. We should not be hesitant to put our trust in Christ; we can take steps of faith and move confidently ahead. The evidence verifying Jesus and his resurrection is profound and consistent with sound reason. The skeptic, however, may ask for indisputable evidence and total understanding. The Christian walks by faith, not by sight. We can choose to follow Christ with confidence and conduct our lives in accordance with his revealed will.

Faith and Sight (Part 2)

*Though you have not seen him, you love him; and even
though you do not see him now, you believe in him and
are filled with an inexpressible and glorious joy...
(1 Peter 1:8)*

Suppose we could transport ourselves back two thousand years
to the time of Christ, and we could hear him teach and see his
miracles. Would we be more likely to believe in him? Would
our faith be any stronger? The apostle Peter was not only an
eyewitness but one of Jesus' closest disciples. Some years later,
in writing to an audience who had never seen Christ and yet was
going through great persecution, Peter commended their
admirable faith. A. W. Tozer commented on this passage.

"The Apostle Peter, who had seen Jesus Christ in the flesh
with his own eyes, passed along to every believing Christian the
assurance that it is possible for us to love the Savior and to live a
life that will glorify Him even though we have not yet seen Him!
It is as though Peter is urging: 'Love Him and work for Him and
live for Him. I give you my testimony that it will be worth it all
when you look upon His face – for I have seen Him with my
own eyes, and I know!'

"In his epistle, Peter, who had known Jesus in the flesh, was
moved to write to the strangers scattered abroad – the Christians
of the dispersion – to remind them that they should love Jesus
Christ even though they had not seen Him in the flesh...

"God has seen fit to give us wonderful and mysterious
faculties, and I truly believe that God has ordained that we may
actually know Jesus now, and love Him better never having seen
Him, than Peter did when he saw Him!"[89]

Lord, we do believe in you! Please open our spiritual eyes,
that we might see you more clearly and trust you more fully.

Faith and Proof

Thomas declared, "Unless I see the nail marks in his hands and put my hand into his side, I will not believe it." .... Jesus told him, "Because you have seen me, you have believed; blessed are those who have not seen and yet have believed." (John 20:24-29)

If we could see Jesus with our physical eyes, would we believe more strongly in him? Doubting Thomas thought so, but Jesus said to him, *"Blessed are those who have not seen and yet have believed."* Here Jesus promises a special blessing – not only for Thomas, but for future generations – for those who believe without seeing the physical evidence.

Have you ever wondered why God has not allowed greater archeological discoveries in order to convince many of the world's skeptics? For example, we have heard of expeditions in the past century which have tried to scale Mt. Ararat in Turkey in order to find the remains of Noah's ark, thus proving the biblical account. There have been some sightings of a large object, and yet conclusive evidence continues to elude all searchers. Could there be a reason God keeps such "proofs" from the human eye? Why have there not been discoveries of Egyptian records verifying the existence of Moses, a *son of Pharaoh's daughter*, and the account of the Exodus? Why has the ark of the covenant been kept from the human eye? It might be that such discoveries will yet be made before our Lord returns, but he may want us to believe without the proof. *Blessed are those who have not seen and yet have believed.*

When I was in college, a student on my hall desperately needed $100 to get a plane ticket home. All of us on the hall were tight financially, but after prayer we took up an offering, and the amount came to $99.86. Now, a skeptic might say, "You were fourteen cents short." Those with eyes of faith, however, quickly said, "God answered our prayer." We will be blessed indeed if we exercise faith in God, despite a lack of proof.

Faith and the Future

> *These little troubles (which are really so transitory) are winning for us a permanent, glorious and solid reward out of all proportion to our pain. For we are looking all the time not at all the visible things but at the invisible. The visible things are transitory; it is the invisible things that are really permanent. (2 Cor. 4:17-18 Phillips)*

Those of us who struggle with our faith in the midst of discouraging or disabling circumstances can be helped by doing three things.

First, even though we haven't seen the provision, the miracle, or the breakthrough we expected, let us remember the Lord – what he has done in the past and what he has promised to do in the future. We might identify with the discouraged psalmist, who had not seen any supernatural intervention: *We do not see our signs, there is no longer any prophet...How long, O God, will the adversary revile?* But his discouragement turned to faith, and he wrote, *Yet God is my king from of old, who works deeds of deliverance in the midst of the earth.*[90] The author went on to recount mighty deeds that God had done. Over and over the Israelites were exhorted to *remember the Lord.*

Second, keep eternity in view. Eternity is going to be a long, long time, and we are in danger of forfeiting the glories ahead if we give up, become bitter toward God, and fail to endure present suffering. Meditating upon the reality of eternity and God's future promises will be a strong motivator to hold on to the Lord.

Third, we can take comfort in knowing that God's future promise is out of all proportion to any present pain. Paul stated our worst troubles are *little* and *transitory.* If we continue in faith, we will soon obtain *a permanent, glorious and solid reward out of all proportion to our pain.* Such a promise may sound almost too good to be true, but elsewhere Paul echoed this truth: *I consider that our present sufferings are not worth comparing with the glory that will be revealed in us.*[91] Hold on in faith; it will be worth it in the end!

Faith and Promise

*What I have said, that will I bring about; what I have
planned, that will I do. (Isaiah 46:11)*

Faith is much more than just our positive imagination or trying
to convince ourselves mentally that something is so. When an
engagement ring is given, it is an indication that a promise is yet
to be fulfilled and that the best is yet to come (marriage). When
God gives us the gift of the Holy Spirit in our hearts, the Bible
says it is *God's guarantee that he will give us everything he
promised* (Eph.1:14 NLT). The Greek word for *guarantee* is also
translated "deposit" (NIV), "pledge" (NAS), or "down payment"
(AMP). In modern Greek, the word is used for an engagement
ring. God's people are described as the "bride of Christ." God
has given us his "engagement ring" – the Holy Spirit residing in
our hearts – which we must accept by faith. It is his pledge that
we will one day be joined together forever.

Suppose a godly young man became engaged to a girl and
then went off to active duty in the military. While he was gone,
some critical friends said, "He'll never come back for you;
you're just kidding yourself. He isn't really that serious." The
young lady could become quite upset by those comments and
worry for some time. Or, instead she could simply gaze at the
engagement ring. "No, I have absolute confidence in my man.
He said he would return, that we will be married, and I believe
him – absolutely."

The ring is not the man; but it is a constant reminder of the
man and his loving promise to her. In the same way, as we
exhibit our faith in Christ, we are saying, "I believe in what my
Lord has said. The 'lover of my soul' has said he loves me; he is
preparing a place for me; and he has promised to come back
again and take me to himself. No matter what the skeptics may
say, I choose to believe him instead. This is not just my
imagination or wishful thinking. I have been given his word and
his pledge. The Holy Spirit confirms to my spirit that these
promises are true and will surely come to pass. I believe him!"

Day Thirty-Eight
Faith and Bargaining

*Then Jacob made a vow, saying, "If God will be with
me and will watch over me on this journey I am taking
and will give me food to eat and clothes to wear so that
I return safely to my father's house, then the LORD will
be my God... (Genesis 28:20-21)*

Jacob, at this time of his life, had only a limited relationship with
God. Basically he was saying, "If you do this…and do
that…then you will be my God." One way we, too, compromise
the life of faith is by "bargaining with God." Here are a few
examples of how it's done.

- "Lord, if you get me out of this mess, I'll serve you for the
  rest of my life…"
- "Lord, if you meet this financial crisis, I'll start tithing …"
- "Lord, if you heal my wife, then I can really trust you…"

By thinking like this, we operate in what Philip Yancey has
called "contract faith." He remarked, "I have observed that
people involved in ministry, perhaps more so than most people,
live with an unstated 'contract faith.' After all, they're giving
time and energy to work for God; don't they deserve special
treatment in return? My wife would get irritated when she got a
parking ticket while stopping to pick up meat for a soup kitchen
or while visiting a shut-in at the hospital. The meter expired for
the very reason that she had sensed a need to devote more time
to doing God's work. Her reward: a fine and a half-day trip to
the city courthouse! Bud, one of the true 'saints' in urban
ministry in Chicago, nearly cut off his hand on a power saw
while demonstrating to volunteers how to build houses for the
homeless…" [92]

To avoid a mentality of "contract faith," we can remember a
few basic truths: (1) God is God and He will do as he pleases; [93]
(2) We live in a sin-infested world that is not fully redeemed
yet; [94] (3) Accidents and tragedies occur to good people as well
as bad; [95] and (4) Regardless of what we encounter, *nothing* will
ever separate us from the love of God in Christ Jesus. [96]

Faith and Silence

Now we see but a poor reflection; then we shall see
face to face. Now I know in part; then I shall know
fully, even as I am fully known. And now three remain:
faith, hope and love... (1 Corinthians 13:12-13)

Ronald Dunn said, "I have been to the bottom, and I'm here to tell you it's solid." Dunn suffered great personal grief through the tragic death of his son, who committed suicide at the age of eighteen. Dunn wrote about his times of depression, guilt, and feeling the "silence" of God. As a pastor, Dunn also had to answer the question some would ask, "Why would God allow something like this to happen to a man of God like you?"

In his book, *When Heaven is Silent: Live by Faith, Not by Sight,*[97] Dunn shared this insight, "In the aftermath of tragedy, to gather up the debris of our faith, we call God on the carpet and demand he explain himself, and he had better have a good reason for doing what he did. But the truth is that God, being God, doesn't need to explain his actions to anyone."[98] Dunn, who related other unexplained experiences of suffering, including being shot at by a gunman, concluded his book by emphasizing the Christian walk is by faith, not by sight.

One of his last chapters is entitled, "The Most Unbelievable Verse in the Bible," which he stated is Romans 8:28: *And we know that in all things God works for the good of those who love him, who have been called according to his purpose.* Dunn explained, "Paul is not saying that whatever happens to a Christian is good. A lot of bad things happen to us. We cannot say that what happens is best. But, it will be worked out for our good, the best. The bad things that happen to us have no weight in thwarting the good God intends for us. Paul doesn't mean that God works out all things for our comfort, convenience, health and wealth...Whatever 'good' Paul has in mind has to do with our salvation and our relationship to the God who saved us...Things do not work out for good. *God* works things out for good...The faith expressed here is faith not in things but in God."[99] Our faith continues even when God seems to be silent.

Faith and Receiving

Yet to all who received him, to those who believed in his name, he gave the right to become children of God... (John 1:12)

Suppose a father, desiring to show his love to a son, went to much time, trouble, and expense to procure a valuable and meaningful gift. And suppose that when the wrapped gift was finally presented to the boy, he just folded his arms and casually replied, "Dad, I will need to pay you first for the gift..." or "Dad, I haven't lived a good enough life yet to accept such a gift..." or "Dad, I'm just not ready; after I get a few things right in my life, then I want that gift." All these responses, of course, are ridiculous, but some of us have similar difficulty in knowing how to receive.

Learning to receive by faith is essential to salvation: *the free gift of God is eternal life in Christ Jesus our Lord.*[100] Pride and self-sufficiency may make it difficult for some people simply to receive.

"While Andrew Jackson was President of the United States, a man was given a court trial and condemned to die. President Jackson offered to pardon him, but the condemned man refused the pardon. Prison authorities, the Attorney General of the United States, and others earnestly endeavored to convince the man to accept the pardon. They tried to impress upon him that it would not only spare his life, but that if he did not accept the pardon it would be an insult to the President. The man persisted. The Attorney General consulted the Supreme Court, asking whether legal authorities could not force the man to receive the pardon. The court ruled that the pardon was merely a printed statement until the man accepted it. If he rejected the pardon, it remained printed matter."[101]

The Lord Jesus Christ has shed his very blood to pardon our sins, but this pardon will not be forced upon anyone. We can refuse it if we so choose. Even though we may intellectually assent to the fact that Jesus secured the pardon, we must still take a deliberate step of faith to *receive* God's free gift of salvation.

Day Forty-One
Faith and Facts

The fool...won't face facts. (Proverbs 14:8 TLB)

No serious, conservative scholars are going to claim the New Testament is a mere collection of fables or fabrications made up by radical followers of a self-proclaimed messiah. No, there is simply too much historical and archeological support for the biblical texts as well as hundreds of reputable eye-witness accounts. We are not exercising "blind faith;" there are plenty of facts to support our belief in Christ. This is not to say there are still questions to be answered and mysteries about the faith. However, the Bible says a man is a *fool* who refuses to face the overwhelming factual evidence and blatantly declares, *"There is no God."*[102] Ultimately, we must decide if we will embrace Christ by faith, or will we stubbornly refuse to face the facts?

After the tragic 1999 earthquake in northwest Turkey, many newscasts asked how towns could have been better prepared. A National Public Radio program broadcasted one of the most unfortunate stories of all. Apparently, some thirty years previously the people in one of the small towns in that region had been informed by authorities that the town was situated right on top of a major fault line. The danger was so significant that authorities suggested that the community relocate. The citizens gathered to discuss the issue. Their response was a solemn town council vote to move the fault line on the map, rather than to move the town.... Sadly, many paid for that unfortunate decision with their lives.[103] They had simply refused to face the facts!

There is no merit in us being naïve and avoiding careful investigation of truth claims. When Luke wrote his gospel about Jesus, he did not go into a trance or find mysterious gold plates "dropped out of heaven;" he said, *I myself have carefully investigated everything from the beginning...*[104] Luke, deemed a "first-rate historian" by many classical scholars, included multiple, historical facts in his writing.[105] He wanted his readers to *know the certainty of the things you have been taught.*[106] Today we certainly have enough facts; we can take a step of faith to follow Jesus Christ as Lord.

Faith and Experience

He has also set eternity in the hearts of men; yet they cannot fathom what God has done from beginning to end. (Ecc. 3:11)

We believe many things, even though we have never personally seen the physical evidence or experienced them. Josh and Sean McDowell apply this thinking to the afterlife. "Virtually every culture from the very dawning of civilization has believed in a life beyond the grave in which some type of soul survives death of the body. It is amazing, when you stop to think about it, that a universal belief in the after-life has dominated historical thinking in spite of having little empirical evidence to justify it. Of course, people do have reason to believe some things they have not experienced. They believe there is a Mount Everest even if they haven't climbed its rugged heights. They believe in the Great Barrier Reef off the coast of Australia even though they have never swum the depth of the Coral Sea. It is universally accepted that hundreds of swallows travel like clockwork in a 12,000-mile round-trip from Argentina to San Juan Capistrano each year, even though most people haven't witnessed the event firsthand. In spite of the fact that most people have neither seen nor experienced these events directly, they can be empirically observed and have been for many years – some for centuries....

"But it is another matter when all cultures in history up to the present affirm their belief in something that seems impossible to record or experience and live to tell about it. Why is the belief that there is life after death affirmed almost unanimously among every culture in history without empirical evidence? It seems clear that the 'sense' there is a life after death has been implanted deeply within the heart of humans... God 'has planted eternity in the human heart, but even so, people cannot see the whole scope of God's work from beginning to end' (Ecc. 3:11). Though humans cannot see into the next life, the vast majority believe it's there, and they have believed that since the dawn of time."[107]

Faith and Feeling

For we walk by faith, not by sight. (2 Corinthians 5:7)

Feelings cannot be neglected, but neither can they be central to our faith. Our Christianity was never meant to be a cold, unhappy religion with no display of emotion. Scripture points out that after believing in Christ, we are filled with *a joy that words cannot express and which has in it even a hint of the glories of Heaven.*[108]

We must also be careful of the other extreme. We cannot trust our emotions to guide us. Our emotions can be very erratic, as unstable as the wind. Too many people make decisions merely on their sense of happiness. But our confidence has to be in the person of Christ and the facts of the gospel message found in the Bible. For many years this train diagram has been used by Campus Crusade for Christ in explaining salvation[109].

The train will run with or without the caboose. However, it would be useless to attempt to pull the train by the caboose. As someone has said,

Feelings come and feelings go, and
Feelings are deceiving.
Our warrant is the word of God;
Nothing else is worth believing.

After a peace treaty was signed, ending the American Civil War, there were soldiers who remained in hiding. They might have returned to their homes to enjoy happy reunions with wives and children. But they subsisted on a diet of berries and other wild foods. They either didn't have the facts or failed to believe the good news of the war's ending. In like manner, we must first have the facts about Christ and then believe the Good News before we enjoy the blessed benefits of our salvation.

Faith and Foundation

Behold, I lay in Zion a stone for a foundation, a tried stone, a precious cornerstone, a sure foundation; Whoever believes will not act hastily. (Isaiah 28:16 NKJV)

Have you ever been told, "As long as you have faith, that's what's important"? But more important than faith is the foundation on which faith is established. We can have great faith in a promising business stock and it can become worthless. We can believe strongly in a dream of success and it can quickly come tumbling down. We can have a strong faith in something other than Christ and yet perish for eternity. Only Jesus Christ is the *sure* foundation. Charles Spurgeon related a sad story that underscores the need of a sure foundation:

"There was an architect who had a plan for building a lighthouse on the Eddystone Rock. It quite satisfied his mind, and as he sat by the fire looking at his plans, he was quite sure that no storm that ever came could shake that building. He applied for the contract to build the lighthouse, and did build it, and a very singular-looking place it was. There were a great many flags about it and ornaments, and it looked very promising. Some shook their heads a little, but he was very, very firm, and said he should like to be in it himself in the worst wind that ever blew. He was in it at the time he wanted to be, and he was never heard of again, nor was anything more ever seen of his lighthouse. The whole thing was swept away. He was a man of great faith, only it happened to be founded on mistaken principles."[110]

We must be careful to build upon the right foundation. We tend to put faith in what is visible – large churches, successful ministries, and dynamic pastors. But, the stability of a building can best be measured by the *unseen* foundation. Let us resolve...

On Christ the Solid Rock I stand;
All other ground is sinking sand.

Day Forty-Five
Faith and the Bridge

For there is one God and one mediator between God and men, the man Christ Jesus. (1 Timothy 2:5)

Our faith can rest in Christ, our mediator between God and man. He is like a "bridge over troubled waters" that keeps us connected to God. Jesus is a bridge that is most secure, unlike other "bridges" which are insubstantial and unsafe to travel on. D. James Kennedy shares a lesson about faith and bridges.

"It was a dark night on the main road from Jackson to Vicksburg, Mississippi. It had rained heavily, but the storm had finally broken, and the pavement was not so slippery. A truck driver traveled down that stretch of highway, and since conditions had improved, he began to relax a bit. Suddenly he saw the twin taillights of the car in front of him melt into the road and disappear. The truck driver sat bolt upright with his startled eyes wide open. Such a thing could not happen! In the next fraction of a second, he saw the gaping black hole where once a bridge had spanned the river. The truck driver slammed on his brakes, and the wheels stopped instantly, but there was no longer a road beneath them. His truck sailed silently and eerily into the black void before him. As the truck sank into the water, the driver broke out the window, got out of the truck, and managed to swim to shore. Like a dripping scarecrow, he scrambled up the embankment to the road. As he climbed, he heard one car after another zoom smoothly into the gap and disappear. The only trace was a booming splash preceded by startled shrieks or cries. Finally, the truck driver made his way to the road and frantically waved his hands at the oncoming cars in the dark. But they did not stop. Sixteen people died that night because *they had faith in a bridge that was no longer there.*

"In life, we maintain faith in many bridges – the bridge of successful achievements, the bridge of good deeds, the bridge of 'I tried as hard as I could' – but all of these bridges are out. Faith in Christ is the only bridge we can rely on."[111]

Faith and Truth

To the Jews who had believed him, Jesus said, "If you hold to my teaching, you are really my disciples. Then you will know the truth, and the truth will set you free." (John 8:31-32)

True faith must always be connected with truth. In the above passage, Jesus was talking to religious people who believed in him; these Jews had a certain measure of faith. Yet, they were not yet disciples; they still had to come to a fuller knowledge of the truth. Faith itself is nothing; faith must lead to truth, and truth will always be centered in Jesus. A. W. Tozer confronted some popular but false ideas of faith:

"There is a nebulous idea accepted by many in our day that faith is an almighty power flowing through the universe which anyone may plug into at will! It is conceived vaguely as a subrational creative pulsation streaming down from somewhere Up There, ready at any time to enter our hearts and change our whole mental and moral constitution as well as our total outlook on man, God and the cosmos.

"When it comes in, supposedly out go pessimism, fear, defeat and failure; in come optimism, confidence, personal mastery and unfailing success in war, love, sports, business and politics.

"All of this is, of course, a spider-web of self-deception woven of the unsubstantial threads of fancy spun out of minds of tenderhearted persons who want to believe it! What is overlooked in all this is that *faith is good only when it engages truth*: when it is made to rest upon falsehood it can and often does lead to eternal tragedy.

"For it is not enough that we believe; we must believe in the right thing about the right One!"[112]

The more we read Scripture, the more likely we will discover truth, and the more likely we will come to know Christ. Just believing is never sufficient; let's indeed *believe in the right thing about the right One!*

Faith and Substance

Faith is the substance of things hoped for...(Heb. 11:1 KJV)

Our faith is no ethereal thing. It is something which has *substance,* or as Greek translations say, *substantial nature, essence, actual being, reality, confidence, assurance.*[113] A secular Greek usage of the word is *title-deed*[114] – used of documents establishing ownership, deposited in an archive and proving the owner's rights; hence it's a guarantee for the future.[115] The Amplified Bible brings this out, *Faith is the assurance (the confirmation, the title deed) of things we hope for...*

For any property owner, having a *title-deed* is essential. If at any time some question or controversy is raised concerning ownership or the present or future status of the property we have, all we have to do is produce the *title-deed,* and the matter is settled. When we are saved, born-again by the Holy Spirit, something happens inside our hearts. We have a new sense of *reality.* We now possess something of a *substantial nature.* As we receive Christ's free gift by faith, it is as if the Holy Spirit puts a *title-deed* in our hand. He says to us, "Now, you are mine and you are guaranteed the possession of eternal salvation. This title-deed is my free gift to you. It is signed in my blood, sealed by the Holy Spirit, and is something about which you can be absolutely sure." This is why many translators use the word *assurance* in this verse describing faith.

If a man had a title-deed which guaranteed him the most wonderful inheritance, it would be hard to imagine him ever wanting to give it up. God has reserved for us such an inheritance – one that can never perish, spoil or fade – and our faith is the title-deed. [116] This is why we want to hold forever – in faith – the initial commitment we make to Christ. This same Greek word is used in the following verse, *We have come to share in Christ if we hold firmly till the end the confidence* [the title-deed] *we had at the first.*[117] When doubts or disturbing circumstances come our way to test our belief in him, let us *hold firmly till the end.* Let us keep grasping the title-deed!

Faith and Roots

And now, just as you accepted Christ Jesus as your Lord, you must continue to follow him. Let your roots grow down into him, and let your lives be built on him. Then your faith will grow strong in the truth you were taught... (Colossians 2:6-7 NLT)

The deeper a tree's roots go into the ground, the more difficult it will be to try to uproot it. As we become more and more acquainted with Christ, our spiritual roots of faith will only grow stronger. Robert Murray M'Cheyne described the process, "The only way to hold fast is to believe more and more. Become better acquainted with Christ – with His person, work, and character. Every page of the gospel unfolds a new feature of His character; every line of the epistles discloses new depths of His work. Get more faith, and you will get a firmer hold. A plant that has a single root may be easily torn up by the hand, crushed by the foot of the wild beast, or blown down by the wind. But a plant that has a thousand roots struck down into the ground can stand.

"Faith is like the root. Many people believe a little concerning Christ: one fact. Every new truth concerning Jesus is a new root struck downward. Believe more intensely. A root going in a right direction but not striking deep is easily torn up.

"Pray for deep-rooted faith. Pray to be established, strengthened, and settled. Take a long, intense look at Jesus – often, often. If you wanted to remember a man again, and he was going away, you'd take an intense look at his face. Look then at Jesus – deeply, intensely – until every feature is engraved on your heart."[118]

Probably the best way we "look at Christ" is by regularly reading the Scriptures. From Genesis through Revelation, we can see something of the person of Christ. When Jesus walked with two disciples on the road to Emmaus, *beginning with Moses... he explained to them what was said in all the Scriptures concerning himself.*[119] Lord, we want our faith roots to go deeper!

Day Forty-Nine
Faith and Surrender

For the eyes of the LORD move to and fro throughout the earth that He may strongly support those whose heart is completely His. (2 Chronicles 16:9)

People of pronounced faith are not necessarily those with the best biblical knowledge, most consistent disciplines, or the greatest spiritual gifts. Often, great faith is seen in those ordinary believers who are simply *fully surrendered to the Lord.* These will be believers who know…

- We are poor in spirit, desperately needing the Lord.[120]
- We are dependent; apart from Him we can do nothing.[121]
- We are like fragile "clay pots," but we contain a most magnificent treasure (Christ).[122]
- We are weak, yet his power is displayed in us.[123]

When a policeman points a gun directly at a thief, the criminal normally puts his hands up in the air – signifying, "I surrender!" Likewise, when we surrender to the Lord, we are yielding; we are taking a "hands-off" approach to controlling our lives; and by faith we are entrusting ourselves into his hands. I can remember very clearly in March 1971, when I took this step of faith and fully surrendered to the Lord. I came to the place where I basically said, "Lord, I'm not going to run my life any longer; I give myself entirely to you – spirit, mind, and body; I am no longer my own. I will live for you the rest of my days." Although that decision may have been costly in terms of friends and income, I have never had any regrets. The Lord is good!

Andrew Murray, in his excellent book entitled, *Absolute Surrender*, wrote, "The condition for obtaining God's full blessing is absolute surrender to Him."[124] William Booth, founder of the Salvation Army, and very fruitful in his ministry in London and then around the world, was asked near the end of his life about the secret of his spiritual success. He said, "I made up my mind that God Almighty should have all there was of William Booth."[125] Can each of us make the same faith determination – that God will have all there is of me!

Faith and Satisfaction

Then Jesus declared... "He who believes in me will never be thirsty...." (John 6:35)

Every man on earth has a "God-shaped vacuum" in his heart that will never be fully satisfied until he surrenders to Christ. Before Christ, *we used to live in sin...following the passionate desires and inclinations of our sinful nature.*[126] Yet, sin never fully satisfied. We were *like the restless sea, which is never still but continually churns up mud and dirt.*[127] We may have enjoyed sin for a season, yet we were discontent, with *a continual lust for more.*[128] Solomon wisely said, *All man's efforts are for his mouth, yet his appetite is never satisfied.*[129] Saint Augustine said, "O Lord, you have made us for Thyself, and our hearts are restless until they find their rest in Thee."[130] Mick Jagger, in his classic rock song, said it concisely, "I can't get no satisfaction."

When we are justified through faith, we obtain a most incredible gift – *we have peace with God through our Lord Jesus Christ.*[131] This is an inner satisfaction, a peace *which transcends all understanding.*[132] This is not to say we do not long for more spiritually; the longer we live, the more we ought to hunger for a greater experiential knowledge of Christ.[133]

If we are not careful, we can become covetous and become dissatisfied with all that we have.

- "If only I had a better job..."
- "If only we had a bigger house..."
- "If only I had a different husband..."
- "If only I looked younger..."

The biblical word for satisfaction is *contentment*. This is something we appropriate by faith. We must continually resist the lusts of the world and determine to be content. This is a learning process, as the apostle Paul said, *I have learned how to be content (satisfied to the point where I am not disturbed or disquieted) in whatever state I am.*[134] Let us be at peace, satisfied and thankful for all God has given us. By faith, we can rest in his bountiful provision and his providential plans for us.

Faith and the Cross

For what I received I passed on to you as of first importance: that Christ died for our sins according to the Scriptures, that he was buried, that he was raised the third day according to the Scriptures....And if Christ has not been raised, our preaching is useless and so is your faith. (1 Corinthians 15:3-4, 14)

Any faith which is not centered in the cross of Calvary is a *useless* faith. We do not merely believe in the fact that God exists, but in the fact that He came to earth as a man, the very Son of God, who sacrificed his life for us – dying a painful death nailed to a cross. Without a faith in Christ's death and resurrection, our faith is in vain. *God will credit righteousness for us who believe in him who raised Jesus our Lord from the dead. He was delivered over to death for our sins and was raised to life for our justification.*[135]

Faith cannot be vague, or a sort of "faith-in-faith." Francis Schaeffer wrote, "True Christian faith rests on content. It is not a vague thing which takes the place of real understanding, nor is it the strength of belief which is of value. *The true basis for faith is not the faith itself, but the work which Christ finished on the cross.* My believing is not the basis for being saved – the basis is the work of Christ. Christian faith is being turned outward to an objective person: 'Believe on the Lord Jesus, and you shall be saved.'"[136]

The cross of Christ is either something at which we become offended, or something we boast about. *We preach Christ crucified: a stumbling block to Jews and foolishness to Gentiles...May I never boast except in the cross of our Lord Jesus Christ, through which the world has been crucified to me, and I to the world.*[137] This is the acid test of our Christianity, and we need to determine how we really feel about the cross. It cannot just be a lovely idea or religious inspiration. The cross must always be at the very center of our faith.

Faith and Finished Work

... Jesus said, "It is finished." With that, he bowed
his head and gave up his spirit. (John 19:30)

Our faith can be greatly encouraged as we look to the cross and
Jesus' finished work. There is a lot of deep meaning in Jesus'
simple utterance: *"It is finished."* Consider three truths:
1.   PAID IN FULL!
    The Greek word used is *tetelestai*, which meant "to carry
out; to accomplish, to fulfill obligations."[138]   Ancient papyri
receipts for taxes have been recovered with the word *tetalestai*
written across them, meaning "paid in full."[139]   In Jesus' death
on the cross, our enormous debt of sin was fully paid and put
away forever!
2.   IT STANDS FINISHED!
    This Greek word is in the perfect tense, which is very
expressive. Kenneth Wuest clarified, "It speaks of an action that
took place in the past, which was completed in past time, and the
existence of its finished results....So, when our Lord cries from
the Cross, *'It is finished,'* it refers to His work of procuring for
lost sinners a salvation from sin through the blood of His Cross.
The entire sense is, 'It was finished and as a result it is forever
done.' 'It stands finished' would be a good translation. The
priests in the tabernacle always stood when ministering in the
sacrifices. But our great High Priest is seated. His work is
finished. He need never arise and offer another sacrifice."[140]
3.   A SHOUT OF TRIUMPH!
    In the other three gospels, these words, *'It is finished'*, are
not recorded, but they all say Jesus *shouted* or *cried out with a
loud voice* as he died.[141] This is no contradiction, as William
Barclay explained, "*'It is finished'* is one word in Greek –
tetelestai – and Jesus died with a shout of triumph on his lips. He
did not say, *'It is finished,'* in weary defeat; he said it as one who
shouts for joy because the victory is won… *'FINISHED!'* "[142]
    Our faith can rest assured – Jesus has finished the work for
our salvation forever, and we can share in his great triumph!

Faith and Repentance

Repent and believe the good news! (Mark 1:15)

Faith and repentance are like Siamese twins – they are inseparable in the Christian walk. If we emphasize *believing* to an inquirer of Christianity without mentioning *repenting*, we are presenting an incomplete – if not false – gospel message. Jesus' final words to his disciples as part of the great commission included: *...that repentance and forgiveness of sins will be preached in His name to all nations...*[143] The apostle Paul's message stated both: *I have declared to both Jews and Greeks that they must turn to God in repentance and have faith in our Lord Jesus.*[144] Charles Spurgeon commented, "Repentance and faith must go together to complete each other. I compare them to a door and its post. Repentance is the door which shuts out sin, but faith is the post on which its hinges are fixed. A door without a doorpost to hang on is not a door at all, while a doorpost without the door hanging on it is of no value whatever."[145]

Repentance is not just emotional experience, it involves a willful turning from going one's own direction to going God's direction. It literally means "to change one's mind." A. W. Tozer said, "Faith is a redirecting of our sight, a getting out of the focus of our own vision and getting God into focus."[146]

Repentance is not a word just for the sinner. In writing to seven churches in Revelation, the apostle John exhorted five of them to *repent*. Repentance is also not just an initial action, it is an ongoing action in the Christian life. On October 31, 1517, Martin Luther posted his Ninety-five Theses on the door of Castle Church in Wittenberg, Germany. His challenge to the Catholic church began the Reformation, one of the pivotal points in church history. Luther began his list of ninety-five statements by saying, "Our Lord and Master Jesus Christ, in saying 'Repent ye, etc.,' meant *the whole life* of the faithful to be an act of repentance."[147] We must therefore view repentance as a vital part of our faith, something that will greatly affect our *whole life*.

Day Fifty-Four
Faith and Works

Faith, if it has no works, is dead, being by itself. (James 2:17)

Trying to find the balance between faith and works can be difficult. But, Scripture is clear – no one will ever earn salvation from God by merely doing good deeds. *He saved us, not because of righteous things we had done, but because of his mercy...*[148] Our primary work is simple: *The work of God is this: to believe in the one he has sent.*[149]

Any true faith, however, will have good works as a natural result. This should not be something for which we have to strive. Jesus said, *"If you love me, you will keep my commandments."*[150] This is no mere commandment. If we have the love of Jesus in our hearts, we will find ourselves automatically loving the unlovable, even our enemies. We will find ourselves with greater inner motivation to be compassionate and to care for the needy. We will have a greater desire to please the Lord by abstaining from immoral and evil deeds. (This does not negate our need to obey the Lord – at times we follow his word simply because he has told us to do it.) A fish does not need to be commanded to swim; he swims because he has a "fish nature." Likewise, we who have a new nature will begin to display fruit of the Spirit.

Works are to faith like thunder is to lightning. When we see a flash of lightning across the horizon, we know that thunder will soon follow. The lightning is the cause of the thunder, and we never hear thunder preceding lightning. After a person has become a born again Christian, we should automatically expect to hear some "thunder." We are not saved *by works*, but created *for works* (Eph. 2:8-10). Works will naturally follow and confirm true faith. We can never say works are unimportant in the Christian life. The Lord addressed five of seven churches in the book of Revelation, saying, *"I know your works..."*[151] He did not say, "I know your spiritual talk," or "I know your good intentions." We must avoid being like those who *profess to know God, but in works they deny Him...*[152] May our works validate the faith we profess.

Faith and Action

By faith Abel offered...
By faith Noah...built
By faith Moses' parents hid him...
By faith Rahab...welcomed the spies... (Heb. 11:4,7,23,31)

Faith can be best understood in the context of actions rather than words. The eleventh chapter of Hebrews is a remarkable record of various men and women who were quite active in demonstrating their faith in God. We read in Scripture that when Abraham offered his son Isaac on the altar in obedience to God, *his faith and his actions were working together, and his faith was made complete by what he did.*[153] It seems that God often puts his people in situations where they will have to perform some action to demonstrate the faith they profess. For example, when Moses was backed up against the Red Sea with the Egyptians in pursuit, the Lord could easily have parted the sea right then. But, he first said to Moses, *"Why are you crying out to me? Tell the Israelites to move on. Raise your staff and stretch out your hand over the sea to divide the water..."*[154]

God frequently chooses not to intervene before his people act. He could have easily caused the defeat of the city of Ai by the Israelites. Yet, he first told Joshua, *"Hold out toward Ai the javelin that is in your hand, for into your hand I will deliver this city."*[155] It seems the Lord often asks us to perform actions which we could question or deem foolish (like holding out a javelin). What God is after is an outward demonstration of faith in Him.

As we act boldly in faith, God is pleased and we are more apt to see results. When friends of a paralytic man could not get into a house to see Jesus, they went to the trouble of going up on the flat rooftop, taking off some roof tiles, and lowering the man on a mat down to Jesus. Removing tiles would have made dust and caused possible danger to people below, but urgency may require risk and radical action. It is recorded that *Jesus saw their faith,*[156] and the man was both forgiven and healed that day.

Faith and Commitment

Commit your way to the LORD, Trust also in Him,
and He will do it. (Psalm 37:5 NAS)

In the nineteenth century there was a famous acrobat, who was known all over the world. His real name was Jean Francois Gravalet, but he was known by his stage name – Blondin. Born in France in 1824, Blondin became well known in France while still a child. As he grew older his skill plus his flair for the spectacular soon brought him the acclaim of many in Europe and then in America. His most spectacular feats, those that also drew most attention, were his crossings of the gorge below Niagara Falls on a tightrope 1,100 feet long and 160 feet above the water. Once he pushed a wheelbarrow across. On another occasion he stopped halfway and cooked an omelet.

Once, in an unusual demonstration of skill, Blondin carried a man across Niagara Falls on his back and then turned around and carried him back. After he had put his rider down, the acrobat turned to the large crowd that had been watching and asked a man who was near at hand, "Do you believe that I could do that with you?"

"Of course," the man said. "I've just seen you do it."

"Well, hop on," said Blondin, "and I'll carry you across." The man answered, "Not on your life!"[157]

Faith cannot just be intellectual; it also involves commitment. James Boice, after sharing this story, wrote, "To believe in the biblical sense is to commit yourself to Christ, to trust him to carry you over the churning cataracts and wild whirlpools of life. The other belief is only intellectual assent."[158]

When we commit to something (or someone) it narrows our daily choices and courses of action. When I committed myself in marriage to my wife, I basically said, "It's going to be you and no one else – and if trials come our way, I am committed to 'walk that tightrope.'" As we commit ourselves to Christ, we do not always know what tomorrow will bring, but we know there are steady hands on the wheelbarrow.

Faith and Testing

In this you greatly rejoice, though now for a little while you may have had to suffer grief in all kinds of trials. These have come so that your faith – of greater value than gold, which perishes even though refined by fire – may be proved genuine and may result in praise, glory and honor when Jesus Christ is revealed. (1 Peter 1:6-7)

Believers may encounter unpleasant circumstances which they would have never chosen to experience. During such times, God is not absent, but he is putting faith to the test. God tests our faith just as the goldsmith puts metal in the fire to see what is genuine (the imitation is quickly burned). Job would never have chosen to have his ten sons and daughters killed, all his servants and livestock destroyed, and his health ruined. Yet, Job held on to the Lord through it all, and in faith declared, *"He knows the way that I take; when he has tested me, I will come forth as gold."*[159]

There are several reasons for God's testing us, a primary one being that God wants to reveal whether or not our faith is *genuine*. We say we believe God. Then we lose our job. Do we get upset and worry, or do we have confidence that God will provide? Why did God allow his people, as they traveled about in the desert, to go hungry at times? Was he trying to make them miserable or play some cruel game with them? No, an explanation is given: *Remember how the Lord your God led you all the way in the desert these forty years, to humble you and test you in order to know what is in your heart...*[160] The words of our mouths will reveal our hearts – whether we will trust God or grumble and complain.

Let us not shrink away from the *refiner's fire.* Then one day we can confess with King David, *"Though you probe my heart and examine me at night, though you test me, you will find nothing..."*[161] Let us never resent trials which come our way; they help strengthen our faith.

Day Fifty-Eight
Faith and Obstacles

Without warning, a furious storm came up on the lake, so that the waves swept over the boat. But Jesus was sleeping. The disciples went and woke him, saying, "Lord, save us! We're going to drown!" He replied, "You of little faith, why are you so afraid?" Then he got up and rebuked the winds and the waves, and it was completely calm. (Matthew 8:23-26)

Samuel Ward, a seventeenth-century Puritan pastor, talked about the kind of faith that stands up and faces great obstacles. "O how faith can shine and triumph over nature and reason – not just persevere, but conquer and rejoice in tribulation! Faith can make you hard as an adamant stone, like a palm that does not break with the heaviest burdens, or oil that ever out-swims all the water that is poured over it. This is the crown and glory of faith. Faith tackles great obstacles. Small boats do fine in a calm, and ordinary men can stand up to a light breeze, but when a heavy tempest blows, and wave after wave crashes, nature yields, the spirit faints, a heart fails. To stand up against such storms and to live and reign is the work of faith. This faith has the Word as its compass, and Christ directing the helm. The greatest adversities are but the exercise and lustre of faith. Men glory when they can tame the tigers, but what is that compared to faith that makes shame, poverty, sickness, persecutions, banishment, yea, death itself calm and bearable? Christians have great advantage because of their faith. Their only error is the lack of skill or failure to use the shield of faith when a dart comes suddenly upon them. When a storm rises, immediately run and awaken your sleeping faith. Knock at its door. Do your work, O faith! Consider this medicine for your faith to drink in comfort: not the slightest trouble befalls you without the overruling eye and hand of God. He is not only our wise God, but a tender Father..."[162]

Heavenly Father, as obstacles come our way, help us not to shrink back in fear, but in faith to tackle them head on!

Faith and Dry Times

God left him to test him and to know everything that was in his heart...(2 Chronicles 32:31)

King Hezekiah was one of the few good kings in Israel's recorded history, yet there was a time he felt God was a million miles away: *God left him.* Sometimes our faith is likewise tested as God withdraws the sense of his presence. God has promised, *"Never will I leave you; never will I forsake you,"*[163] so he does not actually leave. Yet, we *feel* God is far away or that he does not care. These unpleasant occasions are no accidents; God will test our hearts at such times to see if we will continue to walk in faith.

Job, too, felt the absence of God's presence: *"But if I go to the east, he is not there; if I go to the west, I do not find him; when he is at work in the north, I do not see him; when he turns to the south, I catch no glimpse of him."*[164] However, Job refused to follow his feelings or to give in to despair. He continued after the Lord: *"My feet have closely followed his steps; I have kept to his way without turning aside. I have not departed from the commands of his lips; I have treasured the words of his mouth more than my daily bread."*[165] In the end, Job saw the Lord in a new way and was abundantly rewarded by Him.

Many men and women of God have experienced months and even years of "dry seasons" when God seemed oblivious to their needs. Yet they remained faithful. Adam Clarke, a famous Bible teacher of the nineteenth century and author of a popular evangelical Bible commentary, went through a dry period of two years when he got little out of the word of God. However, he faithfully studied the Scriptures daily. One day God rewarded him as the word of God opened with "light from heaven." From then on he began to experience the hidden wisdom of God's word in a fresh way.[166]

Dry times can destroy a plant or cause its roots to go deeper as it seeks for underground streams. Let us not despair in dry times, but instead go deeper in faith.

Faith and Crisis

If you are weak in a crisis, you are weak indeed.
(Proverbs 24:10 Today's English Bible)

A crisis will reveal much about our faith. If we put a teabag into a cup of hot water, we find out what is in the bag! If hard times come and we completely fall to pieces emotionally or just hang on by the skin-of-our-teeth, we realize that our faith is lacking.

Jesus' disciples had been with him for some time and had seen his power demonstrated. One day as they were out in a boat with the Lord, a furious storm came over the lake, and the terrified disciples actually reproved the Lord, who was sleeping, *"Teacher, don't you care if we drown?"* Jesus got up, rebuked the wind and spoke to the waves to be quiet. He then rebuked his disciples: *"Why are you so afraid? Do you still have no faith?"*[167] In every critical situation we are to call out to the Lord, not just cry out in fear. *Why do you now cry aloud – have you no king?*[168] Jesus is our king. He is close to us, and he can still calm any storm. Therefore, we are to *pray in the Spirit on all occasions.*[169] Oswald Chambers says we should act as believers, instead of pagans in times of crisis: "When we are in fear...we go back to the elementary prayers of those who do not know Him, and prove we have not the slightest atom of confidence in Him and in His government of the world...and we sit down in nervous dread. God expects his children to be so confident in Him that in a crisis they are the ones upon whom He can rely."[170]

It is important to be walking in faith today so we won't falter if hard times come tomorrow. The prophet Jeremiah said, *"If you have raced with men on foot and they have worn you out, how can you compete with horses? If you stumble in safe country, how will you manage in the thickets by the Jordan?"*[171] If we cannot handle minor difficulties, what will we do with major ones? Some believers pout over a petty disagreement, fuss over a broken dish, or get agitated at the slightest inconvenience. Let us prepare mentally to suffer; we cannot be strong in a crisis if we are chronic doubters in the small, daily struggles.

Faith and Suffering

Others were tortured and refused to be released, so that they might gain a better resurrection. Some faced jeers and flogging, while still others were chained and put in prison. They were stoned; they were sawed in two; they were put to death by the sword. They went about in sheepskins and goatskins, destitute, persecuted and mistreated – the world was not worthy of them....These were all commended for their faith, yet none of them received what had been promised. (Hebrews 11:35-39)

This is one portion of the great faith chapter that we tend to skip over. We like the dramatic faith stories – the angelic rescue of Daniel, the heavenly demolition of the walls of Jericho, and the supernatural parting of the Red Sea. But then we get to this portion where it mentions *others*. These *others* were also heroes of faith who did *not* escape confiscation of goods, bodily suffering, and intense persecution. Such events (which continue to this present day) bring tears to our eyes as we see extraordinary grace given to believers to endure horrible suffering. *These were all commended for their faith.* The way some died *in faith* caught the baffled attention of those who were eyewitnesses, and many persecutors were converted. *The world was not worthy of* such suffering saints.

Few of us would deliberately choose to suffer for the cause of Christ. But in the sovereignty of God some of us may have to undergo terrible afflictions which can be endured only by our faith and the sustaining grace of God. We must not be unduly surprised if it happens: *Therefore, since Christ suffered in the body, arm yourselves also with the same attitude, because he who has suffered in his body is done with sin...Dear friends, do not be surprised at the painful trial you are suffering, as though something strange were happening to you. But rejoice that you are participating in the sufferings of Christ, so that you may be overjoyed when his glory is revealed....*[172]

If you are suffering, hang in there! You will soon see God's glorious deliverance day – either in this life or the life to come!

Faith and Adversity

Then his people believed his promises. Then they sang his praise. Yet how quickly they forgot what he had done! (Psalm 106:12-13 NLT)

The late David Wilkerson, pastor of Times Square Church in New York, was a man who learned to walk in faith in the midst of a lot of adversity. He wrote, "Nobody had ever seen as many supernatural works as Israel. God provided miracle after miracle for them – and yet each work left the people as faithless and unbelieving as before! You would think that the ten plagues on Egypt would have produced faith in the Israelites….Even after God opened the Red Sea, Israel's faith lasted only three days. Scripture says: 'They did not remember the multitude of your mercies, but rebelled by the sea – the Red Sea' (Psalm 106:7). They even doubted God at the Red Sea – the place where He performed His greatest miracle! We are so like Israel. We want God to speak a word, grant us a miraculous deliverance, quickly meet our needs, and remove all our pain and suffering. In fact, you may be saying right now, 'If God would just get me out of this mess – if He'd give me this one miracle – I would never doubt Him again!' Yet, what about all the miracles He has performed for you? They haven't produced in you any faith to help you in your present trouble!

"Two precious men of God from the Zulu tribe in Africa visited Times Square Church. An incredible revival was taking place among the eight million Zulus, and God was doing miraculous things among them. Yet that is not what these men wanted to talk about. Rather, what impressed them most about the revival were the 'overcomer Zulus' – those who stood for Christ, even though they were being tested and tried severely….I believe the greatest sign or wonder to the world in these last days is not a person who has been raised from the dead. No, what truly makes an impact on the mind and spirit of the ungodly is the Christian who endures all trials, storms, pain and suffering with a confident faith. Such a believer emerges from his troubles stronger in character, stronger in faith, and stronger in Christ."[173]

Faith and Tragedy

"The LORD gave and the LORD has taken away.
Blessed be the name of the LORD." (Job 1:21 NAS)

I have always been amazed by stories of Christians who continue to display great faith despite horrible, personal tragedy. One such example is seen in the life of Maude Smith, who had three sons – Paul, Bill, and Charles. Charles, or Chuck Smith, would eventually be the founder of the popular Calvary Chapel in Costa Mesa, California. Here is part of Maude's testimony:

"Charles…went on into Bible college after high school, finished his education, married in June 1948, and then went into the pastorate. Paul, likewise, went into full-time Christian service. Maude and her husband had a keen interest in the ministries of their sons. The years moved along.

"It was in 1959 that her youngest son, Bill, and her husband were killed in an airplane crash. Bill had a private plane and was flying it. He and his father were returning from San Diego in a storm and crashed on the Camp Pendleton base.

"Maude's faith never wavered, and even before she received official notification, she told Chuck, 'God has spoken to me in prayer. "The Lord has given and he has taken away. Blessed be the name of the Lord." I know they are with the Lord now.' A few hours later the CAP called to say they'd found the plane and that there were no survivors.

"It was Maude's brave example that made the loss easier for her children to bear. She didn't indulge in self-pity but bravely set about to make a new life for herself."[174]

In tragic times, we must either maintain faith in a sovereign God or we may likely become bitter. Maude Smith made the right choice – to praise God even though nothing about the accident made any sense. Her faith not only eventually made her future life much brighter, but had a tremendous effect on her surviving sons, especially Chuck – who has had a major impact in the body of Christ around the world.

Faith and Patience

We do not want you to become lazy, but to imitate those who through faith and patience inherit what has been promised. (Hebrews 6:12)

Patience is one of the hardest lessons for Christians to learn. Someone has defined patience as "accepting a difficult situation from God without giving Him a deadline to remove it."[175] God promised Abraham a son, but Abraham had to wait twenty-five years for the fulfillment of the promise. Abraham is called the father of the faith[176], but it took faith plus patient waiting for Abraham to receive God's answer. *Then Abraham, after patient endurance, found the promise true.*[177]

Our faith can go for naught if it is not matched with a patient spirit ready to wait for God's timing. Many promises of God go unrealized because his people have been too impatient to wait for the answer. We may become frustrated by inconvenient calls, unusual delays, long lines, and slow-talking people. We need more than mere faith to follow God successfully; we also need patience. The patient man will not be a hurried man.

We are living in a generation which emphasizes the easy and expedient; we want results *right now* and therefore avoid long-range goals and seasons of waiting. A. W. Tozer said, "It will cost something to walk slowly in the parade of the ages while excited men of time rush about confusing motion with progress. But it will pay in the long run, and the true Christian is not interested in anything less than that."[178]

Biblical patience means *steadfastness,* not passive resignation. William Barclay said the Greek word implies "spiritual staying power...it is not the patience which grimly waits for the end but the patience which radiantly hopes for the dawn."[179] Such patience never comes from ourselves; it must be a fruit of the Holy Spirit that is developed over time as we are put in trying situations: *The testing of your faith produces patience. But let patience have its perfect work, so that you may be perfect and complete, lacking nothing.*[180] If we add patience to our faith, we will inherit God's promises.

Faith and Endurance

For you have need of endurance, so that when you have done the will of God, you may receive what was promised. (Hebrews 10:36 NAS)

A study of church history reveals that most pioneers of the faith did not achieve instant success. Rather, they inherited the promises of God through much suffering and endurance. Consider the following examples:

- William Carey sailed to India from England in 1793. He lost a five-year-old son, and as a result his wife became mentally ill. Until her death twelve years later, Mrs. Carey raged so violently that she had to be restrained. Carey also survived a flood which swept away his home and later a fire which burned manuscripts of ten versions of the Bible that had taken him years to translate. He labored thirteen years before seeing his first convert. But in time he became known as the "father of modern missions."
- Robert Moffatt, "the patriarch of South African missions" and father-in-law of David Livingston, labored ten years to see his first baptism.
- Adoniram Judson, "America's first foreign missionary," went to Burma in 1814. He lost a six-month-old baby boy, spent a year and a half in a "death prison," lost his wife from fever, suffered a mental breakdown, and waited five years for his first convert.

The Christian race is not a 100-meter sprint; it is more like a cross-country marathon: long, hard, and painful. Scripture says, *Let us run with endurance the race that is set before us, fixing our eyes on Jesus, the author and perfecter of faith.*[181] Some of us may have become weary because we have not seen the fruitfulness we desire. But, *let us not get tired of doing what is right, for after a while we will reap a harvest of blessing if we don't get discouraged and give up.*[182]

Day Sixty-Six
Faith and Warfare (Part 1)

> *Put on the armor of God...take up the shield of faith,
> with which you can extinguish all the flaming arrows of
> the evil one. (Ephesians 6:11-16)*

Christians are not to be passive. We have an enemy of our souls who is actively seeking to destroy us or at least distract us from serving God effectively. We cannot be casual about spiritual warfare: *Be self-controlled and alert. Your enemy the devil prowls around like a roaring lion looking for someone to devour. Resist him, standing firm in the faith...*[183] Our primary posture in warfare is standing.[184] It requires faith on our part to stand against Satan and the world system which is so antagonistic toward Christian beliefs: *This is the victory that has overcome the world, even our faith.*[185] Faith is our shield that wards off onslaughts of our enemy, the *accuser of the brethren.* By faith we use *the sword of the Spirit, the word of God,* and verbally respond to Satan's fiery darts.

- When Satan says we are worthless and God does not care, we respond, "We are *God's children...a chosen people, a royal priesthood, a holy nation, a people belonging to God..."* (Rom. 8:16; I Pet. 2:9)
- When Satan says we should fear, we boldly declare, *"The Lord is my light and salvation–whom shall I fear?"* (Ps. 27:3)
- When Satan says we are failures and ought to quit, we confidently say, *"Do not gloat over me, my enemy! Though I have fallen, I will rise. Though I sit in darkness, the Lord will be my light."* (Mic. 7:8) Even if I *fall seven times, I will rise again!* (Prov. 24:16)
- When Satan says we will die prematurely, we combat that thought with faith, *"I will not die but live, and will proclaim what the Lord has done."* (Ps. 118:17) *My times are in HIS hands.* (Ps. 31:15)
- Finally, we can always say, *Thanks be to God! He gives us the victory through our Lord Jesus Christ!* (I Cor. 15:57)

Faith and Warfare (Part 2)

David said to the Philistine, "You come against me with sword and spear and javelin, but I come against you in the name of the LORD Almighty, the God of the armies of Israel, whom you have defied. This day the LORD will hand you over to me, and I'll strike you down and cut off your head. Today...the whole world will know that there is a God in Israel...the battle is the LORD's..." (1 Sam.17:45-7)

The story of David and Goliath is one of the most dramatic battle scenes in all of history. The Philistines were lined up on one side of the valley and the Israelites on the other side. The "champion" of the Philistines was Goliath, a man over nine feet (or three meters) tall, with his coat of bronze armor weighing about 125 pounds and the iron end of his spear weighing 15 pounds!

Goliath, the giant enemy of Israel is a good representation of Satan, the great enemy of our souls. Goliath was not only intimidating in presence, but he used methods common to Satan:

- He struck fear in the hearts of God's people (v. 24).
- He had no respect for the living God of Israel (v 43).
- He intended great physical harm to David (v. 44).

David is listed as one of the outstanding heroes of faith in the Bible.[186] Out of all the paralyzed bystanders, only David stepped forth in faith: *"Let no one lose heart on account of this Philistine; your servant will go and fight him."*[187] David trusted in his God and had already proven his faith in smaller battles. There was no hesitation in his faith; equipped with the proper weapons, he *ran* toward his enemy. His first stone hit the mark; Goliath was stopped in his tracks and soon decapitated.[188]

David is an example to us in our own spiritual warfare. He did not fight the enemy on his terms; he used his own tried weapons. We too have been given weapons – but spiritual ones, not natural.[189] David did not succumb to fear; he faced his enemy in faith. His confidence was not in himself, but in the Lord. We, too, can be brave and realize *the battle is the Lord's!*

Faith and Confession (Part 1)

If you confess with your mouth, "Jesus is Lord," and believe in your heart that God raised him from the dead, you will be saved. For it is with your heart that you believe and are justified, and it is with your mouth that you confess and are saved. (Romans 10:9-10)

Our verbal confession is very much linked to faith residing in our hearts. A person might say, "Well, I believe, but I just don't like to talk about it." Others might think, "My religion is private. What matters is between God and me." Biblical salvation, however, is incomplete without confession from the mouth.

One question I had to decide at the beginning of my Christian journey was this: "Am I too embarrassed to name the name of Christ?" I received Christ in an evangelistic meeting when I was just entering my freshman year in college. My sinful and selfish behavior did not immediately change, but I started reading the Bible, and God began speaking to me. For six months I did not say a word to anyone about my faith in Christ. Then, two verses came to my attention in a powerful way: *Every one therefore who shall confess me before men, I will also confess him before My Father who is in heaven. But whoever shall deny Me before men, I will also deny him before My Father who is in heaven....If anyone is ashamed of me and my words in this adulterous and sinful generation, the Son of man will be ashamed of him when he comes in his Father's glory with the holy angels.*[190]

At that time I felt this was no small issue; for me it was a choice either for Christ or against Christ; to confess him or deny him. I started talking to friends about my new "religion" and "the man upstairs," but I was convicted again. I needed to confess the name of JESUS CHRIST, the only name by which we can be saved. By the grace of God, I began to talk about Jesus and my faith in him. My life has never been the same since.

Faith and Confession (Part 2)

How, then, can they call on the one they have not believed in? And how can they believe in the one of whom they have not heard? And how can they hear without someone preaching to them? (Romans 10:14)

A popular saying, attributed to Francis of Assisi in the thirteenth century, is "Preach the Gospel at all times and when necessary use words." The problems with this quote are: (1) We have no record of Francis ever saying it; (2) It is contrary to what Francis lived – he was as well known for his spoken words as he was for his lifestyle, sometimes preaching in five villages a day.[191]

It is true that we ought to live the gospel if we are going to tell others about it. There is no worse testimony to Christ than the man who loudly preaches to others and yet is much lacking in the character of Christ. We are also living in a day in which it is often necessary to build a relationship with someone before sharing about Christ. However, we who love Jesus cannot be silent. If the world does not hear the message of good news from us, how will they hear? What person do you know who has become a Christian without at least one person talking to them?

We must be careful of being cowardly and "hiding our light under a basket."[192] I have heard people warning about "preaching fire and brimstone," yet in the past twenty years I have rarely seen anyone preaching that way; in fact, I don't see many people sharing their faith at all. If Christ is the most important thing in our life, how can we *not* talk about him? We must not let the *fear of man* stop us. The gospel will offend some folks, but if a friend was dying of a deadly disease and we had knowledge of the cure, would we refuse to give it to them?

Christ's final instructions for his followers was, *"Go into all the world and preach the good news to all creation."*[193] The Greek word for "preach" implies the use of words; it is the word "to herald" – i.e., to bring an important announcement from a special dignitary. We cannot be silent; let's share the good news!

Faith and Confession (Part 3)

*It is written: "I believed; therefore I have spoken."
With that same spirit of faith we also believe and
therefore speak. (2 Corinthians 4:13)*

Our words are probably more important than we realize: *For by
your words you will be acquitted, and by your words you will be
condemned...*[194] *The tongue has the power of life and death*[195]
Every one of us has given in at times to negative confessions
which seem to leave God out of the picture: "Oh, I'm just a
bum".... "I'm worried about the doctor's visit, something terrible
might happen"... "That boy is a hopeless case..." Our words do
indeed express what's inside us; for *out of the overflow of the
heart the mouth speaks.*[196]

Is our vocabulary more influenced by the world's values, by
natural circumstances, or by what God thinks? Twelve spies
were sent by Moses to check out the land of Canaan, God's land
of promise. They came back and ten were quite distraught,
speaking of the great walled cities and giant-like men in the land:
*"We can't attack those people; they are stronger than we
are."*[197] But two spies, Joshua and Caleb, had eyes of faith and
saw the situation from a heavenly perspective. *"We should go up
and take possession of the land, for we can certainly do it...Do
not be afraid of the people of the land, because we will swallow
them up. Their protection is gone, but the Lord is with us."*[198]
These two men, clearly a minority, were later rewarded for their
faith with entrance into the new land – the only men out of the
entire company of over 600,000 who left Egypt.

We should not encourage blind optimism, but we are not to
complain or fret when all circumstances seem against us. Where
is the Lord? Have we sought him and waited for his help? Let
us confess our confidence in him. *The LORD your God is in your
midst, a mighty one who will save...Seek the Lord and His
strength... say with confidence, "The Lord is my helper; I will
not be afraid. What can man do to me?"*[199]

Faith and Confession (Part 4)

Let us hold fast the confession of our hope without wavering, for He who promised is faithful. (Heb.10:23)

The word *confess* can mean "to acknowledge, to own up to a sin or wrongdoing, or to publicly declare one's belief." The Greek word is *homologeo*, from *homos*, "the same," and *legeo*, "to say," thus it means "to say the same thing as another," or "to agree with another."[200] In other words, for believers to *confess* means to say the same thing God is saying. Joseph, a servant in Potiphar's house, had a golden opportunity to commit adultery with his master's wife when no one was around, but instead of justifying a "personal choice" or a "sexual addiction," he called sin by its right name – *"How then could I do such a wicked thing and sin against God?"*[201]

Some feel confessions from Christians should never be negative. Again, the issue is not what we deem positive or negative, but rather, what is God saying? The apostle Paul once said to the Thessalonians, *"We kept telling you in advance that we were going to suffer affliction; and so it came to pass, as you know."*[202] God had shown Paul persecution was coming, and he was simply saying what God was saying. Paul's confession was not a falling away from faith. Notice in the same chapter, Paul mentioned concern for the Thessalonians' *faith* five times.[203]

If we speak of suffering or an unpleasant circumstance, that is not necessarily a lack of faith. The psalmist said, *"I kept the faith, even when I said, 'I am greatly afflicted.'"*[204] Jesus told his disciples they would have tribulation.[205] He also said that Peter would die by a terrible method – crucifixion.[206] Jesus was not overly concerned about negative talk – he only wanted to say what his Father was saying.[207]

Believers are not to avoid facing reality, but we must walk in faith. We are not to be pessimistic, easily defeated, or governed by mere circumstances. As it is written, *we also believe and therefore speak.*[208]

Faith and Confession (Part 5)

If you had faith...you would say....(Luke 17:6)

There is power in confessing the word of God in faith. When confronted with Satan's three temptations in the wilderness, Jesus quoted Scripture all three times, and the enemy had to flee. The *sword of the Spirit* is most effective as we speak the word in faith. The effective confession will be words imparted by the Holy Spirit. One translation says, *For sword, take that which the Spirit gives you – the words which come from God.*[209] The Greek word here for *word* is *rhema*, which means "a saying, that which is uttered by the living voice."[210] This is the word made alive in our spirit as God speaks to us. Scripture says man lives not by bread alone, but *on every word* [rhema] *that comes from the mouth of God.*[211] Some make the mistake of thinking that a mere confession of the word of God has power in itself. They might quote Isaiah, *So shall My word be that goes forth from My mouth; it shall not return to me void, but it shall accomplish what I please...*[212] This kind of word which *goes forth from My mouth* is a Scripture which the Holy Spirit makes alive to us. This personal word will produce an effective result.

The word of God may actually cause more harm than good if it is used by a man with selfish motives or in a wrong spirit. Apart from the Spirit, the word is the *letter of the law*, which causes spiritual death.[213] However, *The Word that God speaks is alive and full of power – making it active, operative, energizing and effective; it is sharper than any two-edged sword...*[214]

Some view faith as a "force" which is released through faith-filled words. We cannot presume, however, that spoken words (even biblical ones) in themselves have power. Ezekiel reproved some arrogant, false prophets by saying, *"They expect their words to control the event..."*[215] We are to come to the throne of God boldly, but we also must come humbly; for, *Who can speak and have it happen if the Lord has not decreed it...?*[216] Let us therefore wait for God to impart his word to our hearts.

Faith and Praise

Then they believed his promises and sang his praise.
(Psalm 106:12)

Praise is vitally connected to faith. If we believe the Lord, we can begin to sing his praises. When the great armies of Moab and Ammon came against the Israelites, King Jehoshaphat encouraged them to stand in faith. *Do not be afraid or discouraged because of this vast army. For the battle is not yours, but God's...Take up your positions; stand firm and see the deliverance the Lord will give you...Have faith in the Lord your God and you will be upheld...*[217] Then, the Lord gave his people an unusual battle strategy. *Jehoshaphat appointed men to sing to the Lord and praise him for the splendor of his holiness as they went out at the head of the army, saying: "Give thanks to the Lord, for his love endures forever."*[218]

To the natural mind, this kind of strategy would make no sense. *Yet, as they began to sing and praise, the Lord set ambushes against the men of Ammon and Moab and Mount Seir who were invading Judah, and they were defeated.*[219] The worship of God's people confused the enemy so much that they actually turned against and slaughtered one another! This battle was won by praising, not by fighting. When we, too, face overwhelming obstacles, we can begin praising the Lord. "Jesus, I praise you that you are the Master, the one who is in control. Thank you that you have my best interests at heart. You have promised never to leave me or forsake me. Nothing is too difficult for you. Thank you that *in all these things we are more than conquerors through him who loved us.*"[220]

We may tend to praise the Lord after our battles, but we can also begin to praise the Lord *before* the battle, when he has given us the assurance in our hearts. Paul Billheimer says, "Praise is the sparkplug of faith. It is the one thing needed to get faith airborne, enabling it to soar above the deadly pollution of doubt... The secret of faith without doubt is praise – triumphant praise, continuous praise, praise that is a way of life."[221]

Faith and God's Leading

> *Now faith is...the proof of things we do not see and the
> conviction of their reality [faith perceiving as real fact
> what is not revealed to the senses]. Hebrews 11:1 The
> Amplified Bible*

Faith is not superstition. Faith sees the invisible, but not the
nonexistent. *Faith is...the proof of things we do not see.* "The
eyes of faith see something that is real, although invisible. What
superstition sees is unreality and nonexistent. As we learn to
discern between unreality and invisible reality, we discover a
world of difference between the two."[222] If we are to step out in
faith, it is important to spend time with the Heavenly Father and
sense what he is saying. Jesus said, *"The Son can do nothing by
himself; he can do only what he sees his Father doing..."*[223]

One man, used frequently in healing ministry, would wait on
God before any public ministry and ask, "Father, what are you
wanting to do today?" This is a good pattern, for Jesus said,
"...apart from me you can do nothing..."[224]As we pray to the
Heavenly Father, we must not glibly "claim" his promises or
demand that he answer all our demands. God is not a celestial
Santa Claus, waiting to fill our wish lists. A wise man once
shared with me his important discovery that "God is God and I
am not."

In order to pray effectively, we must sense the leading of
God's Spirit. In his classic book, *How to Pray*, R. A. Torrey
explains: "Many people make a collapse of faith altogether by
trying to work up faith by an effort of their will...Trying to
believe something you want to believe is not faith. Believing
what God says in His Word is faith. Faith furthermore comes
through the Spirit. The Spirit knows the will of God, and if I
pray in the Spirit, and look to the Spirit to teach me God's will,
He will lead me out in prayer along the line of that will, and give
me faith that the prayer is answered; but in no case does real
faith come by simply determining that you are going to get the
thing that you want to get."[225]

Day Seventy-Five
Faith and the Holy Spirit (Part 1)

Jesus stood up and said in a loud voice, "If a man is thirsty, let him come to me and drink. Whoever believes in me, as the Scripture has said, streams of living water will flow from within him." By this he meant the Spirit, whom those who believed in him were later to receive. Up to that time the Spirit had not been given since Jesus had not been yet glorified. (John 7:37-39)

God never intended us to be "half-filled" Christians; he wants us to be filled, overflowing with *streams of living water*, which describe the power and operation of the Holy Spirit. Our faith is vital in receiving the Holy Spirit. As a young Christian, I heard quite a few different views on the Holy Spirit. I was told by some that I already had Him; I was told by others to seek for Him. Still others told me I should speak in tongues. For a while I was quite confused! But, I knew I needed the power of the Holy Spirit in order to live an effective Christian life. I also knew the Spirit was not an antiquated promise, *the promise is for you and your children and for all who are far off...*[226]

There should be greater simplicity in seeking to be filled with the Holy Spirit. A few things are clear: (1) The gift is only for those who are *thirsty* for more of God. It is not for those who are simply curious or seeking a mystical experience; (2) The gift is for *believers* – those who have repented and been baptized in water;[227] (3) The gift is freely available simply because Christ has been glorified;[228] (4) The gift is not for selfish purposes or personal gain; it is to empower us to become more effective witnesses for Christ and bring glory to his name;[229] and, (5) The gift is given to all who simply *ask* the Father, who loves to give good gifts to his children.[230]

If these things are not true, striving or tarrying will not avail. It is *by faith we might receive the promise of the Spirit.*[231] God is much more willing to give than we are to receive. Let's not hesitate to ask.

Faith and the Holy Spirit (Part 2)

*If you then, though you are evil, know how to give good
gifts to your children, how much more will your Father
in heaven give the Holy Spirit to those who ask him!
(Luke 11:13)*

There is often much complexity and confusion about receiving
the Holy Spirit. These words by F. B. Meyer may be helpful.

"Many Christians, seeking this blessed fullness, make the
same mistake as is so constantly made by seekers after
forgiveness and acceptance with God. They look within for
evidences of the reception and indwelling of the Spirit, and
refuse to believe in His presence unless they detect certain
symptoms and signs which they consider befitting. This is
entirely wrong. The reckoning is not of feeling, but of faith.

"If we have complied with God's directions, we must
believe, whether we feel any difference or not, that God has done
His part, and has kept His promise, given us through Jesus
Christ; and that He has not been slower to give the Holy Spirit
than earthly fathers to give bread to their hungry children (Luke
11: 13). When we... have solemnly dedicated ourselves to God,
and sought to be filled with the Spirit, we must not examine our
feelings to discover whether there is such a difference in us as
we might expect; but we must cry, in the assurance of faith: 'I
praise You, blessed One, that You have not failed to perform
Your chosen work; You have entered my longing heart; You
have made your home in me. From now on, You will have Your
way with me, to will and do Your own good pleasure'...

"A little child was once asked her age; and she replied, 'I
don't feel like seven. I feel like six; but mother says I'm seven.'
Here was the reckoning of faith, putting her mother's word
before her own feeling. And thus we must refuse to consider
ourselves, diagnose our symptoms, or feel our pulse; but just
launch out on the deep of God's truthfulness, and let down our
nets for a great catch of power and blessing."[232]

Faith and Power

...that you may...realize...how tremendous is the power available to us who believe in God. That power is the same divine power which was demonstrated in Christ when he raised him from the dead... (Ephesians 1:15-21 Phillips)

God's power is never given to us for selfish purposes. It is when we realize our own limitations and frailty, that we acknowledge how much we need divine power manifested in us. *We have this treasure in jars of clay to show that this all-surpassing power is from God and not from us.*[233] This is a fitting description of us – fragile clay pots – yet as we hold this glorious treasure (Christ), we display his power.

The Greek word for "power" is *dunamis*. One English derivative from this word is the word *dynamite*, and some tend to emphasize the power of God in explosive ways – like dramatic healings or spectacular miracles. Such events certainly happen in our day, but they are more exceptional than the norm in our Christian experience. A second English derivative is *dynamo*, which is a kind of motor. A dynamo is just as strong as dynamite, and maybe more so. But, the power of a dynamo is not explosive; it is quiet, controlled, and steady. This is the kind of power that we believers see more readily displayed in our lives.

Why do we pray to see God's power – even his *tremendous power* – manifest in our lives? So that we might...

- Live a godly life in the midst of wickedness. (2 Pet. 1:3)
- Accomplish all he wants us to do. (Phil. 4:13)
- Be consistent witnesses of Jesus. (Acts 1:8)
- Endure suffering and persecution. (2 Tim. 1:8)
- Overcome our deficiencies. (2 Cor. 12:7-10)
- Be enabled to live in undesirable circumstances and/or with unlikable people. (Col. 1:11-12)

Lord, how desperately we need your help! Fill us with your power that we might live for you and serve more effectively!

Day Seventy-Eight
Faith and Guidance

Faith is our guide, not sight.
(2 Corinthians 5:7 Revised English Bible)

Guidance is not an agonizing search for God's secret plans for our lives. It is first and foremost a relationship with the Guide. Jesus is the Good Shepherd who has promised to lead me beside *quiet waters* and *guide me in the paths of righteousness.*[234] He does not enjoy playing guessing games with us; he wants to reveal his will: *"I will not leave you as orphans: I will come to you."*[235] Our problem is that we like to look too far ahead, but the Lord seems to lead us step by step, and not reveal the big picture of his will. *The mind of man plans his way, but the Lord directs his steps.*[236]

We often face decisions where we are not certain about which direction to take. We have a promise, *In all your ways acknowledge him, and he will make your paths straight.*[237] After waiting on God, suppose we make a decision as best we can, and step out in faith. Then the job does not seem as good as we hoped, or the relocation seems to be less than desirable, or the person we marry suddenly shows flaws we did not know existed. Did we make a mistake? Did we make a bad move? Did we marry "the wrong person?" It is always possible we did, because we are fallible. But it is also possible we are exactly in the place where God wants us – it just didn't turn out the way we expected. At times God says, *"Nor are your ways my ways."*[238]

We do not need to be anxious about missing the center of God's will. Instead of God's will being a detailed blueprint which must be followed in slavish detail, it is more like a mighty river which carries a boat along and even incorporates mistakes into its ultimate direction.[239] It is best not to second-guess the many decisions that have to be made in life. *We walk by faith,* and little benefit ever comes from dwelling on the past. To be useful in the kingdom, we must be like the man who *sets his hand to the plow and does not look back.*[240]

Day Seventy-Nine
Faith and Provision

If that is how God clothes the grass of the field, which is here today and tomorrow is thrown into the fire, will he not much more clothe you, O you of little faith? So do not worry, saying, "What shall we eat?" or "What shall we drink?" or "What shall we wear?" For the pagans run after all these things and your heavenly Father knows that you need them. (Matthew 6:30)

Life is uncertain and at any time we may find ourselves facing economic difficulties and lacking basic necessities. What will we do in such times – wring our hands like pagans who do not know God, or deepen our roots of faith? Scripture says we can learn from the animals, who *all look to* [God] *to give them their food at the proper time.*[241]

In the Old Covenant, God's people discovered that the Lord was *Jehovah-Jireh,* which means *the Lord will provide.*[242] An estimated two million Israelites left Egypt to travel and live in a barren wilderness. Their faith was put to the test. They asked, *"Can God prepare a table in the wilderness?"*[243] God was faithful and daily provided bread from heaven – manna – and water from a rock. He also gave another amazing provision: *For forty years you sustained them in the desert; they lacked nothing, their clothes did not wear out...*[244] However, instead of trusting God and *giving thanks in all circumstances,*[245] God's people constantly complained and missed his future promises.

In times of famine, God's people do not escape all suffering, but he wonderfully provides: *The eyes of the Lord are on those who fear him...to keep them alive in famine.*[246] Elijah had bread and meat delivered by ravens.[247] The gracious widow who showed Elijah hospitality received a supernatural promise, *The jar of flour will not be used up and the jug of oil will not run dry until the day the Lord gives rain.*[248] Hudson Taylor went to China with little money but a lot of faith; he said, "God has plenty of ravens in China."[249] In hard times, let's believe God!

Faith and Prosperity

*In the day of prosperity be happy, But in the day of
adversity consider – God has made the one as well as
the other... (Ecclesiastes 7:14 NAS)*

Some teachers say if we have enough faith, we will prosper
financially. After all, Jesus promised us "abundant life"[250] and
we are assured that *God will supply all your needs according to
His riches in glory in Christ Jesus.*[251] So, what are we to think
about prosperity? Is it a sure promise for those who believe the
word of God? Consider three thoughts.

First, God's idea of prosperity may be different from ours.
The most often quoted verse about prosperity is: *Beloved, I pray
that you may prosper in all things and be in health, just as your
soul prospers.* (3 John 2). The Greek, however, means "to grant
a prosperous and expeditious journey."[252] The NIV translates
this meaning better: *I pray that you may enjoy good health and
that all may go well with you*...(emphasis mine). The same Greek
word is used when Paul asks prayer for his trip to Rome – that he
might *have a prosperous journey...*[253] Paul's journey was
recorded in Acts 27-28. It included a terrible storm at sea for two
weeks, a shipwreck, a snakebite, and being chained to a guard.
Yet, Paul arrived safely to his destination! That's prosperity!

Second, God does not favor poverty and oppose riches.
Some of God's servants had much wealth – like Abraham,
Solomon, Lydia, and Joseph of Arimethea. Others did not have
much wealth–like Peter,[254] Paul,[255] and the church in Jerusalem.[256]
If we are blessed financially, we must give glory to God, not
congratulate our laborious self-efforts. *It is [God] who gives you
the ability to produce wealth...*[257] Those who are rich must also
always be on guard against the inherent dangers of money.
Money is not evil, but *the love of money is a root of all kinds of
evil.*[258] Wealth can become an idol in our lives.

Third, the biblical attitude is *contentment* – whether we have
a lot or a little.[259] We should desire to have the *right* amount –
enough to meet our needs and some left over to bless others![260]

Faith and Giving

Moreover, your very giving proves the reality of your faith, and that means that men thank God that you practice the Gospel that you profess to believe in, as well as for the actual gifts you make to them and to others. (2 Cor. 9:13 Phillips)

If Jesus Christ is to be *Lord of all*, this must include our money. *No one can serve two masters . . . You cannot serve both God and money.*[261] The idea of tithing originally was to teach God's people *always to fear the Lord*[262] – or, to put God first.

The New Testament does not teach a legalistic tithe (giving 10%), although tithing is a principle throughout the Scripture, even before the law was given (e.g., Gen. 14:20). It is also an assumed practice in the N.T. (e.g., Matt. 23:23). Therefore, we believe that tithing is a good principle of giving for the believer. The New Testament emphasizes *generous giving*, which ought to go beyond tithing.[263]

God's people were commanded to bring to him their "first fruits" – i.e., the first and best part of their produce. If they obeyed, God promised to abundantly provide for their needs.[264] This is not to encourage selfish giving to get something back; it is simply a principle that God blesses generous people. *Whoever sows generously will also reap generously.*[265]

At times, Christians who are on tight budgets stop tithing "because we can't afford to." Someone wisely responded to this by saying, "You can't afford *not* to tithe." In other words, 90% with God's blessing will go further than 100% without God's blessing. But, it takes faith to tithe, to give the Lord the *first portion*, when we don't know how we will pay the bills. The way we handle our money *proves the reality of our faith.* Is the Lord truly *first* in our lives, or do we just pay lip-service? Are his promises true concerning his provision for his people? Let's not hold back; let's honor God with our generous giving.

Faith and Family

By faith Isaac blessed Jacob and Esau in regard to their future. By faith Jacob, when he was dying, blessed each of Joseph's sons, and worshiped as he leaned on the top of his staff... (Hebrews 11:20-22)

It is amazing how much in the "Faith Chapter" has to do with the relationships of parents and children. By faith, men and women of God can bring blessing – both physical and spiritual – to their children through their prayers, their own obedience, and their godly examples in the home. A parent's faith does not just affect himself/herself; it will affect those who live in the same house.

The meaning of *blessing* has been greatly diminished in our modern day, even among God's people. If we enjoy something, we exclaim, "What a blessing!" Or if someone sneezes, we say, "God bless you." The idea of *bless* is almost like "luck" in the way it is used. Even when we say in parting, "God bless you," the words are seldom said in faith and are just a polite way of saying good-bye.

The traditional Hebrew idea of blessing is a bestowing of God's goodness and favor upon another. The blessing is not just pleasant words, it is actually something transmitted. In his study of *Judaism*, George Moore said that a spoken blessing "is not a mere articulate sound conveying a meaning; it is a thing and does things. A blessing or curse, for example, is not the expression of a benevolent or malevolent, but impotent, wish; it *is* a blessing or curse. Once uttered, it is beyond the speaker's power to revoke or reverse it."[266]

The patriarchs of old *blessed* their children by faith. We read of Simeon who took Jesus in his arms and blessed him and his parents.[267] Jesus also *took the children in his arms, put his hands on them and blessed them.*[268] A blessing is often in the form of a prayer.[269] We fathers, especially, should lay hands on our children at times and by faith and the leading of the Holy Spirit pray a blessing from God upon them.

Day Eighty-Three
Faith and Childbearing

And Adam was not the one deceived; it was the woman who was deceived and became a sinner. But women will be saved through childbearing – if they continue in faith, love and holiness with propriety. (1 Tim. 2:14-15)

This puzzling passage of Scripture emphasizes the importance of mothers continuing in faith, but several things need to be explained. First, the context is not talking about women's eternal salvation. If so, it would imply a salvation by works (e.g., having children), instead of through faith alone.[270] The Greek word for *saved* can also mean "delivered, preserved, kept safe, restored."[271] The word is used in other contexts that are *not* about eternal salvation (e.g., Matt. 8:25; 9:21; 24:22).

John MacArthur gives further explanation, "Paul is teaching that, even though a woman bears the stigma of being the initial instrument who led the race into sin, it is women through childbearing who may be preserved or freed from that stigma by raising a generation of godly children (cf. 5:10).

"Because mothers have a unique bond and intimacy with their children, and spend far more time with them than fathers do, they have far greater influence in their lives and thus a unique responsibility and opportunity for rearing godly children. While a woman may have led the human race into sin, women have the privilege of leading many out of sin to godliness."[272]

We can also say Paul is speaking in general terms; in the providence of God we know *all* women will be not married, and *all* married women will not have children.[273] But the emphasis in this passage is that godly women can help undo the damage that Eve caused by her original sin; in the New Covenant, godly women can *preserve* (save) not only themselves but many others as they function in their God given roles – like childbearing – and pointing others to Christ as they *continue in faith* as well as *love, holiness, and propriety.* Thank God for such women of faith!

Faith and Eating

But the man who has doubts is condemned if he eats, because his eating is not from faith; and everything that does not come from faith is sin. Romans 14:23

Eating is a daily part of our lives, but have you ever considered what it means "to eat from faith?" Some years ago I heard the following teaching by Derek Prince on this subject that radically changed the way I approach eating. I hope it is helpful to you as well. So, what does it mean to 'eat from faith'?

"First, it implies that we acknowledge that God is the One who has provided us with the food we eat. Thus, the provision of nourishing food for our bodies is an example of the principle stated in James 1:16-17, *Every good gift and every perfect gift is from above, and comes down from the Father of lights...*

"Second, because we acknowledge that God is the One who provides our food, we naturally pause before eating to thank Him for it. In this way, we obey the commandment contained in Colossians 3:17. *And whatever you do in word or deed, do all in the name of the Lord Jesus, giving thanks to God the Father through Him.* In this way, too, we are assured of God's blessing upon the food that we eat, so that we obtain the maximum amount of nourishment and benefit from it. This is explained by Paul. *For every creature of God is good, and nothing is to be refused if it is received with thanksgiving; for it is sanctified by the word of God and prayer* (1 Tim. 4:4-5). Thus, through our faith and prayer, the food we eat is blessed and sanctified to us.

"Third, eating in faith implies that we acknowledge that the health and strength we receive through our food belong to God and must be used in His service and for His glory. *Now the body is not for sexual immorality, but for the Lord, and the Lord for the body* (1 Cor. 6:13)."[274]

It's so easy for us to race through a meal and hardly give God any consideration for all the good things we enjoy. Let's remember to give thanks to God at mealtimes and "eat from faith."

Faith and Sleeping

*I will lie down and sleep in peace, for you alone, O
Lord, make me dwell in safety. (Ps. 4:8)*

Each of us spends approximately one third of our lives sleeping.
(If we are extra busy people, maybe it's one-fourth!) Do we view
these hours spent sleeping as wasted time? The Bible says, *"The
righteous will live by faith."*[275] Do we ever consider the Lord as
we go to sleep or exercise faith as we conclude the day and lay
down to sleep? Can we honestly say, *"The day is yours, and
yours also the night"*?[276]

Sleep disorders have hit the American culture in epidemic
proportions. Respected psychologist Archibald Hart said, "About
half of all adult Americans cannot fall asleep at night…suffering
from insomnia. One in six American adults suffer from chronic
insomnia."[277] Sleeping pills are one of the most popular
prescription drugs. Americans currently spend over $100 million
annually on a variety of medications which promise restful sleep.
I believe the Lord can help us!

So how can we honor God – by faith – as we go to sleep?

First, we can cast all our cares of the day upon the Lord. As
we said in an earlier devotion, we can *deposit* any worries or
fears we might have. We can simply leave them with the Lord.

Second, we can thank God for his gift of sleep. Scripture
says, *He grants sleep to those he loves.*[278] It is not a waste of
time; God designed us to sleep and knows we need it! Sleep is a
reminder that only He is God, and we are not! God never needs
to sleep! He is continually taking care of the universe; we don't
have to! His care even includes all our concerns.

Third, we can ask God to watch over us and our house. This
includes any intruders or natural disasters. God has promised: *He
who watches over you will not slumber; indeed, he who watches
over Israel will neither slumber nor sleep.*[279]

Fourth, we can ask God to bless our dreams, keep us from
the evil one, and even speak to us as we sleep (Job 33:14-18).

Lord, we thank you for this wonderful gift of sleep!

Faith and Signs

Many people saw the miraculous signs he was doing and believed in his name...(John 2:23)

Signs and wonders are often a real faith-booster, and we should be very open to God's demonstration of them in our midst. We may tend to be skeptical if we have not personally witnessed supernatural manifestations or have only been exposed to the work of charlatans. Miraculous signs do not always authenticate the gospel of Jesus. Satan can also do *all kinds of counterfeit miracles, signs and wonders.*[280] This fact, however, should not make us skeptics. Satan, like any counterfeiter, only copies what is genuine. We never see counterfeit three dollar bills.

We do not need signs and wonders to believe, and we do not ever need to seek such confirmations of faith. Jesus said, *"A wicked and adulterous generation asks for a miraculous sign."*[281] However, God sometimes uses signs and wonders to build faith. When God miraculously delivered Daniel from a den of lions, pagan King Darius acknowledged, *He is the living God...He rescues and saves; he performs signs and wonders...*[282]

When Elijah cried out to the Lord to return a dead boy's life to him, God miraculously answered, and the thankful mother responded, *"Now I know that you are a man of God and that the word of the Lord from your mouth is true."*[283] When I was a new Christian, I attended a conference where the sick were visibly healed and demons were cast out with strong manifestations. I remember seeing a young lady's withered arm actually grow new, pink skin before my eyes. Such signs confirmed my new-found faith in a powerful way.

Though there are abuses, we should not oppose signs and wonders in our day. We should desire that God manifest his power to us and through us in order to produce faith in Christ and bring glory only to him. *Lord...enable your servants to speak your word with great boldness. Stretch out your hand to heal and perform miraculous signs and wonders through the name of your servant Jesus.*[284]

Faith and Healing (Part 1)

Daughter...your faith has healed you...(Matthew 9:22)

Faith is often connected with healing. God may choose to heal a person who never asks. He may also heal indirectly through the instrument of medicine. The biblical record indicates that most people who received a direct, physical touch from God were in some way asked to demonstrate *faith*. The woman who had been subject to bleeding for twelve years was in a crowd around Jesus, but she alone reached out to touch the edge of his cloak. In her heart, she was expecting an answer: *"If I only touch his cloak, I will be healed."*[285] Because of her expectant, active faith, she received healing. When Jairus asked Jesus to come and heal his dying daughter, Jesus responded, *"Don't be afraid; just believe, and she will be healed."*[286]

Persons with a passive approach –"Well, God is sovereign; if he wants to heal me he will"– seem rarely to receive direct, supernatural healing. God looks for hearts who earnestly look for his help. Namaan, a highly regarded military officer, who was suffering from leprosy, came to Elisha for help. He was commanded to dip in the dirty Jordan River seven times. After some initial resistance, he humbled himself and obeyed. The result was a miraculous touch from God.[287]

Blind Bartimaeus shouted loudly for Jesus' help – despite the reproof of Jesus' disciples – and he received his sight. Possibly many silent people that day remained in their sickness, but Jesus told Bartimaeus, *"Your faith has healed you."*[288]

Jesus and the disciples did not heal every sick person; they were led by the Spirit and *healed those who needed healing.*[289] When Paul looked at a man crippled in his feet, Paul *saw that he had faith to be healed, and called out, "Stand up on your feet."*[290] The man *jumped up and began to walk.*[291]

Sincere and desperate action often leads to frustration and disappointment. But *faith* in the heart, demonstrated by sincere and desperate action, will often bring a healing touch from God.

Faith and Healing (Part 2)

Is any one of you sick? He should call the elders of the church to pray over him and anoint him with oil in the name of the Lord. And the prayer offered in faith will make the sick person well; the Lord will raise him up. (James 5:14-15)

If a man has a serious sickness he is instructed to call the elders (leaders) of the church. Sometimes God heals through the faith of a sick person, sometimes through the faith of the elders. It requires faith for a person to call the elders. I heard of one sick lady who had a pastor who did not believe in modern-day healing. Yet, in faith she called him to come pray for her and reluctantly he did. Even though his prayer was feeble, God honored the faith of the lady and she was healed!

God will also look to the faith of church elders. Should anyone be called to pray for healing from sickness, it is important to go and pray in faith. *The prayer offered in faith will make the sick person well.* Unless specifically requested, this is not the time to pray for God to bless the doctor's hands, to bless the recovery time in the hospital, or for God's grace in this time of suffering. Such prayers may indicate unbelief. If a person has surgery scheduled and asks us to pray for the surgery, we certainly should. But a sick person who calls God's leaders to come pray is usually looking for *God's* direct help, not a hospital stay! We should simply pray in faith, in obedience to God, and look to him for a supernatural touch. We do not need to pronounce a person healed. The results are entirely up to God.

It is the *prayer of faith* that produces results, not the *prayer of perhaps*. We should not pray the timid prayer, "Lord, if it is your will, please heal this person." It is good to want the will of God, but no father would enjoy his child's having a dose of cancer. Thus, we can generally assume that healing, not sickness, is the will of our Heavenly Father.[292] So, unless God gives a definite check, we pray in faith, expecting him to move.

Faith and Healing (Part 3)

"Men of Israel, why does this surprise you? Why do you stare at us as if by our own power or godliness we have made this man walk? The God of Abraham, Isaac and Jacob, the God of our fathers, has glorified his servant Jesus...It is Jesus' name and the faith that comes through him that has given this complete healing to him, as you can all see..." (Acts 3:12-16)

The early apostles refused to take credit for any healing accomplished through them. They were humble men who were quick to focus on the Healer more than the healing. Men who desire to be used by God in healing ministry must keep Jesus at the forefront. A. B. Simpson was such a man, as described by a close associate: "At 36, Simpson was a Presbyterian preacher so sick that he said, 'I feel I could fall into the grave when I have a funeral.' He could not preach for months at a time because of his sickness. He went to a little camp meeting in the woods and heard a quartet sing, 'No man can work like Jesus. No man can work like Him.' Simpson went off among the pine trees with that ringing in his heart: 'Nobody can work like Jesus; nothing is too hard for Jesus. No man can work like Him.' The learned, stiff-necked Presbyterian threw himself down upon the pine needles and said, 'If Jesus Christ is what they said He was in the song, heal me.' The Lord healed him, and he lived to be 76 years old. Simpson founded a society that is now one of the largest evangelical denominations in the world, The Christian and Missionary Alliance."[293]

Simpson, who was used much in ministering healing, learned to seek the Healer, not just the healing. He focused men's attention on Jesus Christ, not just his benefits. He wrote:

Once it was the blessing, now it is the Lord.
Once it was the feeling; now it is His word.
Once His gifts I wanted; now the Giver own;
Once I sought for healing, now Himself alone.[294]

Faith and Healing (Part 4)

He called his twelve disciples to him and gave them authority to drive out evil spirits and to heal every disease and sickness... (Matthew 10:1)

Our Lord is still looking for disciples who can be instruments of his healing power. Sometimes it takes him a while to prepare a useful vessel. Jesus will not share his glory with another. Yet, few men can be used in supernatural ways without becoming proud or promotional. Those of us who have been repulsed by showy or emotional evangelists might have no interest in such a ministry. Or, perhaps we feel that we are not especially gifted in healing.[295] But, our Lord still looks for *vessels* he can use.

False humility may be another hindrance to God's ministry through us. We may look for spiritually impressive saints, but God uses ordinary men. The Book of Acts is a record of Jesus' ongoing ministry through ordinary, human vessels like you and me. They were simple believers empowered with the Holy Spirit, sensitive to his leading, and bold to pray in Jesus' name.

When Paul and his companions were shipwrecked on the island of Malta, he discovered that the father of the island's chief official was sick in bed, suffering from fever and dysentery. He waited for no invitation. *Paul went in to see him and, after prayer, placed his hands on him and healed him.*[296] Paul knew where the healing came from, yet the Scripture says, *Paul...healed him.* God does the healing, but frequently uses willing, faithful vessels.

One's obedient action, under the nudging of the Spirit, can produce significant results. Notice what followed Paul's prayer and healing of this man. *When this had happened, the rest of the sick on the island came and were healed.*[297] Whenever Jesus sent out his disciples to preach the gospel, healing was part of the package.[298] As we share the gospel with friends and neighbors, let us step out in faith and pray for the sick. Not all whom we pray for will be healed, but some will be.

Faith and Miracles

"Now, Lord...stretch out your hand to heal and perform miraculous signs and wonders through the name of your holy servant Jesus." (Acts 4:29-30)

We have no biblical reason to believe that miracles were only confined to apostolic times, that they no longer occur today, or that they will never be part of our experience. Indeed, *Jesus Christ is the same yesterday and today and forever.*[299] J. I. Packer has stated, "Belief in the miraculous is integral to Christianity... There is nothing irrational about believing that God who made the world can still intrude creatively in it."[300]

Miracles are more than just "answers to prayer" and they are different from physical healing (although they may include extraordinary healing, like healing a man who has been an invalid his whole life). Wayne Grudem, in his *Systematic Theology,* provided an excellent definition in his chapter titled "Miracles:" "A miracle is a less common kind of God's activity in which he rouses people's awe and wonder and bears witness to himself."[301] Another definition is, "God working in the world without using natural means." Examples of miracles would include Elijah praying for rain to stop and start again; angelic release of Peter from prison; Jesus' raising Lazarus from the dead; and wild lions kept from harming Daniel.

If anyone has doubt about miracles occurring today I encourage you to read the most comprehensive study of miracles in print, Craig S. Kenner's *Miracles,* a 1,172 page, two-volume book.[302] Keener discusses common objections and sets forth a very balanced approach to miracles. The strength of this work, however, is the thousands of testimonies of miracles – from past ages to present. He has collected testimonies from around the world, many accompanied by reputable eyewitness accounts and medical verification. This book is an eye-opener to God's miracle-working power in our world today.

We realize miracles are unusual, not our daily experience; but, let's believe God to grant his miracles whenever needed.

Supernatural Gifts of Faith

There are different kinds of gifts...to one there is given...faith by the same Spirit. (1 Corinthians 12:4,9)

Faith is listed among the gifts of the Holy Spirit. This is not ordinary faith, for each believer has been given a *measure of faith*.[303] The gift of faith, however, comes when special circumstances require it, or it may reside in certain people who are called to minister in unusual ways, often when they are encountering impossible obstacles or apparently overwhelming opposition. We could think of it as extraordinary faith, which is given to individuals by the sovereignty of God.

Elijah displayed the gift of faith on a number of occasions. In his dramatic encounter with the false prophets of Baal on Mount Carmel, Elijah boldly declared the true God would reveal himself by sending fire upon an altar.[304] After this declaration, he told the people to drench the altar with water three times. Then, God sent fire from heaven. Most believers would never attempt such a thing – it would take supernatural faith to perform such an action.

Elijah *was a man just like us*.[305] God still chooses ordinary believers upon whom he bestows his gifts and through whom he displays his power. It is often surprising the people he uses. Rees Howells, a common Welsh coal miner, became known as a man of mighty prayer. By faith, he founded the Bible College of Wales, even buying buildings in the midst of a national financial depression. Hudson Taylor, a man lacking in the expected education and credentials of his day, went by faith to China and pioneered a successful mission. George Muller, in his care for hundreds of orphans, displayed exceptional faith in the way he believed God would provide their daily bread. When God calls a man to a particular task, he prepares him and equips him for that work. When needed for his service, he may grant any of us the gift of faith for a special time.

How Faith Develops:
Knowing the Author of Faith

*Let us fix our eyes on Jesus, the author and perfecter of
our faith...(Hebrews 12:2)*

Faith is developed by growing nearer to the Author of faith.
Martin Luther said, "Faith is an unceasing and constant looking
which turns the eyes upon nothing but Christ, the Victor over sin
and death and the Giver of righteousness, salvation, and life
eternal."[306] We do not have to strain to believe God, it does not
take frantic effort on our part. The closer we are to Jesus, the
more readily faith comes. Oswald Chambers said, "You can't
pump up faith out of your own heart. Wherever faith is starved
in your soul, it is because you are not in contact with Jesus; get
in contact with Him and lack of faith will go in two seconds."[307]

In the natural realm, it is difficult to have much confidence
or trust in a person we scarcely know. Scripture says, *Now
acquaint yourself with Him, and be at peace.*[308] Abraham is
referred to as the "father of faith,"[309] and is also the only man in
the Bible called *God's friend.*[310] This is a key to faith: Knowing
whom we believe is as important as knowing *what* we believe.

I heard of an elderly Christian lady whose mental faculties
had begun to fail. She had once known much of the Bible by
heart, but as she deteriorated only one verse stayed with her: *For
I know whom I have believed, and am persuaded that He is able
to keep what I have committed to Him until that Day.*[311] As time
went on, she began to forget the one remaining verse, but she
remembered a portion which she would quietly repeat: *what I
have committed to Him.* Near the end of her days, as she hovered
between this world and the next, her loved ones noticed her lips
moving. When they bent down to see if she needed anything,
they heard her repeating over and over again to herself the one
word left in her memory: *"Him, Him, Him."* This dear saint had
lost the whole Bible except one word, but she still possessed the
essence of the Bible in that one word.

How Faith Develops:
Meditate on God's Attributes

O God, we meditate on your unfailing love. (Psalm 48:9)

David Clarkson wrote over three centuries ago, "It is our privilege to live by faith. Living by faith is not a single act, but something habitual and permanent. Faith is a constant dependence upon God, as he is known by his attributes. The divine attributes are the pillars and grounds of our faith. Faith believes them and claims them. Study the attributes of God. Labor to know them distinctly and effectually. The more we know, the more we trust....

"Faith not only holds to the fact that God is able, but that he is willing to do what you seek. Grip two handles with your faith. Take hold that he is able, omnipotent, omniscient, and all sufficient; but also take hold that he is willing to meet your needs by his mercy. Learn to draw arguments from these attributes. When you hold on to both his power and his mercy, faith can easily draw sweet and strong assurances from these. It is true that we are prone to doubt God's willingness, but the Lord has provided for this remarkably. Where there is but one attribute to describe God's power, there are many titles that prove his willingness: mercy, goodness, bounty, grace, love, loving-kindness, compassion, bowels of compassion, patience, and long-suffering. Fix your faith upon this double basis and it will stand firm. God is able and willing. Focus on God's attributes to strengthen faith.

- I am sinful, but God is merciful.
- I am unworthy, but he is gracious.
- I abused patience, but he is love.
- I am unfaithful, but he is faithful.

"Fix on the attribute of God that most suits your condition. In him, there is more than we need, more than we desire, more than we can imagine, infinitely more!"[312]

How Faith Develops:
Hearing the Word of Christ

So faith comes by hearing, and hearing by the word of Christ. (Romans 10:17 NAS)

Faith develops as God speaks a living word by the Holy Spirit to the heart of man. *Even as he spoke, many put their faith in Him.*[313] We must be careful how we respond; the word of God will produce very little spiritual fruitfulness unless it is received with faith. In recounting the history of the Israelites, the author of Hebrews stated, *The message they heard was of no value to them, because those who heard did not combine it with faith.*[314]

Faith is the catalyst which keeps God's word growing in our hearts. If we have a steady diet of reading, studying, meditating upon, and practicing the word of God, faith will rise in our hearts. Those who spend more time watching or listening to the world's news will probably find their hearts more full of fear, doubt, and anxiety than of confident trust in Almighty God.

One of the primary purposes of the gospel accounts is to inspire faith in our hearts. The apostle John said, *Jesus did many other miraculous signs in the presence of his disciples, which are not recorded in this book. But these are written that you may believe that Jesus is the Christ, the Son of God, and that by believing you may have life in his name.*[315] If we ever want to encourage more faith in a man's heart, we can direct him to read the gospels with an open heart, and simply to consider Christ and all that he said.

Each time we approach Scripture, we should not be too casual or presume we will gain something from it. We should humbly pray, "Lord, speak to me, make your word come alive; help me to understand by the Holy Spirit." Charles Spurgeon, a diligent student of Scripture, emphasized the Holy Spirit, "Better six words of one verse saturated by the Holy Spirit than to routinely read one hundred chapters of the Bible."[316] As we continually seek God and abide in his word, faith will grow.

How Faith Develops:
Using What We Have (Part 1)

He who is faithful in a very little thing is faithful also in much; and he who is unrighteous in a very little thing is unrighteous also in much (Luke 16:10)

Rees Howells, a British intercessor and founder of the Bible College of Wales, learned to be faithful in small matters. In his early years as a Christian, Rees met a young man, Will Battery, who was dirty and unshaven, alcoholic, and stricken with meningitis. Although Rees had no natural desire to be with this man, the Holy Spirit birthed a supernatural love in his heart. He began spending time with Will, making him his friend. Rees stated at this time that he had more joy in spending time with this one needy man, than at church in the company of the other believers. He said, "I started at the bottom and loved just one; and if you love one, you can love many; and if many, you can love all."[317]

Some believers are unwilling to exercise faith first in small ways and want to move on to great exploits "for God." However, it is the humble, faithful, and patient man that God will promote in due time.[318] Someone has said, "If you are too big for a little place, you are too little for a big place."

The early disciples who *turned the world upside down* were not extraordinary believers; they were Christ-centered men who simply used what they had: The apostle Peter said to the lame man,. . .*but what I have I give unto you.*[319] Are we willing to use the little we have when God beckons us?

If there is a contentment and willingness to be faithful with the small, God can entrust us with the larger. Susanna Wesley, the mother of John and Charles, spent a good part of her adult life confined to many routine tasks, most involving raising her fifteen children. She once said, "I am willing to fill a little space if God be glorified."[320] Let us, too, be faithful in the small tasks God has given us.

How Faith Develops: Using What We Have (Part 2)

God wants you to give what you have, not what you haven't. (2 Corinthians 8:12 TLB)

We can take great inspiration from three people who, despite severe visual handicaps, used what they had.

Philip Yancey said he read a book "written" by a Frenchman who could only blink his left eyelid. A nurse would run her finger across the alphabet on a poster board until he blinked at the letter he wanted, then begin all over again until he signaled the next letter of the word.[321] Amazing!

A. J. Freeman went blind at age seventeen and was so depressed that a few years later, he decided to jump out a five story window and end his life. At the last minute, however, a nurse jerked him in off the window ledge. Immediately he fell on his knees and prayed to God to save him. With a new lease on life, Freeman learned the trade of making brooms, which provided support for his family. More importantly, he began taking every opportunity to share his faith in Christ. In 1903, Freeman, at the age of thirty-five, was ordained as an evangelist by the Swedish Free Church. He began serving as a full-time evangelist and over his lifetime, an estimated 12,000 persons came to Christ through the preaching of this blind Swede.[322]

Fanny Crosby, blind at six weeks, began writing poetry as a young girl. After becoming a Christian, she became a prolific writer. One of the most influential Christians of the nineteenth century, she published more than 2,000 hymns, including such favorites as "Blessed Assurance" and "To God be the Glory."

In a cemetery in Bridgeport, Connecticut, where she was buried, one will pass by many large and ornate tombstones before arriving at Crosby's. Her small and simple marker lists her name and humbly reads: "SHE HATH DONE WHAT SHE COULD." At the end of our lives, will it be said of us – that we *did what we could* for the glory of God?

How Faith Develops:
Taking Risks for God

Now the Jordan is at flood stage all during harvest. Yet as soon as the priests who carried the ark reached the Jordan and their feet touched the water's edge, the water from upstream stopped flowing. It piled up in a heap... (Joshua 3:15-16)

In the first step to conquering the land of promise, God had commanded the priests to cross the Jordan River during the flood stage. As these priests approached the edge, they would not be able to put just a foot in or wade in slowly; they would have to step in over their heads while carrying the ark of the covenant – taking not just a step, but a plunge!

Faith at times will require us also to take a "plunge" – stepping into an unknown arena, not knowing what's ahead or the risks involved. Corrie ten Boom once described faith as a...

Fantastic

Adventure

In

Trusting

Him[323]

The life of faith often has a certain risk element to it. God delights neither in foolishness nor presumption, but we tend to arrange ways of escape in case "God fails." The natural man does not like to depend on God and wants to avoid any sense of failure. As God leads, we must be willing to "step in over our heads" and believe that he is able to do what is humanly impossible. Jamie Buckingham once said, "Attempt something so big that unless God intervenes it is bound to fail."[324] Great pioneers did not always take the easy, safe, and popular way. President Theodore Roosevelt did not fear failure in attempting great things. He wrote, "Far better to dare mighty things, to win glorious triumphs, even though checkered by failure, than to take rank with those poor spirits who neither enjoy much nor suffer much because they live in the gray twilight that knows neither victory nor defeat."[325]

How Faith Develops:
Standing on His Promises (Part 1)

*And because of his glory and excellence, he has given
us great and precious promises. These are the promises
that enable you to share his divine nature and escape
the world's corruption caused by human desires.
(2 Peter 1:4 NLT)*

The promises of God are fundamental in faith. We can trust the promises because of the One who made the promises! There is no one more truthful and more able to fulfill his promises than God. J. I. Packer wrote, "In the days when the Bible was universally acknowledged in the churches as 'God's Word written,' it was clearly understood that the promises of God recorded in Scripture were the proper, God-given basis for all our life of faith, and that the way to strengthen one's faith was to focus it upon particular promises that spoke to one's condition."[326]

Therefore, as the Holy Spirit illuminates a promise from God's word to our hearts, we can say, "Yes, Lord, I believe your promise and I look to you to fulfill your word." Many of God's promises will sustain us all through this life as we realize God is preparing us for much better life to come. Charles Spurgeon, in *The Check Book of the Bank of Faith* wrote, "God has given no pledge but He will not redeem, and encouraged no hope which He will not fulfill."[327]

There will be much value as we ponder God's promises. Puritan Samuel Clark, in the introduction to his *Scripture Promises,* wrote, "A fixed, constant attention to the promises, and a firm belief of them, would prevent solicitude and anxiety about the concerns of this life. It would keep the mind quiet and composed in every change, and support and keep up our sinking spirits under the several troubles of life.... Christians deprive themselves of their most solid comforts by their unbelief and forgetfulness of God's promises. For there is no extremity so great, but there are promises suitable to it, and abundantly sufficient for our relief in it."[328]

How Faith Develops:
Standing on His Promises (Part 2)

The LORD is faithful to all his promises... (Psalm 145:13)

Faith will grow as we meditate on and memorize the precious promises of God. Here are some of my favorite verses.

GOD'S DIRECTION
Trust in the Lord with all your heart, and lean not on your own understanding; in all your ways acknowledge Him, and He shall direct your paths. (Prov. 3:5-6 NKJV)

GOD'S FREEDOM
Therefore, there is now no condemnation for those who are in Christ Jesus. (Romans 8:1)

GOD'S KEEPING POWER
But the Lord is faithful, and he will strengthen and protect you from the evil one. (2 Thes. 3:3)

GOD'S PEACE
Peace I leave with you; my peace I give you. I do not give to you as the world gives. Do not let your hearts be troubled and do not be afraid. (John 14:27)

GOD'S SUPPORT
So do not fear, for I am with you; Do not be dismayed, for I am your God. I will strengthen you and help you; I will uphold you with my righteous right hand. (Isaiah 41:10)

GOD'S PROTECTION
The Lord will keep you from all harm, he will watch over your life; the Lord will watch over your coming and going both now and forevermore. (Psalm 121:7-8)

GOD'S PRESENCE
Never will I leave you; never will I forsake you. So we say with confidence, "The Lord is my helper; I will not be afraid. What can man do to me?" (Heb. 13:5-6)

Day One Hundred One
Enemies of Faith:
Unbelief

Take care, brethren, lest there should be in any of you an evil, unbelieving heart, in falling away from the living God...those who came out of Egypt..were not able to enter because of unbelief... (Hebrews 3:12-19)

The greatest sin for the Christian is unbelief. Unbelief is everything that is diametrically opposed to faith, and it has deadly consequences. The Israelites missed out on God's provision because of unbelief and were compared to broken branches: *they were broken off because of unbelief, and you stand in faith.*[329] When Jesus performed miracles, the demons of hell could not hinder him; but amazingly, he was stopped by the unbelief of his home-town people. *He could not do any miracles there, except lay his hands on a few sick people and heal them. And he was amazed at their lack of faith.*[330]

Unbelief is a constant danger for us, and it is no small thing. The above verse from Hebrews says each one of us should be careful *lest there should be in any of you an evil, unbelieving heart...* Unbelief is our root problem and it will show itself in a multitude of ways. In the next few pages we will examine eight branches of the barren tree of unbelief. Let us be careful to guard against every manifestation of unbelief.

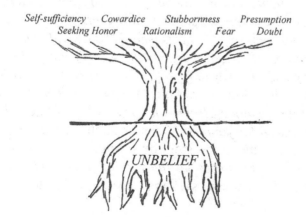

Self-sufficiency   Cowardice   Stubbornness   Presumption
Seeking Honor   Rationalism   Fear   Doubt

UNBELIEF

Enemies of Faith:
Self-sufficiency

Has not God chosen those who are poor in the eyes of the world to be rich in faith and to inherit the kingdom he promised those who love him? (James 2:5)

Why are poor people in the world often deemed *rich in faith*? It is simply because they are more aware of their need for the Lord. Jesus said, *"Blessed are the poor in spirit, for theirs is the kingdom of heaven,"*[331] or as the *New English Bible* says, *"How blest are those who know their need for God..."* Those who have a lot tend to be self-sufficient and say, *"I am rich, I have acquired wealth and do not need a thing."*[332] A man who "has it all" will rarely find room for God in his busy life caring for all his goods and projects. He may also trust his riches more than he trusts Christ. Possibly one reason God does not allow many believers to prosper more is that it might hinder faith.

Jesus targeted the poor in his preaching ministry.[333] As he spoke, *the common people heard him gladly.*[334] Howard Snyder wrote, "From the beginning and throughout history, the most rapid, enduring and society-transforming church growth has normally occurred among the poor."[335]

Scripture is not against believers being wealthy. God *richly provides us with everything for our enjoyment.*[336] Wealthy believers, however, are encouraged to be both cautious and generous.[337] It is the selfish man, however, who is rebuked. *A certain rich man said, "This is what I'll do. I will tear down my barns and build bigger ones, and there I will store all my grain and my goods. I'll say to myself...Take life easy; eat, drink and be merry." But God said to him, "You fool! This very night your life will be demanded from you. Then who will get what you have prepared for yourself?"* Notice all the references to *I* and *my.* Jesus concluded this story by saying, *This is how it will be with anyone who stores up things for himself but is not rich toward God.*[338] May we seek the true riches of faith.

Enemies of Faith:
Seeking Honor

How can you believe, who receive honor from one another, and do not seek the honor that comes from the only God? (John 5:44 NKJV)

In this present life, we will live either for our own honor or for the honor of God himself. The man who lives for the approval of man will have great difficulty developing faith in God. Some Jews in Jesus' day were more concerned with keeping everybody happy than acknowledging Christ. *Many even of the rulers believed in Him, but because of the Pharisees they were not confessing Him, lest they be put out of the synagogue; for they loved the approval of men rather than the approval of God.*[339]

Men and women who have been used by God in his kingdom have been those who refused to seek their own glory. At the end of his recent autobiography, Billy Graham reflected on why God chose him, a simple North Carolina farm boy, to preach to so many people. He said, "I cannot take credit for whatever God has chosen to accomplish through us and our ministry; only God deserves the glory, and we can never thank Him enough for the great things He has done."[340] Mr. Graham's humble and sincere attitude and gratitude is probably why God used him. Charles Colson related a time when he was asked to host a Christian television program. Each day he was greeted by the makeup artist, the wardrobe person, briefing papers, and everyone showing deference to the "star." He confessed he enjoyed the glory, glamour, and all the personal attention, but after two weeks he had to leave. He said, "I know some of my own weaknesses, and I don't trust myself."[341] John Wesley, when seated in a special pew beside a city mayor, exclaimed, "What is this? What have I to do with honor? Lord, let me always *fear*, not *desire* it."[342] True servants of God will be distinguished by a desire to seek God's honor. *If I were still trying to please men, I would not be the servant of Christ.*[343]

Enemies of Faith: Doubt

When they saw Him...some were doubtful....He reproached them for their unbelief and hardness of heart, because they had not believed those who had seen Him after He had risen. (Matthew 28:17 NAS; Mark 16:14 NAS)

Some years ago, a man in Texas received word that he had inherited a large fortune from a relative in England. This Texan, a recluse living in poverty, had never heard of the English relative and was skeptical. Even though he was on the verge of starvation, he would not believe such good news. Disbelief deprived him of a million dollars. He died poverty stricken.[344]

Doubt is not "having honest questions;" it is hesitation, wavering, wondering, and even skepticism at times. It is a refusal to see God's evidences and to exercise faith after assurance has come. The angel Gabriel told Zechariah of a special son to be born, but he responded, *"How can I be sure of this?"*[345] The angel said he would be stricken dumb until the birth of that son *because you did not believe my words.*[346]

Scripture describes the doubtful man: *...he who doubts is like a wave of the sea, blown and tossed by the wind. That man should not think he will receive anything from the Lord; he is a double-minded man, unstable in all he does.*[347] In the Greek, he who doubts literally means "a man of two minds." This man will think faith-filled thoughts for a brief time, then thinks the way of the natural, worldly man. Peter walked on the water when the Master said, *"Come,"* but then focused on the water, and began to sink. Jesus offered no sympathy to Peter: *"You of little faith...why did you doubt?"*[348]

The reason the Lord strongly reproves doubt is that it is unbelief and an insult to his holy name. How do we feel when we tell something true and people do not believe us? How do we feel if a family member or mate is skeptical and even scoffs at what we said? Let us not doubt, but respond to God in faith.

Enemies of Faith:
Stubbornness

They refused to give up their evil practices and
stubborn ways. (Judges 2:19)

"In the summer of 1986, two ships collided in the Black Sea off the coast of Russia. Hundreds of passengers died as they were hurled into the icy waters below. News of the disaster was further darkened when an investigation revealed the cause of the accident. It wasn't a technology problem like radar malfunction – or even thick fog. The cause was human stubbornness.

"Each captain was aware of the other ship's presence nearby. Both could have steered clear, but according to news reports, neither captain wanted to give way to the other. Each was too proud to yield first. By the time they came to their senses, it was too late."[349]

Stubbornness is no mere character quirk; the Bible says, *Stubbornness is as iniquity and idolatry...*[350] As we observed in the story above, it can have deadly effects – affecting not only ourselves, but others as well.

How is stubbornness a barrier or even an enemy of faith? There are several ways it may manifest itself:

- We refuse to face up to the light God is giving us. (This is often because we made serious moral compromises.[351])
- We are unteachable and do not listen to anyone who contradicts what we prefer to believe.
- We remain unyielding and, even when a truth is obvious, we simply refuse to accept it.
- We insist on our own ways and will not defer to others.
- We accept no correction or reproof and as a result we may suffer quite seriously. Scripture says, *Whoever stubbornly refuses to accept criticism will suddenly be destroyed beyond recovery.*[352]

Instead of becoming stubborn, let us walk humbly before our God, face the facts before us, and choose to obey his word.

Enemies of Faith:
Rationalism

"As the heavens are higher than the earth, so are my ways higher than your ways and my thoughts than your thoughts." (Isaiah 55:8-9)

Webster's Unabridged Dictionary defines rationalism as "the principle or habit of accepting reason as the supreme authority in matters of opinion, belief, or conduct."[353] God never intended mindless Christianity; we are called to love God *with all our minds.*[354] Our minds are to be used to consider, calculate, ponder, or deliberate a matter. Christians are not to be lazy intellectually; we are exhorted: *prepare your minds for action.*[355] When we try to figure everything out in the kingdom of God, however, we get in trouble if our minds become the "supreme authority."

With God, we are not dealing with an idol or an Olympian god made in the image of man; we are dealing with the all-powerful, all-knowing, and all-seeing God of the universe. His ways and thoughts are too much for our mortal minds to grasp. *Oh, the depths of the riches of the wisdom and knowledge of God! How unsearchable his judgments, and his paths beyond tracing out! Who has known the mind of the Lord? Or who has been his counselor?*[356]

Some steps of faith we take might not always seem "reasonable," but when we are dealing with the supernatural realm, at times we must step forth in faith though our minds tend to hesitate and rationalize. Much in Abraham's faith journey did not seem reasonable. He was asked to leave his hometown, though he did not know where he was going. He was asked to father a son, though he was past his prime age and his wife, Sarah, was barren. Then, in his ultimate test of faith, Abraham was asked to sacrifice his only son, Isaac. In all these requests, a man's rational mind would have wanted to act contrary to God's will. Our faith will also be tested at times, and when it is, the most rational thing to do is to believe God.

Enemies of Faith:
Cowardice

For God did not give us a spirit of cowardice, but rather a spirit of power and of love and of self-discipline. (2 Timothy 1:7 NRSV)

On the evening of October 8, 1871, a fire started in Chicago that burned for over twenty-four hours, destroying the downtown area and most North Side homes, leaving 90,000 homeless. It is reported that two hundred men committed suicide the day after the Great Chicago Fire. *The Chicago Tribune* came out immediately with a big red letter headline, "Any coward can commit suicide, but it takes a MAN to live under these conditions." The suicides stopped as this one voice of courage seemed to check the tidal wave of cowardice.

Left to ourselves, we would each tend to be cowardly when facing great dangers and difficulties. The disciples all fled when Jesus was arrested, and Peter denied him three times because of cowardice. We are no different. But courage is the opposite of cowardice. When our natural tendency is to be timid or frightened, we need to look to the Lord and be courageous: *Say to those with palpitating heart, "Take courage, fear not."*[357] *Wait for the Lord; be strong, and let your heart take courage.*[358]

Joshua could have been overwhelmed when Moses entrusted to him the task of conquering and possessing the land of Canaan. Four times, God brought a special word of encouragement to Joshua, *"Be strong and courageous."*[359] Joshua would not need to be cautious in his obedience, for he had been told, *"The Lord your God goes with you; he will never leave you nor forsake you."*[360] Courage is not the absence of fear; it's boldly facing life in spite of fear, because we know God is with us.

Martyn Lloyd-Jones said, "Faith is a refusal to panic."[361] We need not panic; *those who are with us are more than those who are with them*[362]...*So we say with confidence, "The Lord is my helper; I will not be afraid."*[363] Let us therefore *stand firm in the faith; be men of courage; be strong.*[364]

Day One Hundred Eight
Enemies of Faith:
Fear (Part 1)

Do not be afraid, only have faith...(Lk. 8:50 Jerusalem Bible)

Fear is probably faith's greatest enemy leading to emotional turmoil and robbing many believers of receiving the provision and promises of God. It is no wonder that over a hundred times in Scripture we are told to *fear not.*

Having a proper "fear of the Lord" may be the remedy to much of the fear that we face: *Do not fear what they fear, and do not dread it. The Lord Almighty is the one you are to regard as holy, he is the one you are to fear, he is the one you are to dread.*[365] Jesus always reproved those who were motivated by the fear of man, *"Do not be afraid of those who kill the body but cannot kill the soul. Rather, be afraid of the one who can destroy both soul and body in hell."*[366]

Most of our fear is imagining negative events which never will happen: *they were overwhelmed with dread, where there was nothing to fear.*[367] We must keep an optimistic attitude that God is a good God and has good plans for our future. We also must be careful with what we focus our minds on while reading and engaging in various media. Do we spend more time dwelling on God's good news or the world's bad news? *Great peace have they who love your law, and nothing can make them stumble.*[368]

Judson Cornwall contrasted faith and fear in this way: "Fear says, 'It won't be done,' while faith says, 'It shall be done'...Fear and faith are diametrically opposed to each other. Fear deprives man of his reason, while faith gives man a reason. Fear terrorizes; faith stabilizes. Fear excites the human nature, but faith calms man better than any medicinal tranquilizer. Fear brings sickness; faith brings health. Fear causes insanity, while faith gives man a sound mind. There just is no common ground on which fear and faith can rest, unless it is the 'fear of the Lord.'"[369]

We never will be immune to fear, but in troublesome times, let us turn to the Lord, *"When I am afraid, I will trust in you."*[370]

Enemies of Faith:
Fear (Part 2)

The LORD is my light and my salvation – whom shall I fear? The LORD is the stronghold of my life – of whom shall I be afraid? Though an army besiege me, my heart will not fear; though war break out against me, even then will I be confident. (Psalm 27:1, 3)

One of my good friends once suffered from a phobia that was so severe he could not drive a car outside our city limits. Anytime he would attempt to drive out of town, he would start sweating, feel his throat tighten, and his heart would start racing. He felt paralyzed and feared that he might even die. He was a serious Christian, and our church leaders and friends sought the Lord with him and his wife to find God's remedy. We tried fasting and prayer, deliverance from demonic influence, and made sure there were no "spiritual loopholes" that would give the enemy an opening. As time went on, we felt that God's answer was: "You will not get immediate freedom; but face this fear head-on; walk in faith; and *little by little you will possess the land.*"[371]

So, a couple times a week, I or another of his friends would take a drive with him and during the drive we would sing praise songs and quote Scripture. It was quite difficult and outside the city limits, as he began to "freeze," he would be urged to go a little farther each time. After several months of facing this tough fear, he could drive a hundred miles to another city. The victory was coming, little by little, step by step. In recent years, this brother has even traveled overseas on several missions trips and we all give God the glory. Faith must often be displayed in the midst of fear, as this acrostic (by an unknown author) implies.

Feeling
Afraid
I
Trust
Him

Enemies of Faith:
Presumption

Nevertheless, in their presumption they went up toward the high hill country, though neither Moses nor the ark of the Lord's covenant moved from that camp. (Numbers 14:44)

When we run ahead of the Lord or take upon ourselves an action which God has not ordained, we are guilty of presumption. Many mistakes have been made in the name of "faith" when one arrogantly moves ahead, even "in the name of the Lord," and yet misses the will of God.

Sometimes presumption is simply a matter of missing God's timing. The Israelites moved out of their camp into battle, but there was one major problem – God's presence (the ark) and his ordained leadership (Moses) did not go with them. As a result, they were soundly defeated and reproach came upon them.

Pride is the basis of presumption; in fact, in the Hebrew language the two words are identical.[372] We can fall into presumption when – out of subtle pride – we want to make God look good. I remember having a vivid daydream of an open air meeting in which I was being used in dramatic healings and miracles. There was one basic problem, however – the people seemed to be very impressed with *me*. Even though I was "God's humble servant," I seemed to be enjoying the fanfare. So, I have learned to pray this biblical prayer, *Keep back your servant from presumptuous sins; let them not rule over me.*[373]

Jack Hayford commented about this great enemy of faith. "Presumption is rooted in fear and fostered in pride. It begins when I am afraid that God won't swing into action fast enough if I don't do something to prove my faith. And it flourishes when I foolishly make high sounding noises about 'faith' and 'trusting God.' Human pride always has to prove itself. But not so with the praying servant of God. The signs *follow*. It is wise to wait for them rather than try to make them happen."[374]

Levels of Faith

In the light of the grace I have received I want to urge each one among you not to exaggerate his real importance. Each of you must judge himself soberly by the standard of the faith God has given him. (Romans 12:3 Jerusalem Bible)

It is amusing to see a little girl, wanting to act like a grown-up, stumbling around in her mother's shoes and looking out from under an oversized hat. God may be amused as well to see some of his children trying to act much more mature in faith than they actually are. I remember as a younger Christian being greatly impressed by men with unusual healing ministries. One day I visited a sick relative, an unbeliever, and boldly declared to him that I was going to pray that God would heal him. He meekly replied, "Oh, I don't have that kind of faith." I unabashedly said, "Well, you may not have the faith, but I've got it!" I then followed with a fervent prayer, rebuked the sickness, and declared him healed. Not one thing happened, and realizing he was no better, I made some feeble comments and departed from my befuddled relative. This was a good lesson in humility for me, desperately needed at that time.

It is important that we develop in faith, but operate on the present level of faith that God has given: *let us keep living by the standard to which we have attained.*[375] Some brothers may have faith to trust God for unusual financial supply; some will not. Some may have faith for healing; others will not; each must walk in *the standard of faith God has given him.*

One of the greatest mistakes we make as Christians is comparing ourselves with others. *What fools they are to measure themselves by themselves, to find in themselves their own standard of comparison.*[376] Comparison with others is unwise because God has made us unique and equipped us with various gifts of his grace.[377] Therefore, we thank God for other gifted persons, but we walk in our own level of faith.

Journey of Faith

As Jesus walked beside the Sea of Galilee, he saw Simon and his brother Andrew casting a net into the lake, for they were fishermen. "Come, follow me," Jesus said... (Mark 1:16-17)

When Peter saw him, he asked, "Lord, what about him?" Jesus answered, "If I want him to remain alive until I return, what is that to you? You must follow me." (John 21:21-22)

Jesus' first and last words to Simon Peter were, "Follow me." Today some people have been told to just "ask Jesus into your heart and you will have a home in heaven." Jesus never said anything like that; his message was *"If anyone would come after me, he must deny himself and take up his cross daily and follow me."*[378] What does it mean to "follow" Christ? William Barclay, in his study of *New Testament Words,* shared several common usages of the Greek word for *follow*:

- For soldiers following their leader and commander;
- For a slave following or attending his master;
- A person sticking to or attaching himself to someone in order to extract some favor which is desired. One writer, in advising someone, said, *"Stick to* Ptollarion all the time ...*Stick* to him so that he might become your friend."[379]

Each of these usages shines some light on our Christian journey. We are soldiers following our commander, Jesus. We are slaves doing the will of our master, Jesus. We also follow hard after him, desiring all the grace, favor, and help he will give us. We also want to be the friends of God!

The life of faith for each of us is a day by day journey. As Tozer explained, "In the Book of Acts, faith was for each believer a beginning, not an end; it was a journey, not a bed in which to lie while waiting for the day of our Lord's triumph. Believing was not a once-done act; it was more than an act, it was an attitude of heart and mind which inspired and enabled the believer to take up his cross and follow the Lamb wherever He went."[380] Jesus' call today is still the same, "Follow me!"

School of Faith

To the Jews who had believed him, Jesus said, "If you hold to my teaching, you are really my disciples..." (John 8:31)

When we truly believe in Jesus Christ, we automatically enroll in the Lord's "School of Faith." To understand this idea, we must ask: "What is the most commonly used word in the New Testament to describe those who follow Christ?" Here are some answers, followed by the number of times each word is used.

- "Christian" – 12 times in the N.T.
- "Believer" – 27 times in the N.T.
- "Pentecostal" – 0 times in the N.T.
- "Baptist" – 0 times in the N.T.[381]
- "Disciple" – 283 times in the N.T.

The word *disciple* best describes those who follow Christ. Do you consider yourself a disciple of Jesus? A disciple can best be defined as "a learner, a student, a follower of a leader, one who wholeheartedly adheres to the teachings of another." In other words, we are continually learning; we are in the Lord's "School of Faith." Discipleship is not an option; Scripture says, *The disciples were first called Christians in Antioch.*[382] What else might characterize a *disciple* of Jesus?

- A disciple of Jesus is daily becoming more personally acquainted with him (Mk. 3:14-15; Lk. 9:23-24).
- A disciple of Jesus obeys his command to be baptized (Matt. 28:19-20).
- A disciple of Jesus is one who is committed to the word of God (John 8:31-32).
- A disciple of Jesus will show love to all men (John 13:34-35).
- A disciple of Jesus is one who pays the price to make him top priority (Luke 14:25-33; Matt. 10:37).

In the "Lord's School of Faith," there are no fees – the teacher has paid them for us; we have the best teacher and best curriculum; as long as we stay in the class, there are no failures; and, if we struggle, the Holy Spirit is the most helpful tutor!

Keeping the Faith:
Not Departing

Now the Spirit expressly says that in latter times some will depart from the faith, giving heed to deceiving spirits and doctrines of demons. (1 Timothy 4:1 NKJV)

A primary reason Paul wrote this first letter to Timothy was to warn against apostasy – falling away from the faith. Notice the verbs used in various warnings to believers (emphasis mine): *Some have <u>shipwrecked</u> their faith* (1:19); s*ome will <u>abandon</u> the faith* (4:1); *he has <u>denied</u> the faith* (5:8); *they have <u>broken</u> their first pledge* (5:12); *some have already <u>turned aside</u> to follow Satan* (5:15); and, *some have...<u>wandered</u> from the faith* (6:10).

Some are quick to jump into heated arguments regarding the doctrine of "once-saved-always-saved." God in his wisdom chose not to organize the Bible as a systematic theology book, thoroughly answering all our questions. It seems the Lord gives believers both needed reassurance concerning our eternal destiny as well as precautions concerning spiritual dangers.

We must not be naive about warnings concerning departing from the faith. They should cause us to walk humbly. If every believer has the potential to turn from the Lord, then we must be careful. *See to it, brothers, that none of you has a sinful unbelieving heart that turns away from the Living God.*[383] The word *apostasy* in Greek has two root words: *away from* and *standing*. In other words, the one who apostatizes no longer stands for things he once did. Often, moral failure or intellectual pride causes this to happen. Departing from the faith usually does not happen overnight; it is a gradual slipping away. *We must pay more careful attention, therefore, to what we have heard, so that we do not drift away.*[384] The word *drift* in the Greek language describes a boat which has been carelessly allowed to float past its harbor, drifting to destruction, because the pilot is negligent or sleeping.[385] May we *see to it*, brethren, that none of us departs from the faith.

Keeping the Faith:
Not Depressed

Why are you so downcast, O my soul?
Why so disturbed within me?
Put your hope in God,
for I will yet praise him,
my Savior and my God. (Psalm 42:5)

Depression is common to the human experience – we will all feel low, dejected, or "blue" at one time or another. There can be many causes: physical disorders, hormonal imbalance, job stress, relational conflicts, setbacks in life, or unconfessed sin.

Christians are not immune to depression. Many men of God in the Bible suffered depression, including Moses,[386] Elijah,[387] Job,[388] David,[389] and Paul.[390]

We should not be unduly alarmed if we fall into depression, and we should certainly not look down on those who suffer from it. But, it does seem that long term depression is not the will of God: *Wherein ye greatly rejoice, though now for a season, if need be, ye are in heaviness through manifold temptations.*[391] (The words, *for a season,* imply short term, rather than long term.) Dr. Martyn Lloyd-Jones wrote an excellent book, *Spiritual Depression,* which dealt with this problem. According to Lloyd-Jones, a type of person who is particularly prone to spiritual depression is the introvert – one who "tends to be always analyzing himself, analyzing everything he does, and worrying about all the possible effects of his actions, always harking back, always full of vain regrets."[392]

Our remedy begins when we turn our focus away from ourselves back to God in faith: "It is because we listen to the devil instead of listening to God that we...fall before his attacks ...You must exhort yourself, say to yourself: *Put your hope in God* – instead of muttering in this depressed, unhappy way. And then you must go on to remind yourself of God, who God is, and what God has done, and what God has pledged to do."[393]

Keeping the Faith:
Not Despairing

"Simon, Simon, Satan has asked to sift you as wheat. But I have prayed for you, Simon, that your faith may not fail. And when you have turned back, strengthen your brothers." (Luke 22:31)

After Peter denied the Lord three times, his faith was certainly sifted. When he heard the rooster crow, he realized the severity of his failure, and he was given to despair. *And he went outside and wept bitterly.*[394] When we suffer from despair, we have a sense of hopelessness as circumstances seem to overwhelm us. This might occur during a time of personal failure, as with Simon Peter. In such times we will be tempted by our enemy to abandon all hope and give up. If we avoid turning to God in faith, self-pity and deep gloom will reign, and we will be of little use to God or anyone else.

The apostle Paul and Timothy each experienced despair as they reached out to help folks in Asia. *We were under pressure, far beyond our ability to endure, so that we even despaired of life. Indeed in our hearts we felt the sentence of death.*[395] God, however, had not forgotten these devoted workers, and had a purpose in the midst of their insurmountable hardships. *But this happened that we might not rely on ourselves but on God, who raises the dead.*[396] Even though the full deliverance had not yet come, Paul determined to believe God. *On him we have set our hope that he will continue to deliver us, as you help us by your prayers.*[397] God will use all kinds of experiences to teach us a vital lesson: *that we might not rely on ourselves.*

When we become aware that a fellow Christian is despairing, we can *help...by...prayers.* This is not the time for advice or reproof, but rather, kindness and prayer. Job said, *For the despairing man there should be kindness from his friend, lest he forsake the fear of the Almighty.*[398] When brethren are suffering, we may be led to pray for deliverance. We can also pray that God will sustain them, that *their faith may not fail.*

Keeping the Faith:
Not Destroyed

We are... persecuted, but not abandoned; struck down, but not destroyed... (2 Corinthians 4:8-9).

In the classic boxing movie, *Rocky,* we see the local and relatively unknown hometown fighter, Rocky Balboa, go up against the great world champion, Apollo Creed. For many rounds Rocky is pulverized and is on the verge of being knocked out. Amazingly, he takes the hardest of blows and keeps standing. In the end, he makes a dramatic comeback, and as the final bell rings, he even injures the champion.

There are some similarities between such a boxing match and the Christian's experience. Satan's objective is to destroy us. We can be compared to the boxer who is almost demolished in the ring of life, but he keeps getting up and returning to the ring. *The Living Bible* says, *We get knocked down, but we get up again and keep going.* J. B. Phillips' translation says, *We may get knocked down, but we are never knocked out!*

Probably no other experience in life will threaten a knockout as will the untimely death of a mate, child, or very close friend. We will never fully empathize with such loss and suffering unless we have "been there." C. S. Lewis married Joy Davidman while she lay in a hospital bed dying of cancer. She recovered and the couple enjoyed three years together before Joy died at the age of 45 on July 13, 1960. Their story was popularized in the film *Shadowlands.* Lewis later wrote out of the anguish of his pain, "You never know how much you really believe anything until its truth or falsehood becomes a matter of life and death to you. It is easy to say you believe a rope to be strong and sound...but suppose you had to hang by that rope over a precipice. Wouldn't you then first discover how much you really trusted it?...Only a real risk tests the reality of a belief."[399] Through this very sad experience, C. S. Lewis was sustained by his faith. He shared the common experience of many a believer: *knocked down, but not knocked out!*

Keeping the Faith:
Not Disappointed

Though the fig tree does not bud
and there are no grapes on the vines,
though the olive crop fails
and the fields produce no food,
though there are no sheep in the pen
and no cattle in the stalls,
yet I will rejoice in the Lord,
I will rejoice in God my Savior.
(Habakkuk 3:17-18)

I can remember vividly the day I received a phone call from my wife – in her fourth pregnancy – announcing in a somber tone that our baby had died. This was a great blow to us – probably the greatest disappointment in my life. This Christian life has its delights, but it is also full of setbacks, reversals, and unexpected failures. Charles Spurgeon said, "I do not know into what trade you can enter to be secure against losses, not what profession you could follow in which you would escape disappointments. I know no corner of the earth without its night, no land without its stones, no sea without its storms."[400]

There are events that baffle any believer. How about the times we have patiently sought God, and things seemed to be lining up the way we had hoped; then, at the very last moment, circumstances changed, and somehow we were "left out in the cold?" In such times we can become confused, even embittered, or, in faith we can embrace the sovereignty of God.

Disappointment – His appointment
Change one letter, then I see
That the thwarting of my purpose
Is God's better choice for me.[401]

The prophet Habakkuk experienced ruined crops, barren livestock, and financial failure; yet, he exercised faith. He made a choice to leave his affairs with God and even rejoice: *yet I will rejoice in the Lord, I will rejoice in God my Savior*. In our times of disappointment, let us demonstrate "Habakkuk's faith."

Keeping the Faith:
Not Disillusioned

We are perplexed because we don't know why things
happen as they do, but we don't give up and quit.
(2 Corinthians 4:8 The Living Bible)

We cannot live very long without discovering that life does not treat everyone the same. A child dies at an early age from a horrible cancer and yet a smoking alcoholic lives to a ripe old age. A God-fearing man works diligently and is barely able to pay his bills, and yet a lazy gambler strikes it rich. Because of the apparent unfairness of life, some become disillusioned in their faith and live in resentment, blaming their misfortunes on God. Philip Yancey, in *Disappointment with God,* has written: "No matter how we rationalize, God will sometimes *seem* unfair from the perspective of a person trapped in time. Only at the end of time, after we have attained God's level of viewing, after every evil has been punished or forgiven, every illness healed, and the entire universe restored – only then will fairness reign. Then we will understand what role is played by evil, and by the Fall, and by natural law, in an 'unfair' event like the death of a child. Until then, we will not know, and can only trust in a God who does know.

"We remain ignorant of many details, not because God enjoys keeping us in the dark, but because we have not the faculties to absorb so much light. At a single glance God knows what the world is about and how history will end. But we time-bound creatures have only the most primitive manner of understanding....Not until history has run its course will we understand how 'all things work together for good.' Faith means believing in advance what will only make sense in reverse."[402]

Our Lord can empathize with our perplexities. His death on the cross, from a natural standpoint, was one of the most unfair events in human history. We must be willing to leave some questions unanswered in this present life and to walk on in faith. We must hold on; one day we will see all things clearly.

Keeping the Faith: Not Deterred

If you do not stand firm in your faith, you will not stand at all. (Isaiah 7:9)

Those who keep the faith will learn to trust God and not be deterred in doing his will, despite any adverse circumstances they encounter. General William Booth was a man of faith who founded the Salvation Army. In his later years, he lost his eyesight. He visited the doctor for help, but the doctor could not do much for him. His son, Bramwell, gave his father the final report: "I am afraid that there is little that they can do for you." General Booth said, "You mean that I will never again see your face?" His son replied, "I am afraid the likelihood is that you will never again see my face in this world." To this, General Booth declared, "Well, I have served God and the people with my eyes, and now I will serve God and the people without my eyes." What an incredible example of faith in the midst of a tremendously adverse circumstance![403]

Richie Skerbitz is another man who has not been deterred despite a physical handicap. You cannot help but notice Ritchie – all sixty pounds and two and a half feet of him. His father had been exposed to Agent Orange in Vietnam, which caused a severe birth defect in Ritchie – born without any legs and only one arm. To add to his troubles, Ritchie became an orphan at eleven years of age, as both his parents were instantly killed in a head-on collision with another car. Over the years, Ritchie has determined not to feel sorry for himself or wish things had been different. Rather, he desires to make an impact in his world. He has a good sense of humor. He enjoys life, hunts, fishes, and even skis. (He said, "When I fell, it was a massive wipeout!") He plays the trumpet, keyboard, and omnichord. He spoke at a pro-life rally in Washington to 650,000 people. Ritchie often shares his faith in Christ and believes God has a purpose for his life.[404]

Like Ritchie and General Booth, let us not be deterred from our faith in God, despite whatever adversaries we face.

Keeping the Faith:
Not Distracted

I have fought the good fight, I have finished the race, I have kept the faith. (2 Timothy 4:7)

Starting a race accomplishes nothing unless one finishes. *The end of a matter is better than its beginning.*[405] Every person who attempts a task in this world makes a start, but not all finish. This is also true of those in the Christian race: many starters, but not all finishers. In writing what many believe was his final letter, Paul said he had finished his race. In his earlier letter to Timothy, he mentioned two men in contrast, Hymenaeus and Alexander, who probably started well, but later *shipwrecked their faith.*[406]

The Bible records some men who started their "race of life" terribly, but later humbled themselves and finished God's way. A good example is King Manasseh, one of the most wicked kings in Judah's history – a man given to gross idolatry and witchcraft, even sacrificing his own sons in fire. Yet in the end, Manasseh *sought the favor of the Lord his God and humbled himself greatly.*[407] Remarkably, this repentant man crossed the finish line by the grace and mercy of God.

One of Satan's great tactics is to distract believers from pursuing their God-ordained course. Paul mentioned Demas, a man who had once been his *fellow worker,*[408] but who, in the end, *deserted me for love of this present world.*[409] Two common distractions are obsessive work and excessive entertainment. We can all get busy in worldly "trivial pursuits." When a man finds himself with no concern for the unsaved and no heart for service in a local church, he is in spiritual danger.

Constantly looking to Jesus will ensure our continuation of faith: *let us run the race...looking unto Jesus, the author and finisher of our faith.*[410] We can be thankful Jesus is the *author* – in Greek this is "one who begins something in order that others may enter into it...one who blazes a trail for others to follow."[411] Jesus is also the *finisher,* so we can be confident that *He who began a good work in you will carry it on to completion...*[412]

Lord, Strengthen Our Faith

MY GOD,
I bless thee that thou hast given me the eye of faith,
>> to see thee as Father,
>> to know thee as a covenant God,
>> to experience thy love planted in me;
For faith is the grace of union
>> by which I spell out my entitlement to thee:
Faith casts my anchor upwards where I trust in thee
>> and engage thee to be my Lord.
Be pleased to live and move within me,
>> breathing in my prayers,
>> inhabiting my praises,
>> speaking in my words,
>> moving in my actions,
>> living in my life,
>> causing me to grow in grace.
Thy bounteous goodness has helped me believe,
>> but my faith is weak and wavering,
>> its light dim,
>> its steps tottering,
>> its increase slow,
>> its backslidings frequent;
It should scale the heavens but lies grovelling in the dust.
Lord, fan this divine spark into glowing flame.
When faith sleeps, my heart becomes an unclean thing,
>> the fount of every loathsome desire,
>> the cage of unclean lusts
>> all fluttering to escape,
>> the noxious tree of deadly fruit,
>> the open wayside of earthly tares.
Lord, awake faith to put forth its strength
>> until all heaven fills my soul
>> and all impurity is cast out.

(An old Puritan prayer, author unknown[413])

Faith and Encouragement

See to it, brothers, that none of you has a sinful, unbelieving heart that turns away from the living God. But encourage one another daily, as long as it is called Today, so that none of you may be hardened by sin's deceitfulness. (Hebrews 3:12-13)

We all need encouragement on a daily basis to continue in our faith. If we are open to the Lord, he may use us in one-on-one situations to rescue those who are wandering from faith: *My brothers, if one of you should wander from the truth and someone should bring him back, remember this: Whoever turns a sinner from the error of his way will save him from death and cover over a multitude of sins.*[414]

The professing believer who chooses to engage in deliberate sin may need simply to be left alone.[415] But we can help restore the faith of those who slip, or get caught up in a sin. *Brethren, even if a man is caught in any trespass, you who are spiritual, restore such a one in a spirit of gentleness; looking to yourselves, lest you too be tempted.*[416] The Greek word for *restore* also means "to repair, to mend" and is used in a passage which describes the disciples' mending their fishing nets.[417] This Greek verb was also used to describe setting a broken bone. If my arm is broken, I want a doctor who knows what he is doing, and preferably one who is gentle, not rough! The Greek tense also implies it is a continual process; healing a broken bone or mending a torn net takes time.

When we restore a fallen brother, we do so in a spirit of gentleness, *meekness,*[418] and *without any sense of superiority.*[419] This means we are aware that apart from the grace of God, we could just as easily fall. John Newton, composer of "Amazing Grace," believed in showing grace to others. "Whoever is truly humbled will...be compassionate and tender to the infirmities of his fellow-sinners, knowing, that if there be a difference, it is grace that has made it, and that he has the seeds of every evil in his own heart."[420] May we gently encourage others in their faith.

Faith and Fellowship

And I pray that the fellowship of your faith may become effective through the knowledge of every good thing which is in you for Christ's sake. (Philemon 6 NAS)

The New Testament idea of fellowship is not just social interaction, visiting over a cup of coffee, or even attending Bible studies together. The NIV translation of the above verse says, *that you may be active in sharing your faith...* The word *sharing* might suggest evangelism, but the Greek word, *koinonia,* implies a deeper level of sharing. The *sharing* being described is that of a common life together, based on our relationship with Christ. The *New English Bible* brings out this idea: *"My prayer is that your fellowship with us in our common faith may deepen the understanding of all the blessings that our union in Christ brings us."* The word *koinonia* was found in a fourth century inscription. A doctor wrote of his beloved wife who had just died: "As with you alone I have *shared* my life."[421] This is the idea of fellowship. In the verse above, Paul encourages Philemon to share his faith in a practical way. His escaped slave had become a believer and Paul's friend. Paul was asking Philemon to receive his returning slave, but as a fellow believer.

Those with true faith become personal with others. One of the great deficiencies in the modern day church is that too often we emphasize meetings and programs, but not true fellowship. We tend to say, "Accept Jesus as your *personal* Savior," but our Christian faith is not meant to remain an individualistic faith. Michael Green wrote, "Our fellowship is never from the alone to the Alone. It is jointly held with others, which makes the Christian faith so different from all the self-improvement cults and faiths that seek fulfillment or enlightenment 'for myself alone.' The Christian faith is inescapably corporate. You cannot have fellowship with the triune God who *is* fellowship without that fellowship spilling over to others in the same family."[422]

Faith and Dwelling

...so that Christ may dwell in your hearts by faith...(Eph. 3:17)

I can go into many homes, enjoy myself, become somewhat acquainted with the surroundings, even be treated with royal hospitality, and yet, not feel completely at home. There is only one place where I ever feel completely at home – in my own permanent residence. There I can kick off my shoes, put my feet on the coffee table, and not worry one bit about disrupting another's possessions or imposing upon one's schedule. I am home!

Jesus wants to be a permanent resident in our hearts, not a temporary visitor. *The Amplified Bible* says, *May Christ through your faith actually dwell (settle down, abide, make his permanent home) in your hearts!* Jesus does not want to come into our lives when it suits us or on special occasions; he wants to "unpack his suitcases" and stay for a long, long time! This is an amazing thought – the God who created the universe will also dwell in our hearts! It is a comforting thought if we ever feel he might only visit temporarily. He has said, *"Never will I leave you; never will I forsake you."*[423]

Jesus wants to feel completely at home when he is invited to dwell in our hearts. In his translation, Kenneth Wuest said, *that the Christ might finally settle down and feel completely at home in your hearts.*[424] We may say, "Jesus, you can have access to the living room, the kitchen, the bedroom ...but just do not open the closet on the second floor." Well, guess which door Jesus will want to open? The closet on the second floor! We cannot ask Jesus into our lives and expect to keep any rooms closed. As someone has said, "If He is not Lord *of all*, then he is not Lord *at all*." Do we have any secret sins or idols in our hearts, any "closets" which we have not submitted to his lordship? Jesus says to us all: *Behold, I stand at the door and knock. If anyone hears my voice and opens the door, I will come in to him and will dine with him, and he with Me.*[425] Let us open our hearts fully so Jesus will feel welcome – even *completely at home.*

Faith and Reputation

First, I thank my God through Jesus Christ for all of you, because your faith is being reported all over the world... (Romans 1:8)

If someone were to write one statement that characterizes your life, what would you be remembered for? "This was a wealthy man of great prestige and power...;" or "This was a funny man with loads of humor...;" or "This was a brilliant man with incredible knowledge...." If people were to visit our church and write a summary sentence, what would our group be noted for? There was a heavy-set man, who only had a reputation for eating. His epitaph read:

> *Gentle reader, gentle reader,*
> *Look on the spot where I do lie,*
> *I always was a very good feeder,*
> *But now the worms do feed on I.*[426]

Then, there was a woman who was remembered for her loose tongue. Her tombstone read:

> *Here lies, returned to clay,*
> *Miss Arabella Young,*
> *Who on the first day of May*
> *Began to hold her tongue.*[427]

In writing his letters, the apostle Paul commended two main qualities in the lives of believers: faith and love. In writing to the Ephesians, Paul said, *For this reason, ever since I heard about your faith in the Lord Jesus and your love for all the saints, I have not stopped giving thanks for you...*[428] In writing to the Thessalonians, he said, *"But Timothy has just now come from you and has brought good news about your faith and love....In all your distress and persecution we were encouraged about you because of your faith."*[429] In writing to Philemon, Paul once again thanked God because, *"I hear about your faith in the Lord Jesus and your love for all the saints."*[430]

Lord God, may we too have a reputation for the right virtues – our faith in God and love for all the saints.

Faith and Love (Part 1)

The only thing that counts is faith expressing itself through love. (Galatians 5:6)

Faith and love are often connected in the Scriptures. A man may exercise faith apart from love, but it will be limited in its effectiveness. *The Amplified Bible* here reads, *Faith activated and energized and expressed and working through love.* William Tyndale's translation: *Faith which by love is mighty in operation.*[431] A true indication that faith is increasing in one's heart will be a parallel increase of demonstrative love. Paul commended the church of the Thessalonians: *Your faith is growing more and more, and the love every one of you has for each other is increasing.*[432]

If faith is not matched by love, men will likely be more susceptible to the spiritual dangers of arrogance and pride. If we had great miracle working faith, but no heart to love people, we would become absorbed with our power and popularity. If we study the great men of faith, we will see they were motivated for the glory of God and the love of his people. The apostles of faith were motivated initially by a love for the Jews, and then later for the Gentiles. Hudson Taylor was motivated by love for the Chinese. Nate Saint and Jim Eliot were driven by compassion for the Auca Indians. George Muller was moved by faith for the needs of countless, destitute orphans. Smith Wigglesworth performed great exploits of faith out of his love for lost souls. He once said he would rather see one soul won for Christ than a thousand healed.[433] Through our faith we should expect to see God's *love...mighty in operation.*

Great faith must have the companion of great love: *If I have a faith that can move mountains, but have not love, I am nothing.*[434] May God fill our hearts with mountain-moving faith, and may He motivate our hearts by his own love which *bears all things, believes all things, hopes all things, endures all things.*[435]

Day One Hundred Twenty-Eight
Faith and Love (Part 2)

My command is this: Love each other as I have loved you. (John 15:12)

Bill Bright, founder of Campus Crusade for Christ, emphasized the practice of loving others *by faith*. There were two gifted attorneys in the same firm who hated each other, constantly criticizing each other. Then, one of the two men received Christ and came to Bright for counsel.

"I have hated and criticized my partner for years," he said, "and he has been equally antagonistic toward me. But now that I am a Christian, I don't feel right about continuing our warfare. What shall I do?"

"Why not ask your partner to forgive you and tell him that you love him?" I suggested.

"I could never do that!" he exclaimed. "That would be hypocritical. I don't love him. How could I tell him I love him when I don't?"

I explained the greatest lesson I had ever learned: God commands His children to love even their enemies, and His supernatural, unconditional love is an expression not of our emotions, but of our will, which we exercise by faith.

Together we knelt to pray, and my friend asked God's forgiveness for his critical attitude toward his law partner and claimed God's love for him by faith.

Early the next morning, my friend walked into his partner's office and announced, "Something wonderful has happened to me. I have become a Christian. And I have come to ask you to forgive me for all that I have done to hurt you in the past and to tell you that I love you."

His partner was so surprised and convicted of his own sin that he responded by asking my friend to forgive him. Then, to my friend's surprise, his partner said, "I would like to become a Christian, too. Would you show me what I need to do?"[436]

Is there someone we do not like who we can begin to love…not because we feel it, but by our actions – done in faith?

Faith and Relinquishing

When Peter saw him, he asked, "Lord, what about him?"
Jesus answered, "If I want him to remain alive until I return,
what is that to you? You must follow me." (John 21:21-22)

In this last recorded conversation with Jesus, Peter is told that he will also follow Jesus in death by crucifixion (and this prediction was confirmed by early church writers). Peter immediately looked at his fellow disciple, John, and asked, "Lord, what about this man? Will he suffer too?" Jesus basically replied, "Peter, what happens to John is none of your business. I will determine his future destiny as well as yours. But as for you, follow me."

It is human nature that when we face upcoming difficulty and suffering, we sometimes look to other believers and say, "Lord, what about that man? He seems to be so carefree. I have so much stuff "on my plate" and he has nothing. I feel like I'm in a whirlwind of trouble and he seems so cozy and comfortable!" In such cases, our focus is entirely wrong. We are looking at people instead of looking to our Master.

The fact is: Jesus Christ is Lord of all and his sovereignty in the affairs of other men is something we must accept by faith.

- God may allow you to endure terrible suffering, but some friends will not suffer much at all.
- God may prosper a fellow believer with a very nice home and two cars, and yet you struggle financially.
- A friend, who does not seem "as spiritual as you," seems to enjoy happy family life, and yet your wife and kids have serious issues. It does not seem fair!

If we are not careful, we may become resentful when others are blessed. This is the sin of *envy*. The bottom line is this: By faith, are we willing to leave the welfare of others in the hands of God and concentrate on our own walk with God? Sometimes this is an issue of forgiveness. One Greek definition of *forgive* is to "let go, leave it." Can't we just leave others in the hands of God? He certainly knows what is right in life for each of us!

Faith and Leaving

*But Ruth replied, "Don't urge me to leave you or to
turn back from you. Where you go I will go, and where
you stay I will stay. Your people will be my people and
your God my God..." (Ruth 1:16)*

Ruth had lost her husband and was now a young widow. Her
mother-in-law, Naomi, was about to leave the land of Moab and
return to her homeland, Israel. By faith, Ruth also chose to leave
her familiar surroundings and set out on a long journey – simply
because she wanted to stay with Naomi. God was orchestrating
events and, after she settled in Israel with little outward hope for
the future, she met a kind and benevolent man. Boaz, a distant
relative, would eventually marry Ruth. This couple was no
insignificant couple; they would become the great-grandparents
of King David, the greatest king of Israel.

Another lady who had to leave her family by faith was
Rebekah. As an old man, Abraham sent a servant to a faraway
relative to obtain a wife for his son, Isaac. When the servant met
Rebekah in that household, God confirmed she was the one. The
final decision, however, belonged to her. *So they called Rebekah
and asked her, "Will you go with this man?" "I will go," she
said.*[437] Rebekah made her decision by faith; she would have to
travel about 450 miles, a month's journey in dangerous
territories, to live in an unknown land and marry a stranger!

Sometimes we, too, have to make a decision by faith, leave a
comfortable place, and travel into the unknown. All brides must
choose to leave their homes[438] and marry a husband, a choice
that certainly involves some "unknowns." Other people may
have to exercise faith to move to a new locality or commit to a
new job. I knew one family who wanted their children in a
Christian school. To do so, they had to search for a different
locality where they found a Christ-centered church and a good
Christian school. The father had to take a decrease in salary. It
was a big step of faith, but their family was greatly blessed.

Faith and Leadership

Remember your leaders, who spoke the word of God to you. Consider the outcome of their way of life and imitate their faith. Jesus Christ is the same yesterday and today and forever. (Hebrews 13:7-8)

The best way to lead others is by personal example. If we are to lead the flock of God, we should be humble in spirit, holy in character, and exhibiting a faith worth imitating. Brethren may remember our messages and advice, but they will remember our faith (or lack of it) even more. God can put us in undesirable and trying situations so that our faith can be developed and may be displayed to others. When we put a tea bag in hot water, we find out what is in the bag. In like manner, our faith is displayed by what we experience. Those brethren close to us will remember how we responded in the "hot water" – times of dealing with sickness, times of financial pressure, and times of church conflict and stress.

A good example will have greater influence on younger believers than a seminary education or the right Bible study courses. Paul said, *"You became imitators of us and of the Lord."*[439] He also said, *"Follow my example, as I follow the example of Christ."*[440] What an amazing statement! How many of us are willing to repeat such a challenge: *"Follow my example..."* This should not be a rarity in the body of Christ; people need to see Christianity lived out in flesh-and-blood examples of the faith. I remember as a youngster growing up in a church for twenty years and not seeing one man of whom I could honestly say, "That is a man of God." I saw no model of the faith for me to imitate.

None of this is to suggest that we unduly focus on ourselves. The above verse concludes with: *Jesus Christ is the same yesterday and today and forever.* A godly leader will not seek to draw men to himself. Any true example of the faith will always point to Jesus: *For we do not preach ourselves, but Jesus Christ, and ourselves as servants for Jesus' sake."*[441]

Faith and Humility

"Yes Lord," she said, "but even the dogs eat the crumbs that fall from their masters' table." Then Jesus answered, "Woman you have great faith! Your request is granted." And her daughter was healed from that very hour. (Matthew 15:27-28)

There are only two occasions in the Bible when Jesus mentioned *great faith*, and both times faith is linked with humility. The Canaanite woman cried out to the Lord, desperate for an answer for her demon-possessed daughter. Jesus' disciples were ready to get rid of this emotional woman, but she kept crying for his help. She was not like many of us who quit praying when an answer does not come quickly. When Jesus spoke to her about not throwing a child's bread to dogs, he was implying that his ministry at that time was for the Jews (the "children"), not the Gentiles (the "dogs"). Then the woman responded in humility, *"Yes Lord... but even the dogs eat the crumbs that fall from their masters' table."* Her humility and persistence brought great commendation from the Lord: *"Woman you have great faith!"*

In the second example of great faith, a Roman centurion requested that Jesus heal his servant. The centurion did not want to trouble the Master, knowing that he had the authority to simply speak healing and it would be accomplished. *"Lord, I do not deserve to have you come under my roof. But just say the word, and my servant will be healed."*[442] When Jesus heard this humble reply, he was astonished and said, *"I have not found anyone in Israel with such great faith."*[443]

John Calvin said, "The beginning of faith. . . is humility, by which we yield our senses as captives to God."[444] Andrew Murray added, "We need only think for a moment what faith is. Is it not...in itself the most humbling thing there can be, the acceptance of our place as dependents, who can claim or get or do nothing but what his grace bestows?"[445] Persistent faith and genuine humility are an essential combination.

Faith and Forever

Truly, truly, I say to you, he who believes has eternal life.
(John 6:47 NAS)

The promise of *eternal life* is the greatest promise for those who believe. We are also given the promises of *eternal dwellings,*[446] *eternal redemption,*[447] an *eternal gospel,*[448] an *eternal covenant,*[449] and entry into the *eternal kingdom.*[450] Jonathan Edwards is reported to have prayed, "Lord, stamp eternity on my eyeballs." Probably most of us live too much for the present, not for eternity. The many pleasures and pursuits in this realm of time can distract us from eternal priorities.

God himself is the *eternal God*, who has no beginning nor end; He is called *"I AM"*[451] and he is the One *who is, and who was, and who is to come.*[452] In God, past, present, and future meet – everything is *now.* One day believers will live with him in a realm where there is no more time. That is why, from God's perspective, *a day is like a thousand years, and a thousand years are like a day.*[453]

This idea of eternity should motivate us. If we are going to live forever in the eternal realm with or without God, how much should we seek to be right with him in the temporal realm?

When I taught elementary age children I explained the word *eternal* as that which is "a long, long time." One might illustrate this concept by unrolling a very long roll of paper and placing a tiny quarter inch line in the middle of it. If we were to pretend that the roll of paper had no beginning and no end, then that little mark would represent our short, finite life on earth.

The idea of *eternity* in Scripture means more than just "a long, long time"; it also means a different dimension of living, a type of life unique to God and his heaven. Scripture says, *Now this is eternal life: that they may know you, the only true God, and Jesus Christ, whom you have sent.*[454] As we come to know God by faith, we begin to experience eternity. This is why Jesus said, "W*hoever lives and believes in me will never die.*"[455] In the spirit, by faith, we can now touch the eternal!

Faithful in Him

*If we are faithless, he will remain faithful, for he cannot
disown himself. (2 Timothy 2:13)*

Hudson Taylor was a famous pioneer missionary to China. In his
biography, his crisis of faith is shared in which he came to
realize he did not have to strive for more faith, but simply rest in
the Faithful One. "I strove for faith, but it would not come; I
tried to exercise it, but in vain. Seeing more and more the
wondrous supply of grace laid up in Jesus, the fullness of our
precious Savior, my guilt and helplessness seemed to increase.
Sins committed appeared but as trifles compared with the sin of
unbelief which was their cause, which could not or would not
take God at His word. . . . I prayed for faith, but it came not.
What was I to do?

"When my agony of soul was at its height, a sentence in a
letter from dear McCarthy was used to remove the scales from
my eyes, and the Spirit of God revealed to me the truth of our
oneness with Jesus as I had never known it before. 'But how to
get faith strengthened? *Not by striving after faith, but by resting
on the Faithful One.*'"[456]

This was to become a revolution in the thinking and work of
Hudson Taylor. He was discovering at this time the truth of
Jesus' words about abiding, *"I am the vine; you are the
branches. If a man remains in me and I in him, he will bear
much fruit; apart from me you can do nothing."*[457] He would no
longer have to strive for faith, but simply be a branch that was
connected to the Vine, allowing the sap of the Vine to flow
through him. The life of faith, for Taylor, became a much
simpler concept: just staying connected.

The truth that Hudson Taylor learned ought to encourage us
as well. We don't always need great faith, but simply remain
connected to the Faithful One, allowing his life flowing through
us. Even when we are not so faithful, he remains faithful!
Hallelujah!

Faithful in Our Walk

My eyes are on the faithful in the land... (Ps. 101:6)

If we are going to walk in faith, we will be described as being "faithful." This word is used 160 times in the Bible to describe God and his followers. Various dictionary definitions of this word include, "dependable, reliable, trustworthy, devoted, loyal, constant (not fickle), true to one's word, steady in allegiance."

Faithfulness is extremely important in our relationship with the Lord. Here are just a few Scriptures to attest to this:

- *The Lord preserves the faithful... (Ps. 31:23)*
- *The Lord ...will not forsake his faithful ones. (Ps. 37:28)*
- *He guards the lives of his faithful ones... (Ps. 97:10)*
- *Well done, good and faithful servant! (Matt. 25:21-23)*

Faithfulness is also extremely important in our relationships with people. Consider just three examples:

- In marriage: Suppose when a man said his wedding vow, "I will be 90% faithful to you..." That would not get it! Without faithfulness, no marriage will last.
- In work: Suppose an employee is interviewing and says, "I will be dependable every day except on Mondays..." or suppose a boss asks for a job to be done, and the employee responds, "Hopefully, I might be able to do it..."
- In friendships: Faithful friends are rare, but can be found. Scripture says, *Many a man claims to have unfailing love, but a faithful man who can find?*[458]

What kind of friends do we want to walk with: Dependable or undependable? Loyal or those who would betray you? Those who will stick with you in good times and bad, or those who are fickle? We must desire to be the right kind of friends – faithful to the Lord and faithful to those people that he has connected us with. We can be faithful because the Lord is faithful!

Faithful and Not Fickle

For the word of the LORD is right and true;
he is faithful in all he does. (Ps. 33:4)

The reason we can be faithful is simply because we have come to know God, and God is faithful. This fact is indeed some of the best news we will ever know!

How many times have we been disappointed by other people? A friend says "I'll see you at the meeting…" and then he doesn't show up. When we ask what happened, he says, "Yeah, I just wasn't feeling that well…" Or, someone is asked to do a task, and later they admit, "I'm sorry, I forgot…" Or, we tell someone, "I'll pray for you," and five minutes later we have dismissed it from our minds. We are pretty fickle, aren't we? I am glad God is not influenced by the weather, or that he doesn't have days when he "doesn't feel very well," or "forgets"? No, Our God is always fully dependable, loyal, and trustworthy! *The LORD is faithful to all his promises;*[459] *He never changes or casts a shifting shadow.*[460] *He is faithful in all he does.*[461]

One of Satan's great strategies is to make us doubt the faithfulness of God. Satan would have us believe that God is not true to his character or that he may fail us or that he really is not committed to us. "God may desert you! He may just leave you even though he said he never would. God can't be trusted!" But, we come back and say, "No, I don't accept those lies; my God is a faithful God!"

Daniel, having been taken captive with other Israelites, could have doubted the faithfulness of God. Daniel, however, displayed great courage and faith within a pagan environment. Later, when given responsibility in the Babylonian government, he proved to be a faithful employee while remaining faithful to his God. When evil men, disturbed by his faith, tried to discredit him, *they could find no ground of accusation or evidence of corruption, inasmuch as he was faithful, and no negligence or corruption was to be found in him.*[462] May God help us to be more like Himself – faithful, not fickle.

Faithful in Small Things

Whoever can be trusted with very little can also be trusted with much, and whoever is dishonest with very little will also be dishonest with much. So if you have not been trustworthy in handling worldly wealth, who will trust you with true riches? (Luke 16:10-11)

Our faithfulness starts with small things, not big things; we will be tested in material matters, before we are entrusted with spiritual matters. Some believers are unwilling first to be used in small ways and want to go quickly to the top. Someone has said, "If you are too big for a little place, you are too little for a big place." F. B. Meyer wrote, "We are called to be faithful in performing our assigned duties. Not brilliance, not success, not notoriety, but the regular, quiet and careful performance of trivial and common duties. Faithfulness in that which is least is as great an attainment in God's sight as in the greatest."[463]
How about us? How faithful are we in small matters?

- Do we pay our bills on time? Do we borrow things and not return them? (Or return them in bad shape?)
- Do we keep confidences? Are we trustworthy?
- Do we keep our appointments on time?
- Do we keep our commitments?

Suppose you have planned to spend time one evening with a person who could benefit from your friendship, and you receive a phone call. Two of your favorite couples invite you over for a big dinner party... What do you do?

Or, as a young person, you have promised to babysit for a family, a family who usually depends on your help, and unexpectantly someone offers you a free ticket to a big concert... What do you do?

Being faithful in small matters is more important than we may realize. The greatest accolade any of us will ever hear from our Master is: *"Well done, good and faithful servant!"*[464]

Faithful Until Death

Do not be afraid of what you are about to suffer. I tell you, the devil will put some of you in prison to test you, and you will suffer persecution for ten days. Be faithful, even to the point of death, and I will give you the crown of life.... You remain true to my name. You did not renounce your faith in me, even in the days of Antipas, my faithful witness, who was put to death in your city – where Satan lives. (Revelation 2:10,13)

I hope this test never comes to any of us, but it could. This is the ultimate of faithfulness: Will we be faithful to the Lord, even unto death? Are we willing to die rather than renounce our loyalty to Christ? If so, Christ says, *I'll give you a crown of life.* One such a man is mentioned – *Antipas, my faithful witness...*

When Emperor Antonius Pius resumed the persecution of Christians in Rome in the mid-second century, a prominent Christian widow, Felicitas, and her seven sons were brought before Publius, chief magistrate of Rome. When he threatened her, she boldly responded, "I am neither moved by your flatteries and entreaties, nor am I intimidated by your threats, for I experience in my heart the working of the Holy Ghost, which gives me a living power and prepares me for the conflict of suffering..." Filled with rage, Publius ordered her beaten and also threatened her sons. Each son boldly declared his faith. The oldest son told him, "You advise me to do a thing that is very foolish, and contrary to all reason, but I confide in my Lord Jesus Christ..." The magistrate then ordered the sons brutally killed, before the eyes of their mother. Four months later she too was executed.[465] The entire family was faithful to the end!

Great persecution continues today. Over 200 million Christians today in at least 60 countries are denied fundamental human rights solely because of their faith. David Barrett and others estimate that approximately 176,000 Christians were martyred from mid-2008 to mid-2009, compared to 34,400 at the beginning of the 20th century.[466] Many today are remaining faithful to death. Would we also be willing to remain so faithful?

Faithful at the End

...I have finished the race, and I have remained faithful...
2 Timothy 4:7 NLT

At the end of your life, *how will you be remembered?* One day, as people are gathered around your casket, what words will be said about you? How will close family and friends *really* remember you?

Billy Graham, when asked about the legacy he hopes to leave, responded, "I want to be remembered as a person who was faithful to God, faithful to my family, faithful to the Scriptures, and faithful to my calling. I want the world to remember Billy Graham as a man that dedicated his life to the Lord and never looked back."[467]

Charles Colson is another man who accomplished much in his life. As a former aide to President Nixon, four decades ago, he said, "When you lower me six feet under, I will go away a Nixon loyalist." Colson, however, was right in the middle of the Watergate investigation. He was convicted and sent to prison. During his incarceration, he became a Christian and eventually established Prison Fellowship. In the past three decades, Colson was an excellent spokesman for Christian worldviews and apologetics and accomplished much good in the body of Christ. Someone asked him just a year before he passed away, "How do you want to be remembered now?" This is Colson's humble response. "I would just like to be remembered as one sinner who was rescued by God's grace, who tried, imperfectly as it was, to do his duty and live his life faithfully."[468]

Although we are certainly lesser known persons with lesser responsibilities than these two outstanding, godly leaders, we can imitate their heart desires. Agree with me in prayer, "Lord, we make the same request.... Remember me as one sinner who was rescued by God's grace, who tried, imperfectly as it was, to do his duty and live his life faithfully.... Help me to finish my race well, loving you and faithful to the very end. Amen."

Part Two

Daily Encouragement
For Bringing

Hope

*And hope
does not
disappoint us.
(Romans 5:6)*

Understanding Hope

I pray also that the eyes of your heart may be enlightened in order that you may know the hope to which he has called you... (Ephesians 1:18)

The word "hope" is probably one of the most neglected and misunderstood of all biblical words. Hope is listed in First Corinthians, chapter 13, as a primary characteristic of the Christian life, along with faith and love. Hope is one of the believer's greatest treasures. "Without it life in a fallen world would be unbearable; without it the zest for living would disappear almost at once; without it one hour of adversity would break our spirits and drive millions to suicide.... If all hope were destroyed within the human breast, mankind would die out altogether in a very few years."[1]

Hope, if properly understood and implanted in our minds, is something that can make disciples of Christ confident, encouraged, and able to smile at the future. When we begin to see the hope we have in Christ, it can transform our thinking and become a strong, motivating force in every area of life.

How we define hope can make the difference between a weak, theological concept and a life-producing force. Here is a simple definition of hope: *Hope is the continued expectation of good; a settled confidence that God has good plans for our future.* Even in one of Israel's darkest moments – held captive for seventy years in Babylon – God told them, *"I know the plans I have for you, declares the Lord, plans to prosper you and not to harm you, plans to give you hope and a future."*[2]

Biblical hope is not the same as our current English usage, e.g., "I hope so!" It is not just a desire, a crossing of one's fingers and wishing something might turn out for the good. Biblical hope points us to the promises of God which are absolutely trustworthy, irrevocable, and certain to come to pass. Even in the worst of circumstances, a believer who has the hope of Christ will be motivated to keep going because he knows the best is yet to come. God says, *there is hope for your future.*[3]

Without Hope

Remember at that time you were separate from Christ...without hope and without God in the world. (Ephesians 2:12)

We were *without hope* before we met Christ. What a horrible state! *Without hope!* Without anything of eternal significance to look forward to – either in this life or the next! Dante portrayed this hopelessness in a description of the entry sign of the Inferno: "Abandon hope, all ye who enter here..."[4]

Yet, we need not despair, for this passage continues with God's good news. *But now in Christ Jesus you who were once far away have been brought near through the blood of Christ.*[5] Before coming to Christ, we have absolutely no hope concerning our eternal destiny – God seems to be far removed from us. *But now...* Thank God the Scripture continues. After we surrender to Christ's lordship, we are *brought near* to him, and he now becomes a personal God to us. Our whole perspective changes and we are *born again into a life full of hope.*[6]

If your hope is not in Christ, let me ask you to be honest. What is your hope? Charles Spurgeon asked a series of questions that deserve our consideration: "Now, then, you who do not believe in God, tell us what your hope is...What is your hope? To live long? Yes, and what then? To bring up a family? Yes, and what then? To see them comfortably settled in life? Yes, and what then? To be a grandfather to numerous progeny? Yes, and what then? To reach extreme old age in peaceful retirement? Yes, and what then? The curtain falls. Let me lift it. The cemetery. The throne of God. Sentence on your soul. The trumpet of resurrection. Final doom. Body and soul in hell forever. You have no better prospect. Please look out of the window, and see what is to be seen. The Lord have mercy upon you, and give you a better hope..."[7]

We do not need to despair. Through his death, Christ has made it possible for us to be *born again into a life full of hope.*

The Treachery of Hope

Sustain me according to your promise, and I will live;
do not let my hopes be dashed. (Psalm 119:116)

Hope is both precious and treacherous. The cynical poet Dryden said bluntly, "When I consider life, it's all a cheat; Yet fooled with hope, men favor the deceit." Tozer commented on this treachery of human hope:

"Hope has sustained the spirit of many a shipwrecked sailor by painting for him a tender picture of rescue and reunion with loved ones, only to leave him at last to die of thirst and exposure on the vast bosom of the sea. Hope has kept many a prisoner believing he could not hang, that a pardon would surely come, and then stood calmly by and watched him die at the end of a rope. Hope has cheered a thousand victims of cancer and tuberculosis with whispered promises of returning health who were never again to know one single day of health till they died. Hope has told the mother that her son missing in action was surely alive, and kept her watching till the end of her days for the letter that never came because the boy that might have written it had long been sleeping in an unmarked grave on a foreign shore."[8]

I heard of a man who was strongly motivated by the hope of a grand retirement. For over forty years, Bob rarely took a vacation. He worked long hours and family life was sacrificed. As years were spent, Bob and his wife began to dream together of all the places they would travel and the projects they would finally have time to enjoy. In his sixty-fifth year, he walked out of the office for the last time, ready to begin enjoying the good life of retirement. Two weeks later, Bob suffered a sudden and massive heart attack. Despite all the medical maneuvers, he was dead within hours. As we look at the big picture of Bob's life, we could say it was a life tragically ruined by false hope.

Only the Christian can truly hope. We can bear anything because we have the glorious and secure hope of heaven. Any lesser hope is a false and treacherous hope.

Vain Hope

He who works his land will have abundant food, but he who chases fantasies lacks judgment. (Proverbs 12:11)

When I was in high school I knew one young man who had a dream to become a great basketball player. His work ethic was impeccable and he practiced harder than anyone I have ever seen. I'm sure someone had told him the old adage, "If you just set your heart on it, you can achieve whatever you want!" There was one basic problem; he just wasn't that good. He did not have the right physical make-up nor the skills. He struggled on a high school level and never played any college ball.

Today many are driven by false hopes for the future, especially athletes. I like the commercial by the National Collegiate Athletic Association (NCAA) which provides a more realistic hope: "There are over 400,000 NCAA student-athletes, and most of us will go pro in something other than sports." Consider these statistics from the NCAA.

- Less than one in 35 (or 3.1%), of high school senior boys playing basketball will go on to play at a NCAA college.
- About one in 75 (or 1.2%), of NCAA male senior basketball players will be drafted by a professional (NBA) team.
- Three in 10,000 (or 0.03%), of high school senior boys playing basketball will eventually be drafted by the NBA.[9]

All of us should pursue hopes that are obtainable, not just fantasies. Such unrealistic hopes can be quite a distraction. Many a musician has wasted years pursuing a lofty dream of "making it big." Many a single person has avoided developing deeper relationships because they're looking for that "perfect one." Vain dreams are often rooted in our own egotism.

As we look to Christ, there *are* hopes that can be realized:
- We can receive the free gift of eternal life (Rom. 6:23).
- We can have all of our sins completely forgiven (I Jn. 1:9).
- We can be transformed daily into all that we ought to be through the power of the Holy Spirit (2 Cor. 3:18).

Let's make sure we pursue such hope in Christ, not a vain hope!

Dashed Hope

...We are perplexed because we don't know why things happen as they do, but we don't give up and quit.... We get knocked down, but we get up again and keep going. (2 Corinthians 4:8-9 TLB)

Many of us have experienced dashed hopes. The job we really wanted was given to someone else. The boy we were pursuing ends up with another girl. Or some other dream for our lives ended up becoming a "shattered dream." In such cases we may be tempted to quit living altogether and let despair win the day. God, however, speaks to us in our pain. He encourages us to get up and keep going – as Larry Crabb has expressed in this "word from the Lord" to us.

"Some of your fondest dreams will shatter, and you will be tempted to lose hope. I will seem to you callous or, worse, weak – unresponsive to your pain. You will wonder if I cannot do anything or simply will not.

"'As you struggle with dashed hopes, you will fail, just as My servant Peter did. You will feel discouraged with yourself to the point of self-hatred. And I will seem to withdraw from you and do nothing.

"When all of this comes to pass, My word to you is this: Do not lose hope. A plan is unfolding that you cannot clearly see. If you could see it as I do, you would still hurt, but you would not lose hope. You would gladly remain faithful to me in the middle of the worst suffering. I guarantee you the power to please me, not to have a good time. But pleasing me will bring you great joy.

"In the deepest part of your soul, you long more than anything else to be a part of My plan, to further My kingdom, to know Me and please Me and enjoy Me. I will satisfy that longing. You have the power to represent Me well no matter what happens in your life. That is the hope I give you in this world. Don't lose it."[10]

Realized Hope

*For my eyes have seen your salvation, which you have
prepared in the sight of all people. (Luke 22:30-31)*

I can remember as a child the great anticipation that developed
in my heart at the beginning of every December. I would spend
hours pondering all the gifts I hoped to receive. When
Christmas finally rolled around and all the gifts had been
opened, there always seemed to be a measure of disappointment, even when I received exactly what I had longed
for. Possibly the Holy Spirit was indicating to me, even as a
young child, that my heart would only be fully satisfied when I
received the ONE GIFT that really matters – the Lord Himself.

Simeon was a righteous and devout man, who had been
told by the Holy Spirit that he would not die until he had seen
the long awaited Messiah. For years the hope of the promised
Messiah had been lingering in his heart and he was *waiting for
the Consolation of Israel.*[11] When that day finally arrived,
Simeon was supernaturally instructed to go into the temple
courts to meet Mary and Joseph. Here, Simeon's expectant
hope was finally realized. Taking the baby Jesus into his arms,
he joyfully exclaimed, *"My eyes have seen your salvation..."*

No holiday season and no human resource will ever deliver
what we all ultimately long for. Our heart's greatest hope will
only be fulfilled in Christ himself and his salvation. This hope
is what Charles Wesley expressed in his great hymn:
> Come, Thou long-expected Jesus,
>> Born to set Thy people free;
> From our fears and sins release us;
>> Let us find our rest in Thee.
> Israel's Strength and Consolation,
>> Hope of all the earth Thou art,
> Dear Desire of every nation,
>> Joy of every longing heart.[12]

May the greatest longings of our hearts find their fulfillment in
Jesus, the "Hope of all the earth...Joy of every longing heart."

History and Hope

From one man he created all the nations throughout the whole earth. He decided beforehand when they should rise and fall, and he determined their boundaries. (Acts 17:26 NLT)

Edward Gibbon, the renowned British historian, once wrote, "History is indeed little more than the register of crimes, follies, and misfortunes of mankind."[13] The Christian, however, views history in a much more hopeful light. History has been rightly called "His story," and we see in Scripture that history is not an aimless, hopeless, repetitive series of events with no ultimate purpose. God has a plan from beginning to end. *He controls the course of world events; he removes kings and sets up other kings.*[14] He will one day conclude human history with the second coming of Christ and establish his own kingdom of perfect righteousness and peace. This is the hope to which Christians cling, as Malcolm Muggeridge explained.

"We look back upon history and what do we see? Empires rising and falling, revolutions and counter-revolutions; wealth accumulated and wealth dispersed. I heard a crazed, cracked Austrian who announced to the world the establishment of a Reich that would last a thousand years. I've seen an Italian clown say he was going to stop and restart the calendar with his own ascension to power. I met a murderous judge and brigand in the Kremlin proclaimed by the intellectual elite of the world as wiser than Solomon, more humane than Marcus Aurelius, more enlightened than Buddha. All in one lifetime, all in one lifetime, gone – gone with the wind.

"Hitler and Mussolini, dead and remembered only in infamy. Stalin, a forbidden name in the regime he helped found….Behind the debris of these solemn supermen and these self-styled imperial diplomatists stands the gigantic figure of one person because of whom, by whom, in whom, and through whom alone mankind may still have hope. The person of Jesus Christ."[15]

Christ Our Only Hope

Find rest, O my soul, in God alone; my hope comes from him. He alone is my rock and salvation... (Psalm 62:5-6) Jesus Christ our Lord – our only hope... (I Tim. 1:1 TLB)

We do not have a number of options that can produce hope in our hearts; Jesus Christ is our only hope. The Bible is clear – there is only *one way* to God the Father;[16] there is only *one name* by which we can be saved;[17] and there is only *one foundation* upon which we can build our lives – Christ Jesus.[18] We simply have no other options. *He who has the Son has life; he who does not have the Son of God does not have life.*[19]

Mankind tends to add something to Christ. It might be Christ plus the church. It might be Christ plus Mary. It might be Christ plus good works. Our hope, however, is in CHRIST ALONE. A famous hymn says, "My hope is built on nothing less than Jesus' blood and righteousness."[20] Scripture makes this truth abundantly clear: Christ *alone* can forgive sins,[21] Christ *alone* is righteous,[22] Christ *alone* is holy,[23] and Christ *alone* is immortal.[24] In our difficulties, only Christ can save. *Deliver me, O God...for you have been my hope, O Sovereign Lord, my confidence since my youth.*[25]

Our own frivolous pursuits and misplaced priorities can cause us to look more to ourselves, rather than to hope in Christ. Arthur Pink once wrote, "The great mistake made by most of the Lord's people is hoping to discover in themselves that which is to be found in Christ alone."[26] Our hope for success cannot be found only in our own intelligence and abilities; we must look to the Christ, our Wisdom. Our hope for health cannot be found only in our meticulous dieting and exercise regimens (as good as these may be). We must look to the Lord, our Healer. Our hope for happy relationships cannot be found in our own capacity for love; our own good intentions can quickly fade and the original fire of love can be quenched. We must look constantly to the Lord, the Source of lasting love.

May we each constantly affirm: *My hope comes from him. He alone is my rock and salvation...I will not be shaken.*[27]

Rediscovering Hope

At least there is hope for a tree:
If it is cut down it will sprout again... (Job 14:7)

In Bunyan's *Pilgrim's Progress* the main character, Christian, is finally able to cast off his heavy burden at the cross. His sins are forgiven and he is given new white and clean garments, and a book to read along the way. That book is his pass to admit him through the celestial gate; it is his hope.

Shortly afterwards as Christian has climbed half way up the Hill Difficulty, he stops at the Restful Arbor, falls asleep, and the book falls out of his hand. Startled by a voice, he wakes and hastens on his way. At the top of the hill he meets Timorous and Mistrust, who warn Christian that there is great danger ahead – fierce lions who will tear them to pieces. Here he reaches into his coat for the book and finds it missing – to his great distress. With a heart of regret and fear, Christian travels back to look for the book, "doubting that he would ever find it and, if not, that there was any hope for him."[28] He is finally able to recover the lost treasure: "Then his sadness turned to gladness, and he thanked God for leading him back."[29]

Some of us may need to do the very same thing. Possibly at one time we came to Christ and experienced his forgiveness and the newness of life. Then somewhere along our journey, as we traveled up a "Hill Difficulty," we fell asleep spiritually and soon lost our hope. When we were later confronted with a crisis situation, like the "fierce lions," we could not face it because we had lost our hope. In such a case, we always need to go back and find our hope – which is found only in Christ.

The verse above says that even when a tree is cut down there is still hope because it can *sprout again.* As its roots tap back into the water, new shoots can spring forth. If we have lost our hope, let us reconnect with Jesus, the source of Living Water, and we will experience new life and new hope to face the hard journey ahead. *There is hope...it will sprout again.*

Radiant With Hope

May the God of hope fill you with all joy and peace in your faith, that by the power of the Holy Spirit, your whole life and outlook may be radiant with hope. (Romans 15:13 Phillips)

Richard Baxter, an English Puritan leader in the seventeenth century, was chronically sick and had plenty of reason to be a miserable man during his lifetime. Tubercular from his teens, Baxter suffered constantly from indigestion, kidney stones, headaches, toothaches, swollen limbs, internal bleeding, and enduring all this before the days of pain-relieving drugs. In spite of his physical condition, Baxter was outgoing, energetic, and uncomplaining. By 1661 he had evangelized his entire town of Kidderminster, which had a population of two thousand adults plus children. Baxter also wrote regularly, producing some classic devotional books which are still used by many Christians. In one of these books, *The Saint's Everlasting Rest*, he tells his secret. From his thirtieth year he practiced a habit which he began when he thought he was about to die: for about a half an hour a day Baxter would meditate on the life to come and the glories awaiting him. This practice instilled hope in his heart and gave this radiant servant of Christ the motivation and strength to keep on going. Hope for the future made the difference in the life of Richard Baxter, and it can make a difference in our lives as well.

Subsequent to being filled with the Holy Spirit, we may tend to anticipate supernatural manifestations. Such outward phenomena, however, may become our focus – tending to center us in this present life, rather than instilling hope for the life to come. One major reason for an empowering from above is to make us *radiant with hope*. Hope changes our outlook on all of life. Therefore we can be sustained, as was Richard Baxter, should unexpected and unexplained times of suffering come our way.

Day One Hundred Fifty
The Anchor of Hope

We have this hope as an anchor for the soul, firm and secure. (Hebrews 6:19)

If we were on a boat entering uncertain, treacherous waters, probably our most important possession at that time would be a good anchor.   Hope is called the *anchor for the soul*. The word *soul* represents our emotional and mental make-up where the storms of life take place, where we have our ups-and-downs. God has created us as complicated, emotional beings. At times our emotions serve useful purposes, but at other times they can wreak havoc. Therefore, we cannot trust our emotions, because they are so uncertain.

Our lives are like a boat in water – water is an uncertain quantity, very unstable.   To have stability we must have our anchor in something solid, and that something solid is the Lord. When we hope in God, it is not just a passing whim, it is a connection with Someone solid and certain. Our hope is like a lifeline, and it will keep us from drifting. Derek Prince has commented, "We live in an element that is totally unstable ...Neither money nor real estate nor anything else that we look at can give us stability...If we want stability, we must have an anchor that passes out of time into eternity.   When our anchor is fastened upon the eternal presence of Almighty God, we are secure."[30]

When a dependable anchor is attached to something solid, it is not pulled by gravity or the force of raging waters. Our hope is described as both *firm and secure*.   The word *firm* means "that which will not slip or totter; it can be relied on; it is certain and true."[31] The word *secure* means "it will not lose its grip or let go; it is stable, fast, certain, unshakable, sure and trusty."[32] No matter what storms we face, if our hope is anchored in Jesus, we are in a good place!   There is no one else more solid and secure for us to be connected with!

The Security of Hope

You will be secure, because there is hope...(Job 11:18)

Recently two of my friends both had their homes broken into by thieves while they were away. Some valuable items were taken and the most difficult losses were family jewelry and memorabilia which did not have great monetary value, but much sentimental value. Both my Christian friends had positive attitudes, however, commenting on how the Lord had blessed them despite the loss. They were reminded that all we have in this present life is temporary. The Book of Hebrews reminds us that we are sojourners, just passing through this present world. [33] The author encouraged believers who had been persecuted and had goods confiscated. *You suffered along with those who were thrown into jail, and when all you owned was taken from you, you accepted it with joy. You knew there were better things waiting for you that will last forever.* [34]

Nothing in this present world is secure.

- We can have a great job but then we are suddenly let go.
- We can have perfect health today and be diagnosed with cancer tomorrow.
- We can enjoy the best of married life today and then find ourselves widowed and all alone.

This is why we hope in Christ. Such hope is secure! Charles Colson wrote, "Sadly, people have either trivialized or politicized the word hope. *The American Heritage Dictionary* defines hope as 'the feeling that...events will turn out for the best.' But a Christian hope isn't a feeling. And it's not wishful thinking. Hope comes from the certainty of God's promises.... Promises abound for us about future realities. God has promised believers that Christ will come again, will redeem our bodies, will make us holy, will let us share in His glory, and will give us eternal life. This isn't simple optimism. And it isn't hope pinned to a fallible human leader. This is a firm hope in the Creator....When we don't have a secure hope, we worry excessively about the future. But when our hope is secure, we are free to live in the fruits of hope."[35] Great words of wisdom!

Day One Hundred Fifty Two
The Refuge of Hope

We who have fled to take hold of the hope offered to us
may be greatly encouraged. (Hebrews 6:18)

In ancient Israel God provided an interesting safety measure. If a man killed another person – but not intentionally – his life would still be in great danger. The law of the land was rooted in a concept of tooth-for-tooth and life-for-life, and a relative would soon hunt down the killer for revenge. Even if a man had wanted his case heard by a judge, he might not have lived that long. Therefore, in the law of Moses, God provided for six cities of refuge to be built in various locations of Israel.[36] The cities were strategically located so that no point in the land was more than thirty miles from one of them. The roads to these cities were to be kept in good repair, free from obstruction and well-marked.[37] Any man who fled to a city of refuge would be kept safe until his case could be heard. If he was then declared guilty, he would not escape punishment.

We who have a hope in Christ have a much better refuge. *God is our refuge and strength, an ever present help in trouble.*[38] In the world apart from Christ we too are "marked men" – men who by our very nature are *deserving of the wrath of God.*[39] By our old, selfish nature we are at *enmity with God* and deserve death;[40] however, because of the great mercy of God, we have a great hope and a safe place to flee. *The name of the Lord is a strong tower; the righteous run to it and are safe.*[41] God is not a difficult refuge to find; he is quite accessible through Christ.[42] The best news in this comparison is that we don't ever have to wait anxiously for a future trial. When we repent, we are forgiven of all sins and declared "not guilty!" No charge can now be brought against us. We therefore boldly declare, *If God is for us, who can be against us?...Who would dare to accuse us, whom God has chosen? God himself has declared us free from sin. Who is in a position to condemn? Only Christ Jesus, and Christ died for us, Christ also rose for us, Christ reigns in power for us, Christ prays for us!*[43]

Day One Hundred Fifty Three
The Helmet of Hope

Take the helmet of salvation...(Eph. 6:17)...putting on...the hope of salvation as a helmet. (I Thes. 5:8)

Today mankind is in tremendous spiritual conflict, much of which takes place in the mind. Many of our basic problems affect the mind: worry, depression, stress, and fear. The mind is Satan's target – that is where he will seek to defeat us.

Ronald Dunn has said, "Memory can be a minister one minute and a monster the next. We have memories we run to and memories we run from; we hide them in a closet of busyness, trying to block them out, to head them off at the pass. But eventually they overtake us. At some unguarded moment, they pounce on us bringing with them all the disappointments of their past...You think you have a memory; but it has you!... Memory is the video camera of the mind; it records everything, forgets nothing. You may think it has forgotten, but something, a word, an insignificant incident, a song, a smell – anything can trigger the memory, and suddenly it's dragging barbed-wire through your stomach."[44]

Yet, God has not left us without a remedy. First, we are not to depend on our natural minds: *Trust in the Lord with all your heart and lean not on your own understanding.*[45] Second, we are to cast down ungodly and humanistic thoughts which come to us. *We demolish arguments and every pretension that sets itself up against the knowledge of God, and we take captive every thought to make it obedient to Christ.*[46] This means we refuse to dwell upon thoughts which seek to undermine what God says. Last, we are to take the *helmet of salvation*, also called the *hope of salvation*. We are likened to soldiers in warfare for whom God has provided spiritual armor to protect from the onslaughts of the enemy.[47] A helmet is among the soldier's most prized possessions. A helmet protects the mind, and if we "put on hope," it will protect us against many mental dangers. Having hope in Christ and his good plans for our future will defeat the devil and help settle our troubled minds.

Temporary Hope

So perishes the hope of the godless.
What he trusts in is fragile; what he relies on
is a spider's web. (Job 8:13-14)

"During World War II, a German prisoner of war was being held in a Russian prison camp. His food was the bare minimum for survival substance, his housing was wretched, his clothing tattered and worn. He was mistreated, isolated, and miserable. He was able to make it from one day to the next for four years only by clinging to the hope that one day he would be released and would go home to become a great artist. Finally, the war ended, and he was released to go home.

"The former prisoner arrived in Vienna, Austria, filled with anticipation of seeing his family and beginning the fulfillment of the dream that had kept him alive through his living nightmare. In spite of his malnutrition and ill health, there was a spring in his step and a gleam in his eye as he disembarked from the train from Russia. He was greeted by his wife whom he had not seen since before the war. On the way home from the train station, he confided to her his dream of being a great artist. His wife gave him a look of withering disparagement as she chided, 'Now that you are free, you must give up those foolish dreams.' The German POW did not respond but continued the journey home in quietness. When he arrived home, the spring was no longer in his step, and the gleam was gone from his eye. Within two weeks he died."[48]

The POW had a hope, but it was only a temporary hope, and simply because of the unkind comments of an insensitive wife, hope was shattered, and even proved fatal. Job said that the hope of the natural, godless man is *fragile*, like *a spider's web*. A spider can labor all week, making his intricate design of a web, and yet with one stroke of a broom, it comes to naught. How much better it is to hope in Christ and his promises. Such hope is based on something solid and indestructible. This hope remains forever.

Day One Hundred Fifty Five
Deferred Hope

Hope deferred makes the heart sick, but a longing fulfilled is a tree of life. (Proverbs 13:12)

Steve was a brilliant young man, who traveled to England to attend college on a scholarship. Before leaving, Steve said goodbye to his high school sweetheart, with whom he was deeply in love. The couple parted in tears, declaring their "love would last forever," and Steve had no doubts all would be well when he returned. As months went by, however, his letters were not so quickly answered. Then his phone calls were not returned. When summer arrived and Steve finally returned home, his worst fears were confirmed. His girl had lost her love for him and was now in the arms of another man....

Probably one of the greatest pains in the human experience occurs when we feel we have been jilted by a person we love. Many of us have suffered a fate like Steve's or have known a similar heartache when a big hope was postponed or suspended.

What are we to do when something we really hope for does not happen as we expect? In such sad times we must realize that our ultimate hope is in GOD HIMSELF, not in answers we think are best. King David certainly had his share of disappointments and deferred answers. As a young man he was given a promise by God that he would become king of Israel, yet for the next dozen years he had to run for his life from a madman king while living in a wilderness with a misfit group of followers. In his absence, David's wife – Michal – was given to another man by her father, King Saul. David was surely discouraged and must have wondered at times what had happened to God's promise. Deferred answers, however, did not ruin his relationship with the Lord. During this time he wrote, *I will bless the Lord at all times; his praise will always be on my lips....I sought the Lord and he answered me...This poor man called, and the Lord heard him...The Lord is close to the brokenhearted...A righteous man may have many troubles, but the Lord delivers him from them all.*[49] In our times of deferred hope, we can still hope in our faithful God.

Delayed Hope

*...but we had hoped that he was the one who was
going to redeem Israel... (Luke 24:21)*

Two disciples met Jesus on the road to Emmaus right after he
had risen from the dead. Like the other disciples, they had been
quite despondent as their hopes in Christ had been dashed when
they saw him brutally beaten and then crucified. As they
walked with Jesus, they had no idea that this walking
companion had just risen from the dead! Later in the day as
they broke bread together, *their eyes were opened and they
recognized him, and he disappeared from their sight.*[50]

There are times in which God does not act when we think
he should or when our prayers seem to be ignored. As someone
wisely said, "God's delays are not necessarily his denials." We
must always remember, *As for God, his way is perfect...*[51] If
we think God has delayed in his response to us, we must not
abandon our hope. Let us be encouraged by these words of
wisdom about God's timing and apparent "delays."

- "Heaven's clock goes at a different rate than our little
  timepieces..."[52] (Alexander MacLaren)
- "God's dates are not man's. God seems to pay no
  attention to our calendars. He has a calendar of His own
  in which he suddenly surprises a man in the middle of
  his days. Leave room for God..."[53] (Oswald Chambers)
- "God's time is the best of all times. To obtain the
  highest kingdom results, God may need to delay your
  answer. Included in this timing may be special blessing
  for you."[54] (Wesley Duewel)
- "We should learn to praise and thank God even though
  He does not come to our aid when we would like to have
  Him come. We should accustom ourselves to His way
  and be patient even though he delays....He does not
  permit us to determine the person, the time, and the
  place, the what, the when, and the how, of His giving."[55]
  (Martin Luther)

Sorrow and Hope

I do not want you to be ignorant, brethren, concerning those who have fallen asleep, lest you sorrow as others who have no hope. (I Thes. 4:13 NKJV)

"In 1858 Scottish missionary Jon Paton and his wife sailed for the New Hebrides (now called Vanuatu). Three months after arriving on the island of Tanna, his wife died. One week later his infant son died. Paton was plunged into sorrow. Feeling terribly alone, and surrounded by savage people who showed him no sympathy, he wrote, 'Let those who have ever passed through any similar darkness as of midnight feel for me. As for others, it would be more than vain to try to paint my sorrows....But for Jesus, and his fellowship....I would have gone mad and died.'"[56]

The Christian may suffer and grieve like any mortal man and yet we have hope to sustain us: we do not *sorrow as others who have no hope.* The Son of God himself had emotions common to mankind; he *was deeply moved in spirit* and *wept* when he saw the tomb of his dead friend, Lazarus.[57] The Greek word for *wept* means a silent shedding of tears and it is contrasted with the loud crying or wailing of other Jews present.[58] Godly sorrow is different because we who believe have hope. Jesus told the mourning sister, Martha, *"I am the resurrection and the life. He who believes in me will live, even though he dies."*[59]

Paul Billheimer has written a very encouraging book entitled, *Don't Waste Your Sorrows.*[60] Our times of sorrow can be a reminder of God and future hope. F. B. Meyer said, "Sorrow is necessary to the soul, as a background for the rainbow of hope to rest upon. Sorrow is the furnace that burns our bonds, so that we walk free in the fires. Sorrow is the veil flung over the cage of the songbird while it learns to sing. Sorrow is the excuse for God to draw nearer to us, and for Him to draw us nearer to Himself."[61] When we sorrow, we can do so as those who have a great hope.

Mismatched Mates and Hope

Love...always hopes... (I Corinthians 13:7)
Wives, in the same way be submissive to your husbands so that, if any of them do not believe the word, they may be won without talk by the behavior of their wives, when they see the purity and reverence of your lives. (I Peter 3:1-2)

There are husbands and wives in the body of Christ who feel they are spiritually mismatched with their mates. By spiritually mismatched, I mean a believer is married either to an unsaved mate or to one who is not walking in obedience to the Lord. This person may be very insensitive to his mate's needs, irresponsible in the home, and spiritually negligent.

In these unpleasant situations, such mismatched spouses need hope, else they will be tempted to throw in the towel. God has not promised us an easy way in this life, but he grants us his victory and peace, even in unpleasant circumstances. God has given mismatched wives great hope that a husband can be won as he observes his wife's *purity and reverence.*

I have seen this fulfilled in my own home. For many years my mother tried to win my father to Christ by taking him to meetings or having spiritual men come by the house. When all of her efforts failed, she took a hands-off approach: "Lord, if you don't do it, it won't get done!" My mother faithfully lived with him for the last dozen years of his life, demonstrating the love of Christ in her practical actions. She kept her hope in God and said little unless a door of opportunity was clearly opened. In the last year of my father's life, he became very sick, and this hard man began to respond to the Spirit's workings. He no longer argued, but now talked of the possibilities of faith. A month before he died, I had the privilege of leading my father in a sinner's prayer. His life was changed, he had peace, and he testified of his faith to a few men before passing on to eternity. God is faithful to his promises! Continue to hope, mismatched mates![62]

Wayward Children and Hope

"...Your work will be rewarded," declares the Lord.
"They will return from the land of the enemy. So
there is hope for your future," declares the Lord.
"Your children will return to their own land..."
(Jeremiah 31:16-17)

One of the greatest heartaches for Christian parents is wayward children who deliberately go contrary to the way of Christ. As our children enter their teen years, we realize that we cannot squeeze them into a Christian mold, and they may have to learn some lessons the hard way. Children must be given the freedom to fail and parents must keep the long view in mind.

Luke Short heard John Flavel's gospel message when he was about fifteen years old. The solemn message centered on the verse, *If any man love not the Lord Jesus Christ, let him be accursed* (I Cor. 16:22). Luke went to sea soon after, sailed to America, and there he lived as a sinner for an unusually long time. When he was a hundred years old, he was sitting in his field, his mind still sharp, reflecting on his past life. As he thought of the days of his youth, he remembered John Flavel's sermon, and the truth once again pierced his heart. He was deeply convicted and surrendered his life to Christ. He lived to 116 years, giving every evidence of being born again.[63] If Luke had praying parents, their answer would have taken 85 years!

We must never lose hope for wayward children, but persevere in prayer. William MacDonald wrote, "If Christian parents have done their best to raise a child in the fear and admonition of the Lord, only to have the child later make shipwreck, what then? For one thing, they should remember that the last chapter hasn't been written. No case is too difficult for the Lord. By continuing earnestly in prayer ...many have lived to see their prodigals return. In other cases, the prayers of parents have been answered after they themselves have gone home to be with the Lord."[64] Parents, that wayward child is not beyond hope. Keep praying!

Financial Needs and Hope

*Why art thou cast down, O my soul? and why art thou
disquieted within me? Hope in God... (Psalm 43:5)*

George Müller constantly had to look to the Lord for financial provision. In Bristol, England, in the nineteenth century, he cared for over 10,000 orphans in his lifetime and provided Christian education for over 100,000 students. Müller rarely made any appeal for funds and looked only to God to provide. The verse above was a favorite of his, and his commentary can encourage us likewise to *hope in God.*

"'Hope thou in God.' Oh, remember this: There is never a time when we may not hope in God. Whatever our necessities, however great our difficulties, and though to all appearance help is impossible, yet our business is to hope in God, and it will be found that it is not in vain. In the Lord's own time help will come.

"Oh, the hundreds, yea, the thousands of times that I have found it thus within the past seventy years and four months! When it seemed impossible that help could come, help did come; for God has His own resources. He is not confined. In ten thousand different ways, and at ten thousand different times, God may help us.

"Our business is to spread our cases before the Lord, in childlike simplicity to pour out all our heart before God, saying, 'I do not deserve that Thou shouldst hear me and answer my requests, but for the sake of my precious Lord Jesus; for His sake answer my prayer, and give me grace quietly to wait till it pleases Thee to answer my prayer. For I believe Thou wilt do it in Thine own time and way.'"[65]

So, if we are facing financial need – whether great or small – let's remember these words from Müller, "Hope in God! He is not confined! He has ten thousand ways to help us! In the Lord's own time help will come!"

Economic Collapse and Hope

When my heart is overwhelmed, lead me to the rock that is higher than I.   (Psalm. 61:1-3 NKJV)

The J. C. Penney department store chain is an American institution. In 2010, it had over eleven hundred stores spread across every state of the union, with sales totaling over $1.5 billion. The man who started it all, James Cash Penney, built his business on bedrock Christian ethics – and even named his first store, "The Golden Rule Store." The company vowed to test every policy and act by the question, "Does it square with what is right and just?" This policy invoked much ridicule and at times hurt Penny's profit. When Penney died in 1971, the *New York Times* wrote, "He seemed too good to be true, but he was as he seemed, and others recognized it."

The stock market crashed in 1929 and J. C. Penney stock plunged from 120 points to only 13 points. Penney himself lost $40 million and within three years had to sell out to satisfy his creditors. He was virtually broke. Crushed in spirit from his loss and his health suddenly failing, Penney wound up in a Michigan sanitarium. One morning he heard the distant singing of employees who had gathered to start the day with God. *Be not dismayed, whatever betide; God will take care of you...* Penney followed the music to its source and slipped into a back row. He left a short time later a changed man, his health and spirit renewed. With new hope in his heart, he was ready to start the long climb back at age fifty-six. Penney started anew with money borrowed on his life insurance, regained a foothold in the company, and was soon back as Chairman of the Board.[66]

God has not promised his children freedom from financial trouble, but he has promised to take care of us: *Do not worry about your life, what you will eat or drink...Look at the birds of the air...your heavenly Father feeds them.* [67] If you have suffered a financial setback, draw close to the Lord and do not give up hope. *I have never seen the righteous forsaken or their children begging bread.*[68]

Disabilities and Hope (Part 1)

But we are citizens of heaven, where the Lord Jesus lives. And we are eagerly waiting for him to return as our Savior. He will take these weak mortal bodies of ours and change them into glorious bodies like his own, using the same mighty power that he will use to conquer everything, everywhere. (Phil. 3:20-21 NLT)

The Shepherd's Home in Wisconsin has a problem with dirty windows. Although many of its residents are severely disabled, they love Jesus and understand that he has promised to return someday and give them new bodies. "Every day," said the superintendent, "some of them go to the windows and press their noses against the glass, looking for Him."[69]

Probably the brightest hope for the disabled (and all of us) is the anticipation of obtaining a new, glorious body one day. This hope often becomes more real in the lives of the physically handicapped, burn victims, and the elderly, whose bodies are simply wearing out. The hope of bodily resurrection gives us strength and motivation to continue. One entire chapter in the Bible, I Corinthians 15, teaches about the historical resurrection of Christ and our future, physical resurrection. Our resurrected bodies will be *imperishable* (v.42), *raised in glory* (v.43), *raised in power* (v.43), and *raised a spiritual body* (v.44). *These ugly and weak bodies will become beautiful and strong.*[70] They will no longer embarrass us; *when they come back to life they will be superhuman bodies.*[71] Our new bodies will be like the resurrected body of Jesus–recognizable by fellow disciples, yet different. Jesus' new body was real. It was no phantom, but a body that could be touched and could consume food. It could pass through closed doors and disappear.

What a great promise we have in the resurrection! If it were a lie, we would have every reason to be depressed as our bodies age. But our hope is true! *We will be changed – in a flash, in the twinkling of an eye*[72]*...When he appears we shall be like him... Everyone who has this hope in him purifies himself...*[73]

Disabilities and Hope (Part 2)

Be strong, do not fear; your God will come...he will come to save you. Then will the eyes of the blind be opened and the ears of the deaf unstopped. Then will the lame leap like a deer, and the mute tongue shout for joy... (Isaiah 35:3-6)

Joni Eareckson Tada has been confined to a wheelchair for over forty years, largely paralyzed below the neck. She could easily give into despair, but hope is what has sustained her for all these years. No matter how difficult her days, she knows God has better days ahead. In *Heaven Your Real Home*, Joni wrote,

"I can still hardly believe it. I, with shriveled, bent fingers, atrophied muscles, gnarled knees, and no feeling from the shoulders down, will one day have a new body – light, bright and clothed in righteousness – powerful and dazzling.

"Can you imagine the hope this gives someone spinal-cord injured like me? No other religion, no other philosophy promises new bodies, hearts and minds. Only in the gospel of Christ do hurting people find such incredible hope.[74]

If we live any length of years, we will soon discover that our bodies are suffering wear and tear. Some of us may suffer much greater physical difficulties, like Joni. A good friend of mine just suffered a stroke, and now has to limp with a cane. One of my brothers just endured a battle with throat cancer. One other fellow church member is facing the possibility of prostate cancer. His attitude, however, is quite hopeful. He said, "The Bible says 'to die is gain,' so either way, I win!" Whatever physical challenges we face, we have a great hope!

- The crippled will walk – even run – with new supernatural strength! No more canes or wheelchairs!
- The blind will see – even more clearly than any earthly resident! No glasses or contacts ever needed again!
- The mentally handicapped will think – more soundly than the greatest thinker ever! No more confusion!

No matter what comes our way, let's hope in God's future!

Destructive Choices and Hope

I will not die; instead, I will live to tell what the LORD has done. (Psalm 118:17 NLT)

Kristen Anderson had many dark moments as a teenager. Three friends and a close grandmother all died within a two year period. Then she was raped by a friend she thought she could trust. She spiraled into a deep depression that she thought would never end. So, on a January night at the age of 17, Kristen attempted suicide by laying down on a set of railroad tracks near her parents' home. She was run over by 33 freight cars at 50 mph and both legs were completely severed from her body. Amazingly, she survived!

After this horrific incident, Kristen found new hope through a relationship with Jesus Christ. She has written a book about her story, *Life in Spite of Me,* and she is now a popular speaker, reaching out and offering hope to those who are hurting, depressed, suicidal, and lost. She is lacking a pair of legs because of her destructive choice, but she now has a new and optimistic life perspective. Here are her words.

"I hope my story has shown you that there is always hope. Suicide is never the answer. There is extraordinary hope and life in God's Son, Jesus Christ. Life without measure…

"Please don't give up. You are not alone. There is a God who made you, and he's not as far away as you may think. He is always near. Wherever you go, whatever you do, he will be with you. He loves you, and he wants to comfort you, heal the hurt in your heart and carry you through this life. Let him in.

"God has an amazing plan for your life, even if you don't have a plan for yourself He has hope for you, even if you don't have hope for yourself He loves you immensely, even when you don't love yourself. And he sees beauty in you, even when all you see is a mess.

"Suicide is never the answer. There is too much to live for. Keep fighting. Please don't give up. Reach out for help. You won't regret it. Your heart can be filled with hope, just like mine and so many others have been. Love, Kristen"[75]

Death and Hope

Where, O death, is your sting? (I Corinthians 15:55)

In past centuries hospitals were scarce and death scenes at home were common. Family and friends who witnessed such events often recorded in detail the final words of a loved one. We can read of Christians, full of hope, who seemed to "die well." A good example is the following newspaper obituary that Vermont pastor, Daniel Jackson, prepared about his wife who died on January 27, 1852:

"It becomes my painful duty to record the death of Mary Jackson, my beloved consort in life. She expired on Tuesday, the 27th of January, at half-past ten in the evening. Her disease was consumption, which refused to relinquish its hold until the vital powers of life sunk beneath its final grasp. It is not in the power of my pen to depict the agonies of that memorable deathbed scene. I will therefore hasten to present the reader a more inviting phase of this matter. The triumphant state of her mind softened every agony, hushed every murmur, and completely disarmed the king of terrors. For awhile, she had a sharp conflict with the power of attachment which bound her to family and friends, but by the grace of God she obtained a glorious victory and longed to depart and be with Christ, which is far better.

"I will notice some of her dying words uttered during the last week of her life. Speaking of the happy state into which she was about to enter, she exclaimed, 'O glorious day, O blessed hope, my heart leaps forward at the thought.'…When I spoke to her about her thirst, she said, 'When I have been thirsty I have thought of that river whose streams make glad the city of God.'

"I am left as a lonely pilgrim with no one to count my sighs nor wipe away the falling tear. But hush, my soul, what means this fretting? If you could look beyond the spheres of material worlds, and see the glories of thy departed one, you would say, 'The Lord gave and the Lord hath taken away, blessed be the name of the Lord.'"[76]

Heaven and Hope

He will wipe away every tear from their eyes. There will be no more death or mourning or crying or pain, for the old order of things has passed away...They will see his face, and his name will be on their foreheads... (Revelation 21:4; 22:4)

Imagine a child who has been hospitalized for over three months. Due to unavoidable circumstances, his family has seldom been able to visit; therefore the hospital stay has been quite lonely. One day, to his great surprise his entire family walks in with the doctor and he is given permission to return home immediately. What joy! What a grand family reunion!

It is hard to comprehend exactly what heaven will be like. We are only given glimpses in Scripture. One thing is certain: It will be more delightful than any present experience. *No eye has seen, no ear has heard, no mind has conceived what God has prepared for those who love him.*[77] The hope of heaven should be our greatest inspiration!

Our supreme joy will be to see face-to-face the Lord Jesus, who will gladly welcome us into his heavenly kingdom. Probably our second greatest joy will be the unbelievable reunion of all the saints throughout the ages. This will be the ultimate fulfillment of Jesus' prayer: *May they be brought to complete unity to let the world know that you sent me and have loved them even as you have loved me...*[78] J. I. Packer said, "The experience of heaven will be a family gathering, as the great host of the redeemed meet together in face-to-face fellowship with their father-God and Jesus their brother. This is the deepest idea of heaven that the Bible gives us...What will make heaven *heaven* is the presence of Jesus and a reconciled divine Father who loves us for Jesus' sake no less than he loves Jesus himself. To see and know and love and be loved by the Father and the Son, in company with the rest of God's vast family, is the whole essence of the Christian hope."[79] Thank you Father, for the prospect of this grand and happy family reunion!

Hope Reserved For Us

*For we have heard of your faith in Christ Jesus and
your love for all of God's people, which come from
your confident hope of what God has reserved for you
in heaven... (Col. 1:4-5 NLT)*

One of the mind-boggling truths in Scripture is the fact that God
has *reserved* or *laid up* (NAS) for us some wonderful things in
heaven. The Bible says quite a bit about a future *inheritance* for
all of God's faithful followers. Paul prayed... *that the eyes of
your heart may be enlightened in order that you may know the
hope to which he has called you, the riches of his glorious
inheritance in the saints...*[80]

Suppose one day an official letter arrived stating that it had
been discovered that you were a distant relative of Bill Gates,
and it was his will that all his relatives would one day receive
shares of his vast fortune! So, from conservative estimates, you
figure that you would eventually receive at least several million
dollars! This letter of good news about your inheritance would
drastically change your future outlook!

Now that scenario is imaginary, but several letters written
to us (by Paul, Peter, and John) tell us about a *real* and *certain*
inheritance that is being *reserved* in heaven for us. This
inheritance will not be in millions of dollars which we might
value right now. God's inheritance will be a million times
better; it will include innumerable and incredible spiritual
blessings promised for residents in heaven!

A promised earthly inheritance is not absolutely certain.
Gates, for example, could change his will at the last minute, or
the economy could crash – leaving him penniless and his heirs
with no future hope. Our hope, however, is *confident*! A major
lesson in the book of Hebrews (chapters 8-10) is that God has
established a new will (covenant) for us and it has been
guaranteed for us through the shed blood of Jesus Christ! This
inheritance will never be lost, misplaced, or diminished in
value! Thanks be to God for such an *inheritance that can never
perish, spoil or fade – kept in heaven for you...*[81]

Hope Keeps Us Moving Forward

Christ...whose house we are, if we hold fast our confidence and the boast of our hope until the end. (Hebrews 3:6 NAS)

Ronald Dunn suffered a great setback when his eighteen-year-old son committed suicide. Dunn later wrote of his devastating experience, and said he came to the place where instead of asking, "Why me?" he began to ask, "What now?" Dunn explained, "Self-pity absorbs us, devours us; it warps our thinking and distorts our vision – of ourselves, of others, and of God. Bitter, sour, and cynical – that's the kind of person self-pity creates... When we ask, 'What now?' we shift our focus from ourselves to God and what He is up to in our lives. And He is up to something. But we will never see it with our eyes turned selfward...Not only does 'what now?' save us from self-pity, but it also gives us *something to look forward to.* 'What now?' means we are still moving, still growing. In short, we have *a future.* It means that life can be good again."[82]

Hope in the Lord will keep us moving forward when all natural circumstances tell us to quit. Job lost his family, his possessions, and his health, but he put his trust in God, boldly declaring, *Though He slay me, I will hope in Him...*[83] Tozer said, "Hope is a nurse and comforter and enables us to go on after every reason for going on has disappeared. Hope has sustained the spirit of a shipwrecked sailor and given him strength to stay alive through the long days that seemed years till help and rescue came; hope has steeled the patriot to fight on and win at last against overwhelming odds; hope has saved from insanity or suicide the prisoner in his lonely cell as he checked off the years and months and days on his homemade calendar; hope has enabled the sick or injured man to wait out the pain and the nausea till health returned and the suffering ended...."[84] Hope helps us to keep moving, patiently waiting for the promise, looking forward to the future.

Hope Keeps Us Optimistic

...And hope does not disappoint us...(Romans 5:5)

Hope is different than faith, although the two words are closely related. Faith deals more with the present, hope deals more with the future. *If it is for this life only that Christ has given us hope, we of all people are most to be pitied.*[85] Faith brings the promises of God into present reality, whereas hope awaits future fulfillment. Scripture says, *Now faith is...*[86], indicating that faith operates more in the present.[87] We will likely be constantly disappointed in life if we live only for the present, but fail to hope for the future. Scripture says, *Hope that is seen is no hope at all. Who hopes for what he already has?*[88] Judson Cornwall has pointed out an interesting fact about hope. "Hope is never attributed to Jesus, nor did the word ever cross his lips except for the occasion when he referred to 'your hope.' For Him the realities of the next world and of the future were so completely familiar that He did not need hope."[89]

Hope will keep believers focused positively on the future; it will keep us rightly optimistic. We may have few good job prospects, problems with a child, or a health crisis. Hope will keep us patiently praying – even for the seemingly impossible. Christian optimism is not an unrealistic whistling in the dark, a refusal to face real life problems. Hope is connected to the present world, but it is also in touch with the *God of all hope*, who lives above and beyond our present circumstances.

Even if bleak circumstances never improve while we live out our days on this earth, we can *rejoice in the hope of the glory of God.*[90] The *Living Bible* is more descriptive here. *We confidently and joyfully look forward to actually becoming all that God has had in mind for us to be.*[91] Downcast believers, let us be hopeful. Let us lift up our heads and rejoice forevermore in our God. With him there's no place for pessimism! In all our circumstances let us give thanks, because for believers the best is always yet to come!

Hope Keeps Us Living

What, what would have become of me had I not believed that I would see the Lord's goodness in the land of the living! (Psalm 27:13 The Amplified Bible)

Studies of former prisoners of war reveal that keeping an alert mind and an optimistic view toward the future are two keys to survival during captivity. In 1960 Armando Valladares was arrested by the Cuban government at the age of 23 because he refused to put an "I'm with Fidel" sign on his desk at work and told some fellow workers he was against communism. He was forbidden a fair trial, accused of being a terrorist and eventually spent 22 years in prison. He was terribly abused and tortured by his guards, as he later described in his book, *Against All Hope.* He describes having to eat rotten food, live in indescribable unsanitary conditions, and endure constant pain. He wrote, "For me, it meant 8,000 days of hunger, of systematic beatings, of hard labor, of solitary confinement and solitude ...of testing my religious convictions, my faith, of fighting the hate my atheist jailers were trying to instill in me with each bayonet thrust..."[92]

Although a religious man, Valladares admitted "I held to the religion I had learned at home and at school...without examining them...At first I embraced Christ out of fear of losing my life."[93] But, then he witnessed courageous young men boldly declaring before they were shot, "Long live Christ the King! Down with communism!" Their fearless faith influenced Valladares to embrace Christ in a more personal way. "It was at that moment I am sure...that Christianity became, more than a religious faith, [now] a way of life for me. I would be sustained by a soul filled with love and hope."[94]

Because of Christian hope in his heart and a resolve to live, Valladares survived his horrible ordeal, and with international pressure, he was finally released in 1982, and soon resettled in the U.S. He has become a spokesman against Castro's regime. In 1986, he was appointed by Ronald Reagan to be U. S. Ambassador to the United Nations Human Rights Commission. Hope can keep us living – even in the most horrible places.

Hope Keeps a Spring in Our Step

The LORD is my strength and my shield; my heart trusts in him, and I am helped. My heart leaps for joy and I will give thanks to him in song. (Psalm 28:7)

You can often tell persons who are despondent and lacking hope – their heads are down, they shuffle their feet, and their conversations tend to be rather negative. Unless we have some physical disability that affects our mannerisms, followers of Jesus ought to have a "spring in their step!" We ought to have smiles on our faces, our heads held high, and conversations that are more optimistic than pessimistic. We ought to walk more than we sit, stay active more than inactive, and have an overall enthusiasm about life in general!

Over four hundred years ago, Thomas Brooks, a nonconformist preacher wrote these words, "There is nothing like God-given hope to keep your mind fresh, provide you with a quicker step, offer you restful sleep at night, brighten your eyes, and put a smile on your face.

"A Christian will part with anything rather than his hope; he knows that hope will keep the heart both from aching and breaking, from fainting and sinking. The Christian knows that hope is a beam of God, a spark of glory that nothing can extinguish till the soul is filled with glory."[95]

This description is not unrealistic for followers of Christ; notice these descriptions of those who have their hope in Him!

- *The path of the righteous is like the first gleam of dawn, shining ever brighter till the full light of day.* (Prov. 4:18)
- *She is clothed with strength and dignity, and she laughs without fear of the future.* (Prov. 31:25 NLT)
- *You have turned my mourning into joyful dancing. You have taken away my clothes of mourning and clothed me with joy...* (Ps. 30:11 NLT)
- *The Sovereign LORD is my strength; he makes my feet like the feet of a deer... to go on the heights.* (Hab. 3:19)
  If we hope in God, it ought to keep a "spring in our step!"

Hope Keeps Us Excited About the Future

There is surely a future hope for you, and your hope
will not be cut off. (Proverbs 23:18)

Every one of us has known the excitement after a future event
has been planned. I have always enjoyed planning detailed
vacations. After I have studied the places we would like to go,
set the dates on my calendar, called in reservations, and made
any practical preparations, there is a certain excitement as I
look forward to the future event.

As we consider having a future in heaven one day with
Jesus Christ, it is important that we too make sure we have our
"reservation," that we take care of any practical preparations,
and that we study (i.e., in the word of God) about our
destination so we have some ideas of what we will find there!

J. I. Packer wrote about hope and excitement. "While
there's life there's hope, we say, but the deeper truth is that only
where there's hope is there life. Take away hope, and life, with
all its fascinating variety of opportunities and experiences,
reduces to mere existence – uninteresting, ungratifying, bleak,
drab and repellant, a burden and a pain...

"God made us hoping creatures, creatures who live very
much in their own future, creatures whose nature it is to look
forward, and to get excited about good things that we foresee,
and to draw joy and strength to cope with the present from our
expectations of future fulfillment and delight. In the absence of
anything exciting to look forward to, existence itself becomes a
burden and life no longer feels worth living. To be without hope
is a tragic thing, the more so because it is needless. God never
intended humankind to live without hope, and he has, in fact,
given Christians the most magnificent hope that ever was."[96]

So, because we hope, we can be excited about our future!
Whatever we may have to go through now is less than nothing
compared with the magnificent future God has planned for us.
The whole creation is on tiptoe to see the wonderful sight of the
sons of God coming into their own...[97]

Hope Keeps Us Renewed

*Those who hope in the Lord will renew their strength.
They will soar on wings like eagles; they will run and
not grow weary, they will walk and not be faint.
(Isaiah 40:31)*

If we truly hope in the Lord, then we will do more than just *renew* our strength. The Hebrew word can also mean *exchange*. In other words, we literally exchange our weak strength for the strength of Almighty God. This is a thrilling promise, because if all we can do is to look within to our own strength and resources, we will soon come to a shallow end, and likely become depressed. But, when we exchange our limited strength for God's, it is like exchanging a flashlight battery for the "power plant of heaven!" Then, we begin functioning again; we *run and not grow weary*; we *walk and not faint*. The Hebrew language says we *sprout wings like eagles*. Now our hope produces new growth, new vision, and new God-given ability.

Regardless of age, we can have a youthful spirit. King David, who certainly knew the wears and tears of life, declared, *He... satisfies your desires with good things so that your youth is renewed like the eagle's.*[98] I have read that certain eagles live to be a hundred years old, but sometime around fifty or sixty years they begin to mope and no longer seem interested in riding the air currents. They also have little interest in associating with other eagles. After some time of apparent disinterest in life, the older eagle will suddenly start beating his wings on a rock, knocking off chunks of overgrown cartilage on his beak, and rubbing his tail feathers against the rocks until he looks bruised and beaten. As the old feathers are lost, new feathers begin to grow. The beak becomes sharp and more usable. The tail feathers grow out more thick and beautiful, and soon the old bird has taken on the appearance of a young bird. The eagle has *renewed his youth* and is good for many more years. May this analogy be true for all "eagle Christians" who have lost their spiritual vitality, but who still hope in the Lord.

Hope Keeps Us Praising

Be joyful in hope. (Romans 12:12)

One of the great testimonies of Christians to a watching world occurs as they maintain a deep, inner joy in response to situations that seem to allow only for misery and depression. Hope makes the difference. God spoke through the prophet Hosea, *"I will make... the valley of Achor a door of hope. There she will sing as in the days of her youth..."*[99] The word *Achor* in the above verse means *trouble* or *disaster* in the Hebrew language. Our times of trouble can become a door for hope to enter, and hope puts a song in the most troubled heart.

Most of the psalms were songs or poems written in the midst of very distressing settings. One psalmist, feeling down-in-the-dumps, encouraged himself by asking, *Why are you downcast, O my soul? Why so disturbed within me? Put your hope in God, for I will yet praise him...*[100] This is the attitude Tim Hansel has adopted. Hansel, a mountain climber, once fell the height of three stories and landed on his neck. Miraculously he survived, but for over twenty years he has lived with chronic pain. In his book, *You Gotta Keep Dancin': In the Midst of Life's Hurts You Can Choose Joy,* Hansel wrote: "Whereas happiness is a feeling, joy is an attitude...Pain is inevitable, but misery is optional. We cannot avoid pain, but we can avoid joy. God has given us such immense freedom that he will allow us to be as miserable as we want to be.

"I know some people who spend their entire lives practicing being unhappy, diligently pursuing joylessness. They get more mileage from having people feel sorry for them than from choosing to live out their lives in the context of joy.

"Joy is simple (not to be confused with easy). At any moment in life we have at least two options, and one of them is to choose an attitude of gratitude, a posture of grace, a commitment to joy."[101]

When we have every reason to be down, let us also choose joy, and say, *But as for me, I will always have hope; I will praise you more and more...you will restore my life again.*[102]

Hope Motivates Holy Living

But we know that when he appears, we shall be like him, for we shall see him as he is. Everyone who has this hope in him purifies himself, just as he is pure. (1 John 3:2-3)

The prospect of us one day standing before the throne of God and seeing our Lord Jesus Christ ought to inspire holy living. We will see the resurrected Jesus in all his glory, whose eyes will be *like blazing fire*[103] – eyes that gaze with absolute purity into the very depths of our souls, exposing every hidden deed and motive. Knowing this sobering fact, we should desire to walk uprightly and do nothing deliberately that we might one day be ashamed of.

As we study New Testament Scriptures about the "end times," we will discover there is little emphasis on practical preparation – like storing up food, retreating to the mountains, or gathering as many guns we can find. The emphasis, rather, is being spiritually prepared to meet Christ and to *live holy lives.* Tozer said, "I cannot think of even one lonely passage in the New Testament which speaks of Christ's revelation, manifestation, appearing or coming that is not directly linked with moral conduct, faith and spiritual holiness."[104]

Suppose a man made a proposal of marriage to a young lady he deeply loved. She was delighted because this was a man she greatly respected and loved, and yet she felt quite ill-prepared to become his lifelong marriage partner. However, she had his firm commitment to her and therefore a *solid hope* that they would soon be united together in happy marriage. Her hope would now be a strong motivation and greatly influence her daily living. Her life would now be specially set apart in anticipation of being with her future groom.

The greatest motivation in Scripture for personal holiness is the anticipation of our future groom – our Lord Jesus who will soon return and take us to himself. We cannot be casual or careless about this. *You ought to live holy and godly lives as you look forward to the day of God and speed its coming....*[105]

Hope Comes From Christ's Resurrection
(Part One)

The Spirit of God, who raised Jesus from the dead, lives in you. And just as he raised Christ from the dead, he will give life to your mortal body by the same Spirit living within you. (Romans 8:11 NLT)

A young scholar approached British statesman Benjamin Disraeli one day. He had developed a new religion and written a book to explain its doctrines. The young man claimed that his newly devised creed surpassed in beauty the message of Christ and his sacrificial crucifixion on Calvary. Disraeli asked the young man about the success of the book's sales, only to hear him complain that he couldn't get anyone to buy it or to believe in his religion. The old statesman placed his hand on the young man's shoulder and said, "No, my boy, you will never get anyone to read your book and believe in your religion until you too have been crucified on a cross and risen from a tomb."[106]

Our hope is ultimately in the resurrection of Jesus Christ. Jesus predicted that he would die, be buried for three days, rise again, and then he actually did it! No other religious leader in history has ever been able to equal the claims and deeds of Jesus Christ. Jesus not only defeated death and rose again from the dead, he also now declares to all who believe in him, *"Because I live, you will live also."*[107] At Christ's coming we shall be resurrected and all changed into the likeness of his glorious, resurrected body. Such a hope ought to motivate us!

Biblical hope is tied to the resurrection but it has present, practical applications as well. In his Greek study of the word for hope, *elpis*, James Garrett points out that of the 54 times the word is used in the New Testament, 19 times it refers directly to the resurrection and 25 times indirectly. It is used only 10 times otherwise.[108] The hope of the resurrection is the greatest hope we could possibly have: *Just as he raised Christ from the dead, he will give life to your mortal body by the same Spirit living within you.* It is incredible, but true, to think that the very same Spirit which raised Christ from the dead is living inside us!

Hope Comes From Christ's Resurrection
(Part Two)

*And if our hope in Christ is only for this life, we are more
to be pitied than anyone in the world. (1 Cor.15:19 NLT)*

Many persons in the midst of tremendous disappointment,
suffering, and grief have found great peace and hope through
the reality of Christ's resurrection. The day after Preston
Parrish had attended the funeral of his dearly loved father, he
received a call from a deputy who announced that his twenty-
five year old son, Nathan, had been tragically killed while rock
climbing. Preston described the deep sorrow of his family, "It
was an ocean of grief deeper than anything we were already
experiencing in the wake of Daddy's passing. The grief was
like sliding off the continental shelf and sinking into the abyss."

Preston and his family were sustained, moment-
by-moment. It was the reality of the resurrection, however, that
brought strength and hope to the Parrish family. Preston
continued his story, "Christ's resurrection holds the only
resolution for so many of the regrets, injustices and mysteries
that life in a fallen world inevitably involves. If we're honest,
all of us struggle with those things in one way or another....

"In the weeks following that fateful call about Nathan,
some well-intentioned people urged us to find solace in our
memories of him. To a degree that was helpful; we do have
many fond memories of his time with us, for which we are
grateful. But true consolation requires more than memories. In
fact, memories alone can intensify the pain of a loved one's
death and haunt rather than console. Christ's resurrection
moves us beyond dead memories to living hope – hope of
seeing our believing loved ones again and, more important,
hope of dwelling for all eternity in the glorious presence of the
Lord Jesus Christ Himself. Without this hope, memories of a
departed loved one are a pitiful prelude to an eternity of
unspeakable despair."[109]

Thanks be to God for the hope we have in the resurrection!

Hope Comes From Christ's Resurrection
(Part Three)

But as for me, I know that my Redeemer lives, and he will stand upon the earth at last. And after my body has decayed, yet in my body I will see God! I will see him for myself. Yes, I will see him with my own eyes. I am overwhelmed at the thought! (Job 19:25-27 NLT)

Steven Curtis and Mary Beth Chapman both experienced a parent's worst nightmare on May 21, 2008, when their teenage son, Will, parking their SUV in the driveway, accidentally ran over and killed his five-year-old sister, Maria. Steven tried CPR, but Maria was pronounced dead on arrival at the hospital.

A year and a half after his daughter's death, Steven was interviewed on ABC News, "Good Morning America." He told Robin Roberts that he was "desperately hopeful" about the future. He said it was their faith that is "keeping us going as a family." He also delivered a message from Will: "Tell them I'm hanging in there. I have some really hard days. I have some really good days. I know I'm going to see my little sister again. It really is my faith that keeps me going."[110]

Mary Beth struggled immensely and later wrote a book, *Choosing to See,* detailing her journey. One truth greatly sustained her at the funeral–that Maria would one day be raised with an imperishable body! Her body was like a seed now being planted in the ground, but "that there was in fact a spring ahead. We really will see her again…more alive than ever."[111]

It is their hope in the resurrection that has sustained the entire Chapman family. They firmly believe that one day they will see Maria again. In another interview, Steven concluded with a note of hope, "We just have to remember this is the story God has entrusted to us. We'll go wherever we can to tell it to His glory and to honor our daughter's memory and more importantly to honor the God who's given us the hope that's just kept us alive to this point."[112]

The resurrection can sustain us as well – even in the most terrific and tragic times. It's our only hope, a substantial one!

Hope Comes from Christ in Us

The mystery that has been kept hidden for ages and generations, but is now disclosed to the saints...which is Christ in you, the hope of glory. (Col. 1:26-27)

In the New Testament we have some *mysteries* revealed – important truths hidden in times past, but brought to light in Christ's coming. One of the most glorious mysteries, kept hidden for ages, is *Christ in you – the hope of glory.*[113] The message of *Christ in you* is at the heart of the gospel message.

What does *Christ in you* mean? It means that Christ died not just to save us from a bad past; his intention is to live out his very life in us through the Holy Spirit. *The Spirit...lives with you and will be in you...On that day you will realize that I am in the Father, and you are in me, and I am in you.*[114]

The reason *Christ in you* is such a great hope for us is that Christ is not just an example to be copied. He does not inspire us to try to imitate him – to be "Christ-like." The apostle Paul stated, *I have been crucified with Christ and I no longer live, but Christ lives in me.*[115] Watchman Nee said that in this verse Paul "is showing us how only Christ satisfies God's heart. This is the life that gives God satisfaction in the believer, and there is no substitute. 'Not I, but Christ,' means Christ *instead of* me. When Paul uses these words he is not claiming to have attained to something his readers have not... He is defining the Christian life. The Christian life is the Christ life. Christ *in me* has become my life, and is living my life instead of me."[116] This is why we can pray,

> "O Jesus, come and dwell in me,
> Walk in my steps each day,
> Live in my life, love in my love,
> And speak in all I say;
> Think in my thoughts, let all my acts
> Thy very actions be,
> So shall it be no longer I,
> But Christ that lives in me."[117]

Hope Comes From Knowing Who is in Control

The LORD has established His throne in the heavens,
And His sovereignty rules over all. (Psalm 103:19 NAS)

One of the outstanding heroes during the terrorist attacks on September 11, 2000 was Todd Beamer. After United Airlines Flight 93 was hijacked, Beamer and other passengers talked with people on the ground via cell phones, and learned that the World Trade Center and the Pentagon had been attacked using hijacked airplanes. After the plane made its turn in a southeasterly direction (likely toward a Washington D.C. target), some of the plane's passengers planned to attack the hijackers and stop their deadly plan. Beamer then prayed and his last audible words were "Are you guys ready? Okay, let's roll!" Their effort was apparently successful, but the plane crashed into a Pennsylvania countryside, killing all passengers aboard.

Two years later, Beamer's widow, Lisa, wrote a book entitled, *Let's Roll!* In this story she shares how her Christian hope made a difference in the larger perspective. "The choices for people like me – and for many of us – are to look at all the things we've lost or to look at all the things we have; to become bitter or to become better; to live in fear or to live in hope…I've chosen to live in hope …

"The reason I've been able to do that is not because I'm a strong person….The reason I've chosen to live in hope is because of the heavenly, eternal perspective God has given me. That tells me that fear comes from feeling out of control, and if September 11 has taught us anything, it is that we are never really in control….

"But hope comes from knowing who *is* in control. Hope comes from knowing that we have a sovereign, loving God, who is in control of every event of our lives….

"It's a time of uncertainty, and many people are looking for something to cling to. I hope for you that you can cling to the one who has all the power, and all the love, and all the care, because he's the one who's really in charge."[118]

Hope Comes from God's Faithfulness

*Yet this I call to mind and therefore I have hope:
Because of the Lord's great love we are not consumed,
for his compassions never fail. They are new every
morning; great is your faithfulness. (Lam. 3:21-23)*

Jeremiah wrote the book of Lamentations at one of the lowest
times in Israel's history as well as in his own personal life. For
over forty years Jeremiah had preached in Judah, warning the
nation that unless it repented and turned to God, judgment was
inevitable. In all those years Jeremiah never saw any positive
response to his message and the people's hearts became even
more hardened. Jeremiah thought about quitting more than
once, but God's word was like a *burning fire* in his heart.[119]

Notice how many ways Jeremiah personally suffered: he
was threatened by people from his hometown,[120] betrayed by
his own family,[121] felt alienated and lonely,[122] beaten and put
in stocks,[123] almost murdered by religious leaders,[124] ridiculed
by a false prophet,[125] thrown into a cistern to die,[126] accused of
lying,[127] and constantly laughed at and mocked.[128] Yet,
through it all, Jeremiah endured and maintained his hope in
God. How could he do it? Jeremiah knew the faithfulness of
God.

Scripture declares our God is not disloyal, treacherous, or
untrue. He is utterly faithful. *Your faithfulness continues
through all generations; you establish the earth and it
endures.*[129] *Know therefore that the Lord your God is God; he
is the faithful God, keeping his covenant of love to a thousand
generations of those who love him and keep his commands.*[130]
As was true of Jeremiah, the reason that we can endure the
heaviest trials is because God is faithful to his eternal purposes.
*God is faithful; he will not let you be tempted beyond what you
can bear. But when you are tempted, he will also provide a way
out so that you can stand up under it.*[131] We can be assured:
God will keep us from falling and even when we stumble, he
will lend his support: *If we are faithless, he will remain faithful,
for he cannot disown himself.*[132] Yes, great is his faithfulness!

Hope Comes from the Scriptures (Part 1)

For everything that was written in the past was written to teach us, so that through endurance and the encouragement of the Scriptures we might have hope. (Romans 15:4)

A major purpose of the written word of God is to produce hope in our hearts. When I meet believers who are complaining about some difficult circumstance, I often ask them, in the course of conversation, if they have been abiding in Scripture and spending time with the Heavenly Father. With few exceptions, the reply is in the negative.

The historical accounts of the men and women of faith who endured all kinds of trials and obstacles are recorded in Scripture to inspire hope in our hearts today. J. B. Phillips rendered the above verse, *For all those words which were written long ago are meant to teach us today; so that we may be encouraged to endure and go on hoping in our own time.*[133]

The word of God is meant to sustain and encourage us whenever we are fearful, anxious, or distressed. If we neglect the word of God, then our hope will diminish and we will soon be given over to despair. Charles Swindoll commented, "Every believer in Jesus Christ must ultimately come to the place where he is going to trust God's Word completely before he can experience consistent victory. His Book is our single source of tangible truth. We try every other crutch – we lean on self. . . on others . . . on feelings . . . on bank accounts . . . on good works . . . on logic and reason . . . on human perspective – and we continually end up with the short straw and churning. God has given His written Word and the promise of His light to all His children. WHEN WILL WE EVER LEARN TO BELIEVE IT AND LIVE IN IT AND USE IT AND CLAIM IT? I often wonder how many of His personal promises to His people exist in His Book unclaimed and ignored."[134]

Let us abide in and live by the word of God that we might *go on hoping in our own time.*

Hope Comes from the Scriptures (Part 2)

*My soul faints with longing for your salvation, but I
have put my hope in your word. (Psalm 119:81)*

One reason millions of people have been able to hope in the
Lord is because of the printed Bible. If there had been no
languages established, no printing presses developed, and no
technology encouraged (e.g., computers), then most of the
world would have remained in darkness without any hope.

According to the *Guinness Book of World Records*, "There
is little doubt that the Bible is the world's best-selling and most
widely distributed book. A survey by the Bible Society
concluded that 2.5 billion copies were printed between 1815
and 1975, but more recent estimates put the number above 5
billion. The whole Bible has been translated into 349 languages; 2123 languages have at least one book translated."[135]

Johannes Gutenberg invented the moveable type printing
press and in 1455 printed the first book, the *Gutenberg Bible*.
His motivation for investing so much time and effort in this
new invention was partially economic; he realized there was a
market for books that could be produced quickly at lower cost.

But Gutenberg was also motivated to bring greater hope to
the masses through the Bible. As he explained it, "God suffers
in the multitude of souls whom His word cannot reach.
Religious truth is imprisoned in a small number of manuscript
books which confine instead of spread the public treasure. Let
us break the seal which seals up holy things and give wings to
Truth in order that she may win every soul that comes into the
world by her word no longer written at great expense by hands
easily palsied, but multiplied like the wind by an untiring
machine...Through [the press], God will spread His word; a
spring of pure truth shall flow from it; like a new star it shall
scatter the darkness of ignorance, and cause a light formerly
unknown to shine among men."[136]

Thank God for this most generous gift and unparalleled
treasure ever given to mankind. We put our *hope in your word!*

Hope Comes from Christ's Second Coming
(Part One)

...He will come again, not to deal with our sins, but to bring salvation to all who are eagerly waiting for him. (Hebrews 9:28 NLT)

Eschatology is the study of the "end times" before Christ returns. Believers are often found in one of several extremes. Some think it is all too difficult and neglect the study of more challenging books in the Bible – like Daniel and Revelation. Others have heard an excess of Bible prophecy and may be somewhat fearful or just too skeptical to pursue the subject. Then you have some believers who seem to thrive on Bible prophecy. Anytime there is a natural disaster, they get excited about "the end being near," and they're constantly looking for prophetic signs in the world's news. They also enjoy conspiracy theories concerning dark secrets in our government and a secret "new world order" about ready to take over.

The Bible is a prophetic book. Some have estimated as much as 20% of Scripture deals with events yet to come. We must not ignore these portions of the word of God. A proper emphasis on the end times can build greater hope in our hearts and help us face the future with an optimistic faith.

J. I. Packer wrote, "Eschatology is...the clue to understanding the nature of the Christian life. That life is essentially a life of hope, a life in which nothing is perfect yet, but the hope of perfection is set before us, so that we may forget what is behind and reach out to what lies ahead and press toward the mark for the prize of the high calling of God in Christ Jesus....Eschatology is supremely relevant for teaching the gospel in these days. We face a great deal of pessimistic hopelessness on the part of people who feel they have seen through the false hopes of society and now have no hope at all. We need to speak loudly and clearly about the glory of the Christian hope."[137]

Let us not avoid eschatology; a careful study will cause greater hope to arise in our hearts! Our Lord is coming back!

Hope Comes from Christ's Second Coming
(Part Two)

...While we wait for the blessed hope – the glorious appearing of our great God and Savior, Jesus Christ... (Titus 2:13)

One day human history will come to a glorious climax as a heavenly trumpet sounds, an angelic shout is proclaimed, and Jesus Christ returns to the earth in all his resurrected splendor and glory. Although students of prophecy differ on the details and timing, we know that in the end Christ will appear for the second time, as he has promised. This is *the blessed hope* – our greatest hope as we face the problems of this troubled time in human history. Indeed, *blessed* hope is a fit description!

End-time teaching is often pessimistic – with an emphasis on doom and gloom. But, believers have much to anticipate. When Jesus comes, he will bring the immediate defeat and punishment of Satan, the Antichrist, and all the demonic host. The saints will be resurrected, raptured, and rewarded. The wicked will be resurrected, judged, and punished. At the Great White Throne Judgment, everything that was ever overlooked by finite human judges will be made right, as divine retribution takes place. Believers will be forever united with Jesus, the heavenly Bridegroom, at the grand celebration of the universe – the marriage supper of the Lamb. Human history, as we know it, will come to conclusion, and our Lord will usher in the final state – the New Heaven and New Earth. What a hope we have!

When Christ comes again, there will be no more grace extended. Those who refused his offer of salvation will have no second chances.[138] Nonbelievers will have no hope and will face a most horrible future. "The best we can hope for," said the agnostic philosopher Bertrand Russell, "is unyielding despair."

Those who have followed Jesus Christ, however, have the hope of life everlasting, a home in heaven, and all the promises of God fulfilled. Therefore, *set your hope fully on the grace to be given you when Jesus Christ is revealed...*[139]

Part Three

**Daily Encouragement
For Growing in**

Love

*And now I will show you
the most excellent way...
(1 Corinthians 12:31)*

Love – The Greatest Thing

God is love. Whoever lives in love lives in God, and
God in him. (1 John 4:16)

Henry Drummond, a popular Scottish evangelist, who worked
closely with D. L. Moody during the nineteenth-century revival
campaigns in England, wrote one of the most popular booklets
of all time. It is a message about love and is aptly entitled, *The
Greatest Thing in the World.* In our Christian journey we, too,
will discover time and time again that the priority, the principal
thing in our human experience, is the love of God. We can
easily become focused on meetings, organizations, doctrinal
discussions, and secondary issues, while missing out on the
greatest thing.

In a world dominated by sin and selfishness, those who
know the love of God will distinguish themselves. They will
not be driven to pursue personal fame and fortune, but will seek
first the kingdom of heaven and be characterized in all they do
by a dimension of love which is out-of-this-world. When they
are taken advantage of, they will not have to set the record
straight. When they are mistreated or attacked, they will not
strike back. When they are not loved, they will still display love
– even to the undeserving or the unresponding. They will even
show love to their enemies in the name of the Lord.

A wise man once said, "The greatest tragedy is not what
one may suffer, but what one may *miss*." We could add that
the greatest tragedy in life is to miss God's love. Scripture
says we can be spiritually gifted, understand all mysteries, have
mountain-moving faith, and sacrifice for the sake of the poor,
and yet, if we are missing love in our hearts, these things are
nothing! [1] It is imperative, therefore, that we constantly
consider our priorities and examine our motivations. Love must
be the supreme thing: *Above all things have fervent love for one
another.* [2]

Love – The Hub of Christianity

This is the message you heard from the beginning: We should love one another. (The apostle John, *1 John 3:11*)

The love of God has been compared to a hub of a wheel. It is the center from which all virtues are connected. Peter Kreft taught on the centrality of love. "John, the youngest of Jesus' disciples, was the last to die. As he grew older his teaching grew simpler, as you can see by reading his first Epistle. He spoke always and only of one thing: the love of God. According to an old tradition, one of his disciples complained to him about this: 'Why don't you talk about anything else?' He answered, 'Because there isn't anything else.'

"Christianity is both complex and simple....It is full of mysteries like the Trinity, creation, the Incarnation, atonement, providence, and eschatology. In fact, it is the most mysterious religion in the world. It is not at all obvious, not what we would expect. That is what all the heresies have been: what the human mind naturally expected. Yet Christianity is also supremely simple. John was right. There is, in the last analysis, only one thing: the love of God.

"Christianity is like a wheel as big and as complex as the cosmos. And the love of God is its hub. Everything else is a spoke. The love of God is the point, the final explanation, of everything else in Christianity and in fact of everything else in the cosmos. The love of God is not just one point among many. It is the ultimate cause and reason, the meaning and explanation for everything else. For everything that exists, exists only because of God's will to create, preserve, provide for, guide, and complete it. And God's will is absolutely simple and single in motive: 'God *is* love' (1 Jn. 4:8)."[3]

Love – The Nature of the Trinity

[The Father] has delivered and drawn us to Himself out of the control and the dominion of darkness and has transferred us into the kingdom of the Son of His love... (Colossians 1:13 The Amplified Bible)

It has been stated by some that God created man because "He needed someone to love." John Morrison, in his teaching about the Trinity, explained why this is poor theology for at least two reasons: "First, if God has an unfulfilled need, then He cannot be God. Second, God cannot be love without that love being actualized – that is, there had to be an actual means of love being expressed by God throughout eternity in order for the eternal God to *be* love. And, that love has been expressed eternally through the relationships among the three Persons of the Trinity. As St. Augustine of the fourth century put it, 'God is (at once) Lover, Beloved, and Love itself.' The Father loves the Son, the Son loves the Father, and the Holy Spirit is Love itself – all within His being as three Persons.

"Darrell Johnson stated: 'The living God is not a solitary God. The living God is not an isolated God. From all eternity the living God has lived in relationships....At the center of the universe is relationship. From all eternity the living God has been community, family. From all eternity the living God has been infinitely pleased as Father, Son and Holy Spirit...And here is the gospel: the God who is love draws nears to me, a sinful, mere mortal, to draw me near to himself, in order to draw me within the circle of Lover, Beloved, and Love itself.'"[4]

It is quite thrilling to consider that the very same eternal love that is shared among the three members of the Trinity is something we can experience! Jesus prayed, *"Father, I want those you have given me to be with me where I am, and to see my glory, the glory you have given me because you loved me before the creation of the world."* [5]

Love – The Expression of God's Nature

Dear friends, let us love one another, for love comes from God. Everyone who loves has been born of God and knows God. Whoever does not know love does not know God, because God is love. (1 John 4:7-8)

God's very nature is love and all that he does is an expression of that nature. Henry Blackaby said, "God can never function contrary to His own nature. Never in your life will God ever express His will toward you except that it is an expression of perfect love. He can't! God's kind of love always seeks the very best for a person. Therefore, He can never give you second best. His nature will not let Him."[6] Even when God disciplines us, his actions are based on love.[7]

Love was ultimately expressed in the life and death of Jesus Christ: *This is love: not that we loved God, but that he loved us and sent his Son as an atoning sacrifice for our sins.*[8] We can never separate the idea of love from the Son of God. As John Murray commented, "The love of God from which we cannot be separated is the love of God *which is in Christ Jesus our Lord.* It is only in Christ Jesus it exists, only in him has it been manifest, only in him is it operative, and only in Christ Jesus as our Lord can *we* know the embrace and bond of this love."[9] This is why we must never seek love as something in itself; we must seek Jesus Christ, accept his love, and become rightly related to God the Father.

God is love, but we cannot say the reverse is true – that love is God. Some have mistakenly tried to equate limited, human love with deity. Our best efforts to express love out of our own physical and emotional resolve falls immensely short of God's dimension of love. When we encounter God, we will encounter true love, and we will have a lifetime to learn more and more about this incredible discovery. This is why the apostle Paul prayed for believers *to grasp how wide and long and high and deep is the love of Christ, and to know this love that surpasses knowledge.*[10]

Love – The Reason for Salvation

For God so loved the world that He gave His only begotten Son, that whoever believes in Him should not perish but have everlasting life. (John 3:16 NKJV)

This verse is probably the most popular verse in the entire Bible, and rightly so – it contains the essence of the gospel message about the love of God. Pay close attention to the word, *so*. God *so* loved the world... This little word emphasizes the intensity and great depth that Almighty God went to rescue us. He sent his very own loved son. The term *only-begotten Son* does not mean that Jesus was born or created, as some cults teach; Jesus has always co-existed with the Father and Holy Spirit. *Only-begotten* in the Greek language means, "unique (in kind); that is the only example in its category."[11]

God's salvation is for the *world*. There seems no good reason to limit God's amazing love to a certain segment of the world or "elected" people; his love is for the *whole* world. John Calvin rightly saw this verse meaning that "the Father loves the human race."[12] This is confirmed by other Scripture: *But when the kindness of God our Savior and His love for mankind appeared...*[13] Thank God we are included!

To help us better appreciate the depth of John 3:16, an unknown author has outlined it as follows:

God – the greatest Lover
so loved – the greatest degree
the world – the greatest company
that He gave – the greatest act
His only begotten Son – the greatest gift
that whoever – the greatest opportunity
believes – the greatest simplicity
in Him – the greatest attraction
should not perish – the greatest promise
but – the greatest difference
have – the greatest certainty
everlasting life – the greatest possession

Love – The Keynote of the Bible

In his love and mercy he redeemed them… (Isaiah 63:9)

As we begin to read any of the sixty-six books of the Bible, we will not read very far without discovering something about the love of God. Even when the prophets wrote during the darkest times in Israel's history, they frequently warned and strongly exhorted God's people, yet just about every prophet ends his book on a positive note of hope – that one day God will regather his people and in love redeem them.

R. A. Torrey declared correctly that love is the "keynote" of the Bible. He wrote, "God's love is the keynote of the whole Bible. It was the love of God that led to the creation as described in the first chapter of Genesis. It was God's love that led to the banishment of Adam and Eve from the Garden of Eden when they fell. It was God's love that led to the promise of the Savior, the seed of the woman, immediately after Adam and Eve had fallen.

"It was God's love that led to the call of Abraham and Jacob to be a blessing first to their own descendants and ultimately to the whole human race. It was God's love that led to the planting of Israel in that land so wondrously adapted to be the training place of the nation that would bring blessing to the whole earth, and from which the Savior would be born. It was God's love that sent Jesus Christ to die for sinful men, to rise again from the dead and to ascend to the right hand of the Father in glory.

"And it will be God's love that will send Him back again to earth when the fullness of time for that greatest event in all this earth's history has come. Heaven and all its glories, hell and its horrors, both have their origin in the love of God. Yes, 'God is love' is the secret of history, the explanation of nature and the solution of eternity's mysteries."[14]

Love – The Mark of the Christian

By this all men will know that you are my disciples, if you have love for one another. (John 13:35 NAS)

Love is the mark, the distinguishing feature, of every true disciple of Jesus. This is the characteristic that catches the attention of unbelievers, and confirms that Jesus was sent by the Father. Andrew Murray stated, "We have been taught that the true Church is where God's Word is rightly preached and the holy sacraments are dispensed as instituted by Christ. Christ himself took a much broader view. To Him the distinguishing mark of His Church was not what her ministers taught and performed, but if His followers truly loved one another."[15]

The love of God dwelling in our hearts is a true indicator that we are spiritually alive. *We know that we have passed from death to life, because we love our brothers. Anyone who does not love remains in death.*[16] When I became a Christian, one change that convinced me of the reality of my conversion was that I immediately had a new love for people from a variety of backgrounds. Physical appearances, social status, and racial distinctives no longer made any difference to me. The love of God transcended all these barriers. At times I have been amazed at the love of God manifested through me despite my personal deficiencies.

Every Christian must be careful not to allow his love to grow cold. If we keep close to Jesus, we will have hearts full of love. Jonathan Edwards warned us, "A Christian should at all times keep a strong guard against everything that tends to overthrow or corrupt or undermine a spirit of love...If love is the sum of Christianity, surely those things which overthrow love are exceedingly unbecoming [to] Christians. An envious Christian, a malicious Christian, a cold and hard-hearted Christian is the greatest absurdity and contradiction."[17]

Believers, let us be distinguished by the love of God.

Love – The Law of the Spirit (Part 1)

The commandments...are summed up in this one rule: "Love your neighbor as yourself." Love does no harm to its neighbor. Therefore love is the fulfillment of the law. (Romans 13:9-10)

Christians sometimes debate on whether or not we should keep the law of Moses. Bypassing this debate, let us simply say that believers now operate under a higher law – the law of love. Watchman Nee explained that a law is simply something which happens over and over again.[18] For example, consider the law of gravity. If I drop a handkerchief in New York, it falls to the ground. If I drop it in London, it falls to the ground. No matter where I let the handkerchief go, gravity operates and always produces the same results. This is the "law" of gravity. Now, suppose when I drop the handkerchief, I place my hand under it and catch it. Why does it not hit the ground? The law of gravity is still in place, but a *higher law* is now operating – the law of my hand, which we can call the law of life. Yes, the law of Moses may still be in operation, but we who have faith in Christ Jesus now operate under a higher law: *Through Christ Jesus the law of the Spirit of life set me free from the law of sin and death.*[19] Trying to operate under the law of Moses can only produce a sense of frustration, as it cannot fully deal with the problem of sin and death. Through Jesus Christ, however, we can receive new LIFE and a new law will begin to operate within us – the law of love. If I love my neighbor, I am not going to steal from him or murder him or commit adultery with his wife. I will refrain from such wicked behavior not just because a religious commandment forbids it, but because the love of God operates in my heart: *Love does no harm to its neighbor.*

This is why St. Augustine said, "Love and do what you will."[20] Love is the fulfillment of all divine commandments. If properly understood, love is a most capable and sufficient guide for all conduct. We should therefore choose to operate under this law of love as it has been revealed in Christ.

Love – The Law of the Spirit (Part 2)

The entire law is summed up in a single command:
"Love your neighbor as yourself." (Galatians 5:14)

When we operate under the law, most of our service is a mere *duty*. When we are motivated by the Holy Spirit, however, our service is more likely to be a *delight*. Richard DeHaan shared a great illustration on this point.

"A husband and wife didn't really love each other. The man was very demanding, so much that he prepared a list of rules and regulations for his wife to follow. He insisted that she read them every day and obey them to the letter. Among other things, his 'do's and don'ts' indicated such details as what time she had to get up in the morning, when his breakfast should be served, and how the housework should be done.

"A few years after the husband died, the woman fell in love with another man, one who dearly loved her, and they were married. This husband did everything he could to make his new wife happy, continually showering her with tokens of his appreciation. One day as she was cleaning house, she found tucked away in a drawer the list of commands her first husband had written for her. As she looked it over, she realized that even though her new husband hadn't given her any kind of list, she was doing everything her first husband's list required.

"She was so devoted to this man that her deepest desire was to please him out of love, not obligation. Doing things for him was her greatest joy."[21]

This is the way it should be in our relationship to Christ. He loves us, and therefore we love him and anything we do for him is motivated by our love, not by a mere list of duties to fulfill. Love is thus the fulfillment of the law and provides us a much better motivation to please our Lord and serve others as well.

Love – The Building Blocks of the Church

> *We must grow up in every way into him who is the head, into Christ, from whom the whole body, joined and knit together by every ligament with which it is equipped, as each part is working properly, promotes the body's growth in building itself up in love. (Ephesians 4:16 NRSV)*

God has given us some instruction about building his church and told us to be careful in the *manner* in which we build.[22] Some things ought to be used as building material and some things not used. The one and only foundation we must build upon is Christ Jesus himself,[23] and the most important construction materials are the building blocks of love. We can try to build a church with correct doctrine, a gifted pastor, or a contemporary worship format, but none of these things are as essential as love: *Love builds up.*[24]

When we become part of a local fellowship, we will soon realize the deficiencies and weaknesses of its members. We may tend to be standoffish and fail to bear patiently with one another. The love we profess will certainly be put to the test in the church. Without ever increasing love in our hearts, we will not be able to relate and properly care for one another. Paul Billheimer offers a great description of the church: "The local church, therefore, may be viewed as a spiritual workshop for the development of God's love. Thus the stresses and strains of a spiritual fellowship offer the ideal situation for the testing of [love]....Love, like other graces of the Spirit, grows only under testing....Therefore the local congregation is one of the best laboratories in which individual believers may discover their real spiritual emptiness and begin to grow in God's love."[25] If this definition is true, then we will learn little about the love of God without becoming a committed part of a local church. There our love will be tested and developed, and our goal will be for *all* to be built up together in the love of Christ.

Love – The Perfect Bond of Unity (Part 1)

And over all these virtues put on love, which binds them all together in perfect unity. (Colossians 3:14)

Two different items, which normally would have little attraction for one another, can be strongly bound together by the right kind of glue. God has given us the "right kind of glue" – his own supernatural love dwelling in our hearts. God's love has the potential to bind all Christians together in unity.

We are Christ's only representatives in a wicked world; therefore we need to put Christian love ahead of our strong opinions. The love of Christ in our midst should take precedence over non-essential doctrinal distinctions and personal preferences. Our "oneness in spirit" must practically be demonstrated through the love that Christ has shed abroad in our hearts. Andrew Murray commented, "The hidden unity of life must be manifest in the visible unity and fellowship of love. Most believers consider it impossible to live in the full oneness of love with the children of God around them. Only when they learn that love to each other is their simple duty, and begin to cry to God for His Holy Spirit to work it in them, will there be hope of change in this respect."[26]

In the family of God it is important that we learn to love because we are going to be spending a lot of time together in eternity! Brothers in the same family may not always see things the same way, but they must never forget they are still brothers. Paul Billheimer explained, "There is only one answer to division over non-essentials and that is growth in love, agape love, and it will never come any other way...God is more interested in love between members of His family than in the inerrancy of one's opinions."[27] Scripture says, *Love does not insist on its own rights or its own way.*[28] Biblical doctrine is certainly important, but in God's economy the more important thing is how well we demonstrate love to our brother, rather than how well we convince him of our "correct" view.

Love – The Perfect Bond of Unity (Part 2)

The whole body...grows and builds itself up in love. (Eph. 4:16)

What are we to do in times when we differ and are at an impasse with one another? There is only one thing we can do – we can choose to love! George Whitefield, who walked through some difficult times with other believers, offered this advice, "Why should we dispute, when there is no probability of convincing? …I am persuaded that the more the love of God is shed abroad in our hearts, the more all narrowness of spirit will subside and give way. Besides, so far as we are narrow-spirited we are uneasy. Prejudices, jealousies and suspicions make the soul miserable."[29]

Sometimes our differences as Christians will be so striking that it may be difficult to work closely with each other. Still, we can respect each other as joint-heirs with Christ and participate in cooperative endeavors. In our county, over fifty different churches have joined in several evangelistic efforts which have been very fruitful. Stephen Clark calls this *cooperative ecumenism*: "Cooperative ecumenism proceeds on the presupposition that Christians of various traditions do not have full agreement or unity, and we do not expect it for some time to come. In the meantime, however, we acknowledge the requirement that we should love one another as brothers and sisters, looking forward to the time when the Lord will make greater unity possible. We will cooperate wherever and whenever we can make Christ known and strengthen those who follow him. Our rule is that we will try to do whatever builds up. Sometimes the rule indicates not cooperating in certain ways, though we might personally be inclined to do so, because of the need to take into account others in our churches who do not see things our way and to avoid worsening relations between churches. Nonetheless, the spirit behind cooperative ecumenism urges us to lay down our lives for all those whom we recognize as true brothers and sisters in Christ, and with them to advance the cause of Christ."[30] Great advice!

Love – The Product of the Spirit

And hope does not disappoint us, because God has poured out his love into our hearts by the Holy Spirit, whom he has given us. (Romans 5:5)

We learn very quickly how lacking we are in our love for God and for each other. This reality should drive us to our knees as we beseech the Holy Spirit to manifest the love of God through us. Love is one of the characteristics of the *fruit of the Spirit.*[31] Scripture mentions *the love of the Spirit*[32] and *your love in the Spirit.*[33] We can never claim credit for being loving. The Holy Spirit will manifest through willing vessels a supernatural dimension of love we could never attain to ourselves.

The above verse says the love of God has been *poured out.* In the Greek, this verb is in the perfect tense which means that this action is a fact, a completed action.[34] God has poured out this love at a specific time in the past – when Christ's Spirit came into our hearts – and he has held nothing back. But the perfect tense also implies a present result: his love *still floods* our hearts.[35] Kenneth Wuest's translation says: *The love of God has been poured out in our hearts and still floods them through the agency of the Holy Spirit who was given to us.*[36] God has given us his love without reservation, and it is continually being poured into our lives.

With such a wonderful promise, we do not ever have to pray for love. If so, it would be like a man who lived on the bank of the mighty Mississippi River who prayed for water. Our only response is to draw upon God's supply, and God's endless supply has already been freely given. This is why the beginning of this verse says our *hope will not disappoint us.* Eugene Peterson has paraphrased it: *We're never left feeling short-changed. Quite the contrary – we can't round up enough containers to hold everything God generously pours into our lives through the Holy Spirit.*[37] Let us pray, "Lord, we do not love as we ought. But, we thank you for the abundant source of Holy Spirit love – poured continually in us and through us."

Love – The Motivation of Our Service (Pt. 1)

*If I gave everything I have to the poor and even sacrificed
my body, I could boast about it; but if I didn't love others,
I would have gained nothing. (1 Corinthians 13:3 NLT)*

Any service which truly honors the Lord will be motivated by
love in the heart of the believer. *Let all that you do be done in
love...*[38] Wrong motives which drive us to action may be very
subtle: to look good in the eyes of people, to satisfy a
conscience which tells us something is missing (our need to
know Christ, not more good works), or to alleviate a sense of
guilt (in not doing enough for God). Love, however, is the
only correct motive: *For the love of Christ controls and urges
and impels us...*[39] In Jesus' last conversation with Simon Peter,
he encouraged Peter in his pastoral call to *take care of my
sheep.*[40] Three times, however, he asked Peter, *"Do you love
me?"*[41] Jesus was emphasizing the heart motive necessary in
caring for his followers.

We must continually examine our motives as we work for
Jesus Christ. Martyn Lloyd-Jones commented, "The motive is
all important. We must work because of the love of Christ. We
must not work because we decide to do so or because we are
told that now we are converted we must 'get busy.' Our motive
must not be to fill churches again. That is a travesty of the New
Testament picture and manner, as is the whole idea of training
people to be witnesses and do personal evangelism....Once a
man has the love of Christ in his heart you need not train him to
witness; he will do it. He will know the power, the constraint,
the motive; everything is already there....The man who knows
the love of Christ in his heart can do more in one hour than the
busy type of man can do in a century. God forbid that we should
ever make activity an end in itself. Let us realize that the motive
must come first, and that the motive must ever be the love of
Christ."[42] Lord, search our hearts. In all that we do, may we be
motivated by your love.

Love – The Motivation of Our Service (Pt. 2)

...through love serve one another. (Galatians 5:13 NAS)

The correct order is love first, then service to others. Without love, we will likely only serve out of obligation and often have resentment lurking in our heart. In the story of "The Prodigal Son" (Luke 15), when the wayward son returns and is joyfully embraced by the father, the older brother becomes angry. *He answered his father, "Look! All these years I've been slaving for you and never disobeyed your orders. Yet you never gave me even a young goat so I could celebrate with my friends."*[43] Notice he does even call him, "Father," but just says, *"Look!..."* Yes, the older brother had served the father for many years, yet he was driven by selfish motives and did not consider his years of labor as joyful service, but rather as *slaving for you.*

We must always guard our hearts as we serve the Lord and others. If we are not motivated by love, James Garrett explained what the alternative might be. "The proud cannot serve; the insensitive don't think about it; the self-centered expect to be served. So many people who otherwise are fine citizens in the Kingdom do not have a servant's heart. They are easy to identify, when we are with them for a while. They never open the door for someone else. They are discourteous. They can watch people carrying things without offering to help (assuming that they have the health to do so). They can attend a church dinner and never help clean up the tables, without being asked. Nor would they be found in the kitchen helping to wash the dishes. They don't mind asking for others to do things.... They consider themselves too busy to spend time helping others with menial tasks. Often they are so goal-oriented that they, like the priest and Levite in the parable of the good Samaritan, rush along on the other side, rather than get side tracked in someone's need (Lk. 10:30ff)."[44]

O God, help our focus to be outward. May your "others-centered" love be rooted in our hearts.

Love – The Goal of Our Instruction

The goal of our instruction is love from a pure heart...
(1 Timothy 1:5 NAS)

Whenever we instruct others about the Christian faith, we must make sure we have the right motives. When our Lord Jesus taught, he was motivated by a deep love and compassion for his listeners: *When Jesus landed and saw a large crowd, he had compassion on them because they were like sheep without a shepherd. So he began teaching them many things.*[45] A teacher should not be motivated by his ego or a desire to have people enjoy listening to him. He must be humble and walk in the truth he is teaching others.[46] He must have a genuine interest in those he teaches. Some teachers might be quite gifted in public speaking and yet have a certain coldness, even aloofness, in their teaching.

Whenever we teach others, we tend to reproduce what we are. Scripture says, *Everyone who is fully trained will be like his teacher.*[47] Notice it says *be* like his teacher, not just think like his teacher. An instructor in the kingdom of God should not only be motivated by the love of God in his own heart, but also desire to see that love reproduced in the people he is instructing – both a love for God and love for others. *The goal of our instruction is love....*When our goal is not love, the apostle Paul said, *Some men, straying from these things, have turned aside to fruitless discussion, wanting to be teachers of the Law, even though they do not understand either what they are saying or the matters about which they make confident assertions.*[48]

We can say a lot of words and yet not really say anything significant. If we neglect the love of God, we may easily turn aside into *fruitless discussion.* One translation says, *Some people have gone astray into a wilderness of words.*[49] Another version says, *They don't know what they are talking about, even though they think they do.*[50] May our instruction be marked by humility and motivated by love, also directing people into a greater love of God.

Love – The Corollary of Wrath

Like the rest, we were by nature objects of wrath. But because of his great love for us, God, who is rich in mercy, made us alive with Christ even when we were dead in transgressions... (Ephesians 2:3-5)

The wrath of God is not opposed to the love of God; it is a necessary corollary. The Bible message is that as much as God is good to the one who trusts in Him, he is also terrible to the one who does not: *But the Lord is the true God; he is the living God, the eternal King. When he is angry, the earth trembles; the nations cannot endure his wrath.*[51] *God is a righteous judge, a God who expresses his wrath every day.*[52] If God indeed is *righteous* and perfectly *just,* then he cannot love sin. We can be thankful for the wrath of God, because if wrath were not an aspect of his justice, God would blink at sin and forever tolerate evil. We would never feel secure with such a God.

We cannot compare the wrath of God with the wrath of man. All of God's wrath is righteous and fully justified. Unlike us, there are not selfish reasons for his anger. God's anger does not occur because God is offended, irritated, or taken advantage of. Almighty God has no "fits of temper," or emotional outbursts when events go contrary to his will. When God displays his wrath, it is never to "get even" or "put us in our place." We can think of God's anger as *His consistent and predictable response to anything that is sinful and contrary to his good and holy nature.*

We ought to be glad that God is *slow to anger*[53] and his anger is always overshadowed by his love and favor: *His anger lasts only a moment, but His favor lasts a lifetime.*[54] As sinners, we deserve the wrath of God just as much as anyone on this earth. This is why Jesus' shed blood is the Good News for those who believe: *Since we have now been justified by his blood, how much more shall we be saved from God's wrath through him.*[55] Through His death, Jesus has *become a curse for us*[56] and now *delivers us from the wrath to come.*[57] Good News!

Pursuing Love

Where shall I go from your Spirit? Or where shall I flee from your presence? If I ascend to heaven, you are there! If I make my bed in Sheol, you are there! (Ps.139:7-8 ESV)

If we were to accurately record our history, we would discover it is a history of God pursuing us. We did not seek God; he sought us out.[58] We did not choose him; he chose us.[59] We did not first love him; he first loved us.[60] We can be especially thankful that God never gives up on us when we ignore him or walk contrary to his will: *Surely your goodness and unfailing love will pursue me all the days of my life…*[61] This is why backsliders can never feel completely comfortable in their sin; the verse at the top says we cannot escape his Spirit, and even if we "make our bed in hell," his presence is still there!

Donald Barnhouse wrote, "The pursuing love of God is the greatest wonder of the spiritual universe. We leave God in the heat of our own self-desire and run from His will because we want so much to have our own way. We get to a crossroads and look back in pride, thinking that we have outdistanced Him. Just as we are about to congratulate ourselves on our achievement of self-enthronement, we feel a touch on our arm and turn in that direction to find Him there. 'My child,' He says in great tenderness, 'I love you; and when I saw you running away from all that is good, I pursued you through a shortcut that love knows well, and awaited you here at the crossroads.' We have torn ourselves free from His grasp and rushed off again, through deepest woods and farthest swamp, and as we look back again, we are sure, this time, that we have succeeded in escaping from Him. But, once more, the touch of love is on our other sleeve and when we turn quickly we find that He is there, pleading with the eyes of love, and showing Himself once more to be the tender and faithful One, loving to the end. He will always say, 'My child, my name and nature are Love…and when you are tired of your running and your wandering, I will be there to draw you to myself once more.'"[62]

Undeserved Love

"Come now, let's settle this," says the LORD. "Though your sins are like scarlet, I will make them as white as snow. Though they are red like crimson, I will make them as white as wool." (Isaiah 1:18)

Recently, I talked to a new believer who felt it hard to accept that God loves him and has fully forgiven him. John Owen, the great Puritan writer, wrote, "The greatest sorrow and burden you can lay on the Father, the greatest unkindness you can do to him, is not to believe that he loves you."[63]

Charles Hodge said, "The great difficulty with many Christians is that they cannot persuade themselves that Christ (or God) loves them; and the reason they cannot feel confident of the love of God, is, that they know they do not deserve his love, on the contrary, that they are in the highest degree unlovely. How can the infinitely pure God love those who are defiled with sin, who are proud, selfish, discontented, ungrateful, disobedient? This, indeed, is hard to believe."[64]

Jerry Bridges added this insight, "But when our sense of guilt is taken away because our consciences are cleansed by the blood of Christ, we're freed up to love Him with all our hearts and souls and minds. We're motivated in a positive sense to love Him in this wholehearted way. Our love will be spontaneous in an outpouring of gratitude to Him and fervent desire to obey Him.

"So if we want to grow in our love for God and in the acceptable obedience that flows out of that love, we must keep coming back to the cross and the cleansing blood of Jesus Christ. That is why it is so important that we keep the gospel before us every day. Because we sin every day, and our consciences condemn us every day, we need the gospel every day."[65]

No, we do not deserve a single bit of the grace and goodness of God, but in his great love he freely bestows his wonderful gifts to those who come humbly to him.

Sacrificial Love (Part 1)

Be imitators of God, therefore as dearly loved children and live a life of love, just as Christ loved us and gave himself up for us as a fragrant offering and sacrifice to God. (Ephesians 5:1-2)

If we want to discover what God's love is like, we can look at the cross of Christ. *This is how we know what love is: Jesus Christ laid down his life for us.*[66] We may know love in a general sense, but we will never know love very deeply unless we see God's love in Christ – a love which gives itself away, that sacrifices itself even unto death. At the end of a popular war movie, *Saving Private Ryan*, we see the end of a battle in which several men lay dead after rescuing Private Ryan. As Ryan looks down at the leader of the rescue team, who has just expired, his face reflects deep emotion and thought: "This soldier gave his life for me." It is a small illustration and a pale comparison of a much greater sacrificial death – the Son of God who died to rescue you and me!

The first mention of love in the Bible is found in a story of sacrifice. Isaac is called Abraham's *only son...whom you love.*[67] Abraham, who had waited fifteen years for this promised son, was now asked to give up his precious gift. The offering of Isaac on the altar is a graphic picture of Calvary where God the Father offered his only Son whom He dearly loved. Sacrificial love is the greatest love: *No one has greater love than this, to lay down one's life for one's friends.*[68]

We may never be called to such sacrificial action as Abraham, but at times our love will be put to the test. This is especially true for those who have families. Are we willing to sacrifice our time, our personal interests, our goals, and our money, for the sake of love? At times we will have to *lay down our life* in order to love unselfishly with the love of Christ. A love which is not willing to make sacrifices is no love at all.

Sacrificial Love (Part 2)

They even did more than we had hoped, for their first action was to give themselves to the Lord and to us, just as God wanted them to do. 2 Corinthians 8:5 NLT

Sacrifices in ancient days implied the death of something, and in most cases it was a sacrificial animal to appease one's god. When we love sacrificially, it involves dying *to ourselves*; it means giving up our time, money, personal preferences, and all available resources to benefit some other person(s). Max Lucado told of a father who loved this way. "I know a father who, out of love for his son, spends each night in a recliner, never sleeping more than a couple of consecutive hours. A car accident paralyzed the teenager. To maintain the boy's circulation, therapists massage his limbs every few hours. At night the father takes the place of therapists. Though he's worked all day and will work again the next, he sets the alarm to wake himself every other hour until sunrise."[69]

Maybe we have not had to love in such an extreme manner, but most parents know something about sacrificial love. How many of us can remember getting up at all hours of the night to attend to a crying child? How many hours did we spend over eighteen years or more of transporting children and waiting patiently in their many activities? How about the money to rear a child? According the U.S. Department of Agriculture, a child born in 2010 will cost $226,900. Love costs something!

In a marriage, if there is no sacrificial love, it probably will not be much of a marriage. Husbands are exhorted *to love their wives, just as Christ loved the church and gave himself up for her...*[70] Husbands, consider just how much Christ selflessly loved the church – enough to be nailed to a cross. According to scholar and commentator Harold W. Hoehner, "This exhortation for husbands to their love wives is unique. It is not found in the Old Testament, rabbinic literature, or in the household codes of the Greco-Roman era."[71]

Brethren, by the help of God, may we love others sacrificially – as Christ has loved us.

Sacrificial Love (Part 3)

There is no greater love than to lay down one's life for one's friends. (John 15:13 NLT)

Once in a while we hear a touching story of a human being who voluntarily dies for another. On July 20, 2012, a gunman opened fire in an Aurora, Colorado movie theatre, killing twelve people. The world was touched as it later came to light that four of the men killed made the ultimate sacrifice as they protected their girlfriends from bullets. As moving as this and similar stories are, no example of sacrifice compares to the death of Jesus on the cross. James Boice explained,

"First, when we begin to reflect on Jesus's death, we recognize that his death was exceptional because *Jesus did not have to die.* That is not true of us. We are mortal. We must die. But Jesus was immortal and therefore did not have to die. He could have come into this world, performed a full and varied ministry, and then returned to heaven without ever having experienced death.

"Second, the death of the Lord Jesus Christ is exceptional in that *he knew he would die.* This is not usually the case when a mere man or woman gives his or her life for another...

"There is another area of Christ's exceptional love. The text says that we are Christ's friends. But if we think of this closely and honestly, we must recognize that, when the Lord Jesus gave his life for us, strictly speaking *we were not exactly his friends.* When he died for us, or when in eternity past he determined to die for us, he did so while we were yet enemies. It was 'while we were still sinners, [that] Christ died for us.'

"There is one more reason why the love of the Lord Jesus Christ for his friends, seen in his death for us, is superior to all human loves. The death of the Lord was a spiritual death, whereas ours, if we are Christians, is only physical....The truly horrible aspect of his death was his separation from the Father. when he was made sin for us and bore sin's punishment."[72]

Do we appreciate Him who made such sacrifice for us?

Giving Love (Part 1)

For God so loved the world that he gave his one and only Son, that whoever believes in him shall not perish but have eternal life. (John 3:16)

The love of God is a giving love: *God so loved the world that he gave....* Jesus Christ demonstrated to his disciples the giving nature of God: he gave them his peace in the midst of trouble.[73] He gave them his joy in the midst of sorrow.[74] He gave them the keys of the kingdom – the knowledge of the gospel and power to open doors of faith to the very ends of the earth.[75] Jesus even gave them his own glory which he enjoyed in eternity with the Father, so that they might walk in unity and testify of the love of God.[76] Then, in the ultimate act of love, he gave his very own life on the cross.

The love of God is neither stingy nor conditional. God is much more willing to give than we are to ask. Annie Johnson Flint very aptly described God's giving love:

> His love has no limit, His grace has no measure,
> His power no boundary known unto men;
> For out of His infinite riches in Jesus
> He giveth and giveth and giveth again.[77]

Love is personal and must have an object to give itself away to. It would be difficult to grow close to God and be a hermit. Some folks may naturally prefer isolated, self-contained lives, but the love of God will change that. We will have many opportunities in which we can choose to give our time, attention, and experience. Some parents might be good providers and feel this is demonstrating their love. Most children, however, would tend to spell love, "T-I-M-E."

Paul describes the giving of the Corinth believers as *the proof of your love.*[78] This is true whether we are giving of ourselves or our money. We should avoid being stingy – simply because God is not stingy toward us! And besides, *Whatever measure you use to give – large or small – will be used to measure what is given back to you.*[79] Let us demonstrate our love in a lifestyle of generous giving.

Giving Love (Part 2)

Husbands, go all out in your love for your wives, exactly as Christ did for the church – a love marked by giving, not getting. (Ephesians 5:25 The Message)

Over the years I have seen some wonderful marriages and some miserable marriages. The difference usually lies in the depth to which both husband and wife allow Christ to live through them in selfless, giving ways – constantly seeking the other's best interests above their own. Dr. James Dobson said that one verse in the Bible "contains more wisdom than most marriages combined. If heeded, it could virtually eliminate divorce from the catalog of human experience."[80] The verse is Philippians 2:3: *Do nothing out of selfish ambition or vain conceit, but in humility consider others better than yourselves.*

Timothy Keller, in his excellent book, *The Meaning of Marriage*, discussed how some people simply live together, avoid a legal marriage, and question why a piece of paper has anything to do with love. Keller responded, "But when the Bible speaks of love, it measures it primarily not by how much you want to receive but by how much you are willing to give of yourself to someone. How much are you willing to lose for the sake of this person? How much of your freedom are you willing to forsake? How much of your precious time, emotion, and resources are you willing to invest in this person? And for that, the marriage vow is not just helpful but it is even a test. In so many cases, when one person says to another, 'I love you, but let's not ruin it by getting married,' that person really means, 'I don't love you enough to close off all my options. I don't love you enough to give myself to you that thoroughly.' To say, 'I don't need a piece of paper to love you' is basically to say, 'My love for you has not reached the marriage level.'"[81]

Our love in a marriage must be a *giving* love – enough to commit ourselves totally to our partner for life, constantly willing to lay down our self-interests for the good of our mate. May we have a love that is *marked by giving, not getting.*

Future Love

For this reason a man will leave his father and mother and be united to his wife, and they will become one flesh. (Genesis 2:24)

A Christian marriage occurs when a man and woman make a commitment – before God and witnesses – to grow together as husband and wife in the love of Christ. None of us has all it will take for a great marriage the day we make our wedding vows. This verse, however, implies the process in marriage: *they will become one flesh.* Therefore, we always keep the big picture of marriage in mind. In pre-marital counseling I always tell the couple that if there are no "fireworks" on the honeymoon, not to worry – they will have a lifetime enjoying the process of learning how to love each other. (One friend of mine was physically sick on his honeymoon night.) Therefore, love must never just focus on the *present,* but also live for the future.

Timothy Keller wrote, "Years ago I attended a wedding in which the couple wrote their own vows. They said something like this: "I love you, and I want to be with you.".... They were expressing their current love for each other, and that was fine and moving. But that is not what marriage vows are. That is not how a covenant works. Wedding vows are not a declaration of present love but a mutually binding promise of future love. A wedding should not be primarily a celebration of how loving you feel now – that can be safely assumed. Rather in a wedding you stand up before God, your family, and all the main institutions of society, and you promise to *be* loving, faithful, and true to the other person in the future, regardless of the undulating internal feelings or external circumstances."[82]

Many a couple has spent multi-thousands of dollars on an elaborate wedding; then, within a few years they have "lost their feelings" and are finished. The temptation to call it quits can come to any couple, but true love never focuses just on the present; it is a commitment for the future – for the long haul. *Love never gives up, never loses faith, is always hopeful, and endures through every circumstance.*[83]

Demonstrative Love

But God demonstrates his own love for us in this: While we were still sinners, Christ died for us. (Romans 5:8)

God did not give us love as a theory to consider or a vague idea about which to marvel. God's love was demonstrated in a very specific and personal manner – his Son, Jesus, dying on the cross. When the Bible says, *God is love,*[84] it does not leave love as an abstract concept; the Scripture immediately follows with this statement: *This is how God showed his love among us: He sent his one and only Son into the world...as an atoning sacrifice for our sins.*[85] The cross was the crowning proof, the ultimate demonstration of the love of God.

Believers will have opportunities as well to demonstrate the love of God. In her book, *Living with Love,* Josephine Robertson tells of a youthful clergyman, the Reverend Joe Roberts, who arrived by stagecoach in a blizzard to minister to the Indians of Wyoming. Soon after his arrival the son of the chief was shot by a soldier in a brawl, and the chief vowed to kill the first white man he met. Thinking this could lead to a long, bloody feud, Roberts decided to take action. Seeking out the tepee, fifteen miles away in the mountains, Roberts stood outside and called the chief's name. When the chief appeared, Roberts said, "I know that the other white men have families, but I am alone. Kill me instead." Amazed, the chief motioned him inside his tent, where he asked, "How do you have so much courage?" Joe Roberts told him about Christ: His death, His teachings. When Joe left, the chief of the Shoshones had renounced his vow to kill and resolved to be a Christian. He had seen love in action.[86]

Every person who calls himself a Christian must be prepared to demonstrate love in very tangible and practical ways. We should have plenty of opportunities in our homes, our work places, and the neighborhoods where God has placed us. Unless love becomes visible, it is not love at all.

Compassionate Love

Because of the LORD's great love we are not consumed,
for his compassions never fail....Though he brings grief,
he will show compassion, so great is his unfailing love.
(Lamentations 3:22,32)

God's love will be marked by compassion. If he were not compassionate toward us, we would feel uncertain of his favor toward us, and we would probably find it difficult to trust him. In his book, *The God Who Loves,* John MacArthur wrote, "We must understand that there is nothing in any sinner that compels God's love. He does not love us because we are lovable. He is not merciful to us because we in any way deserve His mercy. We are despicable, vile sinners who if not saved by the grace of God will be thrown on the trash heap of eternity, which is hell. We have no intrinsic value, no intrinsic worth – there's nothing in us to love.

"I recently overheard a radio talk-show psychologist attempting to give a caller an ego-boost: 'God loves you for what you are. You must see yourself as someone special. After all, you are special to God.'

"But that misses the point entirely. God *does not* love us 'for what we are.' He loves us *in spite of what we are*. He does not love us because we are special. Rather, it is only His love and grace that give our lives any significance at all. That may seem like a doleful perspective to those raised in a culture where self-esteem is elevated to the supreme virtue. But it is, after all, precisely what Scripture teaches: 'We have sinned like our fathers, we have committed iniquity, we have behaved wickedly' (Ps. 106:6). 'All of us have become like one who is unclean, and all our righteous deeds are like a filthy garment; and all of us wither like a leaf, and our iniquities, like the wind, take us away' (Isa. 64:6).

"God loves because He is love; love is essential to who He is. Rather than viewing His love as proof of something worthy in us, we ought to be humbled by it."[87]

Inviting Love

Listen! My lover is knocking: "Open to me, my sister, my darling, my dove, my flawless one..." (Song of Songs 5:2)

Jesus, as the "Lover of our soul," always takes the initiative. He is constantly extending us an invitation – *"Come unto me"*[88] – even though we sometimes are reluctant to respond. Several biblical invitations are specifically directed toward those who are spiritually thirsty and hungry, e.g., *"Come, all you who are thirsty, come to the waters; and you who have no money, come, buy and eat!"*[89] Christ's tender, inviting love for those *who are hungry* is expressed quite well in this poem.

LOVE
By George Herbert[90]

Love bade me welcome; yet my soul drew back,
    Guilty of dust and sin.
But quick-eyed Love, observing me grow slack
    From my first entrance in,
Drew nearer to me, sweetly questioning
    If I lacked anything.

"A guest," I answered, "worthy to be here."
    Love said, "You shall be he."
"I, the unkind, ungrateful? Ah, my dear,
    I cannot look on Thee."
Love took my hand, and smiling, did reply,
    "Who made the eyes but I?"

"Truth, Lord, but I have marred them: let my shame
    Go where it doth deserve."
"And know you not," says Love, "Who bore the blame?"
    "My dear, then I will serve."
"You must sit down," says Love, "and taste my meat."
    So I did sit and eat.

Delightful Love

As for the saints who are in the land, they are the glorious ones in whom is all my delight. (Psalm 16:3)

It may seem an incredible thing to us that God not only loves us, but actually delights in us! Yet, our relationship between us and our heavenly Father can be compared to our children and their earthly father. Even though raising two boys had its challenges at times, our sons have always been a great delight to my wife and me. Even now that they are grown men and both living some distance away, any time they return home it is still a great delight. The same is true with our grandchildren. They are quite active and at times may misbehave as all children do. Yet, whenever they come to see us, it is delightful.

Sometimes we view our heavenly Father as being some-what unhappy with our performance or maybe we think he avoids us because of certain deficiencies in our lives. True, we are not to live carelessly and are instructed to *find out what pleases the Lord.*[91] However, consider God's amazing attitude toward us:

- *For the LORD takes delight in his people; he crowns the humble with salvation.* (Ps. 149:4)
- *Never again will you be called "The Forsaken City" or "The Desolate Land." Your new name will be "The City of God's Delight" and "The Bride of God," for the LORD delights in you and will claim you as his bride.* (Is. 62:4 NLT)
- *The LORD your God is with you, he is mighty to save. He will take great delight in you, he will quiet you with his love, he will rejoice over you with singing.* (Zeph. 3:17)
- *He...rescued me because he delighted in me.* (Ps. 18:19)
- *The LORD detests the sacrifice of the wicked, but he delights in the prayers of the upright.* (Prov. 15:8 NLT)

This last verse is particularly encouraging. We often feel our prayers are feeble or ineffective, but if our hearts are sincere, our prayers are actually God's "delight." Incredible!

Individual Love (Part One)

Therefore, my brethren, individually loved ones, and individually and passionately longed for...be standing firm in the Lord. (Phil. 4:1 Kenneth Wuest's translation)

Someone once said, "God counts by ones." He knows us each personally; he knows us by name; and he loves us *individually.* St. Augustine said, "God loves each of us as if there was only one of us to love."[92] God is not a busy executive who has secretaries setting appointments for us to talk to him. Even though he is active in running the universe, he does not keep glancing at a watch or cell-phone schedule to see if he can "fit us in." No, the Lord gives us his undivided and personal attention when we come to him.

When Jesus encountered children, the Son of God was not too important to ignore them. The disciples thought the children might bother Jesus, but *The Amplified Bible* says, *And He took them [the children up one by one] in His arms and (fervently invoked a) blessing, placing His hands upon them.*[93] Jesus did not just invoke a general blessing on the group of children, but he picked them up and blessed them *one by one.*

We too will have opportunities to show love *one by one.* Some Christians look for large groups to minister to, but we will often need to start with *one.* Rees Howells, a British intercessor and founder of the Bible College of Wales, learned to be faithful in ministering to just one. In his early years as a Christian, Rees met a young man, Will Battery, who was dirty and unshaven, alcoholic, and stricken with meningitis. Even though Rees naturally had no desire to be with this man, the Holy Spirit birthed a supernatural love in his heart, and he began spending time with Will, making him his friend. Rees stated at this time that he had more joy in spending time with this one needy man, than at church in the company of other believers. He said, "I started at the bottom and loved just one; and if you love one, you can love many; and if many, you can love all."[94] May we, too, be willing to start by loving just one.

Individual Love (Part Two)

The shepherd...calls his own sheep by name... (John 10:3)

The analogy of the shepherd relating to his sheep reveals much about God's *individual* love and care for each of us. In his book, *Manners and Customs of Bible Lands,* Fred Wright explained,

"Today, the eastern shepherd delights to give names to certain of his sheep, and if his flock is not too large, all of his sheep may be given names. He knows them by means of certain individual characteristics. He names one: 'Pure White'; another, 'Striped'; another, 'Gray-eared.' All this indicates the tender affection which he has for every one of his flock...

"The shepherd is deeply interested in every single one of his flock. Some of them may be given pet names because of incidents connected with them. They are usually counted each evening as they enter the fold, but sometimes the shepherd dispenses with the counting, for he is able to feel the absence of anyone of his sheep. With one sheep gone, something is felt to be missing from the appearance of the entire flock. One shepherd in the Lebanon district was asked if he always counted his sheep each evening. He replied in the negative, and then was asked how then he knew if all his sheep were present. This was his reply: 'Master, if you were to put a cloth over my eyes, and bring me any sheep and only let me put hands on its face, I could tell in a moment if it was mine or not.'

"When H. R. P. Dickson visited the desert Arabs, he witnessed an event that revealed the amazing knowledge which some of them have of their sheep. One evening, shortly after dark, an Arab shepherd began to call out one by one the names of his fifty-one mother sheep, and was able to pick out each one's lamb, and restore it to its mother to suckle. This was done in darkness, and in the midst of the noise coming from the ewes crying for their lambs, and the lambs crying for their mothers. But no Oriental shepherd ever had a more intimate knowledge of his sheep than Jesus our great Shepherd has of those who belong to His flock."[95] He *calls his own sheep by name.*

Amazing Love

I pray that you...grasp how wide and long and high and deep is the love of Christ... (Ephesians 3:17-18)

William MacDonald has written an excellent description of God's amazing love:

"Love is the conquering power in a world of hatred, strife and selfishness. It can do what no other virtue can do, and, in that sense, is the queen of the graces. Love repays abuse with kindness. It prays for mercy for its executioners. It acts unselfishly when all around are clamoring for their rights. It gives until it can give no more.

"An Indian was driving his elephant along the street, goading it continually to increase its speed. Suddenly the steel goad slipped from his hand, tumbling with loud clanging on the pavement. The elephant swung around, picked up the goad with its trunk, and held it out to the master. Love is like that.

"In one of Aesop's fables, there was a contest between the sun and the wind over who could make a man remove his coat. The wind blew furiously, but the more it blew, the more he pulled the coat tightly around him. Then the sun shone down on him and he took off his coat. It changed him through warmth. Love is like that.

"Sir Walter Scott once threw a stone at a stray dog with such power and accuracy that it broke the dog's leg. As Scott stood there remorsefully, the dog limped up to him and licked the hand that had thrown the rock. Love is like that.

"Stanton hurled bitter invective at Lincoln, calling him a 'low cunning clown' and 'the original gorilla.' He said that anyone would be foolish to go to Africa for a gorilla when there was one in Springfield. Lincoln turned the other cheek. In fact, he later appointed Stanton as War Minister, insisting he was the most qualified man for the job. When Lincoln was shot, Stanton stood by his lifeless body, wept openly and said, 'There lies the greatest ruler of men the world has ever seen.' Lincoln had conquered by turning the other cheek. Love is like that."[96]

Immeasurable Love

I want you to know all about Christ's love, although it is too wonderful to be measured... (Ephesians 3:19 Contemporary English Version)

Two of the most popular gospel musicians and prolific songwriters in recent times are Bill and Gloria Gaither. Bill was once asked by John MacArthur what he believed to be the greatest Christian lyrics ever written – aside from the inspired Psalms. Without hesitation, Gaither began quoting the words from F. M. Lehman's song, "The Love of God."[97]

> The love of God is greater far
> Than time or pen can ever tell,
> It goes beyond the highest star,
> And reaches to the lowest hell.
> The guilty pair, bowed down with care,
> God gave his son to win;
> His erring child he reconciled
> And pardoned from his sins.
>
> Could we with ink the ocean fill,
> And were the skies of parchment made,
> Were every stalk on earth a quill,
> And every man a scribe by trade,
> To write the love of God above
> Would drain the ocean dry,
> Nor could the scroll contain the whole,
> Though stretched from sky to sky.
>
> O love of God, how rich and pure!
> However measureless and strong!
> It shall forever endure –
> The saints' and angels' song.

Stop and consider this *boundless* love. Christ's love drove him to live as a man, to become a curse for us, to be persecuted by his own creation, and to suffer, bleed, and die on a cross for us. Thank God his great love is not exhaustible and confined!

Knowing Love

> *...that you...may be able...to know the love of Christ which passes knowledge...(Ephesians 3:16-19 NKJV)*

How can we *really* know the love of Christ? Is it possible we are only fooling ourselves? Maybe God is not personal or maybe he does not even exist? How can we know for sure? When I am going through tough times, why should I think that God still loves me? How can we be *assured* of the love of God? First, we can look at the evidences of God in all his creation. In his creation, God's invisible attributes – including his love – are clearly seen, so that mankind is without excuse.[98] We can look at how he has provided us with a perfect planet to sustain life, or look at a most wonderfully created human body, or look at the marvelous ways God even loves and provides for animals. His great love and care is evident everywhere!

Second, as the children's song says, "Jesus loves me, this I know, for the Bible tells me so..." In the inspired Scriptures, we see the love of God revealed to his creation, and its highest expression is seen in Christ being manifest in human flesh. As we read the Bible we discover that *God so loved the world...*

Third, the Holy Spirit can confirm God's love to our hearts. One of the functions of the Holy Spirit is to make real to us concepts that we might only know intellectually. He brings a deep assurance about what we believe. *But the Counselor, the Holy Spirit, whom the Father will send in my name, will teach you all things and will remind you of everything I have said to you.*[99] *The Spirit himself testifies with our spirit that we are God's children.*[100] I cannot convince you that God loves you, but the Holy Spirit can reaffirm to you the reality of God's love for each of his children. I personally know that God loves me – not by any feelings or what anyone has said, but ultimately because of what I have appreciated in the amazing created world, read about in holy Scripture, seen in the person of Jesus Christ, and confirmed by the Holy Spirit to my own heart. I pray that you, too, would have such assurance in knowing the love of God.

Wedded Love

He has taken me to the banquet hall, and his banner over me is love...I belong to my lover, and his desire is for me. (Song of Songs 2:4; 7:10)

In the Song of Songs, we have a beautiful love song about a bridegroom, most likely King Solomon, pursuing his bride. This book describes such a personal and passionate love the bridegroom has for his bride, that it could be embarrassing for some readers. The book, however, seems also to have a spiritual purpose – to provide a glimpse of King Jesus, a bridegroom deeply in love, pursuing his bride, the church. Charles Spurgeon said, "We see the Savior's face in almost every book of the Bible, but here we see his heart and feel his love to us."[101]

The wedded love Christ has for his bride – his followers – is incredible, beyond our comprehension. In referring to the king, the Song of Songs mentions *the day of his wedding, the day his heart rejoiced.*[102] I can remember the day of my wedding as I stepped into the front of a church and soon looked up at the end of the center aisle as my beautiful, smiling bride began to make her way slowly toward me. My heart was racing a mile-a-minute. I felt like leaping and shouting! The joy was incredible! Being united to this woman in marriage was the happiest day of my life! Knowing such human responses, can we imagine our Lord Jesus *actually rejoicing* – being extremely thrilled about his bride? When we see the condition of the Lord's church, we may tend to be negative and pessimistic. But, consider these other statements the bridegroom makes: *All beautiful you are, my darling; there is no flaw in you...How delightful is your love, my sister, my bride! How much more pleasing is your love than wine...*[103] Because our Lord sees us as a bride redeemed by his own blood, he makes an amazing statement: *there is no flaw in you.* In the day when we are finally joined together, our Lord will receive *a glorious church, without a spot or wrinkle or any other blemish.*[104] Therefore, as the bride of Christ, we should never doubt his love for us. We can say, *"I am my lover's and my lover is mine."*[105]

Verbal Love

Your words show what is in your hearts...(Matt. 12:34 CEV)

I have read many letters penned by soldiers in the Civil War, expressing their love to their wives and families. One such letter, penned by Sullivan Ballou, was written to his wife as he realized the great peril he faced in the looming clash. He wrote, "If I do not return, my dear Sarah, never forget how much I loved you, nor that when my last breath escapes me on the battlefield, it will whisper your name."[106]

Most men are probably not this good with words expressed toward their wives, but love in our hearts must be verbally expressed. One man supposedly told his wife, "When we got married thirty years ago, I told you I loved you. If I ever change my mind, I'll let you know!" Although not all husbands are that insensitive, husbands as well as wives can certainly grow in the way we verbally express our love.

- Does your wife look nice? Tell her she looks great!
- Did you wife cook a tasty meal? Tell her how much you appreciate it. Be specific in your compliments.
- Does your husband work hard to pay the bills? Tell him how grateful you are.

We can develop our thanksgiving to God and people with thoughtful, verbal appreciation. Gratitude which is not expressed is ingratitude. We should never assume someone feels appreciated if we say nothing. Watchman Nee related a sad but true story that underscores this point. "In England there was a Christian couple. The husband never told his wife that she had done something well. Naturally this woman was always worrying as to whether she had failed as a wife and as a Christian. She worried herself to tuberculosis and to death. While she was dying her husband said to her, 'I do not know what to do if you die, for you have done so much good. What will become of this family if you die?' 'Why did you not say this earlier?' asked the wife. 'I always feel I am no good. I blame myself all the time. You have never once said, 'Well done.'"[107] Let us consider who we might need to love *verbally*.

Extravagant Love

David longed for water and said, "Oh, that someone would get me a drink of water from the well near the gate of Bethlehem!" So the Three broke through the Philistine lines, drew water from the well near the gate of Bethlehem and carried it back to David. But he refused to drink it... (1 Chronicles 11:17-18)

In this account, king David just mentioned in passing his love for the water from Bethlehem. His three key soldiers, because of their great love for their king, risked their very lives to fetch this water. When they returned, David was so overwhelmed with their love and devotion to him, he refused to drink it. Their action is an excellent picture of extravagant love – love that goes beyond what is expected or what is usual.

In the New Testament, a woman came to Jesus, as he was reclining at a dinner table, and poured very expensive perfume on his head. *When the disciples saw this, they were indignant. "Why this waste?" they asked. "This perfume could have been sold at a high price and the money given to the poor."*[108] Jesus rebuked the disciples and commended the woman. She was the only person present who was doing anything extraordinary, as she showed *extravagant* love toward her Savior.

Is your love ever *extravagant*? Do you worship God with *enthusiasm*? Do you ever *go an extra mile* to show love toward some person? Is your love for your mate constrained to the usual and expected, or do you ever do anything *out-of-the ordinary*? Are you just stuck in your humdrum, predictable routines, or do you ever *surprise* your mate with a loving action? How about love for a parent or grandparent? Beside the routine birthday gifts and Father's or Mother's Day cards, do you ever show love in some *unusual* or *unexpected* manner?

We can be thankful God's love for us is *extravagant*. His love does not come in some tightly-wrapped, small package. His gifts of grace are *abundant*. His mercy is *new every morning*. His love is *ever growing* in our hearts. May we too, be characterized by this *extravagant* love. Let us ask the Lord to give us creative ways to show such love to those around us.

Merciful Love

But God, who is rich in mercy, out of the great love
with which he loved us... (Ephesians 2:4 NRSV)

During the Napoleonic Wars, a young, battle-weary French soldier fell asleep while on guard duty. He was court-martialed, found guilty, and sentenced to death. His widowed mother somehow arranged an audience with the Emperor Napoleon. Falling prostrate at his feet, she begged for her son's life to be spared, explaining he was her only child and her sole means of support. Napoleon grew weary of her pleas. "Madam, your son does not deserve mercy. He deserves to die," he said coldly. The mother immediately replied, "Of course, sire, you are right. That's why I am asking you to show mercy on him. If he were deserving, it wouldn't be mercy." Napoleon was so touched by the logic of her statement that he pardoned the soldier.[109]

Mercy involves a giving of oneself to another when there is no obligation to give. God did not have to provide animal skins for Adam and Eve to cover their nakedness. God did not have to wait for more than a thousand years to send the flood to destroy vile and wicked men. God did not have to rescue Lot out of Sodom before it was consumed by heaven-sent fire. God did not have to pardon king David's great sins of adultery and murder. God did not have to restrain His hand when boastful men nailed the hands and feet of His precious Son to a cross.

If we love people with Christ's love, then we will have opportunity to be merciful – to be patient and kind to those who do not deserve it. Fenelon said, "The love of God...knows how to love them patiently with all their faults, and does not insist upon finding in our friends what God has not placed there.... The love of God never looks for perfection in created beings. It knows that it dwells with Him alone; and, as it never expects perfection, it is never disappointed."[110] May our love be rich in mercy.

Reaffirming Love

I urge you, therefore, to reaffirm your love for him.
(2 Corinthians 2:8)

In the Corinthian church a man had come under church discipline, and the entire process brought much sorrow to the hearts of the other believers. Some commentators speculate that this is the same man in Paul's earlier letter to the Corinthians who had fallen into sexual immorality and had been properly judged and expelled from the church. [111] Apparently the man later repented and then Paul urged the church *to forgive and comfort him, so that he will not be overwhelmed by excessive sorrow.*[112]

There are times in which we need to reaffirm our love to fellow Christians. The Greek word for *reaffirm* is a legal word used to ratify, validate, or enforce a legal action.[113] In this case at Corinth, it would likely have been a public meeting in which the sinner confessed and repented of his wrongdoing, and the church leaders then declared the man's sins forgiven. The church was urged to embrace the man as a brother once again and, in love, to restore fellowship with him. This type of situation is the practical outworking of Jesus' instruction to his disciples, *"If you forgive anyone his sins, they are forgiven; if you do not forgive them, they are not forgiven."*[114]

Only God can forgive sins,[115] but as God's representatives we may pronounce a person forgiven in the name of the Lord. We may ratify or validate on earth what has already been accomplished in heaven.[116] When a fallen brother genuinely repents, this public action of forgiveness and reaffirmation is a powerful way of demonstrating the love of God.

There will be opportunities for each of us to reaffirm our love for others. A husband may need to reaffirm his love for his offended wife. A parent may need to reaffirm his love for an estranged child. We must not presume that those close to us always sense our love; we must verbally reaffirm it.

Sovereign Love

The Lord did not set his affection on you and choose you because you were more numerous than other peoples, for you were the fewest of all peoples. But it was because the Lord loved you... (Deut. 7:7-8)

The longer we walk with God, the more we realize that there is not one thing we can boast about concerning our salvation. The fact is – God took the initiative. *This is love: not that we loved God, but that he loved us and sent his Son as an atoning sacrifice for our sins.*[117] Today the evangelical church places a lot of emphasis on "accepting Christ." We say, "Ask Jesus into your heart." "Give your life to Jesus." "Open the door of your heart to Jesus." There is a place for such invitations, but we must not over-emphasize what we do for God to the neglect of what he has done for us. *You did not choose me, but I chose you...*[118]

We did Almighty God no favors when we surrendered to his call. We did not just suddenly start loving Jesus one day. *There is none who understands; There is none who seeks after God.*[119] We did not have one ounce of love in our hearts for God before he drew us to himself and placed such a desire within us. The further we go in this Christian journey, the greater we realize the depth of God's love for us – that he chose us before we were born, that he considered us in his eternal plans, that he took the initiative in loving us, that he patiently waited for us while we went our own way, and that he relentlessly pursued us.

Mary Shekleton wrote of God's sovereign love:

I am an empty vessel – not one thought
Or look of love I ever to Thee brought;
Yet I may come, and come again to Thee
With this, the empty sinner's only plea—
   Thou lovest me.[120]

Inseparable Love

For I am convinced that neither death nor life, neither angels nor demons, neither the present or future, nor any powers, neither height nor depth, nor anything else in all creation, will be able to separate us from the love of God that is in Christ Jesus our Lord. (Romans 8:38-39)

Many a martyr has testified to these encouraging words. Probably every Christian has at times questioned the reality of God, or wondered if He is really there. In times of great perplexity or suffering we may be tempted to ask if He really cares. The Word of God is clear – no matter what comes our way, God *does* still love us and will do so for all eternity.

Elsewhere the Scripture says, *"Never will I leave you; never will I forsake you."*[121] In the Greek, there are three negatives before the word *forsake,* accurately translated in *The Amplified Bible* as follows: *"I will not, I will not, I will not in any degree leave you helpless nor forsake nor let you down (relax my hold on you)! Assuredly not!"*

If any man might have had reason to question the love of God, king David certainly would have. As a young man he was anointed by the priest, Samuel, to be king of Israel. Then, during the next dozen years of his life he stayed in the home of a madman, king Saul, and then had a more extended time in the wilderness. David was running for his life and living in caves with a rag-tag group of distressed and discontented followers. David lost the comforts of home, his wife, and his closest friend. Yet, during this time, he never became embittered or questioned the love of God. He could have become angry, "But God, I thought you chose me to be king!" Instead, in the midst of his hard circumstances, he wrote many positive words about God's love: *"I love you, O Lord, my strength...my deliverer..."*[122] *"I have trusted the Lord...for your love is ever before me."*[123] *"The Lord's unfailing love surrounds the man who trusts in him."*[124] *"Because your love is better than life, my lips will glorify you."*[125] David personally knew the truth and we can too – that *nothing* can separate us from God's love!

Quiet Love

The Lord your God is in your midst,
A victorious warrior.
He will exult over you with joy,
He will be quiet in his love... (Zephaniah 3:17 NAS)

There will be times when God seems *quiet in his love* toward us. Even though we will know deep inside that He *does* love us, all evidence may seem to be contrary to that fact. His love may seem distant from us. It may seem that heaven has bypassed us. We may even begin to question his concern for us.

In times of God's *quiet love,* we must walk by faith and remind ourselves, as did the prophet Zephaniah, of these facts:

- *God is in our midst.* We may not feel his love, but he is still *Immanuel*, God with us. Jesus said the Holy Spirit would not only live with us, but that he *will be in you.*[126] He then promised, *I will not leave you as orphans; I will come to you.*[127] God's love for us is not a flighty thing that comes and goes; *Surely I will be with you always, to the very end of the age.*[128]

- *God is a victorious warrior.* Our Lord Jesus won the victory for us on the cross of Calvary. When he declared, *"It is finished,"* it was a complete victory in every regard – final and finished for all eternity. Therefore, we no longer have to fight for victory, but rather fight *from* victory – his victory. Even if God's love seems removed, his triumph stands sure for his children. *Thanks be to God, who always leads us in triumphal procession in Christ*[129] .... *He gives us the victory through our Lord Jesus Christ.*[130]

- *God will exult over us with joy.* What a marvelous statement – that God actually rejoices over us! One version says, *He will take great delight in you.*[131] Even when we feel in a low spiritual state, we can pray, and amazingly, *the prayer of the upright is his delight.*[132] Therefore, let us never question the love of God, even when he is quiet. Let us hold on in faith. God is in our midst; he is the Victor; and, he takes great delight in us.

Chastening Love

My son, do not despise the chastening of the LORD,
Nor be discouraged when you are rebuked by Him;
For whom the LORD loves He chastens,
And scourges every son whom He receives.
(Hebrews 12:5-6 NKJV)

Any earthly father who truly loves his children will at times discipline them.[133] The same is true of our Heavenly Father. Without his chastening, we would be *illegitimate children and not true sons.*[134] His purpose in discipline is not to bring harm or to make our lives miserable; *God disciplines us for our good, that we may share in his holiness.*[135] If we realize that God is only interested in our good, then we will never resent his chastisements. We should look upon them as "friends" because they help deliver us from the old, self-life which stands in the way of God's purposes. John Calvin shared much insight on this subject: "The scourges by which God chastises his children are testimonies of his love....All the chastisements which God by his own hand inflicts on us have this as the object – to heal us of our vices."[136] For example, suppose we are overly dependent upon people for our spiritual support. God may chastise us by allowing us to be disappointed in such people. If this happens, we must not grow resentful. Instead, we should see the hand of the Lord weaning us, so that we can be more dependent upon Him alone.

Perhaps a man has great anxiety about money and always worries about the future. God may chastise this man by allowing him to have a financial setback. Instead of adding more worry, the Holy Spirit will encourage the man to grow in his trust in the Father. If this man fails to listen to the Lord, then he may soon find himself facing another financial trial. God may send chastisements when we are headed for spiritual danger. Calvin said, "Chastisements cure us of the fearfully dangerous disease of apostasy."[137] None of God's children will be immune from his loving chastisement, but we may escape some of them if we learn from his word and listen to his voice.

Higher Love

For as high as the heavens are above the earth, so great is his love for those who fear him. (Ps. 103:12)

Derek Prince observed that in this passage the psalmist David "...is trying to picture the immensity of God's love and God's mercy and he compares it to the height of heaven. Probably today we are in a better position to understand that than when David wrote those words, for astronomers have spoken to us of countless millions of galaxies all far greater than the galaxy which our sun is part of, and they have given statements and figures that no human mind can fully comprehend of the dimensions of the heavens. And David says that just as great as those dimensions of the heavens, so great is God's love and mercy towards them that fear Him."[138]

In 1743, John Brine wrote of God's higher love: "No tongue can fully express the infinitude of God's love, or any mind comprehend it: It 'passeth knowledge' (Eph 3:19). The most extensive ideas that a finite mind can frame about Divine love are infinitely below its true nature. The heaven is not so far above the earth as the goodness of God is beyond the most raised conceptions which we are able to form of it. It is an ocean which swells higher than all the mountains of opposition ....It is the fountain from which flows all necessary good to all those who are interested in it."[139]

Recently I read two accounts of mothers whose children were brutally murdered, but who discovered supernatural love in their hearts toward their killers. Such love enabled each mother to visit the criminal, to forgive him, and in one case even to develop an ongoing, meaningful friendship. How incredible! How high is the love of God! Even though we cannot adequately conceive of such a high level of love, and we are so feeble in our attempts to display it, God will enlarge our capacity for love. *God's love has flooded our inmost heart through the Holy Spirit he has given us.*[140] We can go higher in our love!

Extensive Love

And I pray that you, being rooted and established in love, may have power, together with all the saints, to grasp how wide and long and high and deep is the love of Christ, and to know this love that surpasses knowledge...(Eph. 3:17-19)

John Phillips explained how extensive God's love really is:

- How *long* is God's love? When did his love for us start? When we got saved? When we were born? When he created Adam? No, he loved us before the world was created; He had us in mind from eternity past. *He chose us in Him before the foundation of the world, that we should be holy and without blame before Him in love.* (Eph. 1:4).

- How *wide* is God's love? God's love is not narrow. *God so loved the world...* (Jn. 3:16) He loves the harlot and the Pharisee. He loves the Jew and the Gentile. He loves the prodigal son and the bitter elder brother. He loves Judas as much as he loved John. How wide is his forgiveness that is available to all men? *As far as the east is from the west, so far has he removed our transgressions from us.* (Ps. 103:12)

- How *high* is God's love? *He does not treat us as our sins deserve or repay us according to our iniquities. For as high as the heavens are above the earth, so great is his love for those who fear him.* (Ps. 103:10-11). Jesus not only paid the price for our sins, but he has raised us up and seated us with him in the heavenly places – in order to display his incredible grace to the universe! (Eph. 2:6-7)

- How *deep* is God's love? Jesus stepped off the throne of the universe and came down to rescue us sinners, stuck in our selfishness and degradation. He *made himself nothing, taking the very nature of a servant, being made in human likeness. And being found in appearance as a man, he humbled himself and became obedient to death – even death on a cross!* (Phil. 2:7-8)[141]

Love for God (Part 1)

One of the teachers of the law...asked him, "Of all the commandments, which is the most important?" "The most important one," answered Jesus, "is this: 'Hear O Israel, the Lord our God, the Lord is one. Love the Lord your God with all your heart and with all your soul and with all your mind and with all your strength.'" (Mark 12:28-30)

Of all the priorities in life, loving God must come first. If we love our families, our jobs, or our own lives above God, we have made a tragic mistake. This is why Jesus said, *"Anyone who loves his father or mother more than me is not worthy of me; anyone who loves his son or daughter more than me is not worthy of me..."*[142] Our God is a jealous God, and he will not accept anything else as preeminent in our lives; he wants to *have first place in everything.*[143]

So, if loving God is to be the supreme thing, what does this mean? How can we tell if we love the Lord Jesus? D. James Kennedy provided a good answer: "Of course, we know we love Him when we obey His Word. But we can also tell whether we love Jesus in the same way we know whether we love a human being. When we love someone, we love to talk with that person. We desire to pour out our hearts and souls to them. We feel confident that our beloved understands and likes to listen to us. But we also love nothing more than to hear from our beloved. If he or she is away, we eagerly anticipate phone calls and letters from that person. And each time we interact with our beloved, we want to discover more and more of that person's character, thoughts, likes and dislikes. We're not satisfied until we know that person well, knowing what he or she thinks about everything. And when we really love someone, we want to become the type of person he or she becomes."[144]

If we are lacking love, let us not look inwardly at ourselves, but to the Source and ask the Lord to rekindle a flame of deep and compassionate love in our hearts for him. *Love the Lord, all his saints!*[145]

Love for God (Part 2)

Jesus answered, The first and principal one of all commands is...you shall love the Lord your God... (Mark 12:30 The Amplified Bible)

We are all probably much more self-focused than we realize. We tend to think of ourselves as *recipients* of God's love, but not as *expressing* love back to God. The starting place, for sure, is to *receive* the love of God, for love can only originate from God. But as we grow as Christians an amazing thing happens: we become *partakers of the divine nature.* Part of this new *nature* includes experiencing the highest kind of love a human being could ever experience – the love of God.[146]

A. W. Tozer wrote about this higher love that we can express back to God. "The phrase, 'the love of God,' when used by Christians almost always refers to God's love for us. We must remember that it can also mean our love for God!

"The first and great commandment is that we should love God with all the power of our total personality. Though all love originates in God and is for that reason God's own love, yet we are permitted to catch and reflect back that love in such manner that it becomes our love indeed!

"The Christian's love for God has by some religious thinkers been divided into two kinds, the love of gratitude and the love of excellence. But we must carry our love to God further than love of gratitude and love of excellence.

"There is a place in the religious experience where we love God for Himself alone, with never a thought of His benefits. There is, in the higher type of love, a supra-rational element that cannot and does not attempt to give reasons for its existence – it only whispers, 'I love!'"[147]

This is why we ought to cultivate daily, God-centered worship. Someone once defined worship as "the occupation of the heart, not with its needs, or even its blessings, but with God himself." Declare with me, "O, come let us adore him! He is worthy of all our praise! There is none like him! There is no god like our God! Holy, Holy, Holy is the Lord God Almighty!"

Love for Others (Part 1)

No one has ever seen God; but if we love each other, God lives in us and his love is made complete in us...If anyone says, "I love God," yet hates his brother, he is a liar. For anyone who does not love his brother, whom he has seen, cannot love God, whom he has not seen. (I John 4:12,20)

We can easily test our love for God by our love for other people. I have talked with wayward mates who have pursued their rebellious way, cut themselves off from loved ones, and then dared to say they love God more than ever. Such deception can be confronted by referring to the above verse and saying, "Your mate is your brother or sister in Christ and should be your closest brother or sister. How can you say you love God whom you have not seen if you refuse to love your brother or sister whom you have seen?"

We are called not only to love each other, but to love each other with the *love of Christ*. This is a much higher law of love which goes far beyond the Old Testament law. The law of Moses said, *You shall love your neighbor as yourself.*[148] Christ, however, takes this to a higher level of love: *A new command I give you: Love one another. As I have loved you, so you must love one another.*[149] This is quite challenging when we think of how Christ loved us – the depth of his mercy and forgiveness, and his sacrifice even unto death.

Christ's love needs nothing reciprocal; it is unselfish, and it is without respect to persons. What a high calling – to love each other with Christ's own love! No man in himself will ever be sufficient for such a task, but through the Holy Spirit's dwelling within us, we have the ability to manifest such love. Sometimes it is good to pray, "Lord, in myself I find it impossible to love this person. Manifest your divine love through me." The gospel message often comes to a needy person as the love of God is revealed through weak and ordinary human vessels.

Love for Others (Part 2)

For the body is not one member, but many....Now you are Christ's body, and individually members of it...
(1 Corinthians 12:14,27)

Love is meant to be interactive. There is no place for "lone-ranger" Christianity. There is no "only child" in the church of Jesus. We were meant for community, or according to the biblical analogy, to be members of a body that interact with and complement each other. We need each other!

Our society is gradually sliding away from the sense of being connected in community and instead is living in more individual and isolated settings. This "collapse of community" has been well-documented by Harvard sociologist Robert Putnam, in his book, *Bowling Alone.*[150] In the past fifty years, he shows how American society has declined significantly in the following areas:

- Participating in political and community campaigns
- Membership in civic groups
- Attending PTA meetings at schools
- Entertaining others at home
- Interaction with neighbors
- Social visiting
- Card playing and board games in groups
- Bowling leagues
- Eating together as a family

On the other side, Putnam documents significant increases in the number of people attending spectator sports, playing video games, watching TV, and talking on cellphones.

What is the remedy for followers of Christ? We must constantly strive to keep the same two priorities that Christ had: God and people. We must deny ourselves daily, avoid becoming isolated in our own little world, take initiative to visit people, and especially – in the body of Christ – *stay connected!*

Love for Ourselves (Part 1)

You shall love your neighbor as yourself...(Lev. 19:18)

In this great command, listed eight times in the New Testament, some have assumed that there must first be a love for oneself before there can be love for a neighbor. The Bible does not suggest we should hate and downgrade ourselves, but it does teach us to deny ourselves for the sake of God's kingdom. Jonathan Edwards distinguished between proper and improper self-love: "Christian love is not contrary to *all* self-love. If we hate ourselves, we despise what God has created and redeemed to be a vessel of his Spirit in the world. Contrarily, selfishness is an inordinate self-love. Self-love, when it is inordinate, becomes a greater motivation in life than love for God or neighbor. Concern for one's own happiness may consume a person to the detriment of his soul and the well-being of his neighbor."[151]

We cannot deduce from the above verse that we must love ourselves sufficiently before we ever show love to others. We ought to assume that we already love ourselves sufficiently. When Scripture says we will see terrible times in the last days, the first reason listed is, *People will be lovers of themselves...*[152] The Bible nowhere commands self-love; it simply mentions it as a fact, and not something to be sought after. We are told in Paul's teaching on marriage that *husbands ought to love their wives as their own bodies.*[153] Does this imply husbands must first love their own bodies before they show love to their wives? By no means! We can assume husbands already love their bodies enough: *After all, no one ever hated his own body, but he feeds and cares for it...*[154]

We are commanded to love our neighbors. In the parable of the Good Samaritan, we realize that *neighbors* are those spiritually and perhaps physically needy people whom God brings across our path, and that we are nudged by the Holy Spirit (often at inconvenient times) to aid and show practical love to.[155] Let us not be selfish, but give ourselves to the task of loving others.

Love for Ourselves (Part 2)

We are God's workmanship... (Eph. 2:10 NIV)
We are God's masterpiece... (Eph. 2:10 NLT)
We are God's work of art...(Eph. 2:10 Jerusalem Bible)

We are not to love ourselves too much, but neither are we to despise ourselves. We are the unique and beautiful creation of God – even called *work of art.* Someone has aptly said, "God does not make any junk!" Therefore we should never think that we are worthless or no good.

Due to harsh or abusive upbringings, some folks find it difficult to feel positive about themselves. We may beat ourselves up and even despise ourselves, yet our Lord Jesus thought enough of us to shed his blood for us on the cross! We should not insult the grace of God, who delights to redeem and restore the worst of men! We cannot say, "Well, I know God loves me, but I just can't stand myself." That's a great insult to God and His incredible love.

We are *God's work of art.* We are not just an ordinary piece of carpentry, some cheap painting, or some shanty house; we are the very best the Master can do – his *masterpiece*! On a construction site, we see all the debris and unfinished work. The architect, however, sees the beautiful house. We sometimes see a multitude of problems or weaknesses in our lives and we wonder if we will ever get anywhere. God, however, sees the final masterpiece; he sees a people who will one day be presented to Him as *a radiant church, without stain or wrinkle or any other blemish, but holy and blameless.*[156] We should not lose hope; God sees us differently than we see ourselves. He has also promised not only to begin a good work in us, but also to *continue his work until it is finally finished on the day when Christ Jesus returns.*[157]

We should never despise ourselves when our Lord, from all eternity, has made wonderful plans to call us to himself, to redeem us from all our sins, and to change us, day by day, into his very image. Even when we fail, his grace is sufficient to help us! Let us never loathe God's "work in progress."

Love for our Brothers (Part 1)

Love the brotherhood of believers... (I Peter 2:17)

One of God's greatest blessings to believers is the gift of a family – the brotherhood of believers. When we become born again, we discover a multitude of new brothers and sisters in Christ. As God sets us in a local church, there is sheer joy as we begin to relate to one another without hypocrisy or self-centered motives. As we are united in a common bond in Christ, we discover a warmth, acceptance, and security that many of us lacked in our natural families. The love we find in our hearts for each other is a sure sign that our lives have been supernaturally changed: *We know that we have passed from death to life, because we love our brothers.*[158]

Brotherly love is to be a high priority: *You were cleansed from your sins when you obeyed the truth, so now you must show sincere love to each other as brothers and sisters. Love each other deeply with all your heart.*[159] Loving other Christians is not always an easy task, and the further we go in the Christian life, the harder it gets. One of the hardest tests we will encounter occurs when Christians mistreat us. We may be slandered, insulted, overlooked, or misunderstood. King David experienced this: *If an enemy were insulting me, I could endure it...But it is you, a man like myself, my companion, my close friend, with whom I once enjoyed sweet fellowship as we walked with the throng at the house of God.*[160] In such times, we must not stumble in faith or become embittered. God will often use the failings or weakness of other Christians to deepen our love. Part of bearing our cross means we demonstrate love in times of mistreatment. This kind of love is supernatural and completely contrary to natural reactions of anger or vengeance.

God has given us a wonderful family, but the more we get to know our brothers and sisters, the more flaws we will see, and the greater the opportunity we will have to excel in love: *You have been taught by God to love one another; for indeed you do practice it toward all the brethren...But we urge you, brethren, to excel still more.*[161]

Love for our Brothers (Part 2)

Above all, love each other deeply, because love covers over a multitude of sins. Offer hospitality to one another without grumbling... (1 Peter 4:8-9)

Hospitality is love in action. In the above verse, Peter encourages *deep love*, and the very next verse tells us how: *Offer hospitality to one another without grumbling.* The J. B. Phillips translation is more specific, *Be hospitable to each other without secretly wishing you hadn't got to be!*

Hospitality is a practical way we can love our brothers and sisters in Christ. Repeatedly we are encouraged by Scripture to *practice hospitality.* [162] This means being willing to have people in our homes – even those who are "strangers" to us. [163] There are probably many reasons we are hesitant about pursuing hospitality. [164]

1. Our busy lifestyles: "We just don't have time for it."
2. Self-centeredness: "We just stick to ourselves."
3. Love of comfort: "I work hard and just like to relax when I get home..."
4. Insecurity: "We had a bad experience in the past."
5. Pride: "My house isn't nice enough."
6. Lack of initiative: "We tried that once but nobody ever reciprocated."
7. No interest in new people: "We don't want to mess up our nice little fellowship group."

How do we view our home? Is it *our* home – or is it the Lord's home? We should see our homes not as a possession we own but a gift God has given us to use in his kingdom. Our homes should express the love of Christ. We don't always have to fix a "seven-course-menu." Sometimes my wife and I just invite people for dessert and some games. You can keep it simple. Your house and yard do not have to be in perfect condition. Hospitality is a great way to show love to the brethren and reach out to new people as well. Let's do it!

Love for Friends

A friend loves at all times... (Proverbs 17:17)

Someone once said, "Jesus taught us not only to love our enemies but also to treat our friends a little better." Good friendships are not always easy to come by, but through Jesus Christ we can develop closer relationships. Jesus was not only a co-worker with his twelve disciples, but also their friend.[165] He also calls all his followers *my friends*.[166]

Before I was a Christian, most of my friendships were rather shallow and based on how we might mutually benefit each other. I can honestly say I never thought a lot about putting others' interests above my own. I was basically "looking after #1" – which was me! After becoming a Christian, I discovered genuine friendships for the first time. Even as a Christian, however, friendships need to be cultivated. Some suggestions:

- Pick the right friends. We might casually associate with any person, but the Bible warns against wrong friendships: *Bad company corrupts good morals*.[167] It is better to have few friends (or none) than friends who will bring us down.
- Take initiative with people. Call them; don't wait to be called. Show genuine care and concern.
- Take an interest in *ordinary* people.[168] These might be some who are not the most popular or who tend to be quiet.
- Learn to ask good questions about the other person. Avoid dominating a conversation. Two basic questions to ask: (1) What do you think about...and (2) Why did you...
- Be honest with friends, but not unkind. True friends at times will clash with you – *like iron sharpening iron*.[169]
- Always be loyal and keep confidences.[170]
- Look people in the eye when you talk to them. Remember names. Be a good listener and don't give the impression you are too busy (or too important) to be with them.
- Don't be possessive or wear out your welcome.[171]
- Lastly, make your best friends those who are serious about their relationship with God; we should say, *I am a friend to all who fear you, to all who follow your precepts*.[172]

Love for Sinners

The Pharisees asked his disciples, "Why does your teacher eat with tax collectors and 'sinners'?" (Matthew 9:11)

We can be most thankful the Bible does not record Jesus just loving his father, just loving the angels, or just loving righteous men. He also loves *sinners...* and even the worst of sinners!

- God loved Jacob, a man who was deceitful enough to cheat his own brother twice and deceive his father.
- God loved king Manasseh, a very violent king, who even murdered his own child.
- God loved an immoral Samaritan woman, an outcast that Jews would normally have no contact with.
- God loved Paul, a persecutor of Christians, blasphemer of God, and self-declared "worst of sinners."[173]
- God loved Zacchaeus, a wealthy tax-collector who made his fortune by ripping people off.
- God loved us – even when we gave him little thought, sinned frequently, and lived for our own pleasures.

Because God has loved us, we can love sinners as well. D. L. Moody was the most popular preacher in America in the nineteenth century. As his ministry started to blossom, he learned a valuable lesson about love. His wife, Emma, went to hear a preacher who was visiting Chicago, Harry Moorhouse, a man who Moody did not especially care for.

When she returned from the meeting, Moody asked her about Moorhouse. "They liked him very much," she replied. "He preaches a little different from you. He preaches that God loves sinners." Moody reacted angrily at first, but then he began to consider what this man was preaching, centered in John 3:16. Moody had always taught that God hates the sinner, but now his thinking changed. "This heart of mine began to thaw out. I could not keep back the tears." His biographer said from that time on Moody became "an apostle of the love of God," and his ministry would never be the same again.[174] May we, too, share the love of God with sinners.

Love for All Men

*May the Lord make your love increase and overflow
for each other and for everyone else...(I Thes. 3:12)*

Christians are not called to withdraw from interaction with
non-Christians. We are to love not only *each other* but also
everyone else. We are told to *do good to* all *people, especially
to those who belong to the family of believers.*[175] Sometimes in
a desire to become God's holy people, believers have become
exclusive in Christian communities or withdrawn to mona-
steries or isolated retreats. We cannot be restrictive in our love
or limit it to spiritual people we like. We must reach out beyond
our close friends and associates and engage with people that
God brings into our lives, some of whom might be non-
believers. Such people may not be our natural preference, but
we will feel the Spirit's nudging to love them.

In the first few centuries of Christianity, several
descriptions of believers were recorded which reveal their
outstanding love – toward both believers and non-believers. In
a letter written to the Emperor Pius, the Christian philosopher,
Aristides, wrote the following words in the second century
describing Christians: "They worship no alien gods. They live
in the awareness of their smallness. Kindness is their nature.
There is no falsehood among them. They love one another.
They do not neglect widows. Orphans they rescue from those
who are cruel to them. Every one of them who has anything
gives ungrudgingly to the one who has nothing....And see,
because of them, good flows on in the world!"[176] In another
second century document, Tertullian quoted the verdict of
heathen people as they depicted believers: "Look how they love
one another."[177] What a compliment! If unbelievers today
were to visit our Christian gatherings, or spend some time in
our homes, would they make the same comment?

As we are given opportunity, may we show love to all men.
If we want to win men to Christ, we will not be successful
without deep love overflowing in practical ways. Jesus said, *All
men will know you are my disciples if you love one another.*[178]

Love for Wives

Husbands, love your wives, just as Christ loved the church and gave himself up for her... (Ephesians 5:25)

I was once told that I should always remember that the woman I married was not just my wife, but she was also the King's daughter! I am probably like many husbands in that I have not fully valued the wonderful gift God has given me in my wife. We husbands have a solemn obligation to honor and love our wives. The Greek tense in the verse above implies continual action, and could be translated, *keep on loving.* This is especially challenging when we think of how Christ has loved the church. Christ gave his very life for the church. Christ's love for us is always giving, living, and forgiving. It is never selfish. It is never dull and static. It is never conditional ("I will love you if you will...").

Husbands are also told in this same passage *to love their wives as their own bodies.*[179] Think of all the care we give to bathing, grooming, and dressing our bodies. Many men spend hours each week in an athletic center exercising and building up their bodies. Do we devote the same time and energy to building up our wives? Loving our wives means we will be committed to them – through thick and thin. It means we will devote our time to them. It means we will patiently listen to them – even when their detailed concerns seem trivial to us.

Wives will feel a lot more love if husbands stay close to Jesus. We may provide materially for our wives and feel we have done our duty, but they will suffer if husbands are spiritually negligent. Women enjoy more security in a relationship when their man is seeking to be a man of God, modeling the humble spirit of Christ, and walking in integrity.

One of the best ways we can love our children is to love their mother. Children will learn much about love by observing a father's treatment of his wife. If we are short with or belittle our mates, our children will likely follow our example. May God help every Christian husband to love his wife just as Christ loved the church.

Love for Husbands

These older women must train the younger women to love their husbands and their children... (Titus 2:4 NLT)

Love does not always "naturally happen" in marriage. Both husbands and wives must *learn* how to love each other. Many young wives would profit a good deal by sitting down with an older Christian woman who has a happy marriage and learning the practical "do's" and "don'ts" of pleasing their husbands. Women can also learn from excellent books on marriage. Sadly, too many women become resentful and concentrate on trying to change their husbands, instead of focusing on their own deficiencies. The following are some suggestions (several from my wife) on how wives can love their husbands.

- Keep your own devotional time with Jesus. The more you know the Lord, the more you will express the fruit of the Spirit to your husband and others.
- Speak words of appreciation and encouragement for all that your husband *does* for the family.
- If there is 20% about your husband you don't like, thank God for the 80% that you *do* like! Leave the 20% with God instead of *you* trying to change or control him.
- Work to make the home an inviting place that your husband looks forward to coming after work.
- Don't expect your husband to be a "mind-reader." Sometimes he "just won't get it." If so, don't pout or give him the silent treatment. Gently *talk* and express your concerns, but without nagging or using sarcasm.
- Even in times of disagreement or agitation, be respectful. Respect is a wife's chief task (Eph. 5:33).
- Be considerate of your husband's needs. Find time for him. The last thing on your mind, after a hectic day of changing diapers and wiping noses, is a romantic evening. It's amazing how we are wired differently, but at times we must put our mate's desires above our own.
- Pray for your man daily...and for God to change *you*.

Love for Mates

However, each one of you also must love his wife as he loves himself, and the wife must respect her husband. (Ephesians 5:33)

Gary Chapman wrote a fascinating book, which remained on the national best-selling list for more than fifteen years and is currently translated in 38 languages, entitled *The 5 Love Languages.*[180] Chapman said that marriage should be based on love, but at times it seems as though the husband and wife are speaking two different languages! He said that there are five basic "love languages" that most people "speak" and learning about your mate's primary "language" is "the secret to love that lasts." The five "love languages" are:

- Quality time
- Words of affirmation
- Gifts
- Acts of service
- Physical touch

For example, a man may feel he demonstrates love to his wife as he works hard to clean up the yard and vacuum the house. His love language is "acts of service." Yet, he may not feel fully appreciated or that his wife is any more affectionate as a result after all his labors. His wife, instead, may be looking for "words of affirmation" – kind and encouraging words that bless her, and are given to her throughout their day when he is not expecting anything in return (e.g., sex). The husband may seldom say such loving words, but it is the "love language" that she really needs. I realized some years ago that giving surprise "gifts" to my wife was not that big a deal. What she does love is having her back and head scratched (physical touch). Scratching my back does nothing for me, but for my wife it is certainly a "love language."

By realizing your unique love language and learning your spouse's, it may help you understand each other better and contribute to building a lasting, loving marriage together.

Love for the Prodigal

So he got up and went to his father. "But while he was still a long way off, his father saw him and was filled with compassion for him; he ran to his son, threw his arms around him and kissed him. (Luke 15:20)

This story has commonly been called "The Parable of the Prodigal Son." On the one hand, it is a fitting title as the name "prodigal" means "wasteful or recklessly extravagant." This son asked his father for an early inheritance, received it, and then wasted all his money before coming to his senses. On the other hand, the story could better be titled, "The Parable of the Loving Father." This is a story that every one of us ought to relate to on some level, because it reveals the heavenly Father's great love for us all, even when we reject him or go our own way. Mark Strauss, in *Zondervan Illustrated Bible Background Commentary,* brought out some insights about this story.

"An inheritance was not normally distributed until a father's death; thus, to ask for it early would be a great insult to the father. It would be like saying, 'I wish you were dead.' Upon receiving such a disgraceful request a father would be expected to beat his son or perhaps cut off his inheritance.... Jesus' readers would have been horrified first that the younger son would ask for the division, but then that he would demand power over it immediately. They would be equally shocked that a father would allow himself to be treated in this way."[181]

When the prodigal son repents and returns home, a very touching thing happens. *His father ... ran to his son.*[182] Strauss again commented, "The scene is striking since even today, a distinguished Middle Eastern patriarch in robes does not run, but always walks in a slow and dignified manner. Running was viewed as humiliating and degrading. The man's unrestrained joy and affection – even to the point of humiliation before others – reveals God's over-whelming love and grace for the lost sinner and the joy experienced when a person repents."[183] Our loving, heavenly Father eagerly continues to welcome any desperate person who returns to him.

Love for the Unpleasant

Love knows no limit to its endurance, no end to its trust,
no fading of its hope; it can outlast anything.
(I Corinthians 13:8 Phillips)

God sometimes uses unpleasant circumstances or people to help develop His love in our hearts. Hoosier Farmer said, "Love is the thing that enables a woman to sing while she mops the floor after her husband has walked across it in his barn boots."[184] Wade Taylor illustrates this kind of love:

"A story is told about a housewife who came to the altar after a stirring message on the love of God. She asked the Lord for a revelation of His love. She waited for some time, but nothing happened and she went home disappointed.

"When she arrived at home, she was greeted by her mother-in-law, who had unexpectedly moved in. The next morning, the maid was cleaning the house, when the mother-in-law appeared. She promptly fired the maid and informed her daughter-in-law that she should clean her own house.

"Before long, the housewife was in her bedroom crying, pleading with the Lord to remove her mother-in-law. The Lord reminded her that she had asked for an experience of His love. He told her to go and tell her mother-in-law that she loved her and was glad she was there. But she was unable to do so.

"Later, during the evening meal, her mother-in-law said, 'Is this the best food you can cook? My son deserves a better meal than this.' Again, the wife resorted to her bedroom to plead with the Lord for the removal of her mother-in-law from her home. And again the Lord told her to tell her mother-in-law that she loved her and was glad she was there.

"Finally, she gave in to the Lord. and with His help she was able to do what He asked, and to do it from her heart. Later, her mother-in-law appeared with her suitcase and said she was leaving. The love that this housewife had sought at an altar had been perfected within her in a real life situation. Now she had a personal understanding of the 'love of God.'"[185] God's love for us *knows no limit to its endurance...and no fading of its hope.*

Love for the Ungrateful

> *But love your enemies, do good to them, and lend to them without expecting to get anything back. Then your reward will be great, and you will be sons of the Most High, because he is kind to the ungrateful and wicked. (Luke 6:35)*

This will certainly test our love level – do we love the person who not only fails to appreciate what we do, but even acts ungrateful? It is not easy, but we are to follow Christ's example; he is *kind to the ungrateful and wicked.* One lady chose to show this kind of incredible love.

"Years ago in North Carolina, Judge Clara Warren served in the juvenile court system. She was known for her strict interpretation of the law, but also for her love and compassion.

"One day Judge Warren took reporter Phyllis Hobe on a tour of a correctional facility. Hobe was surprised by the judge's sincere concern for many of the inmates. She was helping them to get into schools and find jobs when they were released. She even continued to care for them if they were readmitted. 'How can you keep on loving them?' the reporter asked. 'They don't seem to appreciate all you've done for them.' The judge explained that she didn't love them because she wanted to receive their thanks. She simply loved them, expecting nothing in return."[186]

We, too, will have opportunity to love ungrateful people:

- Most children will not joyfully thank you for washing their clothes, preparing food, or paying for their education. Yet, we choose to show love to them over many years.
- Many employers will not personally thank you for all your hard work, or the extra, beyond-the-call-of-duty jobs you fulfill. Yet, you choose to work heartily, as unto the Lord.
- Some fellow believers will not verbally express appreciation for all the kind things you do for them or their children, yet you continue to serve them faithfully in the spirit of Christ.

Lord, may our love go this deep – even to the ungrateful.

Love for the Unlovely

A man with leprosy came and knelt down before him and said, "Lord, if you are willing, you can make me clean." Jesus reached out his hand and touched the man...(Matthew 8:2-3)

A Brooklyn pastor told how his own love was tested when a homeless man visited his church. "At the end of the evening meeting I sat down on the edge of the platform, exhausted, as others continued to pray with those who had responded to Christ....I was just starting to unwind when I looked up to see this man, with shabby clothing and matted hair, standing...and waiting for permission to approach me. I nodded and gave him a weak little wave of my hand. *Look at how this Easter Sunday is going to end,* I thought to myself. *He is going to hit me up for money.* That happens often in this church. *I'm so tired....*When he came close, I saw that his two front teeth were missing. But more striking was his odor – the mixture of alcohol, sweat, urine, and garbage took my breath away...this was the strongest stench I have ever encountered. I instinctively had to turn my head sideways, to inhale. I asked his name.

"David," he said softly.

"How long have you been homeless, David?"

"Six years."

"Where did you sleep last night?"

"In an abandoned truck."

I had heard enough and wanted to get this over quickly. I reached for the money clip in my back pocket. At that moment David put his finger in front of my face and said, "No, you don't understand – I don't want your money. I'm going to die out there. I want the Jesus that redhaired girl talked about."

I hesitated, then closed my eyes. *God, forgive me, I* begged. I felt soiled and cheap. Me, a minister of the gospel... had wanted to get rid of him, when he was crying out for the help of Christ I had just preached about. I swallowed hard as God's love flooded my soul...Holding him close, I talked to him about Jesus' love...[187] Jesus, help us, too, to love the unlovable.

Love for the "No-good"

We have been made and are now the rubbish and filth of the world [the offscouring of all things, the scum of the earth]. 1 Corinthians 4:13 The Amplified Bible

God's estimate of people is often different from our own. The world sometimes may look at certain people and consider them *worthless* or even *the scum of the earth.* Yet, God may look at the same persons and see them as "*pearls* in the process" or as "*trophies* of grace" that he will display to the universe. James Kennedy shared this story of God's love for the "no-good."

"Mel Trotter gave a whole new meaning to the terms 'no good.' He was so 'no good' it was almost written on his forehead. He was the very scum of the scum. He abused his family. He neglected his children. He was fired from his jobs. He was a drunkard in the gutter and would do anything for a drink. In fact, one day he came home and found his little daughter very seriously ill. He was so 'concerned' that he took off her shoes and went out and sold them for a drink! When he returned, he found that his little girl was dead. He was so overwhelmed by remorse that he said he was going to end his life. He made his way across one of the worst parts of Chicago, to throw himself into Lake Michigan. But as he passed down the street, he could hear someone preaching over a loudspeaker. He stepped into the building's doorway and heard a man talking about Jesus Christ, who loved sinners. He said to himself, 'Can it be that there is anyone who could love someone like me?' He stood transfixed by that message of love that he heard. The grasp of that addiction suddenly was loosened. Mel Trotter was set free!

"He later established a great mission for the down-and-outers in downtown Grand Rapids, and ultimately established fifty more missions around the nation. Tens of thousands of drunks and ne'er-do-wells had their lives transformed by Christ through Trotter. Take Christ out of the picture, and all you end up with is a drunken suicide!"[188] Thank God! Christ loves and saves even the worst of men – including us!

Love for the Unresponsive

I am glad to give you myself and all I have for your spiritual good, even though it seems that the more I love you, the less you love me. (2 Cor.12:15 TLB)

Christian love shines brightly even when there is no response or gratitude from the recipient. This truth is illustrated by Ed Wheat in a touching example. "A man loved his wife tenderly and steadfastly for a total of fifteen years without any responding love on her part. There could be no response, for she had developed cerebral arteriosclerosis, the chronic brain syndrome....At the onset of the disease she was a pretty, vivacious lady of sixty who looked at least ten years younger. In the beginning she experienced intermittent times of confusion....As the disease progressed, she gradually lost all her mental faculties and did not even recognize her husband. He took care of her at home by himself for the first five years. During that time he often took her for visits, she looking her prettiest although she had no idea of where she was, and he proudly displaying her as his wife, introducing her to everyone, even though her remarks were apt to be inappropriate to the conversation. He never made an apology for her; he never indicated that there was anything wrong with what she had just said. He always treated her with the utmost courtesy. He showered her with love and attention....The time came when the doctors said she had to go into a nursing home for intensive care. She lived there for ten years (part of that time bedfast with arthritis) and he was with her daily....He never made a negative comment about her. He did not begrudge the large amount of money required to keep her in the home all those years, never even hinted that it might be a problem. In fact, he never complained about any detail of her care throughout the long illness....This man was loyal, always true to his wife, even though his love had no response for fifteen years....I can speak of this case with intimate knowledge, for these people were my own wonderful parents. What my father taught me about *agape* love through his example I can never forget."[189]

Love for All Races

He has made from one blood every nation of men... (Acts 17:26)

We are all from one blood. We have one common ancestor. Therefore, there is no one superior race. There is only one race – the human race. We all stand equal in worth before Almighty God and all have the same need of redemption through his grace. Therefore, there is no excuse for racial prejudice. Yet, in the 21st century, racist attitudes remain, and Kerby Anderson has pointed out three main causes: [190]

1. **Pride.** When we are proud of who we are, we can easily look down upon those who are different from us....We can start believing we are superior to another person or race.
2. **Inferiority.** Racism can come from the opposite end of the emotional spectrum. We may not feel good about ourselves, and therefore we ridicule another person or race.
3. **Fear.** We fear what we do not understand, or what is strange and foreign. Racial and cultural differences may even seem dangerous to us.

If we plan to go to heaven, our hearts must be prepared – there will not be even "one ounce" of racial prejudice in heaven. The bride of Christ will be characterized by the heavenly dimension of love and will include the redeemed from *every tribe and language and people and nation.*[191] John Piper wrote, "Being a person [created in the image of God] is infinitely more significant than being a white person or black person. In the real world on this earth, race is significant, but in the more real world of heaven, redeemed personhood is ten thousand times more significant than race."[192]

As Christians, we are to love *all* races. We must avoid subtle superior attitudes, racial jokes and slurs, and making any class distinctions. We are one in Christ! *My brothers, as believers in our glorious Lord Jesus Christ, don't show favoritism....*[193] *There is neither Jew nor Greek, slave nor free, male nor female, for you are all one in Christ Jesus.*[194]

Love for our Enemies (Part 1)

You have heard that it was said, "Love your neighbor and hate your enemy." But I tell you: Love your enemies and pray for those who persecute you, that you may be sons of your Father in heaven. He causes his sun to rise on the evil and the good, and sends rain on the righteous and the unrighteous. If you love those who love you, what reward will you get? (Matthew 5:43-46)

Corrie ten Boom experienced supernatural love toward one who would naturally be an enemy. Both Corrie and her sister, Betsie, had been arrested for concealing Jews in their home in Holland during the Nazi occupation of Holland. Betsie died in the concentration camp, but Corrie was later released. Years later, after the war, Corrie was speaking in a church in Munich when a familiar figure came forward after the meeting – a Nazi guard from that same camp. He said he had become a Christian and knew that God had forgiven him for all the cruel things he did there, but felt he must also ask Corrie to forgive him. After an intense inner struggle, Corrie realized she had to forgive this man as Christ had forgiven her. By an act of her will, she silently asked Jesus to help her. Stretching out her hand, she cried, "I forgive you brother...with all my heart!" She later wrote of that account, "For a long moment we grasped each other's hands, the former guard and former prisoner. I had never known God's love so intensely as I did then."[195]

If we ever want to compare other religions to genuine Christianity, we can look at the way their adherents love their enemies. The early church father, Tertullian, commented, "Our religion commands us to love even our enemies and to pray for those who persecute us....Everyone loves those who love them. It is unique to Christians to love those who hate them."[196] God's love will even enable his disciples to feel toward enemies what other people feel toward friends.

Love for our Enemies (Part 2)

*Forgive as the Lord forgave you. And over all these
virtues put on love... (Colossians 3:13-14)*

Louis Zamperini's incredible World War II story has been
vividly portrayed in the bestseller, *Unbroken,* by Laura
Hidlebrand. Zamperini was a famous Olympic runner, who
joined the U.S. Air Force when war broke out. On one
mission, their B-24 airplane crashed into the Pacific Ocean,
but Zamperini and two other crew members amazingly
survived, living the next 47 days on life rafts. Two of the men
finally reached an island, only to be captured by Japanese
soldiers. Zamperini would spend the next two and a half years
in various prisons, where prisoners were cruelly treated. One
big, sadistic Japanese guard, named Matsuhiro, seemed to
have a demonic hatred bent toward Zamperini. Anytime they
would cross paths, this guard would pound him in the face.

When the war was over, Zamperini returned home and
was an instant celebrity. But, he soon found himself in an
unhappy marriage and addicted to alcohol. Every night, he
suffered nightmares of the guard, Matsuhiro, tormenting him.
All this changed, however, in 1949, when he attended a big
tent crusade in Los Angeles, where young Billy Graham was
preaching. One night, Zamperini went forward and gave his
life to Christ. He returned home, poured out all his liquor, and
slept peacefully for the first time in years. He never again had
a nightmare of Matsuhiro. He was truly a new man in Christ!

A few years later, Zamperini had an opportunity to go
back and visit some of the former Japanese guards, now
imprisoned. He shared the forgiveness of Christ to these
former tormentors, who were greatly surprised by his love.
Zamperini never saw Matsuhiro in his visits, but he sent him a
letter. In it, he said, "I committed my life to Christ. Love
replaced the hate I had for you...I also forgave you and now
would hope that you would also become a Christian."
Matsuhiro never responded, but Zamperini had obeyed the
Lord in loving his former enemy. We can do the same.

Love for our Enemies (Part 3)

Do not be overcome by evil, but overcome evil with good. (Romans 12:21)

There is a love that will stretch us to the limit – love for our enemies. This would include loving those who mistreat you, those who take advantage of you, those who injure you with no regrets, and those who even seem to enjoy making your life miserable. The following is a wonderful example of this love.

"In 1915, during a religious and ethnic conflict in which over a million Armenians were slaughtered by the Turks, a military unit attacked a village, murdering all the adults and taking the young women as hostages. In one home, after killing the parents, the officer in charge gave the daughters to the men in his command but kept the beautiful oldest daughter for himself. After several months of slavery and sexual abuse, she escaped from him and began to rebuild her life. Eventually she attended training school and became a nurse.

"One night several years later, while she was working in a hospital intensive care unit, she recognized the face of a desperately ill patient. He was the officer who had enslaved and abused her and had murdered her parents. His comatose condition required round-the-clock attention and care. Only after a lengthy and difficult time during which he was mostly semiconscious did he begin to recover.

"One day, as he was finally regaining his health, a doctor spoke to him about the nurse who had been caring for him. 'What a fortunate man you are,' he commented. 'Without her constant devotion you would have never made it.'

"Later when alone, the officer stared at the nurse. 'I've wanted for days to ask you, we've met before, haven't we?'

'Yes,' the nurse nodded. 'We've met before.'

'I don't understand,' he continued. 'Why didn't you kill me when you had the opportunity? Why didn't you just let me die?'

'Because I am a follower of one who said, "love your enemies,"' the nurse replied."[197]

Love for our Enemies (Part 4)

Do not repay anyone evil for evil....On the contrary:
"If your enemy is hungry, feed him..." (Rom. 12:20)

If you ever want to know the difference between Christianity and Islam, it is quite simple: Christianity is a religion of love; Islam is not. Love is unique to Christianity; in *no* other religion will you discover the depth of love that Jesus Christ revealed.

Bill Warner, who has done extensive study in the *Koran*, observed, "While there are over 300 references in the Koran to Allah and fear, there are 49 references to love. Of these references, 39 are negative such as the 14 negative references to love of money, power, other gods and status.... There are 25 verses about how Allah does not love kafirs (non-Muslims).... Three verses command humanity to love Allah and 2 verses tell about how Allah loves a believer. This leaves 5 verses about love; 3 of these are about loving kin or a Muslim brother. One verse commands a Muslim to give for the love of Allah. This leaves only one verse about love: give what you love to charity and....Muslim charity only goes to other Muslims. There is not a verse about either compassion or love for a kafir, but there are 14 verses that teach a Muslim is not a friend of the kafir."[198]

If anyone is still trying to decide about these religions, just consider the two founders. Jesus Christ came as the *Prince of Peace,*[199] who was no warrior, but who brought an inner peace for the souls of men. Jesus never raised a weapon, physically hurt a soul, and he even prayed for his enemies while hanging on the cross. The Koran, on the other hand, says more than seventy times that Muslims are to copy Mohammed's life in the smallest detail.[200] It is a historical fact that Mohammed was a violent man and Islam spread through violence, not "peaceful dialogue." Warner said, "Mohammed was involved in an event of violence on average every 6 weeks for 9 years and that does not include assassinations, Muslims raping women, and executions."[201]

So, which religion do we want to choose?

Painful Love

When Israel was a child, I loved him... My people are
bent on backsliding from Me. (Hosea 11:1,7)

At times it hurts to love. Herbert Vander Lugt says, "If you want to go through life with as little sorrow or pain as possible, don't love anybody. Every time you let yourself love, you open the door to pain. A person who falls in love and marries may shed many tears over the illness or death of their spouse. Parents who love their children will suffer many hurts as they watch them grow up. A health-care worker who is genuinely concerned about her terminally ill patients feels grief when they die....We can spare ourselves much pain if we don't let ourselves become emotionally attached to anyone. But we will also miss out on some of the greatest joys in life. The more we love, the more we suffer. That's true. But the path of selfless love is also the path to some of our greatest joys.

"In Hosea 11, God spoke of His love for Israel. He compared Himself to a father caring for a child (vv. 3-4). But the people who should have brought Him joy caused Him pain instead. They rejected His love and guidance and did not honor Him (vv. 5,7)."[202] Our God can sympathize with painful love.

When we give ourselves to truly love another person, we open ourselves up. The results can be painful. C. S. Lewis said, "To love at all is to be vulnerable....The only place outside heaven where you feel perfectly safe from all dangers and perturbations of love is hell."[203]

Even though loving others makes us vulnerable to hurts and disappointments, we need simply to obey our Master. If we love, our reward will be great in heaven and sometimes on earth. The blessings of pouring ourselves out in selfless love far outweigh any potential pain we might experience.

Unconditional Love

Like the rest, we were by nature objects of wrath. But because of his great love for us, God, who is rich in mercy, made us alive with Christ...(Ephesians 2:3-4)

The concept of unconditional love may be hard to grasp, but it can bring freedom to many a bound person. When God says to us, "I love you," he is NOT saying: "I love you *because...*" or "I love you *if...*" or "I love you *when...*"

If any of these statements were true, then God's love would be *conditional*, and we would spend a lifetime always wondering if we were ever pleasing him. Believers from strict, legalistic, and abusive backgrounds often feel compelled to have to work for God. Therefore, any shortcomings or failings can cause them to question the love of God. It is not our goodness, devotion, or sacrifice which earn the love of God. God loves us simply because it is part of his nature to love. He is love. He does not love us because we have done something to merit it. His love is an action, coming entirely from himself. It is not a reaction based on something we have done.

Unconditional love is never an excuse for believers to engage deliberately in sin, to be spiritually careless, or half-hearted toward God. If we do, we reap bad consequences, as Scripture clearly teaches.[204] God is not a senile grandfather in heaven who still smiles as his rebellious children enjoy themselves in sin. God's unconditional love does not mean he winks at sin or that he unilaterally forgives without our repentance, but it does mean his love is still available. Even in our worst state, we can curse God and reject his love, but his arms are still stretched out to us. It is like a fountain of life giving water that ever flows for those who will come and drink. We can walk past it, but the water flows on. Because God loves us unconditionally, we do not need to do a hundred forms of penance or get our lives "all straightened out" first. We can simply come as we are and drink freely of the water of life.

Impartial Love

Isaac, who had a taste for wild game, loved Esau, but Rebekah loved Jacob. (Genesis 25:28)

Partiality was one of the big problems in Isaac's household. Isaac preferred one son and his wife, Rebekah, favored the other. Elsewhere in Genesis, Esau is called *his son*, and Jacob is called *her son*.[205] In a family when parents have favorites and it becomes obvious to the other siblings, it will be certain to cause some strife through feelings of envy, mistrust, and resentment.

In our church congregation, we have a wonderful set of parents, Steve and Karin, who have eight children – four white, biological children and four biracial, adopted children. When I asked Karin about her love for these varied children, this was her response: "Adoption is not for everyone. Steve and I can love these children impartially because of the love of God in our hearts. I do not love any one less than the others. If I have to discipline a strong willed child more often, it may appear as though my love for her is less, but that is not so. Sometimes when an adopted older child comes immediately into a family, it takes time for love to grow, but God's love is immediately present....Recently, when someone wanted to interfere with one of my newly acquired children, I found my motherly protective love arising with an attitude of, 'They are mine...Don't mess with them. I am their mother!'....God's love is an impartial love and that is the way he calls us to love also....If my house was on fire and I had to save my children, I would not think about saving a particular child or my biological children first; I would simply grab whoever I could!....If you ever want to ruffle my feathers just make a comment like, 'Oh, so you have four of your own children plus these four others.' My quick response will be, 'No! They are *all* my own!'"

Impartial love should also be characteristic in our church family. Although we may have special objects of our love, we are told, *My brothers, as believers in our glorious Lord Jesus Christ, don't show favoritism.*[206] Let love be without partiality.

Adoptive Love

See what an incredible quality of love the Father has given...us, that we should be permitted to be named and called and counted the children of God! And so we are! (I John 3:1 The Amplified Bible)

Adoption is an incredible manifestation of love – an act where a husband and wife freely and deliberately take a child who is not biologically their own into their family. It is no required duty, but rather an act of sacrificial kindness. The child has done nothing to merit such generosity; the adoption into a caring family occurs simply because of love. In ancient times, adoption sometimes meant a lowly slave, who legally owned and deserved nothing, would be granted the status of a son – with all the rights and responsibilities belonging to his new family.[207]

We will spend a lifetime only beginning to realize how much the heavenly Father has loved us by sending his Son to die on our behalf, so that we might be adopted as his very own children. *God sent forth His Son...to redeem those who were under the law, that we might receive the adoption as sons...*[208] For some believers, being a Christian centers around an act of "being saved," but our adoption means much more. When parents love a child enough to adopt him, their love does not stop with the completed legal process. This is just the beginning as parents will seek to develop a growing love relationship. They will not be satisfied merely with their child's official status as a new member of the family. As they show more and more love, they hope that love will be returned. They desire a mutual relationship and deep friendship with the one adopted. This is exactly how God relates to his children as well. As he loves us increasingly, our love for him will hopefully grow, and this is only the beginning of an eternity full of the Father's love.

Let us stop and consider what a high privilege we have entered into – becoming God's very own children, part of his eternal family, with all of heaven's blessings available to us!

Restrictive Love

This is love for God: to obey his commands. And his commands are not burdensome. (I John 5:3)

God loves us immensely and has given us certain restrictions, not to hinder us, but to bring us into the full dimension of his love. Henry Blackaby has said, "Life has some 'land mines' that can destroy you or wreck your life. God does not want to see you miss out on His best, and He does not want to see your life wrecked....Suppose you had to cross a field full of land mines. A person who knows exactly where every one of them is buried offers to take you through it. Would you say to him, 'I don't want you to tell me what to do. I don't want you to impose your ways on me?' I don't know about you, but I would stay as close to that person as I could. I certainly would not go wandering off. His directions to me would preserve my life. He would say, 'Don't go that way, because that will kill you – Go this way and you will live."[209] God's restrictions are not intended to make life miserable; they are intended to protect us.

God desires for us to live an abundant life and to know that his commands are for our good.[210] Blackaby illustrated again, "Suppose the Lord says, 'I have a gift for you – a beautiful, wonderful expression of what love is. I will provide you with a spouse – a husband or a wife. Your relationship with this person will bring out the very best in you. It will give you an opportunity to experience some of the deepest and most meaningful expressions of human love....But then He says, 'You shall not commit adultery' (Matt. 5:27). Is that command to limit or restrict you? No! It is to protect and free you to experience love at its human best. What happens if you break the command and commit adultery? The love relationship is ruptured between husband and wife. Trust is gone. Hurt sets in. Guilt and bitterness creep in....Scars may severely limit the future dimensions of love you could have experienced together."[211]

God has our best in mind. If we love him, let us keep his commands. They are not burdensome. They are for our good.

Forsaken Love

Yet I hold this against you: You have forsaken your first love... (Revelation 2:4)

The church in Ephesus was reproved by the Lord because they had abandoned their first love. Think of a husband who has wed the most wonderful girl he has ever met. For several years they enjoy blissful marital intimacy, but then she starts to grow cold. One day he sadly realizes she has lost her first love for him. This illustration is used repeatedly by the prophets describing God's people forsaking their first love of him. It can happen to us as well. How can we tell we are slipping away from our first love? I know I have forsaken my first love for Jesus when...

- I am entangled with cares and anxieties of this life.
- I am grumpy, easily offended, and hard to live with.
- I refuse to forgive, choosing to live in bitterness.
- I seldom read the word of God.
- I seldom talk about the things of God.
- I no longer hate sin and make excuses to justify it.
- I resent serving the body of Christ.
- I no longer give cheerfully to God's work.
- I avoid Christian meetings.
- I no longer care about sinners destined for hell.

In such times of forsaken love, our case is not hopeless. To this same church of Ephesus, our Lord said, *"Remember the height from which you have fallen! Repent and do the things you did at first."* [212] Notice the three verbs: *remember... repent...do.* We must stir our minds and *remember* the days in which we walked closer with the Lord. We must exercise our wills and *repent* – deliberately turning 180 degrees around from going our own way and returning to God's way. Finally, we must *do* those godly duties we did at first. If we have lost our first love for our heavenly Bridegroom, let us take heart; it can be restored.

Worldly Love

Do not love the world or anything in the world. If anyone loves the world, the love of the Father is not in him. For everything in the world – the cravings of sinful man, the lust of the eyes, and the boasting of what he has and does – comes not from the Father but from the world. (I John 2:15-16)

The *world* in this biblical context represents the humanistic system which exalts natural man and de-emphasizes Jesus Christ. Satan is called *the god of this world,*[213] and his system of things, though it may even seem benevolent and religious at times, is wicked to the core. Christians are warned, *Do not conform any longer to the pattern of this world....For this world in its present form is passing away.*[214] We know we have been affected negatively when our love for Christ grows cold and worldly things become more important than him. There are three particular manifestations of the world system:

- *The cravings of sinful man.* Every unregenerate man will have certain cravings, or lusts, which strongly influence him, and yet leave little meaningful satisfaction. These cravings may be for pleasure, possessions, or position. The one who eagerly pursues such things is at enmity with God[215] and lacks the contentment found only in Christ.

- *The lust of the eyes.* This is one of Satan's greatest strategies. The eyes of men can be diverted to seductive ads in newspapers, sex on television, or internet pornography. We need to be on guard constantly and say as Job said, *"I made a covenant with my eyes not to look lustfully at a girl."*[216] Women can lust after men, or be tempted to lust after material things, always looking for something better.

- *The boasting of what he has and does.* The King James Version calls this symptom, *the pride of life.* This is when we speak highly of ourselves, become unduly proud of our accomplishments, or constantly dwell on what people think. Consider: Who do we love the most – Jesus or the world?

Misplaced Love (Part 1)

Anyone who loves his father or mother more than me is not worthy of me; anyone who loves his son or daughter more than me is not worthy of me. (Matt. 10:37)

We can make the mistake of misplaced love – allowing a person to become so important to us that our love for the Lord is replaced. God is certainly not opposed to family love, but the essence of idolatry is when anything, even a close friend or a family member, comes before God. Some parents think they are doing what's best for their children by working two jobs to provide many nice things and then scheduling all their other time around the varied activities in which their kids are involved. As a result of excessive "love," God is often left out. This is idolatry. *The Amplified Bible* says, *Little children, keep yourselves from idols [from anything and everything that would occupy the place of your heart due to God, from any sort of substitute for Him that would take first place in your life.]*[217] A. W. Tozer told the story of a woman whose baby "had a high fever and was really suffering and she knew it. She watched that little suffering face and after having done everything she could do to assuage its pains and sufferings, she turned away to think it over. 'When I turned away,' she said, 'I saw the strain and the pain in the flesh on the baby's face and the two bright eyes and I knew that baby was suffering.' I turned and said, 'God, I'm through with you. You let my baby suffer like that; I'm through! I can't love a God who'll let my baby suffer!'

"She went on to become a rationalist, an unbeliever. Well, she was a poor fool and she didn't understand....She loved her baby more than she loved the God who created her. If the God who created her would let her baby run a fever, she would have nothing to do with Him. That kind of love is not love. It is the extension of her personality, the projection of her personality into that baby and it is sheer pure selfishness."[218]

Let us never allow our love for God to be displaced by love for another person. May the Lord always have first place.

Misplaced Love (Part 2)

Every good and perfect gift is from above, coming down from the Father of the heavenly lights, who does not change like shifting shadows. James 1:17

Do we love the gifts more than the Giver? Too often we are enamored with the things God gives us – material blessings, friends, and family – rather than God himself. Charles Swindoll elaborated on this point:

"Many years ago I called on a man in the hospital. He had suffered a series of heart attacks and had undergone major surgery. During his rehabilitation, he stayed at the dismal Veterans Hospital.

"The day I arrived to visit, I saw a touching scene. This man had a young son, and during his confinement in the hospital, he had made a little wooden truck for his boy. Since the boy was not allowed to go into the ward and visit his father, an orderly had brought the gift down to the child, who was waiting in front of the hospital with his mother. The father was looking out of a fifth-floor window, watching his son unwrap the gift.

"The little boy opened the package and his eyes got wide when he saw that wonderful little truck. He hugged it to his chest.

"Meanwhile, the father was walking back and forth waving his arms behind the windowpane, trying to get his son's attention.

"The little boy put the truck down and reached up and hugged the orderly and thanked him for the truck. And all the while the frustrated father was going through these dramatic gestures, trying to say, 'It's me, son. I made that truck for you. I gave that to you. Look up here!' I could almost read his lips.

"Finally the mother and the orderly turned the boy's attention up to that fifth-floor window. It was then the boy cried, 'Daddy! Oh, thank you! I miss you, Daddy! Come home, Daddy. Thank you for my truck.'

"And the father stood in the window with tears pouring down his cheeks.

"How much like that child we are. We are shut away in our cave of loneliness and discouragement, and then God brings along the gifts of rest and refreshment, wise counsel, and close, personal friends. And we fall in love with the gifts, rather than the Giver!"[219]

Counterfeit Love: Random Force

The grace of our Lord was poured out on me abund-
antly, along with the faith and love that are in Christ
Jesus. (1 Timothy 1:14)

Biblical love is not a vague, random force that we discover or
"fall into." The Scripture says our *faith* and *love* originate *in*
Christ Jesus. The Son of God revealed himself in many
personal ways before coming as a baby – at times in human
form as *the angel of the Lord.*[220]When God revealed himself to
Moses in the burning bush, he declared his name, "I AM WHO
I AM,"[221] suggesting a person, not just a philosophical idea.

Some people try to make "God" equal to "love." God's
attributes, however, should not be exclusively limited to love.
The Bible does teach, *God is love* (I Jn. 4:16), but it also teaches
God is a lot more.   For example,

- God is *light*; in him there is no darkness at all. (1 Jn. 1:5)
- God is *holy* (Ps. 99:9).   This is the only attribute of God
  that is used in multiples of three: *"Holy, holy, holy is the*
  Lord God Almighty..." (Rev. 4:8)
- God is *just.* (II Thes. 1:6). Because he is perfect justice,
  he must deal with evil.
- God is a *consuming fire*, a jealous God. (Heb. 12:29)
  This is why he cannot accept multiple "gods" in our
  lives, just like most wives would be quite jealous if
  there were additional wives in their homes!

Love, therefore, is a major attribute of God, but not his only
one. Almighty God is much greater than we can ever grasp, like
an ant trying to grasp who a human being is. This is why Christ
came, in flesh-and-blood, to reveal God and his love. God had
previously sent prophets, inspired writings, and signs and
wonders, but his ultimate revelation came *personally*–in Christ.

In today's technology-driven world, people are being
increasingly drawn into impersonal means of communication
(rather than face-to-face).   Jesus, however, desires to show his
love personally to each of us and he longs for us to respond.

Counterfeit Love: Sentimentalism

For I wrote you out of great distress and anguish of heart and with many tears, not to grieve you but to let you know the depth of my love for you. (II Cor. 2:4)

There is a vast difference between genuine, heartfelt emotion and the gushy, sentimental feeling that is often confused with love. An old song said, "Love Makes the World Go Round." This is certainly true in our American culture as we see a proliferation of romance novels and films. Our giant entertainment industry is based on this sentimental idea of love. What is the difference between real love and sentimentalism? Basically this: Biblical love may involve the emotions and even have a romantic dimension to it, but at its core is a commitment to walk out love in action – *whether the feeling is there or not.* A sentimental person, on the other hand, is highly motivated by mere emotions and more in love with love itself.

This superficial view of love is influencing some modern day Christian books, songs, and ministry. I heard a Christian praise song which said, "I love loving you Lord." How shallow! What this song is saying is that "I love the experience of loving the Lord," rather than simply saying, "I love you, Lord." (Period!) We are not to focus on our feelings of affection in worship, but on God himself. Another song said, "Heaven meets earth like a sloppy, wet kiss, and my heart turns violently inside my chest." This is sentimental love at its worst – comparing our encounter with God to a "sloppy, wet kiss!"

I can remember being in a church which was lavishly decorated with many beautiful flowers on Easter Sunday. The choir and pastor seemed to go out of their way to have a flawless service. I remember a person afterwards saying, "What a lovely service!" Yet, in the entire message the pastor preached that day, only one half of one Bible verse was used. What stirred people? Was it truth? Was it the reality of Jesus? Or, was it the sentimental feeling of participating in a "lovely service?" Let us not confuse sentimentalism with the love of God.

Counterfeit Love: Limited Love

If you love those who love you, what reward will you get? Are not even the tax collectors doing that? And if you greet only your brothers, what are you doing more than others? Do not even pagans do that? (Matthew 5:46-47)

Jesus taught his disciples not to love as "pagans" – i.e., limiting our love to those who are a lot like ourselves. Charles Price warned Christians of sinking down to this low level of love.

"On one occasion I was leading a two-week conference in Austria…One person in the group was telling me about the tremendous work God had been doing among the young people in his church fellowship, and particularly how they had been bound together with a real love for one another….However, while he was speaking, I noticed that he only mentioned the young people in the church and said nothing about any older ones. Later that day I asked him if there were any older people in the church. He began to smile and said 'Oh, that is a different story. The young people and the older people don't get on in our church, so apart from Sunday morning, we meet separately for all the other meetings.' I said to him that although he had told us in his talk that the Holy Spirit had given the young people such a great love for each other, it was probably a mistake to attribute it to the Holy Spirit. It does not take the Spirit of God to get a group of young people with similar outlook, similar background, and similar experience to develop a love for each other. That will happen naturally. Neither does it take the Holy Spirit to cause the older folk in the church to gang together and find it more comfortable to meet separately….

"The love of God in our lives is not a love that reinforces the natural divisions among people by only making the love we already have for certain people stronger, but it is a love that breaks down natural barriers."[222]

Therefore, let us not limit our love to our own age group, our friends, or the folks we feel more comfortable with. Let the love of Christ go beyond our natural likes and limits.

Counterfeit Love: Materialism

For the love of money is a root of all kinds of evil.
(1 Timothy. 6:10)

It has been said, "Love God, use things…but don't love things, and use God." Our American culture has a way of stimulating a love for things. We are bombarded with ads that make us discontent – telling us we need the newest cars, clothes, cell-phones, etc. so we can feel better about ourselves and join the "in-crowd." Then we have politicians telling us we all need to pursue "the American dream" which nowadays means we spend more than we can afford and in the process we accumulate a mountain of debt.

Some couples spend years building and furnishing a big house and then they never invite anyone to visit. They are always considering a home improvement or some addition. This is what makes their life exciting–something new! Basically, such people love their things more than they love people, and never consider using their home to bless others.

As we have said before, God is not opposed to wealth or nice things – as long as first things are put first. The biblical balance is found in some verses that follow the one at the top. *Command those who are rich in this present world not to be arrogant nor to put their hope in wealth, which is so uncertain, but to put their hope in God, who richly provides us with everything for our enjoyment. Command them to do good, to be rich in good deeds, and to be generous and willing to share. In this way they…may take hold of the life that is truly life.*[223] Material things are temporal and our hope ought to be in the eternal things. If we are blessed financially, we ought to share.

Are we too wrapped up in our materialism? Is our life consumed with maintaining all our "stuff?" The prophet Haggai rebuked God's people who were so busy with their own houses that they forsook the house of God.[224] Today the "house of God" is the people of God.[225] Do we have time for loving God and people, or are we just too busy with our own house?

Counterfeit Love: Common Cause

That day Herod and Pilate became friends – before this they had been enemies. (Luke 23:12)

It is a curious thing that two people who are quite hostile to one another can suddenly find a measure of comradery between them when they have a common enemy to attack. Such was the case of Herod and Pilate – two men who normally despised each other – who became friends as they united against Jesus. Having objects of disagreement in common – something we both agree to dislike – may bring us together, but it is a counterfeit form of love. I have known some wives who have voiced concerns about their husbands facing spiritual problems. Then, when a mature member of their church addressed a problem with a husband, he reacted and the wife stood with her husband. Police sometimes find abused women who have called for help suddenly join with their husbands to attack the policeman! Such couples may seem to enjoy a renewed sense of love between them, but it only lasts as long as they have a common enemy.

Jonathan Edwards witnessed this counterfeit love in his day: "Indeed there is a counterfeit love that often appears among those who are led by a spirit of delusion. There is commonly in the wildest enthusiasts a kind of union and affection, arising from self-love, occasioned by their agreeing in those things wherein they greatly differ from all others, and from which they are objects of the ridicule of all the rest of mankind. This naturally will cause them so much the more to prize those peculiarities that make them the objects of others' contempt. Thus the ancient Gnostics…boasted of their great love one to another; one sect of them, in particular, calling themselves the *family of love.* But this is quite another thing from that Christian love I have just described: it is only the working of a natural self-love, and no true benevolence any more than the union and friendship which may be among a company of pirates that are at war with the rest of the world."[226]

May we be united in God's love, not a common cause.

Counterfeit Love: Infatuation

Your love must be real...(Rom. 12:9 New Century Version)

I recently heard of a man who hired a helicopter to drop 2,500 carnations and 10,000 love letters on the lawn of a woman he loved. The woman, who apparently was not impressed at all, charged the man with littering. Her comment to reporters was, "He has lost his mind." This man may represent extreme infatuation, but infatuation is a common counterfeit to real love. Infatuation is an intense fascination with a member of the opposite sex that sometimes is described as "falling in love." I can remember a friend of mine sharing how he had such deep feelings of love for the opposite sex; the only problem was – it was for *two* different girls! He could not decide whom he liked better and, in time he lost interest in both. What love!

What are some ways we can distinguish between infatuation and the love of God? (1) Infatuation means continual involvement with the opposite sex, and without it the person never quite feels secure or happy. Love means waiting on God, being secure, and trusting him to bring about a lasting friendship in his good time. (2) Infatuation is mainly physical attraction and involvement. Love involves the whole person – spiritual, mental, and physical (with sex limited to the confines of marriage). (3) Infatuation leads to a possessive relationship. The person constantly wonders if his/her loved one is with someone else, and will even check at times to make sure. Love, on the other hand, *is not possessive.*[227] If we want to control or manipulate another person, we are not being motivated by the love of God. (4) Infatuation usually means a lack of confidence in the other person. True love, however, can say, *"I am glad I can have complete confidence in you."*[228] (5)Infatuation makes excuses for the other's spiritual lack, and does not face reality: "He's not a Christian, but he's such a nice guy", or "After marriage, he'll come around." Love, on the other hand, faces the facts and is marked by honesty and spiritual growth. Let us pray for real love and avoid the shallow imitation of infatuation.

Counterfeit Love: Co-dependency

> *This is what the LORD says: "Cursed are those who put their trust in mere humans, who rely on human strength and turn their hearts away from the LORD....But blessed are those who trust in the LORD and have made the LORD their hope and confidence." (Jer. 17:5-7 NLT)*

Many people seem to look for their security in another person, rather than the Lord. In some cases, persons will stay in an unhealthy (maybe even physically dangerous) relationship because they are so starved for love and too insecure to break free. This is called a "co-dependent" relationship. Three Christian doctors/psychologists have together written a helpful book, *Love is a Choice,* about this counterfeit form of love. The following thoughts are adapted from this book.[229]

A CO-DEPENDENT IN A RELATIONSHIP ...
- Cannot be oneself and feels controlled by the other party.
- Conversely, feels inordinately responsible for others.
- Is afraid to cross the other party lest he/she gets angry.
- Feels insecure; can't stand to be alone; gets jealous easily.
- Fears abandonment; "I'm so afraid of losing him."

Co-dependent relationships sometimes occur between mothers and daughters. One mother was concerned about her daughter being sexually active and wanted a school staff person to talk to the daughter. When asked why the mother herself would not talk to her daughter, the mother responded, "I don't want to lose her as a friend." What a sad situation.

What is the remedy for co-dependent people? The answers are not always simple, but at the root of it is their relationship with God. Will they accept the love of a most gracious heavenly Father? Will their ultimate security rest in the Lord, or in some other person? Are they going to continue to live self-absorbed lives, or humble and deny themselves, and be more concerned about pleasing Almighty God than some other person?

Counterfeit Love: Lust

Amnon son of David fell in love with Tamar...Then Amnon said to Tamar, "Bring the food here into my bedroom so I may eat from your hand."....But when she took it to him to eat, he grabbed her...he raped her. Then Amnon hated her... (2 Samuel 13:1-15)

Many men confuse these two words: love and lust. In fact, much of what our media portrays as "love" in reality is only sexual desire, and most of that is dominated by lust. Amnon had feelings of love for his sister, but within hours those feelings turned to hatred. Amnon was a man driven by lust, not true love. Lust is selfish. Amnon had none of Tamar's interests at heart; he only wanted sex with her. Many a man will talk a good line about how much he loves a woman, but in reality he only wants sex. Lust has a sense of urgency: "I must have that woman and have her at once." True love can wait. Sex can be a beautiful thing in the confines of a godly marriage, or it can be a mere animalistic instinct which has nothing to do with love and leads to frustration. Amnon got his wish – Tamar in bed – and yet afterwards there was no satisfaction; after getting his sexual needs met, he hated her.

Every one of us must be on guard against the danger of lust: *Each one is tempted when he is carried away and enticed by his own lust. And when lust has conceived, it brings forth death.*[230] We cannot blame our lust on the devil or anyone else; the Phillips translation says, *No, a man's temptation is due to the pull of his own inward desires which can be enormously attractive.*[231] Satan may put out a lot of bait for us, but we must guard our hearts. Lust can be very subtle and secretive: "I would if I could..." We should ask constantly: "Am I more concerned for the other person's interests than my own?" It is possible for a Christian man to lust after his own wife, if he only shows her consideration when he wants sex. Let's remember the difference between love and lust: *love is never selfish.*[232]

Counterfeit Love: Homosexuality

They exchanged the truth of God for a lie...Even their women exchanged natural relations for unnatural ones. In the same way the men also abandoned natural relations with women and were inflamed with lust for one another. Men committed indecent acts with other men, and received in themselves the due penalty for their perversion. (Rom. 1:24-27)

In the past two decades there has been a tremendous push in our popular culture for a universal acceptance of the homosexual lifestyle and same-sex marriage, including, for the first time, an endorsement from a President of the United States in 2012. Sadly, several major church denominations have softened their view of homosexuality, allowing homosexuals to become church members and even pastors/priests. It is important that Christians have a *clear* and *uncompromising* view of this issue. We can certainly show love to homosexual people, but there are several specific reasons we cannot accept homosexuality.

1. Homosexuality goes against God's natural order and is against his clear commands.[233] This is not a man's biased opinion or a case of homophobia; it is God's opinion.

2. Homosexuals, generally, are *not* moral people and are usually *not* interested in long-term relationships. Over a lifetime, 74% of male homosexuals have more than 100 partners; half of these strangers. 28% report more than a thousand partners.[234] Only 8% of homosexuals and 7% of lesbians have relationships lasting more than three years.[235]

3. The media completely ignores the serious health issues related to homosexual activity.[236]

4. The media implies there is a great demand for homosexual unions, but there is not. Official data reveals that gays and lesbians comprise only about 2 to 4 percent of the American population[237] In 2010, the U.S. Census Bureau counted fewer than 650,000 same sex couples – only 1 out of 167 American households. Why should we allow such a group to set the country's morality? Let's do things God's way!

Counterfeit Love: Sex (only)

*For this reason a man will leave his father and mother
and be united to his wife, and they will become one
flesh. (Gen.2:24)*

God created sex and designed it to be a good and exciting part
of life within the covenant of marriage. The expression above,
one flesh, includes the sexual union.[238] When God created male
and female, with all their body parts, he said, *it was very
good.*[239] To *become* "one flesh" implies an ongoing process;
and it involves the physical, the emotional, and the spiritual.
Sex is meant to be an exciting part of marriage, as the Bible
describes: *May you rejoice in the wife of your youth...may you
ever be captivated by her love.*[240] The word *captivated* is also
translated *exhilarated, intoxicated,* and *transported with
delight.*[241] Christian couples ought to enjoy sex!

Christians must think appropriately on sex issues, and not
base our standards from the popular media, which suggests that
love is all about sex. In reality, sex is a *small* part of married
life. Hollywood gives a false impression of sex...that sex is all
that occupies people's minds and it is *the* major event in their
time together. Yet, it has been estimated that even in the best of
marriages, sex is probably less than 3% of a couple's time
together. So, what is the other 97% of our married life like?
David Letterman once interviewed an actor and asked him how
his love scenes in the films compared to real life. The actor
reminded Letterman he had been married twenty years and then
he said, "Here's the difference in a nutshell. In the movies, life
is mostly about sex and occasionally about children. [Real]
married life is mostly about children and occasionally about
sex."[242] In other words, married love is a lot more than sex!

Married couples can learn how to enjoy God's wonderful
gift of sex. If we are walking in love throughout the day with
each other, considering each other's interests above our own,
then sex ought to be the "icing on the cake" of a good marriage.

Premature Love

Daughters of Jerusalem, I charge you: not to awaken love until it is ready... (Song of Songs NLT)

Some parents think it is cute when their young sons and daughters – even in their preteens – start acting in romantic ways toward the opposite sex. They think it is normal for young teenagers to engage in recreational dating – just dating around until sometime, somewhere (it is to be hoped) they might meet decent marriage partners. This modern dating approach is not good because it leads to a lot of heartache and naturally often leads to premarital sex. God has not designed us to be emotionally involved with the opposite sex without also becoming physically involved. Some parents rationalize dating by saying, "Well, they are both Christians and they will exercise self-control." This is foolish thinking, because young people have the same hormones whether they are Christian or not, and if they are involved in an ongoing relationship, we can reasonably assume they will become physically involved.

There is a proper time to *awaken love.* There is *a time to embrace and a time to refrain.*[243] If young people can enjoy each other in wholesome group social settings, instead of feeling a necessity to pair up with someone special, they will be better off. If you have any doubt about this, just survey the number of people who dated in a serious way in high school and examine the fruit of those relationships several years later. You may find very few ever married each other and even fewer of those who married have remained together. The physical dimension of love is a gift of God to enjoy, but it is best to keep it "sleeping" until the proper time. Statistics indicate the longer young girls wait to engage in romantic relationships, the less likely they will become pregnant out of wedlock.[244] If physical love is enjoyed prematurely, it may lead to emotional hurts, guilt, or permanent ramifications such as an unwanted baby or a sexual disease. It is best *not to awaken love until it is ready.*

Acting Love

Children, love must not be a matter of theory or talk; it must be true love which shows itself in action. (I John 3:18 Revised English Bible)

Love in the New Testament is portrayed more often as a verb than a noun – describing what one does or does not do. If a man speaks forth poetic words about love, but his very actions contradict such words, his love is empty. It is like a cloud without rain or a beautifully wrapped package with nothing inside. When we Christians talk to people about God's love, they will be looking for a demonstration of the same. They will look at our families and church, and be more interested in *love which shows itself in action* than all our religious words.

When we find people difficult to love, we can decide to act in love. Scripture says, *If your enemy is hungry, feed him; if he is thirsty, give him something to drink.*[245] I once told a woman who felt she had lost all love for her husband, "Even if you feel you have absolutely no love for your husband, you can choose to perform actions of love. You can cook his favorite meal. You can act civilly toward him even though the emotions are dead."

C. S. Lewis gave this advice on showing love to difficult people, "Do not waste time bothering whether you 'love' your neighbor; act as if you did. As soon as we do this we find one of the great secrets. When you are behaving as if you loved someone, you will presently come to love him. If you injure someone you dislike, you will find yourself disliking him more. If you do him a good turn, you will find yourself disliking him less. There is, indeed one exception. If you do him a good turn, not to please God and obey the law of charity, but to show him what a fine forgiving chap you are, and to put him in your debt, and then sit down and wait for his 'gratitude,' you will probably be disappointed...Do not sit trying to manufacture feelings. Ask yourself, 'If I were sure that I loved God, what would I do?' When you have found the answer, go and do it."[246]

Doing Love

*Let no debt remain outstanding, except the continuing
debt to love one another, for he who loves his fellow-
man has fulfilled the law. (Romans 13:8)*

Real love is not just refraining from doing harm to our
neighbor; it is also positive. It "does" for the other. This is
what Paul means as he writes of the *continuing debt to love
one another*. James Boice commented on this idea. "Let's
think about this 'continuing debt' positively, and ask, What
does it mean to discharge this debt honestly? Here are some
extremely simple but important and often neglected ways.

1. *Listen to one another.* We live in an age in which few
   people really listen to one another. We talk to or at one
   another, of course. To really love another person, we must
   listen. If we do not know how to listen, we must learn
   how. And we must take time to do it.
2. *Share with one another.* We need to share ourselves with
   one another. But, if we are to be open about our lives,
   including our joys and our struggles, it makes us
   vulnerable.
3. *Forgive one another.* None of us is without sin. Therefore,
   we are all guilty of sinning against others. For this reason,
   listening and sharing also involve forgiveness. Sharing
   means expressing our hurts, and listening means hearing
   how we have hurt the other person.
4. *Serve one another.* This does not come to us naturally,
   which is one reason the Bible mentions and illustrates it so
   often. This was practically the last lesson Jesus left with
   the disciples when he washed their feet. Jesus was giving
   an example of menial service, teaching that we are to serve
   others.

What the world needs is the sincere, selfless, sacrificial,
serving love of God displayed in those who know him and are
determined to obey him faithfully."[247]

Practical Love

Jesus...now showed them the full extent of his love...he poured water into a basin and began to wash the disciples' feet, drying them with the towel...(Jn. 13:1)

Love is not an uncontrolled and unpredictable emotion. Real love involves an exercise of the will more than the releasing of emotions. Jesus demonstrated *the full extent of his love* by performing a slave's task – washing the dirty feet of the guests of the house. There is probably little emotion in washing dirty feet or similar practical duties performed unselfishly for others.

Robert Chapman, a godly leader in 19th century England, had a regular practice of cleaning the dirty boots of his visitors, despite their objections. This was his way of "washing feet."[248]

Brother Lawrence wrote *Practicing the Presence of God*, from his experiences living with a brotherhood at a French monastery in the seventeenth century. His job was cooking and cleaning in the kitchen. He felt no resentment, but saw his service as a way to express his love to God: "I will always continue to act purely for the love of God....The time of business does not with me differ from the time of prayer."[249]

William MacDonald added, "We must...guard against the notion that love is confined to a world of dream castles with little relation to the nitty-gritty of everyday life. For every hour of moonlight and roses, there are weeks of mops and dirty dishes. In other words, love is intensely practical. Love cleans the washbasin and bathtub after using them. Love replaces paper towels when the supply is gone so that the next person will not be inconvenienced....It picks up the crumpled Kleenex instead of walking over it. It replaces the gas and oil after using a borrowed car. Love empties the garbage without being asked. It doesn't keep people waiting. It serves others before self.... Love speaks loudly so that the deaf can hear. And love works in order to have the means to share with others."[250]

Day Two Hundred Seventy-Nine
Voluntary Love

But if serving the LORD seems undesirable to you, then choose for yourselves this day whom you will serve... (Joshua 24:15)

God, in his great love, has created us as moral agents with free will. He did not create us as computerized robots who will just automatically love him. Real love can never be coerced. We can freely choose to reject God, and he will never force us to relate to him if we want to despise him.

Hell will be a continual and miserable existence for people who chose to reject Christ and only live for themselves. Men will *all be brought to judgment, all who do not believe the truth but make sinfulness their deliberate choice.*[251] Self-absorbed people would never be happy in heaven – the home of God and a multitude of people and angelic brings who love him.

Hell is actually a manifestation of God's love, as J. Rodman Williams explained, "Strangely enough, hell may be viewed not only as the result of God's holy judgment upon the unsaved, but also as the consequence of His love and mercy . . . Hell with all its misery will be less torment for still sinful persons than to have to live eternally in the presence of a holy God and of those who are continually praising His name...A loving and merciful God will never force people into a heaven for which they are totally unfit."[252] Peter Kreft also believed that "God's love is the ultimate reason for Hell's existence. The premise of God's love results in the conclusion of Hell through the medium of free choice. If you love someone, you give him his freedom. God could have created good little robots, and then there would have been no Hell because there would have been no real persons. Because God loved free persons into existence, Hell became possible."[253] Mankind is destined to live forever – either with God or without God. Because he loves us, each of us now has that choice. Do you want Christ and heaven...or no Christ and hell? What is your choice?

Day Two Hundred Eighty
Truthful Love

...the beloved Gaius, whom I love in truth. (3 John 1 ESV)

I once knew a man who was obsessed with lying. He didn't just lie about major things, but he would lie about little things. If he bought something extra at the grocery store and his wife asked him about it, he would deny buying anything extra. If he forgot to stop by the post office, he would make up some ridiculous excuse why he did not stop. Needless to say, his wife suffered severely living with a man whom she simply could not trust.

Love cannot be separated from truth. If we are to love God, we must also embrace truth. We cannot say "I love God," but ignore truth, which resides in Christ himself (Jn. 14:6) and his word (Jn. 17:17). Embracing falsehood is a most serious matter. No person who is a continual, deliberate liar will ever enter heaven.[254] As we love each other, we are also to walk in truthfulness with each other. Notice this exhortation, written to Christians. *We will speak the truth in love, growing in every way more and more like Christ.... So stop telling lies. Let us tell our neighbors the truth, for we are all parts of the same body.*[255]

Why do we tell lies? Three common reasons are:

- **Insecurity.** We sometimes lie to make people like us better. Yet, in the love of Christ, we ought to be secure, because he has *made us accepted in the Beloved.*[256]
- **Fear.** To save ourselves in awkward circumstances, we might tend to lie, yet *perfect love casts out fear.*[257]
- **Selfishness/pride**. We may exaggerate to make ourselves look better than we actually are. If you are a "new man in Christ," then *don't lie to each other, for you have stripped off your old sinful nature and all its wicked deeds.*[258]

Being truthful with one another does not always mean being "brutally honest." Some people pride themselves by "telling it just like it is," but that is not always the loving thing to do. To tell a mother "your baby looks ugly" might be a truth, but it certainly would not be loving. Let's speak the truth but in love.

Day Two Hundred Eighty-One
Obedient Love (Part 1)

Whoever has my commands and obeys them, he is the one who loves me. He who loves me will be loved by my Father, and I too will love him and show myself to him. (John 14:21)

We often make love out to be a sentimental or emotional thing, whereas God looks for obedient action to demonstrate our love to him. Imagine a father who instructs his child to take the household trash cans out to the road. The child becomes excited and exclaims, "Oh, goody! Daddy spoke to me! How wonderful – I have heard a word from Daddy!" If such nonsense were uttered by a child, the father would likely say, "Hush up child, and just do as I say – take the trash out!" In church meetings, sometimes folks applaud after a profound or prophetic word comes forth, but our obedient response is what counts.

Much of the love we exhibit will be done as obedient action, not because of the feelings we have. Winkie Pratney defined love as "the rule of unselfishly willing the highest good for God and His universe."[259] In the verse above, we are given a threefold promise for obedient love. First, we will be loved by the Father. Second, Jesus will also love us. Third, Jesus says he will *show* himself to us. The King James Version says, *"I will...manifest Myself to him." The Amplified Bible* adds, *"I will let Myself be clearly seen by him and make Myself real to him."* What a wonderful promise for those who obey the Lord. If we are obedient, we can expect personal revival all the time! We do not have to worship for an hour or wait in lengthy meditation before we experience the presence of God. We simply need to demonstrate our love to the Heavenly Father by obeying what He has told us to do. The Greek word for *obey* means not just "to do or to comply;" but it means, "to listen – like a porter who has the duty to listen when there is a knock at the door."[260] It is used of the servant girl, Rhoda, who *listened* to Peter's knock at the door.[261] May we too, hearken when our Master is knocking.

Obedient Love (Part 2)

If you love me, you will obey what I command. (Jn. 14:15)

William Barclay emphasized the necessity of obedience in the Christian life, as he commented on this passage. "To John there is only one test of love and that is obedience. It was by his obedience that Jesus showed his love of God; and it is by our obedience that we must show our love of Jesus. C. K. Barrett says: 'John never allowed love to devolve into a sentiment or emotion. Its expression is always moral and is revealed in obedience.' We know all too well how there are those who protest their love in words but who, at the same time, bring pain and heartbreak to those whom they claim to love. There are children and young people who say that they love their parents, and who yet cause them grief and anxiety. There are husbands who say they love their wives and wives who say they love their husbands, and who yet, by their irritability and their thoughtless unkindness bring pain to the other one. To Jesus real love is not an easy thing. It is shown only in true obedience."[262]

Now, we cannot stop at this truth; there is some additional good news to know. This verse above in John 14 (about showing our love through obedience) is followed by a verse saying that Jesus will send the Holy Spirit to help us! *I will ask the Father, and He will give you another Helper, that He may be with you forever... He abides with you and will be in you. I will not leave you as orphans; I will come to you* (vv. 16-18). The Greek word for *Helper* is *parakletos* and no single English word can fully translate it. In the Greek it meant, "someone called alongside to help" in a time of trouble or need. It might be someone that would help plead your case in court or someone to stand beside you and encourage you in battle.[263] *The Amplified Bible* gives some of the various meanings: *Comforter, Counselor, Helper, Intercessor, Advocate, Strengthener, and Standby.* Yes, we must show our love by obedience and thank God the Holy Spirit is here to help us.

Emotional Love

During the days of Jesus' life on earth, he offered up prayers and petitions with loud cries and tears... (Hebrews 5:7)

Because love involves a decision and obedient action, we cannot say it is without emotion. Jesus' love was not based on emotion, but on doing the will of the Father. However, his love for people often displayed strong emotion. He wept upon hearing of the death of Lazarus, and he showed affection as he took children in his arms. Jesus as a human was not detached from emotion. He loves us all with a deep, deep affection.

I grew up in a family where little affection or emotional love was shown. Even though I knew my parents loved me, I missed out on something important, and after I became a Christian I had to work on being more expressive in my love. Love was never meant to be something stoical or impassive. It is abnormal for a husband to not display any emotions of love toward his wife. How would any typical wife respond to a listless, dead-panned husband who on rare occasions muttered in a monotone voice, "Honey, you know I really do love you..."? It is doubtful she would be convinced!

In the Bible we are told to *love one another deeply, from the heart.* [264] If we love only as a duty, a command to be fulfilled, we might easily adopt the wrong attitude of "I can love him, but I don't like him." Jerry Bridges confessed his own shortcomings in this regard. "One of the greatest moments of my Christian life occurred one day when I opened my arms and warmly embraced a brother in Christ whom I disliked for several years. God had so dealt with me that I finally realized to think about anyone, 'I will love him, but I can't like him' was a great deal less than God's standard of love and was therefore a sinful attitude on my part." [265] If we are having difficulty in this area, let us not just *decide* to do acts of love; let us *desire* to do them. If we humble ourselves and ask, God will surely help us.

Progressive Love

And this is my prayer: that your love may abound more and more in knowledge and depth of insight. (Philippians 1:9)

When I met Teresa, the girl I would eventually marry, there were many things that impressed me. But, the preeminent characteristic that drew me was her love for God. I detected she had a genuine love in her heart which would grow in the years to come. Teresa had only been a Christian for a year and was just beginning to grow in her knowledge of God. I had been a Christian just four years and was maybe a step ahead of her spiritually. I knew neither of us had *at that time* all the love which would sustain us "in good times and bad." But, I felt I would grow in the love of God and that Teresa had a heart to grow in the same. I had heard a good definition of marriage: "a commitment of a husband and wife to grow together in the love of Christ." This has certainly been true for us and now thirty-seven years later, we are still growing in the love of God (by his grace). On one anniversary, Teresa gave me this lovely poem:

> When I first said that I loved you,
>   there was no way I could know
> How the feelings that I had back then
>   Would deepen and grow –
> Now I realize how true love builds
>   On all that's gone before,
> And I know that with each passing year,
>   I'll love you more and more.[266]

This is an excellent description of the love of Christ in our hearts. His love is not a stagnant, settled, and stunted emotion; it is ever living, moving forward and growing in maturity. When we surrender our lives to Christ, we begin to experience the love of God, but also soon realize our deficiencies in loving others. This realization should not unduly alarm us; nevertheless, we will need to grow in his everlasting love. We should pray for one another–that our *love may abound more and more.*

Desirous Love

One thing I have desired of the LORD, that will I seek:
that I may dwell in the house of the LORD all the days
of my life, to behold the beauty of the LORD, and to
inquire in His temple. (Psalm 27:4 NKJV)

Nancy DeMoss wrote, "As a military strategist and warrior, as a musician and poet, and as a statesman and king – in virtually every way – David stood head and shoulders above the men of his day. This man had it all – fame, popularity, fortune, natural ability, and loyal friends. So when David says, 'One thing have I desired of the LORD, that will I seek after,' we wonder, 'What is the deepest desire and longing of this man's heart? What matters to him more than anything else? What is his highest earthly priority? If only one thing could be said of him at the end of his life, what would he want it to be?'

"By the way, how would you finish that sentence? 'One thing have I desired of the Lord; that will I seek after: _____.' What is the greatest desire and longing of your heart? In the answer to that question lies the explanation for much of what we do – our choices, our priorities, our use of time, the way we spend money, the way we respond to pressure, whom or what we love. David's answer reveals why God could say. 'This man's heart beats like Mine...'

"David had one supreme, driving passion in life: to walk in intimate union and communion with God. It is as if he were saying, 'If I can only accomplish one thing in my life, if nothing else gets done, this is the one thing that really matters to me; this is my highest goal and my number one priority: to live in the presence of the Lord, to look on His beauty, and to learn from Him. I want to know Him, to love Him, to have an intimate relationship with Him. That's the one thing in my life that matters most. And that is the one thing I am going to pursue above all others.'"[267]

May God grant us a heart like David so we can say, "Above all else, I want to know Him and to love Him.

Prayerful Love (Part 1)

Be clear minded and self-controlled so that you can pray. Above all, love each other deeply...(1 Pet. 4:7, 8)

In these verses, there seems to be a close link between love and prayer. When our hearts are full of love toward others, we find ourselves naturally praying for them. If we feel our love for others is lacking, possibly one thing that will kindle greater love in our hearts is deliberate and sincere prayer for such people. This may include people who agitate us, malign us, or even threaten harm to us. Martin Luther once said, "There is no greater love than to intercede before God for bloodthirsty enemies."[268] This follows Jesus' advice, *"Love your enemies and pray for those who persecute you."*[269] We may have no feelings of love whatsoever toward some people, but we can still pray for their welfare. Andrew Murray said, "If you wish your love to grow and increase, you must deny yourself even in prayer, praying earnestly for God's children....Love compels us to pray. The love of God is bestowed upon believing prayer."[270]

Vera McCoy's only son, Mark, was brutally shot and killed by a man named Charles. Vera's heart was filled with anguished grief, and she recorded her struggle as the Holy Spirit nudged her to forgive: "God wanted me to pray for Charles. 'I can't, Lord,' I whispered. 'Mark was my only son.' *But I gave My only Son for you.* 'That's how it started. I began daily praying for the man who killed my son. It was incredibly hard...As I prayed, over and over, the paralyzing coldness in my heart began to lift."[271] Months later Vera visited Charles and as they both wept and hugged, she was fully able to forgive him.

In Samuel's farewell speech to Israel, he expressed his disappointment for their turning away from the Lord. Samuel probably felt disgust and little inclination to pray for them, but he said, *"As for me, far be it from me that I should sin against the Lord by failing to pray for you."*[272] If we need to love others more, let us pray for them, and God's love will grow.

Prayerful Love (Part 2)

One of His disciples said to Him, "Lord, teach us to pray, as John also taught his disciples." So He said to them, "When you pray, say: Our Father in heaven, Hallowed be Your name. Your kingdom come. Your will be done..." (Luke 11:1-3 NKJV)

We are all familiar with "The Lord's Prayer." A better title might be "The Model Prayer," because the disciples had just asked Jesus *how* to pray. Peter Kreft says that "the world's most perfect prayer" is also a prayer full of love in each request:

"We call God 'our Father' because we believe in His fatherly love and care.

"We want His name hallowed and loved and praised, because we love Him and want others to do the same.

"We want His kingdom to come because His kingdom is the kingdom of love.

"We want His will to be done, even in preference to our own – we want the abolition of our own will when it is out of alignment with His – because we know His will is pure love. Ours is not.

"If *this* is done on earth as it is in Heaven, then we will approach heaven on earth, the annihilation of lovelessness.

"We ask for our daily bread because we know His love wants to give it. Love longs to fulfill the needs of the beloved.

"We ask to be forgiven as we forgive because love forgives, 'it is not irritable or resentful' (I Cor 13:5).

"We ask to be delivered from temptations against love and from the evil that comes when love leaves, because we know 'the one thing necessary'.

"Finally, we praise His kingdom, His power, and His glory because they are nothing but the reign of love."[273]

Putting on Love

Above all, clothe yourselves with love... (Col. 3:14 NLT)

Possibly you have been in a public setting, like a restaurant, when a young woman walks in with skimpy clothing, and some older person mutters, "Why doesn't she put some clothing on?" Sometimes, we may also be lacking – in our spiritual clothing.

The book of Colossians, chapter three, compares the Christian life to putting off and then putting on certain "clothing." Some things we are told to put off are *anger, rage, malice, slander, and filthy language.*[274] It is important to "put off" certain things when we follow Christ. Now, there are some folks who think this is enough – that if they just quit cussing, stop doing "bad things," and "clean up their act" a little, things will be OK between them and God. But, this is like a man who takes off all his clothes and thinks he is ready to walk out the door! It is not enough to "take off" certain things; it is equally important that we *put on* some new clothing. Paul, in his letter to the Colossians, gives us the list we are to "clothe ourselves" with:[275]

- *tenderhearted mercy*
- *kindness*
- *humility*
- *gentleness*
- *patience*
- *forgiveness*

How do we do this? It will happen in our daily relationships, for we will have multiple opportunities to choose the "right clothing." We can be harsh, or put on *tenderhearted mercy.* We can remain stubborn or proud, or we can choose to put on *humility.* We can live in bitterness, or we can choose to put on *forgiveness.* In his list of the right spiritual clothing, Paul sums it up with one word: love – our most important garment. *Above all, clothe yourselves with love, which binds us all together in perfect harmony.*[276] Let us never be embarrassed because we have failed to dress adequately; let's put on love.

The Love Chapter (Part 1)

I am writing to God's church in Corinth, to you who have been called by God to be his own holy people... (1 Cor. 1:1 NLT)

It might seem strange that God selected the city of Corinth as the recipient of the most famous description of love – Paul's first letter to the Corinthians, chapter 13. Yet, it should not be surprising, because God's love is so often seen in the lives of exceedingly sinful people. John Stott explained, "Corinth was associated in everybody's mind with immorality. Behind the city, which Julius Caesar had beautifully rebuilt in 46 B.C., nearly 2,000 feet above sea level, rose the rocky eminence called the Acrocorinth. On its flat summit stood the temple of Aphrodite or Venus, the goddess of love. A thousand female slaves served her and roamed the city's streets by night as prostitutes. The sexual promiscuity of Corinth was proverbial, so that the Greek word *korinthiazomai* meant to practice immorality, and *korinthiastes* was a synonym for a harlot. Corinth was 'the Vanity Fair of the Roman Empire.' But the gospel of Christ crucified summoned the Corinthians to repentance and holiness, and warned them that the sexually immoral would not inherit the kingdom of God (6:9ff)."[277]

When Paul wrote his letter to the church in Corinth, he addressed some of their serious problems – division and cliques (1:10-12); jealousy and quarreling (3:1-4); gross sexual immorality – even a male church member living with his stepmother (5:1-13); drunkenness at the communion table (11:21-33); and the misuse of spiritual gifts (Ch. 12, 14). Yet it was this unique group of believers that would receive such special instructions about love. Paul recognized the grace of God that the Corinthians had received[278] and when he wrote of the thieves, drunkards, adulterers, and homosexuals in Corinth, he concluded his statement with these triumphant words, *'...and such were some of you.'* (I Cor. 6:11) Paul witnessed the love and grace of God changing the worst of people. Yes, it is most fitting that God's "love chapter" was written to saved sinners who were being sanctified at Corinth.

The Love Chapter (Part 2)

Follow the way of love and eagerly desire spiritual gifts… (1 Corinthians 14:1)

One of the great controversies in the contemporary church involves the place of spiritual gifts. Some claim that such gifts as tongues, healing, and prophecy passed away in the early church, and are no longer relevant for today. Others over-emphasize the gifts and as a result end up acting in strange ways or neglecting sound theology. It is no coincidence that "The Love Chapter," 1 Corinthians 13, is stuck right between the two chapters that deal specifically with the use and misuse of spiritual gifts – chapters 12 and 14.

In my Christian journey I have been blessed to fellowship with quite a diversity of believers from several nations – both Pentecostal and non-pentecostal. I have been blessed by authors from backgrounds that are active in the realm of the Holy Spirit and others who rarely mention the Spirit. I have pastor friends who are charismatic and some who are not. The love of Christ, however, overrides our differences and is our bond of unity.

On this side of heaven we will never agree with all our Christian brothers and sisters on the use or misuse of gifts. However, we ought to agree on the following:

- Any gift is a simply a manifestation of the *grace* of God (1 Peter 4:10). The word for gift, *charisma,* is derived from the word for "grace" – *charis.* What we have is not our own.
- *Every one* of us has been blessed with certain gifts (Rom. 12:3: 1 Cor. 12:7), and most are probably not spectacular.
- Each one should use whatever gift he has received to *serve others* and spread God's love. Gifts are to bless *others*, not to boost an ego or further selfish purposes. (1 Cor. 14:12)
- The purpose of the Holy Spirit is to *exalt Christ*, not some man or ministry (John 16:13-14).
- *Fruit* of the Holy Spirit is as important as gifts of the Holy Spirit, (Gal 5:22-23) and love is the most important fruit. Despite different views we have, we must not fail to love.

The Love Chapter (Part 3)

Love is patient, love is kind. It does not envy, it does not boast, it is not proud. It is not rude, it is not self-seeking, it is not easily angered, it keeps no record of wrongs. Love does not delight in evil but rejoices with the truth. It always protects, always trusts, always hopes, always perseveres. Love never fails...
(1 Corinthians. 13:4-8)

The "Love Chapter" is probably the most popular chapter in the Bible. It is used frequently in weddings. In reality, however, this passage should be one of the most frightening – as it convicts us of how dreadfully short we fall in displaying this kind of love. How many marriage difficulties would be resolved if both partners operated in this dimension of love?

The love portrayed here is much deeper than the superficial, sentimental type of love so prevalent in our society. This is *agape* love in the Greek language, a heavenly dimension of love which aptly describes the kind of love that God shows each of us. God is incredibly *patient* toward us and so wonderfully *kind.* He is *slow to anger,*[279] and when he forgives us, he *keeps no record of wrongs.* His love for us *never fails.*

When we think of relating to one another in this kind of love, we realize it is impossible for any natural man to manifest it consistently. This "Love Chapter" will serve as a mirror to reveal our blemishes and point us to Christ. Earlier in the passage it says we can have a high level of knowledge, faith, or ability, and yet if we are lacking in love, we have *nothing.*[280]

In the devotions which follow, we will look at each phrase of this extraordinary passage, so we can meditate more fully on each facet of heavenly love. As we realize how needy we are, we can cry out for God to supply our lack. If God's people live in the reality of this chapter, we are bound to influence the world around us. D. L. Moody once said, "When the Church lives in the power of the 13th chapter of First Corinthians I am sure that many will be added daily to the flock of God."[281]

Love Is Patient (Part 1)

When the way is rough, your patience has a chance to grow. So let it grow and don't try to squirm out of your problems. For when your patience is finally in full bloom, you will be ready for anything, strong in character, full and complete. (James 1:2-3 TLB)

Imagine this scene: You are at the checkout counter with only a few items and you have a deadline to meet soon. The lady in front of you with her basket full is chatting casually with the new checkout lady. Just as your gears have really started to grind, it is now your turn to pay, and...the register runs out of tape. The manger is called to fix the machine and you continue to wait...

Billy Graham has defined patience as "the ability to absorb strain and stress without complaint and to be undisturbed by obstacles, delays or failures." [282] In our busy, fast-paced, "get-it-now" society, patience is often lacking. Many a husband has a wife who takes more time than he does to get ready, so he acts short with the woman he should love. Many a person makes a financial mistake, because he was impatient and went quickly into debt. John Bunyan wrote, "Passion wants all of the best things now, while patience is willing to wait."[283] Phillip Keller said, "So often we human beings, rather than exercising patience, prefer to opt out of adversity. Endeavoring to escape from difficult situations, we try to avoid and cut ourselves off from awkward people. We kick over the traces, shake off the harness, and break up anything that might bind us into suffering. Yet the patience of God spoken of in the New Testament is just the opposite. It is a picture of a beast of burden remaining steadily under control. It is an ox yoked to a plow breaking up the stiff soil of its owner's field. No matter whether the plow runs into rocks, stumps or heavy sod, the patient beast just pulls on steadily. Regardless of summer sun, the annoyance of flies or chilling winds, the strong beast goes on breaking ground for its master."[284] True love is steady and patient.

Love Is Patient (Part 2)

*His fellow servant fell to his knees and begged him,
"Be patient with me, and I will pay you back." But he
refused. Instead, he went off and had that man thrown
into prison... (Matthew 18:29-30)*

If we have love in our hearts for our fellow man, then we must
learn to be patient, and we can be certain that our patience will
be tried. It may be that child who acts so contrary, that
employee who makes so many mistakes, that friend we
discover chewing tobacco, or that church member with the
irritating personality. Even close friends may touch a nerve as
we start to see their imperfections. Fenelon said, "It should be
remembered that even the best of people leave much to be
desired, and we must not expect too much. We need to be very
patient with the faults of others....Sometimes we find the most
surprising faults in otherwise good people."[285]

We can be patient with one another if we just stop and
think about how patient God has been with us. If it were not
for God's patience, there would be no salvation: *God is patient
with you, not wanting anyone to perish, but everyone to come to
repentance.*[286] As we look back on our own personal lives, do
we think God has been frequently patient with us? When I
consider my many years of independence – living in pride,
selfishness, and a multitude of sins, and then consider how I
would have fared in the presence of a Holy God, I would have
to say God has been *very* patient with me. Therefore, if God has
been so incredibly patient toward me, I should also be patient
with my fellow man. In the above account from Matthew, a
servant was forgiven of a great debt by his master, but then he
refused to forgive a fellow-servant a smaller debt. When the
master found out about it, he had the unforgiving servant sent to
the torturers. How many times have we been too demanding,
too harsh, too critical of one's poor performance, and just plain
ugly in the way we have acted toward another child of God? We
have no excuse for not showing the patient love of Christ. We
are to be *patient with all men.*[287]

Love Is Kind

*And be kind to one another, tender-hearted, forgiving
one another, just as God in Christ has forgiven you.
(Ephesians 4:32)*

Probably every one of us wants other people to like us, but what is the one quality that will tend to make us more inviting, more desirable in the eyes of other people? Scripture says, *That which makes a man to be desired is his kindness.*[288] Much more than our appearance, our possessions, our knowledge – people will be drawn to us by our kindness. How many husbands would like to be more desirable to their wives? If I were to survey what Christian wives desire in a husband, probably their top answer would be a "man who loves God." Probably next on the list would be a man who was kind and considerate.

Let us think back on our own salvation experience. What is it that drew us to the Lord? Was it the wrath of God? The Bible says, *The kindness of God leads you to repentance.*[289] God is extremely kind to us. Frederick Faber's hymn says, "For the love of God is broader than the measure of man's mind; And the heart of the Eternal is most wonderfully kind."[290]

Kindness should mark our relationships with others. When the apostles were mistreated and slandered, they said, *"We answer kindly."*[291] "The nicest thing we can do for our Heavenly Father," wrote St. Teresa of Avila, "is to be kind to his children." Job's comforters had a lot of advice for a suffering man, but not much compassion or kindness. Job replied to them, *For the despairing man there should be kindness from his friend; lest he forsake the fear of the Almighty.*[292] Kindness is being gracious, mild, sweet, benevolent, and forbearing (instead of being harsh, abrasive, bitter, unfriendly, or spiteful.)[293] Greek scholar Richard Trench says "sweetness" is probably the closest synonym.[294] This Greek word for *kind* is used where it says, "The old wine is *better.*"[295] Have you ever had bitter wine? Or bitter tea? Most people would prefer sweet to bitter. When we are jarred, what will spill over – sweetness or bitterness?

Love Does Not Envy (Part 1)

But if you harbor bitter envy and selfish ambition in your hearts, do not boast about it or deny the truth. (James 3:14)

Many of the worst relational problems recorded in Scripture occurred as a result of envy. Cain killed his brother, Abel, because he envied Abel's more acceptable offering.[296]Joseph's brothers sold him into slavery because they were envious of the extra attention their father showed him.[297] Moses was opposed by Korah and Dathan because they felt envious of his holy position with God. [298] Daniel was persecuted by other administrators envious of his high position and his *extraordinary spirit.*[299] Jesus was handed over for Pilate's judgment because the Jewish leaders envied the large following he had.[300]

Envy can bring great personal harm to us – both spiritually and physically. Scripture says, *A heart at peace gives life to the body, but envy rots the bones.*[301] Some commentators blame the cause of disorder in the Corinthian church on the misuse of spiritual gifts. However, a greater cause of the church disorder at Corinth was envy: *For where you have envy and selfish ambition, there you find disorder and every evil practice.*[302] Paul reproved their immature, schismatic thinking: *"For where there are envy, strife, and divisions among you, are you not carnal and behaving like mere men?"*[303] Envy usually occurs out of insecurity or when we wrongly compare ourselves to someone else. We have potential to envy when someone is honored or prospers more than we do. In such cases, we can either become jealous or *rejoice with those who rejoice.*[304]

The remedy for envy is a larger view of the body of Christ. Scripture says, *Therefore let no one glory in men. For all things are yours: whether Paul or Apollos, or Cephas...all are yours.*[305] In other words, if the Lord blesses the ministry of another brother, I can rejoice; he is actually part of me, and his ministry is part of my ministry. In my human body, my fingers are not envious of my toes. My mouth does not resent my ears. We need never envy another believer: *All things are yours!*

Love Does Not Envy (Part 2)

Love doesn't want what it doesn't have...
(1 Corinthians 13:4 The Message)

This is the essence of envy – wanting what we don't have, and even resenting those who have it! In heaven, there will not be one ounce of envy in any one of the inhabitants because we will be perfectly content in a realm of perfect love. Jonathan Edwards wrote about the absence of envy in our future home: "There is undoubtedly an inconceivably pure, sweet, and fervent love between the saints in glory....For all shall have as much love as they desire, and as great manifestations of love as they can bear. And in this manner, all shall be fully satisfied. And where there is perfect satisfaction, there can be no reason for envy. And there will be no temptation for any to envy those that are above them in glory, on account of the latter being lifted up with pride; for there will be no pride in heaven....

"Heaven itself, the place of habitation, is a garden of pleasures, a heavenly paradise, fitted in all respects for an abode of heavenly love; a place where they may have sweet society and perfect enjoyment of each other's love. None are unsocial or distant from each other. The petty distinctions of this world do not draw lines in the society of heaven, but all meet in the equality of holiness and of holy love....

"The joy of heavenly love shall never be interrupted or trifled by jealousy. Heavenly lovers will have no doubt of the love of each other....There shall be no such thing as flattery or insincerity in heaven, but there perfect sincerity shall reign through all in all. Everyone will be just what he seems to be, and will really have all the love that he seems to have. It will not be as in this world, where comparatively few things are what they seem to be, and where professions are often made lightly and without meaning. But there, every expression of love shall come from the bottom of the heart, and all that is professed shall be really and truly felt....The saints shall know that God loves them, and they...shall have no doubt of the love of all their fellow inhabitants in heaven."[306]

Love Does Not Boast, It Is Not Proud

*Love...is neither anxious to impress nor does it cherish
inflated ideas of its own importance. (1 Corinthians
13:4 Phillips)*

Before I became a Christian, most of my relationships with the
opposite sex were marked by immaturity, selfishness, and a
lack of confidence. Later, after I came to know the Lord and
had met Teresa, the woman who would soon become my wife, I
noticed something different about her. Our relationship with
each other was so forthright and peaceful that neither of us felt
any need to impress the other or act in a phony manner. We
could both just be ourselves. We realized then that love is not
anxious to impress.

If we have love in our hearts we will find little room for
acting in pride or wrongly trying to impress others. Any time
we do a good deed, we must make sure we are doing it out of
love, and not for any personal recognition. Jesus said, *"Be
careful not to do your 'acts of righteousness' before men, to be
seen by them. If you do, you will have no reward from your
Father in heaven."*[307] The humble man is a man who lives his
life to impress God not men. He is more concerned about what
God thinks than what men think. His motivation is not
self-exaltation or self-recognition, but God's glorification.
Jesus said that when we do a good deed, *don't let your left hand
know what your right hand is doing.*[308] The humble man
simply responds to the Lord and goes about his business. He
doesn't keep spiritual statistics, nor does he allow his "feathers
to become ruffled" if his labor goes unnoticed. Scripture says,
*Let another praise you, and not your own mouth; someone else,
and not your own lips.*[309]

The humble man will live for the glory of God. He will
not have a desire to impress others about himself – even his
spiritual accomplishments. He will want to do all things for
the glory of God; his attitude will be, *Not to us, O LORD, not to
us but to your name be the glory...*[310]

Love Is Not Rude

Love...does not act unbecomingly...(1 Cor. 13:5 NAS)
Love...is not rude (1 Cor. 13:5 NIV)
Love...has good manners (1 Cor. 13:5 Phillips)

Good manners are a practical outworking of our love for one another. Good manners are not primarily for ourselves; they are polite actions performed out of consideration for others. The selfish man may not care much about manners, because he may not really care what other people think. Scripture urges us to be *considerate ...toward all men.*[311] In Greek, this word *considerate* means "that which is fitting, right, moderate, orderly, or gentle."[312]

Most of us probably have plenty of room for improvement when it comes to manners. We may tend to think of manners in terms of proper etiquette, like the way we hold a fork at the table or the way we introduce someone. The following are three practical ways we can show good manners and demonstrate love to others:

- **Avoid thoughtless language.** It is common in our culture to use crude or cutting words, or humor that is not proper. Husbands and wives should never belittle their mates, especially when speaking about them publicly. We must seek to edify and defend those whom we love, not tear them down.

- **Be gentle, not rough.** The word "rude" comes from the Latin, *rudis*, which means "rough, raw."[313] We should be gentle and sensitive to one another. Husbands are to *love their wives as they do their own bodies...For no one ever hates his own body, but he nourishes and tenderly cares for it.*[314] Wives, too, must be gentle.

- **Pay attention when people are speaking to us.** There is nothing more discourteous than a person who looks around the room or at his cell phone when we are speaking to him. If we love someone, we value that person's opinions and words to us. We will give him our undivided attention.

Let us always remember that *love has good manners*.

Love Is Not Self-Seeking (Part 1)

Love...does not seek its own (1 Corinthians 13:6 NKJV)

Self-centeredness is a great problem. Even in the body of Christ it is sadly evident when we look at the best-selling Christian books – most of them have to do with solving personal problems (e.g., fixing marriages, healing hurts, solving financial problems, etc.). Whenever we focus too much on ourselves, we will be lacking in love and personal relationships will suffer. When Jesus calls a man to follow him, he calls him to *deny himself.*[315] This is a call for every believer; there are no exceptions for wounded people. *The Amplified Bible* says here, *If any one intends to come after Me let him . . . lose sight of himself and his own interests.* The following is the proper perspective that enables us to experience true peace and joy:

Jesus first

Others second

Yourself last

Some people will only talk of *their* problems, *their* opinions, and *their* concerns. Then, they may wonder why they have a hard time making friends and experiencing true love. Larry Crabb, a respected Christian counselor, points to self-centeredness as a basic cause of marital conflicts: "The Christian life cannot develop without a deepening awareness of what we first recognized at the time of our conversion: self-centeredness still runs deep within us . . . Self-centeredness convincingly and continually whispers to me that nothing in this universe is more important than my need to be accepted and respectfully treated . . . If people were really moral, murmurs self, then everyone who crosses my path, whether shop-keeper, pastor, or spouse, would devote their resources to making me whole, happy, and comfortable."[316]

As we love, let us learn to deny ourselves and seek the welfare of others, not our own welfare.

Love Is Not Self-Seeking (Part 2)

Love...is never selfish (1 Corinthians 13:6 NEB)

Selfishness goes a lot deeper than most of us can imagine, and it takes the "spotlight" of the Holy Spirit to reveal it and his power to turn us from it. Relationships suffer the most when we relate to people selfishly – not thinking of their best interests, but our own. In the 16th century, Teresa of Avila, a devout Spanish nun and mystic, reflected on this selfless love, exhibited perfectly in Christ, but also expected of his followers.

"When we hope to gain affection from others, we always seek it because of some interest, benefit, or pleasure we hope to receive from them. However 'pure' our affection for another may seem in our own eyes, it is natural that we should want them to feel affection for us. Too often, though, we begin to analyze the affection they show us. Do they feel the same toward us as we feel toward them? Would they do as much for us? Soon we determine that, compared with the way we feel for them, compared with what we would do for them, their love for us has little substance....

"The one who truly loves in spirit cares nothing whether he receives the affection of another or not. When I say this, you may think it odd and unnatural. You may think that such a person will be cold and compassionless toward people while they are occupied with loving God.

"Nothing is further from the truth. A man or woman who learns to love in a detached manner, for the sake of God's love, will love others a great deal. They will love with greater compassion and intensity. Their only concern will be to see the person they love grow in the Lord, no matter what it takes.

"To love others for their spiritual profit and not for our own comfort or benefit – that is what love really is. People who love in this way are always more happy to give than to receive, even in their relationship with the Creator Himself!"[317]

So, Lord, help us to love unselfishly – to "love others for their spiritual profit and not for our own benefit."

Love Does Not Demand Its Own Way

Love… does not demand its own way. (1 Cor. 13:5 NLT)

One thing is certain about love – it will not be "pushy" with people or *demand its own way*. Frank Sinatra recorded a hit song years ago, "I Did It My Way." That song is the antithesis of love. Someone has said that in the end, all mankind will be divided into two groups: those who say "My will be done," or those who say to God, "Thy will be done." Our thinking here affects not only the quality of our relationship with God, but with the people we encounter. Larry Crabb wrote, "The necessary foundation for any relationship with God is a recognition that God is God and we are not. We therefore have no business demanding anything of anyone, no matter how fervently our soul longs for relief from pain. It is wrong to internally demand that your loved one become a Christian or your spouse stop drinking or your biopsy be negative or your rebellious child straighten up. Desire much, pray for much, but demand nothing. To trust God means to demand nothing."[318]

Sometimes we demand perfection from others, but we don't require this same high standard of ourselves. I have seen this occur in some husband-wife relationships. A husband may expect a spotless home and ready romance, yet he is very inconsiderate of his wife, seldom talks to her about her interests, and always has a dozen half-finished, messy projects around the house. This is why Jesus said we need to look at the log in our own eye before we worry about a splinter in our brother's eye.[319]

We also sometimes demand love or satisfaction from another human that can only be found in God. If so, we will certainly be disappointed. Oswald Chambers said, "The love which springs from self-conceit or self-interest ends in being cruel because it demands an infinite satisfaction from another human being which it will never get. The love which has God as its center makes no demands."[320]

O God, help us to die to ourselves and to make no demands of others. Help us to love others with the deep love of Christ.

Love Is Not Easily Angered

Love...is not provoked. (1 Corinthians 13:5 NKJV)
Love ...is not irritable or touchy. (1 Cor. 13:5 TLB)
Love is not quick to take offence. (1 Cor. 13:5 NEB)

Sinful anger is often the symptom of a deeper root problem: *self-love*. I might get angry if people don't appreciate or respect *me*; or if someone is honored or preferred above *me*; or if someone eats what belongs to *me* or sits where I ought to sit or damages what belongs to *me*. Jonathan Edwards wrote, "Love is contrary to all sinful anger....The heart of man is exceedingly prone to undue and sinful anger, being naturally full of pride and selfishness; and we live in a world that is full of occasions that tend to stir up this corruption that is within us....Love is a gentle and sweet disposition and affection of the soul. It will prevent...quarrels, and will dispose men to peacefulness, and to forgive injurious treatment received from others..."[321]

When we are lacking in love, we will tend to be touchy and easily offended. Not all anger is sin, but the following conditions, listed by Joseph Butler, can lead to sinful anger:

- When, to favor a resentment or feud, we imagine an injury done to us;
- When an injury done to us becomes, in our minds, greater than it really is;
- When, without real injury, we feel resentment on account of pain or inconvenience;
- When indignation rises too high, and overwhelms our ability to restrain it;
- When we gratify resentments by causing pain or harm out of revenge; or,
- When we are so perplexed and angry at sin in our own lives that we readily project anger at the sin we find in others.[322]

The remedy for sinful anger is for each of us to restrain our spirit and choose love. *He who has a cool spirit is a man of understanding...The fool comes out with all his angry feelings, but the wise man subdues and restrains them...Everyone should be slow to become angry.*[323]

Love Keeps No Record of Wrongs (Pt. 1)

Love... does not take into account a wrong suffered.
(1 Corinthians 13:5 NAS)

True love will not keep a mental record of wrongs. The New King James translation, *Love...thinks no evil,* is not the best translation here because, in reality, some offenses against us may never be completely forgotten. But, we can avoid *dwelling* on them. The NAS version quoted above better communicates the Greek verb, an accountant's word meaning "to compute, calculate, to count over."[324] In other words, if we truly love, we will not keep recording hurts in our minds. Jay Adams illustrated this from a most unusual counseling session. "Sue and Wilbur came for counseling. She sat there with arms defiantly folded, he nervously shifting from side to side....She opened the conversation with these words: 'I'm here because my physician sent me. He said that there is nothing physically wrong with me. He said I'm getting an ulcer, but not from any physical cause.' All the while her husband sat cowering. Sue reached down into what looked like a shopping bag, and she pulled out a manuscript that was at least one inch thick, on standard size paper, single-spaced, typewritten on both sides. She slapped it down on the counselor's desk and said, 'There is why I'm getting an ulcer.' The counselor saw immediately what it was. It turned out to be a thirteen-year record of wrongs that her husband had done to her. They were all listed and catalogued. Now, what would you have said to her? The counselor looked at Sue and said, 'It's been a long while since I have met anyone as resentful as you....This is not only a record of what your husband has done to you [incidentally, subsequent sessions showed that it was a very accurate record], it is also a record of what you have done about it. This is a record of your sin against him, your sin against God, and your sin against your own body. This is a record you cannot deny; you put it down there yourself in black and white. This record of bitterness shows that your attitude has been the opposite of 1 Corinthians 13, which says that love never keeps records...'"[325]

Love Keeps No Record of Wrongs (Pt. 2)

But I tell you that men will have to give account on the day of judgment for every careless word they have spoken. For by your words you will be acquitted, and by your words you will be condemned. (Matthew 12:36-37)

As we consider God's love for us, these words of Jesus may seem to contradict the verse, *Love...keeps no records of wrongs.* I used to have a fear that I would be severely judged after death for careless words I have spoken in this life. However, there are two clarifications which should bring freedom to believers.

First, while this pronouncement by Christ should create a healthy fear in us concerning careless words, he was not addressing his disciples, but the Pharisees–religious hypocrites who had been accusing him of doing his works by the power of Satan.[326] Jesus called them a *brood of vipers* and warned them of blaspheming the Holy Spirit by their slanderous words.[327]

Second, because of Jesus' death on the cross, the believer escapes the judgment which will be common to unregenerate mankind. God's promises seem too good to be true, but our sins will not count against us on Judgment Day. We have passed from death to life, and from judgment to acquittal; *he does not come into judgment, but has passed from death to life.*[328]Through the death of Christ, we who were once enemies of God are now reconciled and declared to be *holy in his sight, without blemish and free from accusation.*[329] This last phrase, *free from accusation*, should thrill any follower of Christ. It means "free from reproach, without stain, guiltless, that which cannot be called to account, that which has no flaws to pick at."[330] Scripture makes it clear that believers have no license to sin,[331] and God's condemnation is for any *who do not believe the truth but make sinfulness their deliberate choice.*[332] It is staggering to realize, however, that Christians will never have to give an account for sins at the final judgment: *Blessed is the man whose sin the Lord will never count against him.*[333] *There is now no condemnation for those who are in Christ Jesus.*[334]

Love Does Not Delight in Evil But Rejoices With the Truth

*Love...does not gloat over the wickedness of other people...
(1 Corinthians 13:6 Phillips)
Love takes no pleasure in other people's sins but delights
in the truth...(1 Corinthians 13:6 Jerusalem Bible)*

I wonder: if we truly believed this, how much television and movies would we enjoy watching? Movies tend to make us enjoy the exploits and words of wicked men and rarely is there a popular movie that does not condone some act of immorality. Believers are not to dwell on evil or delight in evil. *It is shameful to even mention what the disobedient do in secret.*[335] We are instructed to be *wise in what is good and simple concerning evil.*[336] Our thought life is to center around the things that are *true...noble...right...pure...lovely...admirable... excellent...or praiseworthy.*[337] Think of the last movie you enjoyed watching – did it fit these descriptions?

We are also not to rejoice when someone suffers evil. True love will never rejoice in the misfortunes of another, even when it is a person we intensely dislike. When a person has mistreated us or harmed us in some ways, our natural tendency would be toward revenge – to see that person get his fair due and even to be glad when it happens. However, Scripture says, *Do not gloat when your enemy falls; when he stumbles, do not let your heart rejoice.*[338]

Let us rejoice in truth and be lovers of truth. Truth, or reality, is given its fullest revelation in Christ. We must love truth and welcome truth, especially when it is directed toward ourselves. Sometimes God's truth will clash with our personal interests or expose things hidden in our innermost being, but we must not resist this work of the Holy Spirit. We should not say, "What will truth cost me?" Rather, we should say with the psalmist, *"I have chosen the way of truth."*[339] Let us pray, "Lord, reveal truth to me, even though it might not be easy. I choose to not be resistant toward the revelation you bring, but I will accept truth, walk in truth, and even rejoice in the truth."

Love Always Protects

Love...bears all things... (1 Corinthians 13:7 NAS)
Love ...covers all things... (1 Cor. 13:7 NAS margin)
Love...is always slow to expose... (1 Cor. 13:7 Moffatt)

Four times the Bible says, *love covers a multitude of sins.*[340] The Greek word for *covers* means "to hide or bury it in the earth."[341] If something is buried in the earth, it is difficult to find. This is not to imply that Christians should ignore sins in each other or neglect to deal with them. Sometimes God must first *uncover* sin before he can cover it in his forgiveness. What this passage means is that Christians should leave sin buried after it is dealt with, desiring to cover sin rather than expose it. *He who covers a transgression seeks love, but he who repeats a matter separates the best of friends.*[342]

After the account of Noah and the great flood, there is an embarrassing chapter in the life of this man of faith: *Noah, a man of the soil, proceeded to plant a vineyard. When he drank some of its wine, he became drunk and lay uncovered inside his tent. Ham, the father of Canaan, saw his father's nakedness and told his two brothers outside. But Shem and Japheth took a garment and laid it across their shoulders; then they walked in backward and covered their father's nakedness. Their faces were turned the other way so that they would not see their father's nakedness.*[343]

Right after this incident, both Shem and Japheth and their descendants received a blessing from Noah, while Ham and his descendants were cursed because he *told* his brothers about their dad's drunken condition. The Hebrew word for *told* means, "to declare, to betray, or to celebrate with praise."[344] Ham, in his perverted sense of pleasure, apparently *enjoyed telling* his brothers about their father's shameful condition. In contrast, Shem and Japheth, moved by reverential modesty, backed into the tent and covered their father's nakedness. There are times where a person's sin may need to be discussed or dealt with, but may our hearts always be compelled by love which prefers to see a multitude of sins covered by the mercy of God.

Love Always Trusts

Love...always trusts...(1 Corinthians 13:7 NIV)

By nature we do not trust people, and sometimes we have good reason to be skeptical. When we love, however, we will find ourselves more likely to trust and believe the best of others. Floyd McClung, a missionary leader in Youth With a Mission, has provided a good example of this idea. "Shortly before the Russian invasion of Czechoslovakia in 1968, a church just outside Prague experienced a terrible schism. Five elders fought it out, but none of them won. Consequently the flock scattered in several directions. Realizing the devastating effect of their behavior, the elders became ashamed of their actions, but were too proud to reach out to one another. After some time of praying things through, one of the elders took the initiative, went to the others, and admitted his wrong. A spirit of contrition moved through the various factions in the church, and eventually unity and fellowship were restored. Several weeks after this, Russian tanks rolled into the country. Religious and cultural freedom ended abruptly as the new government cracked down hard. Soon all five elders were arrested. The authorities decided to make them a public example of the consequences of being too vocal about religious matters. A high-ranking officer of the secret police was to interrogate them. Confident that he could get them to incriminate each other, he separated them and began to try to undermine their trust in one another. To his amazement it did not work. Every time he tried to use half-truths and innuendos from the past to divide them, each would simply reply, 'I don't believe my brother would say that about me, and even if he did, I forgive him!' Eventually the officer became so frustrated with this unusual response that he called all five of the men into his office and demanded to know why they loved each other so much. It wasn't long before he was on his knees, asking God to fill him with the same love."[345] It is by our loving trust for each other that our genuineness as Christians is demonstrated.

Love Is Ready to Believe the Best

Love...is ever ready to believe the best of every person...
(1 Corinthians 13:7 The Amplified Bible)

In Jesus' day the Rabbis taught that there were six great works which brought a man credit in this world and profit in the world to come – study, visiting the sick, hospitality, devotion in prayer, the education of children in the Law, and *thinking the best of other people.*[346] For the devout Jew, *thinking the best of other people* was a religious duty, but for the Christian it is more. It is an act of love.

If we are to think the best of others, this does not mean we are to be naive about evildoers or fail to differentiate between truth and error. Believers are told to be wise, discerning, and even to avoid certain people.[347] However, we can be optimistic, because we realize the grace of God in our lives and know he can transform the worst of sinners. Therefore, we can be *ready to believe the best.*

Elisabeth Elliot extensively researched the life of Amy Carmichael, an Irish missionary who left a legacy of her godly example as well as numerous devotional books. Amy spent fifty-three years in South India without a furlough and was the founder of the Dohnavur Fellowship, a refuge for children in moral danger. In her biography, Elliot commented, "People who worked closely with Amy Carmichael found it nearly impossible, after her death, to think of any faults. Perhaps memory did its beneficent work of erasure. One man, however, after weeks of thought, volunteered that Amy indeed had at least one weakness: sometimes she misjudged folk. When asked in what way, he said, 'She thought they were better than they were.' If that [was] her single sin... it is rather more endearing than offensive."[348]

Sometimes we are apt to look for faults in friends and those we know well. Amy Carmichael wrote of Calvary love: "If I do not give a friend 'the benefit of the doubt,' but put the worst construction instead of the best on what is said or done, then I know nothing of Calvary love."[349] Well said!

Love Always Hopes, Always Perseveres

Love hopes all things, endures all things. (1 Cor.13:7 NAS)
Love knows no limit to its endurance, no end to its trust, no
fading of its hope; it can outlast anything. Love never fails.
(1 Cor. 13:7-8 Phillips)

Those who love seem to have the capacity to endure and persevere when everyone else would probably quit. This is often seen in the incredible, persevering love a mother has for a wayward son. When circumstances would indicate that all is lost, a mother's love holds on and maintains a glimmer of hope.

The love of God is able to help ordinary people endure when problems come rolling in like a flood: *Many waters cannot quench love; rivers cannot wash it away.*[350] Love is not drowned or defeated by anything it encounters; *it can outlast anything.* When Scripture says love *endures all things*, such love is no passive resignation or acceptance of what happens. The Greek word for *endure* means "to stand still, to await, to hold out...It includes active and energetic resistance to hostile power... the endurance of pains and afflictions with a steadfast spirit, without being bowed down by them."[351] A picture of this heroic quality can be seen in a soldier who has been struck a few blows by his enemy, but he is standing erect, unwavering. Although he has no external indication that his resistance will be successful, he fully expects to win. He does not allow the difficulties of the moment to rob him of his peace or purpose; he fights on unflinchingly. This is how God's enduring love is.

God's love, because it has a positive, enduring quality, has a way of making time stand still. Jacob was tricked into having to work seven years to obtain Rachel, the woman he wanted to marry. Seven years can be a long time, like for someone attending school. The seven years, however, *seemed like only a few days to him because of his love for her.*[352] Love gives us a way of seeing things quite differently. Love does not always change unpleasant circumstances, but it can change us and help us to *endure all things.*

Love Never Fails

Though there be wealth, it shall rust and decay.
Though there be fame, it shall sink into oblivion.
Though there be political power and supremacy, it shall
  burst like a bubble.
Though there be military might, it shall crumble.
Though there be tongues of eloquence, they shall be stilled.
Though there be beauty of face and form, it shall fade.
BUT LOVE IS FOREVER.

When hoary time shall be no more,
When earthly thrones and kingdoms fall,
When the Ancient of Days is set upon His Judgment Seat,
When angel harps are stilled and Heaven's silence fills the
  universe,
LOVE WILL STILL BE YOUNG.

When the last plane has made its flight,
The last satellite circled the globe,
The last rocket has been launched;
When the debris of the melting cosmos has been swept afar
  by the fiery tempest of God's wrath;
When the new heaven and earth leap from the matrix of the
  ages –
LOVE will still be in its infancy.
It will never grow old, never fade, never decay.
It is life's superlative goal.
It is divine.

Therefore, MAKE LOVE YOUR AIM!

Anonymous[353]

Love Through Me

For we know how dearly God loves us, because he has given us the Holy Spirit to fill our hearts with his love. (Romans 5:5 NLT)

As we bring this devotional study about love to a conclusion, we have considered many facets of the love of God in these pages. Perhaps you are like me. As I reflect on God's love, I can feel woefully deficient and at times even despairing. The more we see the limitless love of God, the more likely we are to see how lacking we are! Yet, the Holy Spirit was not sent to discourage us, but to *fill our hearts with his love.* Whenever we feel we do not have sufficient love we need for others, the Holy Spirit can manifest *the love of God* through our finite beings.

Therefore, we do not need to pray for "more love." If we have Jesus Christ dwelling in our hearts, we already have Love Incarnate. His love is a *fruit of the Spirit* that will continually develop in us. So, instead, our prayer ought to be, "God, manifest your great love through me to others." This simple prayer by Amy Carmichael is one we can all pray.

POUR LOVE THROUGH ME[354]

Love of God, eternal Love,
    Sweep my barriers down!
Fountain of eternal love,
    Let Thy power be known;
Fill me, flood me, overflow me;
Love of God, eternal Love,
    Sweep my barriers down!

Love of God, eternal Love,
    Pour Thy love through me!
Nothing less than Calvary love
    Do I ask of Thee;
Fill me, flood me, overflow me;
Love of God, eternal Love,
    Pour Thy love through me!

Day Three Hundred Twelve
Love: Summary

May the Lord direct your hearts into the love of God...
(2 Thessalonians 3:5 NAS)

Who can separate us from the love of God? With all that we have reflected on concerning love, we have only begun to grasp the greatness of this gift. As we conclude this section of devotions on love, let us summarize a few central truths.

- We can *marvel* at the love of God, enjoyed among the three members of the Trinity from eternity, and now shared with his "magnum opus" – the grandest of his creation in the entire, vast universe – mankind. How *privileged* we are to participate in this divine love!

- We can *appreciate* God's love for fallen man. Even though we have sinned exceedingly, even when we turn away from him, and even if our hearts grow cold – his steadfast love remains forever. Thank you, Lord!

- We can only *stand in awe* as we consider the greatest expression of God's love – sending his one and only Son to not only experience life on this earth, but to be ignored, mocked, and eventually tortured and killed by his own creation. Yet, no army of angels was sent for vengeance and no curse called down; while dying in agony he still loved us: *Father, forgive them; they don't know what they are doing...* What amazing love!

- Finally, *stop and reflect* on the fact that Jesus Christ died on the cross for *you.* He loved *you* so much he was willing to suffer on the cross, to pay for *your* sins, and to give *you* the promise of new, abundant life. How can we not be full of constant, heartfelt praise and worship?

> How marvelous, how wonderful
> And my song shall ever be
> How marvelous, how wonderful
> Is my Savior's love for me![355]

NOTES ON FAITH

1. Ewald Plass, *What Luther Says* (Concordia Publishing House, St. Louis, MO, 1959) p. 497

2. Heb. 11:5

3. Gen. 5:21,24

4. Heb. 11:5

5. 2 Cor. 5:7 NAS

6. A. T. Robertson, *Word Pictures in the New Testament - Vol. IV* (Baker Book House, Grand Rapids, MI, 1931) p. 525

7. Rom. 5:2 *Jerusalem Bible*

8. Phil. 3:9

9. Rom. 4:9,16

10. Rom. 1:17

11. *Table Talk*, Theodore G. Tappert, ed. In Helmut Lehmann, Gen. Ed., *Luther's Works*, (Fortress, Philadelphia, 1967) Vol. 54, pp. 308-309

12. Eph. 4:13; I Cor. 13:11

13. I recommend a short biography, Lindley Baldwin, *Samuel Morris* (Bethany House, Minneapolis, MN, 1942)

14. 2 Tim. 1:5

15. 2 Cor. 2:17

16. A.T. Robertson, *The Glory of the Ministry,* (Baker Book House, Grand Rapids, MI, 1979) p. 47

17. 1 Pet. 1:6-7

18. Heb. 10:38

19. Rom. 1:17; Hab. 2:4; Gal. 3:11; Heb. 10:38

20. Eph. 4:14-15

21. 2 Pet. 3:18

22. Mark Buchanan, *Things Unseen* (Multnomah Publishers, Eugene, OR, 2002) pp. 139-140

23. Ibid., p. 141

24. Mk. 9:19

25. A. W. Tozer, *The Root of the Righteous* (Christian Publications, Camp Hill PA, 1955) p. 48

26. William Tyndale, *Prologue to Romans [1534]*, ed. David Danielle (Yale University Press, New Haven, CT, 1989) p. 213

27. From Irving Larson in "Faith is Resting Upon God," source unknown.

28. Lynn Anderson, *If I Really Believe, Why Do I Have These Doubts?* (Howard Publishing, West Monroe, LA, 2000) pp. 125-126

29. Ron Eggert, compiler, *Tozer on Christian Leadership* (Christian Publications, Camp Hill, PA, 2001) Oct. 6 devotional

30. Josh McDowell and Sean McDowell, *The Unshakable Truth* (Harvest House Publishers, Eugene OR, 2010) p. 213

31. 1 Cor. 4:7

32. Judson Cornwall, *Let Us See Jesus* (Fleming Revell, Old Tappan, NJ, 1981) p. 43

33. Charles Price, *The Real Faith* (Logos, Plainfield, NJ, 1940) pp. 11,16

34. Is. 1:18

35. 2 Cor. 5:21; 1 Cor. 1:30

36. Rom. 4:7-8 NLT

37. Ewald Plass, op. cit., p. 515

38. Graham Miller, *Calvin's Wisdom* (The Banner of Truth Trust, Carlisle, PA, 1992) p. 181

39. Rom. 5:9

40. Rom. 5:9-10

41. Rom. 8:33-34 Phillips NT

42. 2 Cor. 9:15

43. Charles Hodge, *Second Epistle to the Corinthians* (Banner of Truth Trust, Carlisle, PA, 1959) p. 150

44. Phil. 3:9 NLT

45. Robert J. Morgan, *The Promise* (B & H Publishing Group, Nashville, TN, 2008) p. 20

46. Ps. 25:8

47. Ps. 145:17

48. Ps. 97:2

49. Rom. 14:17

50. 2 Cor. 5:17

51. On all these verses, the underlining is mine, for emphasis.

52. William Barclay, *The Letter to the Romans* (The Westminster Press, Philadelphia, PA, 1975) p. 73

53. Kenneth S. Wuest, *The New Testament: An Expanded Translation* (William B Erdmans Publishing Co., Grand Rapids, MI, 1961)

54. Phil. 4:6-7

NOTES ON FAITH

55. C. H. Spurgeon, "Sermons to Ministers and Other Tried Believers," *Unusual Occasions* from The C. H. Spurgeon Collection, version 2.0 (AGES Software, Rio, WI, 2001)

56. Jer. 32:8-15

57. Phm. 22

58. Ps. 46:1 (emphasis mine)

59. Heb. 11:6 NAS (emphasis mine)

60. Matt. 7:11

61. Prov. 15:8 NAS

62. Jam. 4:2

63. Heb. 13:8

64. Ex. 3:14

65. Heb. 11:6 NAS (emphasis mine)

66. Ewald Plass, op. cit., p.499

67. Harry E. Jessop, *The Ministry of Prevailing Prayer* (Light and Hope Publications, Bernie, IN, 1941) p. 109

68. Paul Lee Tan, *Encyclopedia of 7,700 Illustrations* (Assurance Publishers, Rockville, MD, 1979) p. 404

69. Philip Yancey, *Reaching for the Invisible God* (Zondervan Publishing House, Grand Rapids, MI, 2000) pp. 38-39

70. Corrie ten Boom, *Amazing Love* (Christian Literature Crusade, Ft Washington, PA, 2007)

71. Oswald Chambers, *Baffled to Fight Better* (Discovery House Publishers, Grand Rapids, MI, 1990) p. 82

72. Ps. 112:4

73. Billy Graham, *Just As I Am* (Harper, San Francisco, CA, 997) p. 139

74. A. W. Tozer, *Man: The Dwelling Place of God*, quoted in *The Best of A. W. Tozer* (Christian Publications, Camp Hill, PA, 1978) p. 169

75. Jn. 1:3

76. Col. 1:16

77. Matt. 19:4-6

78. Rom. 5:12-19; 1 Cor. 15:22

79. For further reading, I recommend *Should Christians Embrace Evolution?* (P & R Publishing, 2011), edited by Norman Nevin. Contributors include six theologians and six scientists. This book was *World* Magazine's "Book of the Year" for 2011.

80. William MacDonald, *True Discipleship* (Walterick Publishers, Kansas City, KS, 1975) pp. 37-38

81. John 7:17 NAS (emphasis mine)

82. Gen. 11:31-12;1; Acts 7:2-4

83. Ps. 37:23 NAS

84. Matt. 14:29

85. Ex. 24:7

86. As quoted in *Ten Homilies on the First Epistle of John*, Tractate XXIX on John 7:14-18, From *A Select Library of the Nicene and Post-Nicene Fathers of the Christian Church,* Volume VII, by St. Augustine, chapter VII (1888) as translated by Philip Schaff

87. Christopher Shaw, *Lift Up Your Eyes* (Christian Literature Crusade, Fort Washington, PA, 2008) May 15 devotional

88. Charles Ryrie, booklet, *Does it Really Matter What You Believe...* (American Tract Society, Garland, TX, 1991) p. 1

89. A. W. Tozer, *Renewed Day By Day* (Fleming H. Revell, Old Tappan, NJ, 1980) April 10 devotional

90. Ps. 74:9-12 NAS

91. Rom. 8:18

92. Philip Yancey, *Church: Why Bother?* (Zondervan Publishing House, Grand Rapids, MI, 2001) pp. 92-94

93. Ps. 115:3

94. Rom. 8:18-25

95. Lk. 13:1-5; Jn. 16:33; the example of Job – a "righteous man."

96. Rom. 8:31-39

97. Ronald Dunn, *When Heaven is Silent: Live by Faith, Not by Sight* (Thomas Nelson Publishers, Nashville, 1994)

98. Ibid., p. 69

99. Ibid., pp. 184-186

100. Rom. 6:23 NAS

101. William McCarrell, *My Favorite Illustration*, quoted in *Our Daily Times With God* (Discovery House Publishers, Grand Rapids, MI, 1988) p. 127

102. Ps. 14:1; 53:1

103. "Turkey Quake," a report by Jennifer Ludden on National Public Radio's All Things Considered program (August 26, 1999), www.npr.org.

104. Lk. 1:3

NOTES ON FAITH

105. Renowned archeologist, William M. Ramsey wrote, "Luke's history is unsurpassed in respect to its trustworthiness...Luke is an historian of the first rank...He should be placed along with the greatest of historians." (See F. F. Bruce, *The New Testament Documents: Are They Reliable?* Inter-Varsity Press, Downers Grove, IL, 1990, pp. 90-91.) Another great classical scholar and historian, Colin Hemer, identifies in great detail 84 facts in the last 16 chapters of Acts that have been confirmed by historical and archeological research. (See Colin Hemer, *The Book of Acts in the Setting of Hellenistic History,* Eisenbrauns, Winona Lake, IN, 1990.)

106. Lk. 1:4

107. Josh McDowell and Sean McDowell, *The Unshakable Truth* (Harvest House Publishers, Eugene, OR, 2010) p. 414

108. 1 Pet. 1:8 Phillips

109. From the *Four Spiritual Laws* booklet (New Life Publications, PO Box 593684, Orlando, FL 32859)

110. *Spurgeon's Expository Encyclopedia, Volume 7* (Baker Book House, Grand Rapids, MI, 1996) pp. 129-130

111. D. James Kennedy, *New Every Morning* (Multnomah Books, Sisters, OR, 1996) July 13 devotional.

112. A. W. Tozer, *Renewed Day By Day,* Jan. 9 devotional (emphasis mine)

113. William Arndt and F. Wilbur Gingrich, *A Greek-English Lexicon of the New Testament* (University of Chicago Press, 1957)

114. Moulton and Milligan, *Vocabulary of the New Testament* (Hendrickson Publishers, Peabody, MA, 1930).

115. Ceslas Spicq, *Theological Lexicon of the New Testament, Volume 3* (Hendrickson Publishers, Peabody, MA, 1994) p. 423

116. 1 Pet. 1:4-5

117. Heb. 3:14

118. Stephen Sorenson, editor, *The Best of Robert Murray M'Cheyne* (Honor Books, Colorado Springs, CO, 2006) p. 101

119. Lk. 24:27

120. Matt. 5:3

121. Jn. 15:1-7

122. 2 Cor. 4:7

123. 2 Cor. 12:9-10

124. Andrew Murray, *Absolute Surrender* (Whitaker House, New Kennington, PA, 1981) p. 8

125. George Scott Railton (First Commissioner to General Booth), *The Authoritative Life of General William Booth* (George H. Donan Co., NY, 1912). Internet version – Preface pp. 1-2

126. Eph. 2:2-3 NLT

127. Is. 57:20 NLT

128. Eph. 4:19

129. Ecc. 6:7

130. St. Augustine, *Confessions* (Penguin Classics, NY, 1961)

131. Rom. 5:1

132. Phil. 4:7

133. Matt. 5:6; Phil. 3:10

134. Phil. 4:11 *The Amplified Bible*

135. Rom. 4:24-25

136. Francis Schaeffer, *The God Who is There* (InterVarsity Press, Downers Grove, IL, 1968) p. 133

137. 1 Cor. 1:23; Gal. 6:14

138. Gerhard Friedrich, *Theological Dictionary of the New Testament, Vol. VII* (Wm. B. Eerdmans Publishing Co., Grand Rapids, MI, 1972) p. 57

139. Edwin A. Blum, "John" in *The Bible Knowledge Commentary*, editors John Walvoord and Roy Zuck (Victor Books, Wheaton , IL, 1983) p. 340

140. Kenneth Wuest, *Golden Nuggets From the Greek New Testament*, Eerdmans Pub., Grand Rapids, MI, 1940) p.119

141. Matt. 27: 50; Mk. 15: 37; Lk. 23: 46

142. Adapted from William Barclay, *The Gospel of John, Volume 2*, The Westminster Press, Philadelphia, 1975) p. 258

143. Lk. 24:47

144. Acts 20:21

145. Tom Carter, compiler, *2200 Quotations from the Writings of C. H . Spurgeon* (Baker Book House, Grand Rapids, MI, 1988) p. 314

146. A. W. Tozer, *The Pursuit of God* (Christian Publications, Camp Hill, PA, 1982) p. 91

147. "The Ninety-Five Theses, 1517," Henry Bettenson, editor, *Documents of the Christian Church*, (Oxford Press, London, 1969) p. 186 (emphasis mine)

148. Tit. 3:5. Also, see Is. 64:6; Rom. 3:10-12; Eph. 2:8-9

149. John 6:29

150. John 14:15

151. Rev. 2:2,19; 3:1,8,15

NOTES ON FAITH

152. Tit. 1:16

153. Jam. 2:22

154. Ex. 14:15

155. Josh. 8:18

156. Lk. 5:18-25

157. James Montgomery Boice, *The Gospel of John, Vol. 2* (Baker Books, Grand Rapids, MI, 1985, 1999) p. 639

158. Ibid., p.639

159. Job 23:10

160. Deut 8:2

161. Ps. 17:3

162. Samuel Ward, *Sermons,* pp. 33-36, quoted in Richard Rushing, editor, *Voices from the Past* (The Banner of Truth Trust, Carlisle, PA, 2009) p. 49

163. Heb. 13:5

164. Job 23:8

165. Job 23:10-12

166. Story told by Bill Gothard in *Men's Manual, Volume One* (Institute in Basic Life Principles, Oak Brook, IL, 1979) p. 55

167. Mk. 4:35-41

168. Mic. 4:9

169. Eph. 6:18

170. Oswald Chambers, *The Place of Help* (Christian Literature Crusade, Ft. Washington, PA, 1935) pp. 39-40

171. Jer. 12:5

172. 1 Pet. 4:1,12-13,19

173. David Wilkerson archive on January 17, 2012, on the web www.worldchallenge.org

174. Helen Kooiman, *Silhouettes* (Word Books, Waco, TX, 1972) p. 157

175. Bill Gothard "Character Clues" definition cards (Institute in Basic Life Principles, Oak Brook, IL)

176. Rom. 4:11,16

177. Heb. 6:15 Phillips

178. James L. Snyder, *In Pursuit of God :The Life of A. W. Tozer* (Christian Publications, Camp Hill, PA, 1991) p. 135

179. William Barclay, *New Testament Words* (SCM Press, London, 1964) p. 144

180. Jam. 1:3-4 NKJV

181. Heb. 12:2 NAS

182. Gal. 6:9 *The Living Bible*

183. 1 Pet. 5:8-9

184. On the cross, Christ won the victory over sin and Satan (Jn. 19:30; Col. 2:15; 2 Cor. 2:14). Therefore, we do not fight *for* victory; we fight *from* [Christ's] victory. This is why in the great chapter about spiritual warfare in Eph. 6:10-18, four times we are told to *stand,* or hold our ground.

185. 1 John 5:4

186. Heb. 11:32-34

187. 1 Sam. 17:32

188. 1 Sam. 17:45-51

189. 2 Cor. 10:3-5; Eph. 6:10-19

190. Matt. 10:32-33 NAS; Mk. 8:38

191. Mark Galli, *Francis of Assisi and His World* (IVP Books, Downers Grove, IL, 2002)

192. Matt. 5:15

193. Mark 16:15

194. Matt. 12:37

195. Prov. 18:21

196. Matt. 12:34

197. Num. 13:31

198. Num. 13:30; 14:9

199. Zeph. 3:17 ESV; Ps. 105:4 NKJV; Heb. 13:6

200. J. Henry Thayer, *Thayer's Greek-English Lexicon of the New Testament* (Associated Publishers, Grand Rapids, MI)

201. Gen. 39:9 (emphasis mine)

202. 1 Thes. 3:4 NAS

203. 1 Thes. 3:2,5,6,7,10

204. Ps. 116:10 RSV

205. John 16:33

206. John 21:18-19

207. John 8:28-29

208. 2 Cor. 4:13

209. Eph. 6:17 *New English Bible*

210. J. H. Thayer, *Thayer's Greek-English Lexicon of the New Testament*

211. Matt. 4:4

NOTES ON FAITH

212. Is. 55:11 NKJV

213. 2 Cor. 3:6

214. Heb. 4:12 *The Amplified Bible* (emphasis mine)

215. Ezek. 13:6 *New English Bible*

216. Lam. 3:37-38

217. 2 Chron. 20:15-20

218. 2 Chron. 20:21

219. 2 Chron. 20:22-23

220. Rom. 8:37

221. Paul Billheimer, *Destined for the Throne* (Bethany House Publishers, Minnesota, MN, 1975) p. 18

222. Paul Little, *How to Give Away Your Faith* (InterVarsity Press, Downers Grove, IL, 1966) p. 107

223. John 5:19

224. John 15:5

225. R. A. Torrey, *How to Pray* (Moody Press, Chicago) pp. 57-58

226. Acts 2:39

227. Acts 2:38

228. Acts 2:33

229. Acts 1:8; John 16:14

230. Lk. 11:9-13

231. Gal. 3:14

231. F. B. Meyer, *Elijah and the Secret of His Power* (Christian Literature Crusade, Ft. Washington, PA, 1971) pp. 36-37 (I have updated a few words into modern English.)

233. 2 Cor. 4:7

234. Ps. 23:1-3

235. John 14:18

236. Prov. 16:9 NAS

237. Prov. 3:6

238. Is. 55:8 NKJV

239. R. Paul Stevens, article on "Vocational Guidance," in *The Complete Book of Everyday Christianity,* edited by Robert Banks and R. Paul Stevens (InterVarsity Press, Downers Grove, IL, 1997) p. 1079

240. Lk. 9:62

241. Ps. 104:27

242. Gen. 22:14

243. Ps. 78:19 NAS

244. Neh. 9:21

245. See I Thes 5:18

246. Ps. 33:19

247. 1 Kings 17:6

248. 1 Kings 17:14

249. Dr. and Mrs. Howard Taylor, *Hudson Taylor's Spiritual Secret* (Moody Press, Chicago, IL, 1932) p. 120

250. John 10:10 KJV

251. Phil. 4:19

252. J. Henry Thayer, *Thayer's Greek-English Lexicon of the New Testament*

253. Rom. 1:10 KJV

254. Acts 3:6

255. 2 Cor. 11:26-29

256. Rom. 15:26

257. Deut. 8:18

258. 1 Tim. 6:10

259. I Tim. 6:6-8; Phil 4:11

260. Prov. 30:8-9 is a good prayer in this regard: ...*give me neither poverty nor riches! Give me just enough to satisfy my needs. For if I grow rich, I may deny you and say, "Who is the LORD?" And if I am too poor, I may steal and thus insult God's holy name.* (NLT)

261. Matt. 6:24

262. Deut. 14:23 NLT

263. 1 Tim. 6:17-19

264. Prov. 3:9-10

265. 2 Cor. 9:6

266. George Foot Moore, *Judaism, Volume One* (Henrickson Publishers, Peabody, MA, 1927) p. 414. A good example of the power of a spoken blessing is seen when blind old Isaac, deceived by Rebecca's ruse and Jacob's falsehoods, bestows on Jacob the blessing he thought he was giving to Esau. He cannot undo what he has done; the best he can do is to invent a second-best blessing for his firstborn and best-loved son (Gen. 27).

267. Luke 2:28,34-35

268. Mark 10:16

NOTES ON FAITH

269. Christian blessings are neither "magic" nor something we can just impart to others at will. Any good thing we can impart to another must come through God. *Every good thing bestowed and every perfect gift is from above, coming down from the father of lights* (James 1:17). Therefore, we address our requests to him. "Lord, I ask your hand of favor to come upon my son..." (e.g., Ruth 2:12; Gen 49:25)

270. Eph. 2:8-9; Tit. 3:5

271. Greek, *sozo*, in Bauer, Arndt, and Gingrich, *A Greek-English Lexicon of the New Testament*

272. John MacArthur, *The MacArthur Bible Commentary* (Thomas Nelson Publishers, Nashville, TN, 2005) p. 1784

273. 1 Cor. 7:25-40

274. Derek Prince, *The Spirit-Filled Believer's Handbook* (Creation House, Orlando, FL, 1993) pp. 120-122

275. Rom. 1:17

276. Ps. 74:16

277. Archibald D. Hart, *The Anxiety Cure* (W Publishing, Nashville, TN, 1999) p. 193

278. Ps. 127:2

279. Ps. 121:3-4

280. e.g., 2 Thes. 2:9; Rev. 13:13-14; 2 Tim. 3:8

281. Matt. 12:38

282. Dan. 6:26-27

283. 1 Kings 17:24

284. Acts 4:29-30

285. Matt. 9:21

286. Lk. 8:41,50

287. 2 Kings 5:1-15

288. Mark 10:46-52

289. Lk. 9:11

290. Acts 14:8-10

291. Acts 14:10b

292. There are many reasons why a person may not receive healing, but unless God gives discernment, we should pray. A person may misuse God's laws of nature and invite trouble. For example, a man might engage in sexual immorality, mistreat the "temple of God," and suffer from gonorrhea and syphilis (1 Cor. 6:18-19). A man may overwork himself to the point of death, even for spiritual causes (Phil 2:26-27). A bitter,

complaining heart may incur physical ailments (Prov. 17:22). God, too, may not answer as we are anticipating for reasons known only to himself (Is. 55:8-9). We should not become "Job's friends" who feel they have to provide religious explanations for unanswered prayer.

293. A. W. Tozer, *Rut, Rot, or Revival* (Christian Publications, Camp Hill, PA 1992) pp. 108-109

294. A.B. Simpson, *Himself* (Christian Publications, Camp Hill, PA, 1991)

295. There are special *gifts of healing* (1 Cor. 12:9) which only some believers have (v.30). This is a supernatural surge of confidence which enables a believer to meet a specific physical need. For example, Peter one day told a beggar, *"Look at us...Silver and gold I do not have, but what I have I give you. In the name of Jesus Christ of Nazareth, walk."* (Acts 3:4-6) Peter and even possibly Jesus had walked by this man at the temple several times before, but this one day Peter felt a strong impression to pray for him. The *gift of healing* may be manifested occasionally in a particular, dramatic healing, like Peter's, or more regularly in believers who seem to have frequent success in healing the sick.

296. Acts 28:8

297. Acts 28:9

298. e.g., Luke 9:1-2; 10:1-12; Mark 16:15-20

299. Heb. 13:8

300. J. I. Packer, *Concise Theology* (Tyndale House Publishers, Wheaton, Il, 1993) p. 58

301. Wayne Grudem, *Systematic Theology* (Zondervan Publishing House, Grand Rapids, MI, 1994) p. 355

302. Craig S. Keener, *Miracles* (Baker Academic, Grand Rapids, MI, 2011)

303. Rom. 12:3

304. 1 Kings 18:16-40

305. Jam. 5:17

306. Plass, op. cit., p.466

307. Oswald Chambers, *Conformed to His Image* (Christian Literature Crusade, Ft. Washington, PA, 1950) p. 60

308. Job 22:21 NKJV

309. Rom. 4:11,16

310. Jam. 2:23

311. 2 Tim. 1:12 NKJV

312. David Clarkson, *Works of David Clarkson, 3 Volumes* (Banner of Truth Trust, Carlisle, PA, 1988) Vol 1, pp. 174-179 (I have changed a few words to make it more readable.)

NOTES ON FAITH

313. John 8:30

314. Heb. 4:2

315. John 20:30-31

316. Anthony Ruspantini, *Quoting Spurgeon* (Baker Books, Grand Rapids, MI, 1994) p. 77

317. Norman Grubb, *Rees Howells: Intercessor* (Christian Literature Crusade, Fort Washington, PA, 1973) pp. 46-47

318. 1 Pet. 5:5-7

319. Acts 3:6 (emphasis mine)

320. Rebecca Harmon, *Susanna, Mother of the Wesleys* (Abington Press, Nashville, 1968) p. 166

321. Philip Yancey, *Reaching for the Invisible God* (Zondervan Publishing House, Grand Rapids, MI, 2000) p. 104

322. E. Michael and Sharon Rusten, *The One Year Christian History* (Tyndale House Publishers, Carol Stream, IL, 2003), Dec. 20 devotional

323. Corrie ten Boom, *Each New Day* (G. K. Hall and Co, Boston, MA, 1977) Sept. 25 devotional.

324. Pat Robertson and Jamie Buckingham, *Shout it from the Housetops* (Logos Int., Plainfield. NJ, 1972) p. x.

325. Maurice Fulton, ed., *Roosevelt's Writings* (MacMillan, New York, 1922) p. 168

326. J. I. Packer, *Knowing God* (InterVarsity Press, Downers Grove, IL, 1973) p. 115

327. Charles Spurgeon, *The Check Book of the Bank of Faith* (Christian Literature Crusade, Ft. Washington, PA, 1857) p. 3

328. You can see Samuel Clark's entire book, *The Scripture Promises* at *whatsaiththescripture.com/Promises/Clarkes_Bible_Promises.html*

329. Rom. 11:20

330. Mark 6:5-6

331. Matt. 5:3

332. Rev. 3:17

333. Matt. 11:5

334. Mark 12:37 KJV

335. Howard Snyder, *The Community of the King* (Intervarsity Press, Downers Grove, IL) p. 120

336. 1 Tim. 6:17

337. 1 Tim. 6:17-19

338. Luke 12:16-21 (emphasis mine)

339. John 12:42-43 NAS

340. Billy Graham, *Just As I Am* (HarperCollins Pub., San Francisco, 1997) p. 723

341. Charles Colson, *The Body* (Word Publishing, Dallas, 1992) p. 311

342. John Wesley, *Journal*, May 1765 (from *The Works of John Wesley*, Baker Book House, Grand Rapids, MI, 1996) p. 211

343. Gal. 1:10

344. Paul Little, *How to Give Away Your Faith* (InterVarsity Press, Downers Grove, IL, 1966) p. 107

345. Luke 1:18

346. Luke 1:19-20

347. Jam. 1:6-8

348. Matt. 14:31

349. David Jeremiah, *Turning Points* (Integrity Publishers, Nashville, TN, 2005) p. 297

350. 1 Sam. 15:23

351. John 3:19-21

352. Prov. 29:1 NLT

353. *Webster's New Universal Unabridged Dictionary* (Barnes and Noble Books, New York, 1996)

354. Luke 10:27

355. 1 Pet. 1:13

356. Rom. 11:33-34

357. Is.35:4 NAS

358. Ps. 27:14 NAS

359. Deut. 31:6; Josh. 1:6,9,18

360. Deut. 31:6

361. D. Martyn Lloyd-Jones, *Spiritual Depression* (William Eerdmans Pub., Grand Rapids, MI, 1965) p. 143

362. 2 Kings 6:16

363. Heb. 13:6

364. 1 Cor. 16:13

365. Is. 8:12-13

366. Matt. 10:28

367. Ps. 53:5

368. Ps. 119:165

NOTES ON FAITH

369. Judson Cornwall, *Unfeigned Faith* (Fleming Revell Co., Old Tappan, NJ, 1981) p. 116

370. Ps. 56:3

371. Ex. 23:29-30; Deut 7:22

372. Hebrew word, *zadon*, is translated as "proud, inflated, insolent, arrogant, haughtiness, or presumption."

373. Ps. 19:13 NAS

374. Jack Hayford, *Prayer is Invading the Impossible* (Logos, Plainfield, NJ)

375. Phil. 3:16 NAS

376. 2 Cor. 10:12 *New English Bible*

377. 1 Pet. 4:10

378. Lk. 9:23

379. William Barclay, *New Testament Words* (SCM Press, London, 1964) pp. 41-43

380. Tozer, *Renewed Day by Day*, Nov. 11 devotional

381. The word "Baptist" is never applied to believers in general; the word is used 14 times in the four gospels to describe the prophet, *John the Baptist.*

382. Acts 11:26

383. Heb. 3:12

384. Heb. 2:1

385. William Barclay, *The Letter to the Hebrews* (Westminster Press, Philadelphia, 1976) p. 21

386. Num. 11:10-15

387. 1 Kings 19:3-5

388. Job 3

389. Ps. 43:5

390. 2 Cor. 1:8; 7:5-6 NAS

391. 1 Pet. 1:6 KJV

392. D. Martyn Lloyd-Jones, *Spiritual Depression,* p. 17

393. Ibid., p.20-21

394. Luke 22:62

395. 2 Cor. 1:8-9

396. 2 Cor. 1:9

397. 2 Cor. 1:10-11

398. Job 6:14 NAS

399. C. S. Lewis, *A Grief Observed* (Bantam Books, New York, 1976) p. 25

400. Al Bryant, comp., *Near the Sun: A Sourcebook of Daily Meditations from Charles Haddon Spurgeon* (Word Books, Waco, 1980) pp. 9-10, 61

401. Author unknown

402. Philip Yancey, *Disappointment With God* (Zondervan Publishing House, Grand Rapids, MI, 1988) pp. 200-201

403. D. James Kennedy, *New Every Morning*, June 30 devotional

404. Ritchie's story was told in the article "Wonderfully Made" by Greg Johnson, *Breakaway* magazine, June 1992 issue (Focus on the Family, Colorado Springs, CO)

405. Ecc. 7:8

406. 1 Tim. 1:19-20

407. 2 Chron. 33:1-13

408. Phm. 24

409. 2 Tim. 4:10 *The Amplified Bible*

410. Heb. 12:2 NKJV

411. William Barclay, *The Letter to Hebrews* (The Westminster Press, Philadelphia, 1976) pp. 25-26

412. Phil. 1:6

413. Arthur Bennett, *The Valley of Vision: A Collection of Puritan Prayers and Devotions* (The Banner of Truth Trust, Carlisle, PA, 1975) p. 160

414. Jam. 5:19-20

415. 1 Cor. 5:9-13; 2 Thes. 3:6,14-15

416. Gal. 6:1 NAS

417. Greek *katartizo* also used in Matt. 4:21

418. Gal. 6:1 KJV

419. Gal 6:1 *The Amplified Bible*

420. *Letters of John Newton* (The Banner of Truth Trust, Carlisle, PA, 1960) p. 134

421. Kenneth Wuest, *In These Last Days* (Eerdmans Publishing Co, Grand Rapids, MI, 1954) p. 96

422. Michael Green, "Fellowship" in *The Complete Book of Everyday Christianity*, op. cit., p. 406

423. Heb. 13:5

424. Kenneth Wuest, *The New Testament: An Expanded Translation*

425. Rev. 3:20 NAS

NOTES ON FAITH

426. C. H. Spurgeon, *John Ploughman's Talks* (Whitaker House, Springdale, PA, 1993) p. 177

427. Ibid., p.180

428. Eph. 1:15-16

429. 1 Thes. 3:6-7

430. Phm. 5

431. David Daniell, *Tyndale's New Testament* (Yale University Press, New Haven, 1989)

432. 2 Thes. 1:3

433. Jack Hywel-Davies, *The Life of Smith Wigglesworth* (Vine Books, Ann Arbor, MI, 1987) p. 139

434. 1 Cor. 13:2

435. 1 Cor. 13:7

436. Bill and Vonette Bright, *The Greatest Lesson I've Ever Learned* (Life ConneXions, Peachtree City, CA, 1990, 2005) pp. 245-247

437. Gen. 24:58

438. Gen. 2:24

439. 1 Thes. 1:6

440. 1 Cor. 11:1

441. 2 Cor. 4:5

442. Matt. 8:5-10

443. Matt. 8:10

444. Graham Miller, *Calvin's Wisdom* (The Banner of Truth Trust, Carlisle, PA, 1992) p. 105

445. Andrew Murray, *Humility* (Fleming Revell Co., Old Tappan, NJ, 1961) pp. 51-54

446. Luke 16:9

447. Heb. 9:12

448. Rev. 14:6

449. Heb. 13:20

450. 2 Pet. 1:11

451. Ex. 3:14

452. Rev. 1:4

453. 2 Pet. 3:9

454. John 17:3

455. John 11:25-26

456. Excerpt from chapter on "The Exchanged Life" in Dr. and Mrs. Howard Taylor, *Hudson Taylor's Spiritual Secret* (Moody Press, Chicago, 1932) pp. 160-161

457. John 15:5

458. Prov. 20:6

459. Ps. 145:13

460. Jam. 1:17 NLT

461. Ps. 33:4

462. Dan. 6:4 NAS

463. Editor Stephen Sorenson, *The Best of F. B. Meyer* (Honor Books, Colorado Springs, CO, 2006) p. 81

464. Matt. 25:21

465. From *The Martyrs Mirror; The New Encyclopedia of Christian Martyrs,* printed in *The Voice of the Martyrs* magazine (Bartlesville, OK), March 2012 issue

466. David B. Barrett, Todd M. Johnson, and Peter F. Crossing, 2009 report in International Bulletin of Missionary Research (Vol. 33, No. 1: 32)

467. Sandra Chambers, article "A Faithful Witness," *Charisma* magazine, July 2005 issue (Lake Mary, FL) p. 43

468. Quote in *World* magazine, Feb. 26, 2011 issue (Asheville, NC)

NOTES ON HOPE

1. A. W. Tozer, *The Size of the Soul* (Christian Publications, Camp Hill, PA, 1992) p.88

2. Jer. 29:11

3. Jer. 31:17

4. Dante Aligheri, *The Divine Comedy* (Simon and Brown Publishers, 2007; originally published about 1550). From Canto III

5. Eph. 2:13

6. 1 Pet. 1:3 Phillips

7. *Spurgeon's Expository Encyclopedia, Volume* 9 (Baker Books, Grand Rapids, MI, 1996) p. 166

8. Tozer, op. cit., p.92

9. *NCAA Research* on internet, last updated Sept. 27, 2011 "Estimated Probability of Competing in Athletics Beyond the High School Interscholastic Level Men's Basketball"

10. Larry Crabb, *Shattered Dreams* (Waterbrook Press, Colorado Springs, CO, 2001) p. 26

11. Lk. 2:25 NKJV

12. Charles Wesley hymn, *Come, Thou Long-Expected Jesus,* 1976 by Paragon Associates, Inc., Nashville, TN

13. Edward Gibbon, *The History of the Decline and Fall of the Roman Empire*, Vol. 1, Ch. 3 (Adamant Media Corp., 2005, facsimile of edition published in 1787 by J. J. Tourneiser, Basil)

14. Dan. 2:21 NLT

15. Malcolm Muggeridge, *The End of Christendom* (Eerdmans, Grand Rapids, MI, 1980)

16. John 14:6

17. Acts 4:12

18. 1 Cor. 3:11

19. 1 John 5:11-12

20. Edward Mote hymn, *The Solid Rock* (public domain)

21. Mark 2:7

22. Is. 45:24; Rom. 3:10; 1 Cor. 1:30

23. Rev. 15:4

24. 1 Tim. 6:15-16

25. Ps. 71:4-5

26. Arthur Pink, *The Doctrine of Sanctification* (Bible Truth Depot, Swengel, PA, 1955) p. 200

27. Ps. 62:5-6

28. John Bunyan, retold by James Thomas, *Pilgrim's Progress in Today's English* (Moody Press, Chicago, 1964) pp. 44-45

29. *Ibid.*, p. 46

30. Derek Prince, article "War on the Mind," in *New Wine Magazine*, March 1983 (Integrity Communications, Mobile, AL)

31. Greek, *bebaian,* in *Thayer's Greek-English Lexicon* (Associated Press Pub.) and A. T. Robertson, *Word Pictures in the New Testament, Volume 5* (Baker Book House, Grand Rapids, 1932) p. 379

32. Greek, *asphale,* in Ibid.

33. Heb. 11:13-16

34. Heb. 10:34 NLT

35. Charles Colson, *Breakpoint* commentary on "Hope," April 7, 2009.

36. These cities were important enough to be mentioned in four books in the Old Testament: Ex. 21:12-13; Num. 35:6-34; Deut. 19:1-4; and Josh. 20.

37. William MacDonald, *Believer's Bible Commentary, Old Testament* (Thomas Nelson Publishing Co., Nashville, 1992) pp. 253-254

38. Ps. 46:1

39. Eph. 2:3-4

40. Eph. 2:14-15 NAS; Rom. 6:23

41. Prov. 18:10

42. Eph. 2:18 NAS

43. Rom. 8:31-34 Phillips

44. Ronald Dunn, *When Heaven is Silent* (Thomas Nelson Publishers, Nashville, 1994), p. 158

45. Prov. 3:5

46. 2 Cor. 10:5

47. Eph. 6:10-19

48. Anne Graham Lotz, *The Glorious Dawn of God's Story* (Word Publishing, Dallas, 1997) p. 217

49. Ps. 34:1, 4, 6, 18-19

50. Lk. 24:31

51. Ps. 18:30

52. Lance Wubbels, editor, *In His Presence* (Emerald Books, Lynnwood, WA, 1998) July 20 devotional by MacLaren

53. David McCasland, editor, *The Quotable Oswald Chambers* (Discovery House Publishers, Grand Rapids, MI, 2008) p. 298

NOTES ON HOPE

54. Wesley Duewel, *Mighty Prevailing Prayer* (Francis Asbury Press, Grand Rapids, MI, 1990) p. 60

55. Ewald Plass, *What Luther Says* (Concordia Publishing House, St. Louis, MO, 1959) p. 629

56. *Our Daily Bread*, August 1992 issue (Grand Rapids, MI)

57. John 11:33,35

58. *Thayer's Greek English Lexicon*, p.347 and A. T. Robertson, *Word Pictures in the New Testament, Volume 5*, p.203

59. John 11:25

60. Paul Billheimer, *Don't Waste Your Sorrows* (Christian Literature Crusade, Fort Washington, PA, 1977)

61. Charles Erlandson, editor, *F. B. Meyer: The Best From All His Works* (Thomas Nelson Publishers, Nashville, 1988) p. 75

62. For more encouragement concerning spiritually mismatched mates, you may want to read my booklet, *There is More to Eternity Than Living Happily-Ever-After With Your Mates*. Available from CFC Literature (address in front of this book)

63. Story told by Robert Murray M'Cheyne, *God Makes a Path* (Ambassador Productions, Belfast, N. Ireland, 1995), p. 9

64. William MacDonald, *One Day at a Time* (Everyday Publications, Scarborough, ON Canada, 1985) p. 309

65. Quote found in Mrs. Charles Cowman, *Streams in the Desert* (Zondervan Publishing House, Grand Rapids, MI, 1925, 1996) Feb. 7 devotional. Original source unknown.

66. Article "J. C. Penney: Living by the Golden Rule," in John Woodbridge, *More Than Conquerors* (Moody Bible Institute, Chicago, 1992) pp. 340-343

67. Matt. 6:25-27

68. Ps. 37:25

69. *Our Daily Bread*, op. cit., June 1995 issue

70. 1 Cor. 15:43 Contemporary English Version

71. 1 Cor. 15:44 The Living Bible

72. 1 Cor. 15:51-52

73. 1 John 3:2-3

74. Joni Eareckson Tada, *Heaven – Your Real Home* (Zondervan, Grand Rapids, MI, 1996) p. 53

75. Kristen Jane Anderson, *Life In Spite of Me* (Multnomah Books, Colorado Springs, Co, 2010) pp. 13, 199-200

76. Robert Morgan, *On This Day*, January 27 devotional (Thomas Nelson Inc., Nashville, 1997). A few words are updated in modern English.

77. 1 Cor. 2:9

78. John 17:23-24

79. J. I Packer, *In God's Presence* (Harold Shaw Publishers, Wheaton, Il, 1986) September 22 devotional.

80. Eph. 1:18

81. 1 Pet. 1:3-4

82. Ronald Dunn, op. cit., pp.76-80

83. Job 13:15

84. A. W. Tozer, *The Size of the Soul*, p.89

85. 1 Cor. 15:19 Revised English Bible

86. Heb. 11:1

87. This is not to say that faith will always receive an answer in this lifetime (cf. Heb. 11:39).

88. Rom. 8:24

89. Judson Cornwall, *Unfeigned Faith* (Fleming Revell Co., Old Tappan, NJ, 1981) p. 44

90. Rom. 5:2

91. Rom. 5:2 The Living Bible

92. David Horowitz, article "Armando Valladares: Human Rights Hero," *Newsmax.* (December 5, 2003). Also quoted in *Wikipedia.*

93. Armando Valladares, *Against All Hope* (Encounter books, San Francisco, 2001) p. 15

94. Ibid., pp. 16-17

95. Thomas Brooks quoted in Paul Miller, compiler, *Fill Me With Hope* (Barbour Publishing, Uhrichsville, OH, 2004) Oct 12 devotional

96. First paragraph from J. I. Packer, *Never Beyond Hope* (InterVarsity Press, Downers Grove, IL, 2000) pp. 9-10. Second paragraph from Packer, *The J. I. Packer Classic Collection* (NavPress, Colorado Springs, CO, 2010) p. 251

97. Rom. 8:18-19 Phillips

98. Ps. 103:5

99. Hos. 2:15

100. Ps. 42:5

101. Tim Hansel, *You Gotta Keep Dancin': In the Midst of Life's Hurts You Can Choose Joy* (David C. Cook Publishing Co., Elgin, Il, 1985), p. 55

102. Ps. 71:14,20

NOTES ON HOPE

103. Rev. 1:14

104. A. W. Tozer, *The Tozer Pulpit*, Vol. 5 (Christian Publications, Camp Hill, PA, 1994), p. 145

105. 2 Pet. 3:10-12

106. *Our Daily Times With God* (Discovery House Publishers, Grand Rapids, MI, 1988) p. 98

107. John 14:19

108. James Garrett, from a spoken message, "The Revelation of Jesus Christ."

109. Preston Parrish, article "Jesus is Enough" in *Decision* magazine (Charlotte, NC), April 2008 issue

110. ABC news interview on Good Morning America, March 14, 2009.

111. Mary Beth Chapman, *Choosing to See: A Journey of Struggle and Faith* (Revell, Grand Rapids, MI, 2010) pp. 181-182

112. Chapman interview in *Charisma* magazine (Ft. Mary, FL) May 2010

113. Col. 1:26-27

114. John 14:17,20

115. Gal. 2:20

116. Watchman Nee, *Changed Into His Likeness* (Christian Literature Crusade, Fort Washington, PA, 1967) p. 81

117. A. B. Simpson, *Victory Over Self* (Christian Publications, Camp Hill, PA) p. 31

118. Lisa Beamer, *Let's Roll!* (Tyndale House Publishers, Wheaton, Il, 2002)

119. Jer. 20:9

120. Jer. 11:21

121. Jer. 12:6

122. Jer. 9:2; 15:17

123. Jer. 20:2

124. Jer. 26:8

125. Jer. 28

126. Jer. 38:6

127. Jer. 43:2

128. Lam. 3:14

129. Ps. 119:90

130. Deut. 7:9

131. 1 Cor. 10:13

132. 2 Tim. 2:13

133. Rom. 15:4 Phillips

134. Charles Swindoll, *Living Beyond the Daily Grind, Book One* (Word Publishing, Dallas, 1988) p. 127

135. From www.guinnessworldrecords.com/records - 1/best-selling book

136. Johannes Gutenberg in the *Mazarin Bible* (1455) Cited in William J. Federer, *America's God and Country Encyclopedia of Quotations* (Fame Publishing, Coppell, TX, 1994) p. 269

137. J. I. Packer, *Honouring the Written Word of God,* quoted in the *J. I. Packer Classic Collection* (NavPress, Colorado Springs, CO, 2010) p. 282

138. Heb. 9:27

139. 1 Pet. 1:13

NOTES ON LOVE

1. 1 Cor. 13:1-3

2. 1 Pet. 4:8

3. Peter Kreft, *The God Who Loves You* (Ignatius Press, San Francisco, 1988) pp. 35-36

4. John Morrison's teaching, "The Trinity, Part 3" was given at Community Fellowship Church, Staunton, VA, Dec. 2010. Darrell Johnson quote taken from his book, *Experiencing the Trinity* (Regent College Publishing; Vancouver, BC, 2002) p. 61

5. John 17:24

6. Henry Blackaby and Claude King, *Experiencing God* (Broadman and Holman Publishers, Nashville, TN, 1994), p. 17

7. Heb. 12:6

8. 1 John 4:10

9. John Murray, *The Epistle to the Romans* (Eerdmans, Grand Rapids, 1959) p. 335

10. Eph. 3:16-19

11. Greek *monogenes* in William Arndt and F. Wilbur Gingrich, *A Greek-English Lexicon of the New Testament* (University of Chicago Press, 1957)

12. John Calvin, *Commentary on a Harmony of the Evangelists,* William Pringle, translator (Baker Books, Grand Rapids, 1979 reprint) p. 123

13. Tit. 3:4 NAS

14. Reuben A. Torrey, "The Keynote of the Bible" in *Decision* magazine (Billy Graham Evangelistic Association, Charlotte, NC), Feb. 2012 issue.

15. Andrew Murray and Jonathan Edwards [edited by Louis Parkhurst, Jr.], *The Believer's Secret of Christian Love* (Bethany House Publishers, Minneapolis, MN, 1990) p. 39

16. 1 John 3:14

17. Jonathan Edwards, *Charity and Its Fruits* (The Banner of Truth Trust, Carlisle, PA, 1852, 1969) p. 23

18. Watchman Nee, *The Normal Christian Life* (Christian Literature Crusade, Ft. Washington, PA, 1957) pp. 125-127

19. Rom. 8:2

20. St. Augustine, *Ten Homilies on the First Epistle of John, VII, 8; NPNF, I,* vii, p. 504

21. Richard DeHaan, devotional in *Our Daily Times With God* (Radio Bible Class, Grand Rapids, MI, 1988) p. 88

22. 1 Cor. 3, esp. v.10

23. 1 Cor. 3:11

24. 1 Cor. 8:1

25. Paul Billheimer, *Love Covers* (Christian Literature Crusade, Ft. Washington, PA, 1981) p. 34

26. Andrew Murray, *The Believer's Secret of Living Like Christ* (Bethany House Publishers, Minneapolis, MN, 1985) p. 80

27. Billheimer, op. cit., pp. 88, 29.

28. 1 Cor. 13:5 *The Amplified Bible*

29. John Pollock, *George Whitefield and the Great Awakening* (Lion Publishing, Belleville, MI, 1972), p. 190

30. Stephen Clark, article in *Pastoral Renewal* (Ann Arbor, MI) April 1987 issue.

31. Gal. 5:22-23

32. Rom. 15:30

33. Col. 1:8

34. H. E. Dana and Julius Mantley, *A Manual Grammar of the Greek New Testament* (The MacMillan Company, Toronto, Ontario, 1927) pp. 200-203

35. W. Robertson Nicoll, *The Expositor's Greek New Testament, Vol. 2* (William Eerdmans Publishing Co, Grand Rapids, MI, 1983) p. 624

36. Kenneth Wuest, *The New Testament: An Expanded Translation* (William Eerdmans Publishing Co, Grand Rapids, MI, © 1961)

37. Rom. 5:5 in Eugene Peterson, *The Message* (NavPress, Colorado Springs, Co, 1993)

38. 1 Cor. 16:14

39. 2 Cor. 5:13 *The Amplified Bible*

40. John 21:16

41. John 21:15-17

42. D. Martyn Lloyd-Jones, *The Unsearchable Riches of Christ* (Baker Books, Grand Rapids, MI, 1979) pp. 252-253

43. Luke 15:28-29

44. James Garrett, article, "The Essential Component of Relationship in the New Testament Church," p. 22 (See www.doulospress.org.)

45. Mark 6:34

46. Rom. 2:1,21; 2 Tim. 2:25 KJV

47. Luke 6:40

48. 1 Tim. 1:6-7 NAS

49. 1 Tim. 1:6 *New English Bible*

50. 1 Tim. 1:6 Contemporary English Version

51. Jer. 10:10

52. Ps. 7:11

53. Ps. 103:8; Ex. 34:6

NOTES ON LOVE

54. Ps. 30:5; see also Is. 54:5-8

55. Rom. 5:9

56. Gal. 3:13

57. 1 Thes. 1:10 NAS

58. Rom. 3:11

59. John 15:16

60. 1 John 4:10

61. Ps. 23:6 NLT

62. Donald Grey Barnhouse, *The Epistle to the Romans, Part 38* (The Bible Study Hour, Philadelphia, 1952) pp. 1843-1844

63. John Owen, *Communion with God*, editor R. J. K. Law (Banner of Truth Trust, Edinburgh, Scotland, 1991) p. 13

64. Charles Hodge, *Commentary on the Epistle to the Romans* (Eerdmans, Grand Rapids, MI, 1955) p. 290

65. Jerry Bridges, *Holiness Day by Day* (NavPress, Colorado Springs, Co., 2008) p. 73

66. 1 John 3:16

67. Gen. 22:1-2

68. John 15:13 NRSV

69. Max Lucado, *3:16: The Numbers of Hope* (Thomas Nelson Publishers, Nashville, TN, 2007) p. 42

70. Eph. 5:25

71. Harold W. Hoehner, *Ephesians: An Exegetical Commentary* (Baker Books, Grand Rapids, MI, 2002) p. 748

72. James Boice, *Come to the Waters* (Baker Books, Grand Rapids, MI, 2011) Sept. 2 devotional

73. John 16:33

74. John 15:11; 17:13

75. Matt. 16:19; 28:19-20

76. John 17:22-24

77. Annie Johnson Flint, "He Giveth More Grace" (Lillenas Publishing Company, 1941,1969)

78. 2 Cor. 8:24

79. Luke 6:38 TLB

80. Dr. James Dobson, *Love for a Lifetime* (Multnomah Books, Sisters, OR, 1987, 1993) p. 57

81. Timothy Keller, *The Meaning of Marriage* (Dutton Books, NY, 2011) p. 78

82. Keller, Ibid., pp. 86-87

83. 1 Cor. 13:7 NLT

84. 1 John 4:8

85. 1 John 4:9-10

86. Story told in Stephen Olford, *Committed to Christ and His Church* (Baker Book House, Grand Rapids, MI, 1991) p. 42

87. John MacArthur, *The God Who Loves* (Word Publishing, Nashville, TN, 1996, 2001) pp. 119-120

88. Matt. 11:28

89. Is. 55:1

90. George Herbert, "Love" in *The Harper Book of Christian Poetry*, editor Anthony Mercante (Harper and Row, NY, 1972) pp. 134-135

91. Eph. 5:10

92. Mark Water, Compiler, *The New Encyclopedia of Christian Quotations* (Baker Books, Grand Rapids, MI, 2000) p. 421

93. Mark 10:16 *The Amplified Bible*

94. Norman Grubb, *Rees Howells: Intercessor* (Christian Literature Crusade, Fort Washington, PA, 1973) pp. 46-47

95. Fred Wright, *Manners and Customs of Bible Lands,* (Moody Press, Chicago, IL, 1953), pp. 155-159

96. William MacDonald, *One Day at a Time* (Everyday Publications, Scarborough, ON, 1985) p. 346

97. John MacArthur, *The God Who Loves,* pp. xi, xii

98. Rom. 1:19-20

99. John 14:26

100. Rom. 8:16

101. Tom Carter, Compiler, *2200 Quotations from the Writings of Charles Spurgeon* (Baker Books, Grand Rapids, MI, 1988) p. 247

102. Song of Songs 3:11

103. Song of Songs 4:10

104. Eph. 5:27 NLT

105. Song of Songs 6:3

106. For the entire letter, see www.civilwardads.com

107. Adapted from Watchman Nee, *Do All For The Glory Of God* (Christian Fellowship Publishers, NY, 1974) p. 55

108. Matt. 26:8-9

109. D. Seamands, *Healing Grace* (Victor Books, Wheaton, IL, 1988) p.111

110. *Fenelon's Spiritual Letters* (Christian Books, Augusta, ME, 1982) p.57

NOTES ON LOVE

111. 1 Cor. 5:1-13

112. 2 Cor. 2:7

113. Gerhard Kittle, *Theological Dictionary of the New Testament, Vol. 3* (William Eerdmans Publishing Co., Grand Rapids, MI, 1965) p. 1098

114. John 20:23

115. Mark 2:7

116. See also Matt. 16:19; 18:18

117. 1 John 4:10

118. John 15:16

119. Rom. 3:11

120. Mary Shekleton, "It Passeth Knowledge," *Hymns* (InterVarsity Press, Downers Grove, IL, 1952) #133

121. Heb. 13:5-6

122. Ps. 18:1

123. Ps. 26:1-3

124. Ps. 32:10

125. Ps. 63:3

126. John 14:17

127. John 14:18

128. Matt. 28:20

129. 2 Cor. 2:14

130. 1 Cor. 15:57

131. Zeph. 3:17 NIV

132. Prov. 15:8 NAS

133. Prov. 13:24

134. Heb. 12:8

135. Heb. 12:10

136. Graham Miller, *Calvin's Wisdom* (The Banner of Truth Trust, Carlisle, PA, 1992) p. 37

137. Ibid., p. 37

138. Derek Prince, www.derekprince.org Weekly e-devotional, Feb. 20, 2012

139. Arthur Brine, quoted in Arthur W. Pink, *The Attributes of God* (Baker Book House, Grand Rapids, MI, 1975) p. 80

140. Rom. 5:5 *New English Bible*

141. John Phillips, *Exploring Here and There Vol. 1* (Ambassador-Emerald International, Greenville, SC, 2000) p. 135

142. Matt. 10:37-38

143. Col. 1:18 NAS

144. D. James Kennedy, *New Every Morning* (Multonomah Books, Sisters, OR, 1996) May 26 devotional

145. Ps. 31:23

146. 2 Pet. 1:4-7 NAS

147. A. W. Tozer, *Renewed Day by Day* (Fleming H. Revell Co., Old Tappan, NJ, 1980) Jan. 13 devotional

148. Lev. 19:18

149. John 13:34. Also see John 15:12.

150. Robert D. Putnam, *Bowling Alone* (Simon & Schuster, NY, 2000)

151. Murray and Edwards, *Believer's Secret*, pp.78-79

152. 2 Tim. 3:1

153. Eph. 5:28

154. Eph. 5:29

155. In the Parable of the Good Samaritan, the question is asked, *Who is my neighbor?* (Luke 10:29).   Jesus' parable implies our love will be that which transcends race, color, or creed.   Our love will not be limited to those we like or to close friends within our church.

156. Eph. 5:27

157. Phil. 1:6 NLT

158. 1 John 3:14

159. 1 Pet. 1:22 NLT

160. Ps. 55:12-14

161. 1 Thes. 4:9-10

162. e.g., Rom. 12:13; I Pet. 4:9: Tit. 1:8; Heb. 13:2

163. The Greek word for hospitality (*philoxenos*) literally means "a love for strangers."

164. I used this list previously in my book, *Church Life: Building on the Foundation of Jesus Christ.* (CFC Literature, Staunton, VA, 2005) p. 108

165. Mark 3:14-15. Notice Jesus did not just call the twelve men to preach and work with him; his first call was for them to "be with him."

166. John 15:15

167. 1 Cor. 15:33

168. Romans 12:16 says, *Live in harmony with one another. Do not be proud, but be willing to associate with people of low position. Do not be conceited.* The NLT says, *Don't be too proud to enjoy the company of ordinary people. And don't think you know it all!*

169. Prov. 27:17

NOTES ON LOVE

170. Prov. 16:28; 17:9; 20:6

171. Prov. 25:17

172. Ps. 119:63

173. 1 Tim. 1:12-16

174. John Pollock, *Moody* (Zondervan Publishing House, Grand Rapids, MI, 1963) pp. 72-75

175. Gal. 6:10

176. Aristides, *Apology 15,16*. From Eberhard Arnold, *The Early Christians* (Plough Publishing House, Rifton, New York, 1970) pp. 105-106

177. Tertullian, *Apology 39,40* From Eberhard Arnold, *The Early Christians*, p.112

178. John 13:35

179. Eph. 5:28

180. Gary Chapman, *The 5 Love Languages: The Secret to Love that Lasts* (Northfield Press, Chicago, IL, 2010)

181. Mark Strauss, article on "Luke" in *Zondervan Illustrated Bible Backgrounds Commentary,* Clinton Arnold, General Editor (Zondervan, Grand Rapids, MI, 2002) p. 447

182. Luke 15:20

183. Strauss, *Zondervan Illustrated Bible Backgrounds Commentary,* p. 448

184. D. James Kennedy, *New Every Morning,* Feb. 11 devotional

185. Wade Taylor, *Waterspouts of Glory* (Pinecrest Publications, Salisbury, NY, 1996) p. 33

186. Vernon Grounds, article "Love Underserved," in *Our Daily Bread* (Radio Bible Class, Grand Rapids, MI) Sept. 10, 2002 devotional

187. Jim Cymbala, *Fresh Wind, Fresh Fire* (Zondervan Publishing House, Grand Rapids, MI, 1997) pp. 141-143

188. D. James Kennedy, *What If Jesus Had Never Been Born?* (Thomas Nelson Publishers, Nashville, TN, 1994) pp. 194-195

189. Ed Wheat, *Love Life for Every Married Couple* (Zondervan Publishing, Grand Rapids, MI, 1980) pp. 120-121

190. Kerby Anderson, *Christian Ethics in Plain Language* (Nelson Publishing, Nashville, TN, 2005) p. 176

191. Rev. 5:9

192. John Piper, *A Godward Life, Book Two* (Multnomah Publishers, Sisters, OR, 1999) p. 261

193. Jam. 2:1

194. Gal. 3:28

195. *Guideposts Magazine* (Guideposts Associates, Inc., Carmel, NY, 1972)

196. David Bercot, editor, *A Dictionary of Early Christian Beliefs* (Henrickson Publishers, Peabody, MA, 1998) p.409

197. Geoffrey Wainright, *Doxology: The Praise of God in Worship, Doctrine, and Life* (Oxford University Press, NY, 1980) p. 434. Also told in Stephen Seamands, *Wounds That Heal* (InterVarsity Press, Downers Grove, IL, 2003) pp. 148-149

198. Bill Warner, *Thirteen Lessons on Political Islam: Islam 101* (Published by CSPI, 2008). See WWW.CSPIPUBLISHING.COM

199. Is. 9:6

200. Warner, Ibid., p. 1

201. Warner, Ibid., p. 4

202. Herbert Vander Lugt, *Our Daily Bread*, April 1992 (RBC Ministries, Grand Rapids, MI)

203. C. S. Lewis, *The Four Loves* (Geoffrey Bles, London, 1960) p. 138

204. Rom. 6:1-2; Gal.6:7-9; Eph. 5:3-7; Heb. 10:26,38; 1 John 3:4-7

205. Gen. 27:5-6

206. Jam. 2:1-4

207. Gal. 4:1-7

208. Gal. 4:4-5 NKJV

209. Henry Blackaby and Claude King, *Experiencing God*, pp. 20-21

210. Deut. 6:20-25

211. Blackaby and King, op. cit., p. 21

212. Rev. 2:5

213. 2 Cor. 4:4 NAS

214. Rom. 12:2; I Cor. 7:31

215. Jam. 4:3-4

216. Job 31:1

217. 1 John 5:21 *The Amplified Bible*

218. A. W. Tozer, *Success and the Christian* (Christian Publications, Camp Hill, PA, 1994) pp. 78-79

219. Charles Swindoll, *Elijah* (W Publishing Group, Nashville, TN, 2000) pp. 121-122

220. Angels appear throughout the Bible, but one particular supernatural being stands out and is distinguished as *the angel of the Lord.* (e.g., Gen. 18-19, 22; Josh. 5; Jud. 13) This being allows himself to be worshipped and called "Lord," which all normal angels refuse. Most evangelical theologians believe these are theophanies – appearances of the pre-incarnate Jesus in human form.

NOTES ON LOVE

221. Ex. 3:14

222. Charles Price, *Stop Trying to Love For Jesus* (Kingsway Books, Eastbourne, UK, 1995) pp. 119-121

223. 1 Tim. 6:17-19

224. Hag. 1:9

225. Heb. 3:6; Eph. 2:22

226. Jonathan Edwards, "The Distinguishing Marks of a Work of the Spirit of God," in *Jonathan Edwards on Revival* (Banner of Truth Trust, Carlisle, PA, 1741, 1965) p. 117-118

227. 1 Cor. 13:4 Phillips

228. 2 Cor. 7:16

229. Dr. Robert Hemfelt, Dr. Frank Minirth, and Dr. Paul Meier, *Love is a Choice* (Thomas Nelson, Nashville, 1989)

230. Jam. 1:14-15 NAS

231. Jam. 1:14 Phillips

232. 1 Cor. 13:5 Revised English Bible

233. See Lev. 18:22; Rom. 1:24-29; 1 Cor. 6:9-10; Rev. 21:8. Scripture is clear about all forms of immorality – including homosexuality – such practices are against the will of God.

234. Dr. Thomas Schmidt in his research concluded, "Promiscuity among homosexual men is not a mere stereotype…it is virtually the *only* experience…" Thomas Schmidt, *Straight and Narrow* (InterVarsity Press, Downers Grove, IL, 1995)   pp. 106-108

235. One of the most carefully researched studies on homosexual couples, *The Male Couple,* was authored by two men who are themselves a professing homosexual couple. Of 156 male couples studied, only seven remained sexually active only with each other. These authors concluded that "outside sexual activity was the rule for male couples." Daniel McWhirter and Andrew Mattison, *The Male Couple* (Prentice Hall Trade, NY, 1985). For additional research on the lack of homosexual fidelity, see internet documentation by Family Research Council, "Comparing the Lifestyles of Homosexual Couples to Married Couples."

236. Jeffrey Satinover, a psychiatrist with degrees from MIT, Harvard, and University of Texas, reported some of the damaging medical consequences (rarely mentioned by mainstream media) from homosexual practices:

    a.   A twenty-five to thirty-year decrease in life expectancy

    b.   Chronic, potentially fatal, liver disease – infectious hepatitis

    c.   Inevitably fatal immune disease including associated cancers

    d.   Frequently fatal rectal cancer

    e.   Multiple bowel and other infectious diseases

    f.   A much higher than usual incidence of suicide

See Jeffery Satinover, *Homosexuality and the Politics of Truth*, (Baker Books, Grand Rapids, MI, 1996) p. 51

237. Sources: The 2006-2008 National Survey of Family Growth found that 3.7 percent of adults aged 18 to 44 were homosexual or bisexual. The University of Chicago's National Opinion Research Center, which has been conducting scientifically designed surveys on homosexuality for close to 30 years found the percentage of gays, lesbians, and bisexuals in the United States in 2008 was 2 percent – a number that has been stable since the late '80s.

238. 1 Cor. 6:16

239. Gen. 1:31

240. Prov. 5:18-19

241. See NAS, NAS margin, and *The Amplified Bible*

242. Philip Yancey, *Rumors of Another World* (Zondervan Publishing House, Grand Rapids, MI, 2003) p. 93

243. Ecc. 3:5

244. See the author's booklet, *Dating, Mating, or Waiting.* Available from CFC Literature.

245. Rom. 12:20

246. C. S. Lewis, *Mere Christianity* (MacMillan, New York, 1943)

247. James Boice, *Come to the Waters* , Oct. 22 devotional

248. Robert Peterson and Alexander Strauch, *Agape Leadership* (Lewis and Roth Publishers, Littleton, Co, 1991) p. 44

249. Brother Lawrence, *The Practice of the Presence of God* (Fleming Revell Co., Old Tappan, NJ, 1958) pp. 14, 29

250. William MacDonald, *One Day at a Time*, Jan. 26 devotional

251. 2 Thes. 2:12 NEB

252. J. Rodman Williams, *Renewal Theology, Vol. 3* (Zondervan Publishing House, Grand Rapids, MI, 1992) p. 477

253. Peter Kreft, *The God Who Loves You* (Ignatius Press, San Francisco, CA, 1988), p. 155

254. This is emphasized three times in the book of Revelation: Rev. 21:8, 27; 22:15

255. Eph. 4:15,25 NLT

256. Eph. 1:6 NKJV

257. 1 Jn. 4:18

258. Col. 3:9 NLT

NOTES ON LOVE

259. Winkie Pratney, *Youth Aflame* (Bethany House Pub.) Minneapolis, MN, 1983) p. 235

260. *Thayer's Greek-English Lexicon of the New Testament* . Greek word "upakouw"

261. Acts 12:13

262. William Barclay, *The Gospel of John, Volume 2* (The Westminster Press, Philadelphia, PA, 1975) p. 166

263. Ibid, pp. 166-167

264. 1 Pet. 1:22

265. Jerry Bridges, *The Practice of Godliness* (NavPress, Colorado Springs, CO, 1983) p. 209

266. Poem by Emily Matthews, "The True Joy of Love," (American Greetings, Cleveland, OH)

267. Nancy Leigh DeMoss, *A Place of Quiet Rest* (Moody Publishers, Chicago, 2000), pp. 39-40

268. Edward Plass, *What Luther Says* (Concordia Publishing House, St. Louis, MO, 1959) p. 832

269. Matt. 5:44

270. Murray and Edwards, *The Believer's Secret of Christian Love*, pp. 85-86

271. Vera McCoy, article "He Killed My Son!" in *Guideposts* (New York, NY), February 1993

272. 1 Sam. 12:23

273. Peter Kreft, *The God Who Loves You,* pp. 46-47

274. Col. 3:8

275. Col. 3:12-14

276. Col. 3:14 NLT

277. John Stott, *The Message of Acts* (InterVarsity Press, Downers Grove, IL, 1990) p. 296

278. 1 Cor. 1:4. It is amazing Paul does not start off his letter with a stinging rebuke, but with thanksgiving to God and encouragement for them!

279. Ps. 103:8

280. 1 Cor. 13:1-3

281. John Pollock, *Moody* (Zondervan, Grand Rapids, MI, 1963) p. 198

282. *The Billy Graham Christian Worker's Handbook*, edited by Charles Ward (World Wide Publications, Minneapolis, MN, 1984) p. 221

283. John Bunyan, *Pilgrim's Progress in Today's English* (Moody Press, Chicago, 1964) p. 33

284. Phillip Keller, *A Gardner Looks at the Fruit of the Spirit* (Tyndale House Publishers, Wheaton, IL, 1991) pp. 512-517

285. Fenelon, *Let Go*, pp. 43, 50

286. 2 Pet. 3:9

287. 1 Thes. 5:14 NAS

288. Prov. 19:22 ASV

289. Rom. 2:4 NAS

290. F.W. Faber, hymn "There's a Wideness in God's Mercy"

291. 1 Cor. 4:13

292. Job 6:14 NAS

293. Kenneth Wuest, *Ephesians and Colossians in the Greek New Testament* (Eerdmans, Grand Rapids, MI, 1953) p. 117, and other books on synonyms and antonyms.

294. Richard C. Trench, *Synonyms of the New Testament* (Eerdmans Publishing Co., Grand Rapids, MI, 1953). Trench says concerning the Greek word for kindness (chrestos): "'Sweetness' has seized more successfully the central notion of the word." p.233

295. Luke 5:39

296. Gen. 4:5; 1 John 3:12

297. Gen. 37:4, 11 NKJV

298. Num. 16:3; Ps. 106:16

299. Dan. 6:3-4

300. Matt. 27:18

301. Prov. 14:30

302. Jam. 3:16

303. 1 Cor. 3:3 NKJV

304. Rom. 12:15

305. 1 Cor. 3:21-22

306. Jonathan Edwards, *A World of Love* (Calvary Press, Amityville, NY, 1999) pp. 25, 29, 34-35

307. Matt. 6:1-3

308. Matt. 6:3

309. Prov. 27:2

310. Ps. 115:1

311. Tit. 3:2

312. Greek word *epieikeia* in Kittle, *Theological Dictionary of the New Testament, Vol. II,* p. 588

313. John Ayto, *Dictionary of Word Origins* (Arcade Publishing, New York, 1990) p. 450

NOTES ON LOVE

314. Eph. 5:28-29 NRSV

315. Mark 8:34

316. Larry Crabb, *Men and Women* (Zondervan Publishing House, Grand Rapids, MI, 1991) pp. 53, 76-77

317. Teresa of Avila, *Majestic Is Your Name,* paraphrased by David Hazzard (Bethany House Publishers, Minneapolis, MN, 1993)

318. Larry Crabb, *Inside Out* (NavPress, Downers Grove, IL, 2007) p. 149

319. Matt. 7:1-5

320. Oswald Chambers, *God's Workmanship,* quoted in David McCasland, *The Quotable Oswald Chambers* (Discovery House Publishers, Grand Rapids, MI, 2008) p. 154

321. Jonathan Edwards, *Charity and Its Fruits*, pp. 197, 201, 8

322. Anglican bishop Joseph Butler (1692-1752), paraphrased from his *Analogy of Religion* (1736), possibly one of the best defenses of the Christian faith in the eighteenth century.

323. Prov. 17:27 NAS; Prov. 29:11 Jerusalem Bible; Jam. 1:19 NIV

324. Greek word, *logizomai,* in *Thayer's Greek-English Lexicon of the New Testament* and J. H. Moulton and G. Milligan, *Vocabulary of the Greek New Testament* (Henrickson Publishers, Peabody, MA)

325. Jay Adams, *Christian Living in the Home* (Baker Book House, Grand Rapids, MI, 1989) pp. 32-33

326. Matt. 12:22-32

327. Matt. 12:30-34

328. John 5:24 RSV

329. Col. 1:22

330. Kittle, *Theological Dictionary of the New Testament, Vol. 1*, p. 356 and A.T. Robertson, *Word Pictures in the New Testament, Vol. 4* (Baker Book House, Grand Rapids, MI, 1931) p. 482

331. Rom. 6:1 ff.; Heb. 10:26-31; Rom. 11:22; Col 1:22-23

332. 2 Thes. 2:12 New English Bible

333. Rom. 4:8

334. Rom. 8:1

335. Eph. 5:12

336. Rom. 16:19 NKJV

337. Phil. 4:8

338. Prov. 24:17

339. Ps. 119:30

340. Prov. 10:12; 17:9; I Pet. 4:8; Jam. 5:20

341. Kittle, *Theological Dictionary of the New Testament, Volume 3,* p.556

342. Prov. 17:9 NKJV

343. Gen. 9:20-23

344. Hebrew *nagad,* in *Gesenius' Hebrew and Chaldee Lexicon* (Baker Book House, Grand Rapids, MI, 1979)

345. Floyd McClung, *Learning to Love People You Don't Like* (YWAM Publishing, Seattle, WA, 1992) pp. 61-62

346. William Barclay, *The Gospel of Matthew* (The Westminster Press, Philadelphia, 1975) pp. 261-262

347. e.g., Rom. 16:17; Matt. 7:15; 2 Thes. 3:6,14-15

348. Elisabeth Elliot, *A Chance To Die* (Fleming H. Revell, Grand Rapids, MI, 1987) p. 327

349. Amy Carmichael, *If* (Christian Literature Crusade, Ft. Washington, PA) p. 43

350. Song of Songs 8:7

351. Greek *hupomeno* in Kittle, *Theological Dictionary of the New Testament, Volume 4,* pp. 581-583

352. Gen. 29:20

353. From Paul Billheimer, *Don't Waste Your Sorrows* (Christian Literature Crusade, Ft. Washington, PA, 1977) pp. 120-121

354. Amy Carmichael, *Mountain Breezes* (Christian Literature Crusade, Ft. Washington, PA, 1990) p. 178

355. "I Stand Amazed," by Charles H. Gabriel, Public Domain

OTHER BOOKS AVAILABLE
By Clay Sterrett

Safeguards for the Saints

Kingdom Priorities

Church Life: Building on the Foundation of Jesus Christ

Growing Old in the Grace of God

FOR MORE INFORMATION OR TO ORDER:

Web: www.cfcliterature.com

For a listing of literature and order form:
CFC Literature
P.O. Box 245
Staunton, VA 24402

Or, order any of the above from amazon.com